DIASPORA JEWS AND JUDAISM

SOUTH FLORIDA STUDIES IN THE HISTORY OF JUDAISM

Edited by
Jacob Neusner
William Scott Green, James Strange
Darrell J. Fasching, Sara Mandell

Number 41
Diaspora Jews and Judaism

edited by
J. Andrew Overman
Robert S. MacLennan

DIASPORA JEWS AND JUDAISM
Essays in Honor of, and in Dialogue with,
A. Thomas Kraabel

edited by
J. Andrew Overman
Robert S. MacLennan

Scholars Press
Atlanta, Georgia

DIASPORA JEWS AND JUDAISM
Essays in Honor of, and in Dialogue with,
A. Thomas Kraabel

©1992
University of South Florida

Publication of this book was made possible by a grant from the Tisch Family Foundation, New York City. The University of South Florida acknowledges with thanks this important support for its scholarly projects.

Library of Congress Cataloging in Publication Data

Diaspora Jews and Judaism : essays in honor of, and in dialogue with, A. Thomas Kraabel / edited by J. Andrew Overman, Robert S. MacLennan.
    p. cm. — (South Florida studies in the history of Judaism ; 41)
    Includes bibliographical references and index.
    ISBN 1-55540-696-3
    1. Judaism—History—Post-exilic period, 586 B.C.-219 A.D.—Historiography. 2. Jewish diaspora—Historiography. 3. Jews in the New Testament. 4. Christianity—Origin. I. Kraabel, A. Thomas. II. Overman, J. Andrew, 1955- . III. MacLennan, Robert S. IV. Series.
BM176.D53 1992
296'.09—dc20   92-3434
                                                       CIP
Printed in the United States of America
on acid-free paper

DIASPORA JEWS AND JUDAISM:

Essays in Honor of, and in Dialogue with, A. Thomas Kraabel

TABLE OF CONTENTS

PREFACE

This volume combines several aims. First is the desire to honor A. Thomas Kraabel for his twenty-five years of work on diaspora Jews in the Roman period. From his dissertation in 1968 on Judaism in the western Asia Minor to this day Tom Kraabel has studied diaspora Jewish communities in the Roman period, and from that time has continued to enrich and challenge all those who have been drawn into the study of *diaspora Jews and Judaism*. Tom's work has focused on the vitality of Jewish communities in the diaspora, the origin and development of the synagogue, the relationship between Jews and Christians in the Roman diaspora, and the prejudices which have too often tended to distort our interpretation of Jewish life from this period and in these places. This unique contribution, and the clarion voice which has shaped it, is honored in this volume.

But *festschriften* and various volumes honoring senior scholars often resonate with the tenor of a valediction. We do not intend this to be the case with this collection. It is clear to all those who work on Judaism or Christianity in the Greco-Roman world that Tom Kraabel is not finished posing the lapidary questions which have characterized his work to date. This is highlighted by the inclusion of the *Afterword* by Kraabel. In light of this fact we have asked a number of scholars to both honor, and enter into dialogue with the work of Tom Kraabel on diaspora Jews and Judaism. This format has, therefore, provided an opportunity to gather some of Kraabel's most significant, although disparate, work in one place. The reader can refer to the views and arguments put forth by Kraabel in these articles, and at the same time read scholars who build upon, and engage these views. It is also for this reason that several articles which appeared elsewhere, but which so clearly build upon Kraabel's work, are included.

The contributions in this book have been divided into three areas of research. These three areas, reflected in the table of contents, reveal, yet in no way do they exhaust, the areas which have guided Tom Kraabel's research. It is hoped that these essays give us a sense of the questions posed and the paths taken by this field over the past few years, and that they also provide us with a sense of where the study of diaspora Jews and Judaism is headed.

We would like to thank the contributors, all of whom gladly contributed to this book. It is a tribute both to Tom Kraabel, and to the vitality and intrigue of the subject matter that so many scholars eagerly agreed to participate in this project. Our task as editors was made immeasurably easier by the quality of these contributions.

J. Andrew Overman
The University of Rochester

Robert S. MacLennan
Hitchcock Presbyterian Church
Scarsdale, NY
January 1, 1992

LIST OF ABBREVIATIONS

A	*Archaeology*
AA	*The Acts of the Pagan Martyrs, Acta Alexandrinorum*, ed. H. Musurillo (1954)
AASOR	*Annual of the American Schools of Oriental Research*
AB	*The Anchor Bible*
ANRW	*Aufstieg und Niedergang der romischen Welt: Geschichte und Kultur Roms im Spiegel der neuren Forschung*. Edited by Hildegard Temporini and Wolfgang Haase. Berlin and New York: de Gruyter, 1984
ASR	*American Sociological Review*
AJ	Josephus, *Antiquitates Judaicae*
AJA	*American Journal of Archaeology*
Ap.	Josephus, *In Apionem*
ATR	*Anglican Theological Review*
Answer	Tertullian, *Answer to the Jews*
AusBR	*The Australian Biblical Review*
BA	*Biblical Archaeologist*
Barn.	*The Epistle of Barnabas*. In *The Apostolic Fathers*. LCL
BASOR	*Bulletin of the American Schools of Oriental Research*
BAR	*Biblical Archaeology Review*
BJ	Josephus, *Bellum Judaicum*
BJRL	*Bulletin of the John Rylands University Library of Manchester*
BJS	The Brown Judaica Series
BT	*The Babylonian Talmud*, followed by the name of the tractate; English translation ed. I. Epstein (1935-48)
CBQ	*Catholic Biblical Quarterly*
CC	*Christian Century*
CCARJ	*Central Conference of American Rabbis Journal*
CH	*Church History*
CIJ	*Corpus Inscriptionum Judaicarum*, ed. J.B. Frey (1936-1952)
ConJ	*Conservative Judaism*
CPJ	*Corpus Papyrorum Judaicarum*, editors, V.A. Tcherikover, A. Fuks and M. Stern, (1957-1964)
CQ	*The Classical Quarterly*
CQR	*Church Quarterly Review*
CW	*Classical World*
Dio	*Dio's Roman History*
EJ	*Encyclopaedia Judaica*, 16 vols. Jerusalem: Keter Publishing House Jerusalem Ltd., 1972
Eus., DE.	Eusebius, *Demonstratio Evangelica*
___, HE.	_____, *Historia Ecclesiastica*
___, PE.	_____, *Praeparatio Evangelica*

Fl.	Philo, *In Flaccum*, ed. H. Box (1939)
HTR	*Harvard Theological Review*
HUCA	*Hebrew Union College Annual*
ICC	*The International Critical Commentary*
IDBS	*Interpreter's Dictionary of the Bible, Supplement*
Int	*Interpretation*
IEJ	*Israel Exploration Journal*
JBL	*Journal of Biblical Literature*
JE	*The Jewish Encyclopedia* (1901-6)
JEA	*Journal of Egyptian Archaeology*
JEH	*Journal of Ecclesiastical History*
JES	*Journal of Ecumenical Studies*
JJS	*Journal of Jewish Studies*
JQR	*Jewish Quarterly Review*
JRH	*Journal of Religious History*
JRS	*Journal of Roman Studies*
JSJ	*Journal for the Study of Judaism in the Persian, Hellenistic and Roman Periods*
JSNT	*Journal for the Study of the New Testament*
JTS	*Journal of Theological Studies*
Dial.	Justin Martyr's *Dialogue with Trypho the Jew*
LCL	Loeb Classical Library
NT	Novum Testamentum
NTS	New Testament Studies
Numen	Numen: International Review for Religions
Orig., *Cel.*	Origen, *Contra Celsum*
PEQ	*Palestine Exploration Quarterly*
PG	J. Migne, *Patrologia Graeca*
PL	J. Migne, *Patrologia Latina*
PRS	*Perspective in Religious Studies*
RE	*Paulys Realencyclopadie der classischen Altertumswissenschaft*
RSR	*Religious Studies Review*
RB	*Revue biblique*
RHE	*Revue d'histoire ecclesiastique*
RHPhR	*Revue d'histoire et de Philosophe religieuses*
SA	*Scientific American*
SBL	*The Society of Biblical Literature*
Scr.Hier.	*Scripta hierosolymitana*
SEv.	*Studia Evangelica*
Semeia	*Semeia*
SJT	*Scottish Journal of Theology*
SPB	*Studia postbiblica*

SP	*Studia Patristica*
T	*Theologia*
TDNT	*Theological Dictionary of the New Testament*, eds. G. Kittel and G. Friedrich
Tert. *Ad.Jud.*	Tertullian, *Adversus Judaeos*
___. *Ad.Mar.*	Tertullian, *Adversus Marcionem*
TS	*Theological Studies*
TT	*Teologisk Tidsskrift*
TU	*Texte und Untersuchungen*
TZ	*Theologische Zeitschrift*. Basel 1945ff
USQR	*Union Seminary Quarterly Review*
V	Josephus, *Vita*
VC	*Vigiliae christianae*
VT	*Vetus Testamentum*
ZNW	*Zeitschrift für die neutestamentliche Wissenschaft*

CONTRIBUTORS

John J. Collins
>University of Chicago Divinity School

Douglas R. Edwards
>University of Puget Sound

William Scott Green
>University of Rochester

Daniel J. Harrington, S.J.
>Weston School of Theology

Howard Clark Kee
>Professor Emeritus,
>Boston University

A. Thomas Kraabel
>Luther College,

Ross S. Kraemer
>Franklin & Marshall College

Amy-Jill Levine
>Swarthmore College

Robert S. MacLennan
>Hitchcock Presbyterian Church
>Scarsdale, New York

Jacob Neusner
>University of South Florida

J. Andrew Overman
>University of Rochester

Calvin Roetzel
>Macalester College

Anthony J. Saldarini
>Boston College

A.T. Kraabel: An Appreciation
William Scott Green

Although humanistic scholarship often appears an affair of solitude, of working alone, it really is the product of a sustained and special collaboration. To be sure, advances in humanistic understanding frequently derive from the imaginative and synthetic powers of a single researcher, but every new scholarly generalization—particularly about the past—builds and depends heavily on myriad specialized studies carried out by others. Like the rest of humanities, the study of ancient Judaism is a collective exercise that requires—indeed, assumes—a substantial division of labor. The richness and diversity of the primary data—linguistic, textual, artificial—to say nothing of the theories and methods needed to decipher and make meaning from them, demand a multiplicity of investigative and interpretive skills that no individual scholar can be supposed to possess.

In the case of Tom Kraabel—whose scholarship this volume celebrates—the notion of an academic division of labor has at least a double meaning. In the first instance, Kraabel's pioneering work in the study of the so-called "diaspora" Judaism—a term at least as theological as geographical—exhibits the interdisciplinarity and multiple interests scholars in this field must have. Kraabel's well-known ability to work effectively in different subfields—particularly archaeology and social history—gives his scholarship considerable gravity and influence. In the second instance, the increasingly collective nature of research on ancient Judaism is evident in the varied areas of expertise manifested by those who have contributed to this volume. Not all studies of Judaism in antiquity can engage the interest of a wide range of scholars, but Kraabel's do. In important ways, his work exemplifies the study of "diaspora" Judaism and establishes durable and instructive models for other scholars to follow.

Kraabel's work on the excavations of Sardis, his research on the "God-fearers," and his studies of "diaspora" synagogues and communities have made his a leading intellectual voice in the study of ancient Judaism. He has effectively and convincingly challenged the inherited consensus about Jewish social and religious life outside of the land of Israel, and he has laid the foundations for a more variegated and nuanced picture than previous research could provide. His studies draw our attention to the importance of local context in the development of Jewish religious and social life in antiquity, and his research exposes a diversity in the Jewish Roman diaspora that earlier scholarship, shaped primarily by the literary evidence, could not envision.

A particular merit of Kraabel's work is it sustained concern with the problems of Judaism as a religion. Although his work exhibits a keen sense of the relationship between religion and social history, it is able to keep the two distinct and not collapse one into the other. In the same way, he consistently offers a mature and seasoned view of the relationship of archaeology to literature, showing how archaeology challenges and refreshes texts without setting one sort of evidence over the other. This commitment to balance—an admirable trait of mind—combined with a concern for the importance of the local, allows Kraabel's scholarship to avoid the monolithic assumptions about Judaism—which usually are grounded in theology—typical of earlier scholarship. The lens Kraabel provides lets us see various Judaisms in context—he writes of "a dozen major forms" of Judaism under Roman rule—as responding to discrete circumstances. This perspective creates a complex setting for our understanding of Jewish religion and lets Judaism be seen in relation to other Greco-Roman religions, not only Christianity. Thus, Kraabel insists that Judaism be studied in its own right, not merely as a vehicle for understanding Christianity.

In a field highly susceptible to hidden agenda, Kraabel's scholarship stands out for its discipline and clarity. Kraabel is neither an opinion-passer nor a word-waster. His writing is laconic and forthright, and he labors to make his presuppositions clear. This is one of the reasons that Kraabel's scholarship has been so instructive to a younger generation of researchers in ancient Judaism. Because he eschews special pleading and insists on clarity of both purpose and inference, his scholarship exhibits a refreshing self-consciousness that makes the thinking behind it accessible to readers. That is why so many of us have learned so much from Tom Kraabel and why it is such a pleasure to be able to express appreciation and admiration for what he has done.

A. Thomas Kraabel and Judaism
Anthony J. Saldarini

Upon completion of my dissertation, when I asked my director to suggest another project, he replied, "Tony, your heart will tell you what to do." Tom Kraabel's heart clearly told him to explore the hidden character of diaspora Judaism and in doing so to heal the Christian mind of its prejudicial preconceptions of Judaism. His work has helped the scholarly community see old things in a new way and find new things it might have ignored. From his work and that of colleagues a new paradigm for understanding Judaism, and indeed a new Judaism has gradually emerged.

Through his work on the excavation of the Sardis synagogue Tom early understood that Jews within the Roman Empire lived as a politically and socially powerful and respected ethnic community, not as a "religious" group which could be caricatured and dismissed by Christian theology. A careful reading of all texts showed that Jews were not alien curiosities to most of their neighbors in the Roman Empire, but important members of a complex society. Furthermore, the Jewish way of life, bound together by monotheism and commitment to the Biblical tradition, manifested itself in richly diverse ways during the Greco-Roman period, as does Judaism today. Any intellectual construction of a normative Judaism, so convenient as a foil to Christian theology, did violence to the lived reality of thousands of Jewish communities throughout the diaspora, each of which had developed its own grasp of the tradition and created its own accommodations with the local communities and cultures.

To correct misconceptions and explore the riches of diaspora Judaism Tom has written about a variety of communities, their social systems, their relationships with gentiles and about distortions of Judaism in the New Testament and Christian interpretation. He has challenged the neat category of "God-fearers" in favor of a more diverse and flexible set of relationships between Jewish communities and their neighbors. He has contributed additional evidence that evolving Rabbinic Judaism in Palestine did not strongly influence, much less control, diaspora communities and showed that, therefore, diaspora Jews were not syncretistic or heterodox, but vital and creative groups living within the Roman Empire, fully in accord with their ancestral laws. In the last twenty-five years many other scholars have listened to the voice of diaspora Judaism and joined Tom in his quest to understand Judaism as a living and vital tradition. We thank him for helping to lead the way.

The Roman Diaspora:
Six Questionable Assumptions[1]
A. T. Kraabel

Among the inscriptions recovered by Austrian archaeologists at the beginning of this century was an open letter "to the faithful in Ephesus" from the sixth-century bishop Hypatios which refers to *philargyria Ioudaike*, "Jewish greed." It was noted by Juster and Schürer,[2] and included as no. 747 in the *CII* of J.B. Frey. It is usually taken as direct evidence of the historical situation of Jews in Ephesus at the time. That is incorrect. The document is concerned wholly with the affairs of the Church, in particular with the proper cost of burial for Ephesian Christians. The text is laced with biblical language; earlier editors[3] recognized allusions to three New Testament verses, but they missed a fourth: *philargyria Ioudaike* echoes the *Pharisaioi philargyroi* of Luke 16:14. The bishop has turned "greedy Pharisees" into "Jewish greed" to make a point among Christians; they are not to be greedy like the Jews *of the Bible*. The use of this text to show that Ephesian Jews in the sixth century had a reputation for avarice, or even that they were involved in the business of burial,[4] is unwarranted.

Nor does the inscription belong in *CII*. Frey included it because he shared the traditional view. In a way, the older interpretations of *CII* 747 typify that view. But in the last half-century a series of discoveries has forced a thorough reconsideration of traditional views about the Jews of post-biblical times, first for Hellenistic and Roman Palestine, then for the rabbinic communities. The intent of this essay is to extend that review to Ephesus and the other sites in the west, between Dura Europos and Spain, in which Jewish communities were located.

These discoveries are of two kinds. The first come from the archaeologists and palaeographers. Prof. Yadin has been responsible for a larger portion of

---

1 Editor's note: This essay first appeared in *Essays in Honour of Yigael Yadin*, edited by G. Vermes and J. Neusner (= *Journal of Jewish Studies* 33.1-2, 1982): 445-464. This project was made possible by the support of the American Council of Learned Societies and the Graduate School of the University of Minnesota, the assistance of W.E. Ziezulewicz (History) and P.S. Stuehrenberg (Ancient Studies) of the University of Minnesota, and the hospitality of Wolfson College, Oxford. G. Vermes, W.S. Green and G.E.M. de Ste. Croix suggested improvements to an early draft. Any errors or infelicities are my own.

2 E. Schürer, *Geschichte des jüdischen Volkes im Zeitalter Jesu Christi III* (Leipzig, 1909[3-4]) 717; J. Juster, *Les Juifs dans l'Empire romain* (Paris, 1914) I 190.

3 H. Gregoire, *Recueil des inscriptions grecques chrétiennes d'Asie Mineure*, 1 (Paris, 1922) no. 108; J. Keil in *Forschungen in Ephesos* IV.I (Vienna, 1932) no. 35.

4 In *Ephesus after Antiquity* (Cambridge UK, 1979) C. Foss calls this "conventional ecclesiastical rhetoric," 45. But according to J. Starr, the inscription shows that Jews "served the city as undertakers," *The Jews in the Byzantine Empire* 641-1204 (Athens, 1939) 197.

this wealth than any other scholar alive today, witness—for post-biblical Judaism alone—his excavations at Masada and in the Judaean caves, and his contributions to the manuscript evidence for that explosive period. Most of the other new sources of information are in the Holy Land as well, the Dead Sea Scrolls and, from the archaeologists, the Old City and Temple Mount projects in Jerusalem, the explorations at Beth Shearim and particularly the many excavated synagogues.[5]

The new evidence from the Diaspora is made up chiefly of the synagogues excavated at Ostia in Italy, Stobi in Macedonia, Saris in Lydia and Dura in Syria,[6] the papyri published comprehensively two decades ago as *CPJ*, and scattered inscriptions faithfully logged and wisely interpreted by Louis Robert.[7] While this new information is less abundant than that for Palestine, it is more important on an item-for-item basis. This is because what had been available from the Diaspora previously was quite sparse; any new datum substantially increases the total. What was known before World War II was chiefly inscriptions, along with small finds often of uncertain provenance. Rome, Dura and Egypt apart, no ancient community was "documented" with more than a very few items, perhaps only a single artifact. Reconstructions of community life and piety could be no more than speculative. As it turned out, they were also dominated by faulty preconceptions of what these Jews might or "should" have been.

The other *novum* in the understanding of ancient Jewry is as important as the new material evidence: it is a new point of view, new presuppositions and new methodology. For over a millennium the study of Judaism was dominated by the Church; her interests were paramount, her issues were the ones explored. Even today in many American libraries and curricula, Jewish Studies is an aspect of Religious Studies; that is a legacy of the old view. Non-Christian academics, including not a few Jews, also played by the Church's rules and on the playing field she defined, if they worked in the mainstream of western scholarship. Long after the Renaissance, while the academy became more

---

5 Convenient review in the relevant chapters of *Early Judaism and Its Modern Interpreters*, edd. R.A. Kraft and G.W.E. Nickelsburg, vol II of *The Bible and Its Modern Interpreters*, ed. D.A. Knight (Philadelphia, 1982). More generally, M. Avi-Yonah, *The Jews of Palestine* (Oxford, 1976) and E.M. Smallwood, *The Jews under Roman Rule* (Leiden, 1975).

6 A.T. Kraabel, 'The Diaspora Synagogue,' *ANRW* II 19.1 (1979) 477:510; and 'Social Systems of Six Diaspora Synagogues,' in *Ancient Synagogues*, ed. J. Gutmann (Chico CA, 1981) 79-91.

7 See his "Bulletin épigraphique" annually in *REG*, under the heading "inscriptions greco-juives."

independent of the Church, distortion continued; ancient Jewry was not looked at directly, but "in the light of" something else.[8]

The new methods were developed first for the study of Israelite history and the Bible; that story is a familiar one and need not be repeated here. Post-biblical Judaism is a more complex matter. The rabbinic tradition developed its methods early and sustained them in relative isolation from the larger academy.[9] Some aspects of Jewish history and thought became important for students of the New Testament and the early Church, but their findings were bound to produce an imperfect view of ancient Judaism since they were interested in it less for its own sake than as the background for understanding early Christianity.

It was almost inevitable that the western Diaspora would be misunderstood: for rabbinics it was far from the centres of activity in Palestine and especially in Babylonia; references to the west were rare, usually obscure, and often without much historical concern.[10] New Testament studies took (and still takes) its evidence chiefly from written texts, and there was not much textual evidence from the Judaism west of the Holy Land. When archaeology was utilized, the data were almost always drawn from the Holy Land. This was a striking self-limitation considering the archaeological richness of the Greco-Roman world, and in view of the fact that the New Testament itself is not least the record of an ancient religion moving *out of* Palestine into the rest of the Roman Empire.

---

8 G. Langmuir, 'Majority History and Post-Biblical Jews,' *Jour Hist Ideas* 27 (1966) 343 64; H. Liebeschütz, *Das Judentum im deutschen Geschichtsbild von Hegel bis Max Weber* (Tubingen, 1967); C. Klein, *Anti-Judaism in Christian Theology* (London 1978); G.F. Moore, 'Christian Writers on Judaism,' *HTR* 14 (1921) 197-254; G. Vermes, 'Jewish Studies and New Testament Interpretation,' *JJS* 31 (1980) 1-17. A. Momigliano illustrates the historian's problem in 'Jacob Bernays,' *Mededelingen der Koninklijke Nederlandse Akademie van Wetenschappen* 32 (1969) 151-78, and 'J.G. Droysen between Greeks and Jews,' in *Essays in Ancient and Modern Historiography* (Oxford, 1977) 307-23.

9 For a very long time studies of the rabbinic literature tended both to overestimate its value as direct historical evidence, and to miss the schemes of organization and classification which gave it its own coherence. The work done today tends to be much more useful, due to the application of more generally accepted methods for the study of history, literature and ancient society. For recent examples and further bibliography see the essays of J.Z. Smith (on classification and epitaphs), W.S. Green (on rabbinic "biography"), P. Schäfer (on Aqiva) and G. Bowersock (on the Bar Kochba war) in W.S. Green, ed. *Approaches to Ancient Judaism, Volume II* (Chico CA, 1980).

10 G. Vermes, 'Ancient Rome in Post-biblical Jewish Literature,' in *Post-biblical Jewish Studies* (Leiden, 1975) 215-24; G. Stemberger, 'Die Beurteilung Roms in der rabbinischen Literatur,' *ANRW* II. 19.2 (1979) 338-96; N.R.M. der Lange, 'Jewish Attitudes to the Roman Empire' in P.D.A. Garnsey and C.R. Whittaker, eds. *Imperialism in the Ancient World* (Cambridge, UK, 1978) 255-81, 354-57.

This deficiency in New Testament studies is explained in part by the fact that the third group of scholars, the classical archaeologists, were usually unprepared for the Jewish material they did turn up in Diaspora sites; frequently they missed it, or misinterpreted it. Dura was the glorious exception, the first[11] ancient synagogue excavated and published scientifically, and interpreted within a broad historical context. Priene in Ionia is more typical; the excavators of this building were competent archaeologists, but they identified their synagogue as a "house church" despite clear Jewish evidence *in situ*.

The pre-critical approach to the Hebrew Bible, Israelite history and religion has all but disappeared from western universities. Post-biblical Judaism -—what used to be called *late* Judaism—is thus also the latest part of the field to be reached by new data and methods, but there are clear signs that here too change is well advanced, particularly in rabbinics. The traditional approach to rabbinic literature is still to be found in many *yeshivoth;* such sectarian activity (like the Christological interpretation of the "Old Testament" in Christian seminaries) has its place, and doubtless will continue. But the critical and interdisciplinary study of the same literature becomes more common with every passing academic year; in the US at least, most Jewish and Gentile students now exposed to rabbinics learn the methods pioneered by the American editor of this volume.

But the movement from old to new is far from completed. For those areas of the Jewish world which were within the Roman Empire, the most tenacious part of the old view is what might be called the "New Testament" approach to Jewish texts and other evidence. Recent reviews of two major synthetic works serve to indicate how deeply imbedded the old consensus was.

Martin Hengel's indispensable *Judaism and Hellenism* has been evaluated by two prominent ancient historians. Arnaldo Momigliano locates the book within nineteenth- and twentieth-century German Protestant theology; he questions whether Hengel himself realized the implications of this context when drawing conclusions from his careful collection of the primary data.[12] Fergus Millar makes a similar point more gently, then suggests an entirely different reconstruction of the evidence for a central thesis of the book.[13]

Jacob Neusner is more direct in his review of the other volume, E.P. Sanders' *Paul and Palestinian Judaism*; in his judgment the book is deeply flawed

---

11 The second was of course Yadin's Masada, the third Khirbet Shema, cf. E.M. Meyers, A.T. Kraabel, J.F. Strange, *Ancient Synagogue Excavations at Khirbet Shema'*... (Durham NC, 1976). In all probability the fourth will be Sardis, see G.M.A. Hanfmann, ed. *Sardis from Prehistoric to Roman Times* (Cambridge, MA, in press).

12 *JTS* 21 (1970) 149-55.

13 'The Background to the Maccabean Revolution: Reflections on Martin Hengel's *Judaism and Hellenism,*' *JJS* 29 (1978) 1-21.

because "Sanders...has not asked what is important and central in the system of Tannaitic-Rabbinic writings. All he wants to know is what, in these writings, addresses questions of interest to Paul."[14] Neusner's accurate critique is made all the more startling by the fact that Sanders had set out to "destroy" earlier, inaccurate views of rabbinic Judaism carried along in New Testament scholarship.[15] Sanders was aware of many of the critical problems and moved farther from the old consensus than had Hengel, but what he calls an analysis of ancient rabbinic Judaism was still controlled to too great an extent by the priorities and presuppositions of another field.

These reviews are nevertheless an indication that in the study of Palestinian Judaism and in rabbinics some progress has been made; other essays in the present volume provide further evidence to the same point. But in the analysis of the western Diaspora, reappraisal has only begun. There are several reasons for the delay. Rabbinic and biblical studies are disciplines each with its arena of discourse and debate and its own internal momentum. "Diaspora Judaism" is an interdisciplinary field or area; such things are cumbersome and often far from cohesive. Further, the scope of Jewish historiography always narrowed after the destruction of the Jerusalem Temple; at that point its centre of interest shifted eastward, while the eastern boundary of the Roman Empire was moving steadily west.The Jews of the Roman Diaspora began to drop from sight. But perhaps most significant is the fact that, since the traditional view of the Diaspora was really only a *by-product* of biblical and rabbinic studies, new approaches could correct and deepen the understanding of those literatures while leaving Diaspora Judaism unexamined on the periphery.

In part, this was because a new view of the Diaspora will not be due primarily to further study of the ancient texts, but to the new data from excavation, and the contributions of ancient historians. The disciplines which created the old consensus will not arrive at a more accurate conception unaided.

According to that consensus, the Jews of the western Diaspora eagerly offered the Gentile world a debased form of their ancestral religion, paganized to make it attractive to non-Jews. Their primary allegiance, political as well as religious, was to the Holy Land, but due to their separation from that land and their lack of status among Gentiles, they lived anxious lives in a world which could never be their home.[16] Since Judaism is a religion first of all, the

---

14 'Comparing Judaism,' *HR* 18 (1978-79) 177-91, expanded and reprinted in the volume edited by Green (*supra* note 8) with a reply by Sanders. The quotation is from 180f. = 50.

15 E.P. Sanders, *Paul and Palestinian Judaism* (London, 1977) xii.

16 "The Diaspora is the beginning of the Jewish tragedy, alienation together with self-preservation through isolation," W. den Boer, *Mnemosyne* 29 (1976) 450, in a review of J.N. Sevenster, *The Roots of Pagan Anti-Semitism in the Ancient World* (Leiden, 1975).

activities of these Jews and the actions toward them by Gentiles are best understood on religious terms. To take the six main points of this bald summary in order:

The Jewish Diaspora was *syncretistic* (I). Substantial elements of pagan piety were mixed in with the ancestral religion. A frequently used piece of evidence was the fragmentary text of Valerius Maximum (1.3.3 = S147b),[17] which seemed to say that *Jewish* missionaries of the Anatolian deity Sabazios were active in Rome in 139 B.C.E. But a recent study has shown that this text had suffered in transmission and originally made no connection whatever between Jews and Sabazios.[18]

On the strength of a text in the Historia Augusta (Quadr. Tyr. 8.4=S 527), it was thought that Diaspora syncretism had become so powerful that even the Patriarch, visiting Egypt from Palestine, would worship the local deity Sarapis; but this story was made up as a playful jab at the instability of the Egyptian character, and lacks historical foundation.[19]

Anatolian Judaism was thought to be particularly weak in this regard,[20] as the Talmud seemed to indicate: *bShabbath* 147b states that "the wines and baths of Perugitha" contributed to the apostasy of the Ten Tribes of Israel. *Perugitha* was long thought to be Phrygia in Anatolia; that view is still being repeated.[21] In actuality it is a town of the Galilee, near Tiberias. Citing this text, Cumont argued that the Jewish missionaries of Sabazios known from Valerius Maximus (!) were from Phrygia, where Sabazios was popular and the Jews close to apostasy; his 1906 statement on the matter was frequently cited.[22] The influence of "syncretistic Anatolian Jews" was widely recognized: in the fascinating frescoes of the Tomb of Vincentius in Rome (because of a clear reference to Sabazios plus several features that appeared Jewish,),[23] in

17 S = the number of the entry in M. Stern, *Greek and Latin Authors on Jews and Judaism I* (Jerusalem, 1974), II (1980).

18 E.N. Lane, 'Sabazius and the Jews in Valerius Maximus: A Re-examination,' *JRS* 69 (1979) 35-38.

19 R. Syme, 'Ipse Ille Patriarcha,' in *Emperors and Biography* (Oxford, 1971) 17-29.

20 G. Kittel, 'Das kleinasiatische Judentum in der hellenistisch-römischen Zeit,' *TLZ* 69 (1944) 9-20; F. Blanchetiere, 'Juifs et non Juifs: Essai sur la diaspora en Asie-Mineure,' *RHPR* 54 (1974) 367-82, cf. A.T. Kraabel, *'Paganism and Judaism: The Sardis Evidence,'* in *Paganisme, Judaisme, Christianisme...Mélanges offerts à Marcel Simon*, edd. A. Benoit et al. (Strasbourg, 1978) 25-31. Generally, A.T. Kraabel, *Jewish Communities in Western Asia Minor*, forthcoming.

21 A.R.R. Sheppard, 'Jews, Christians and Heretics in Acmonia and Eumeneia,' *AnatStud* 29 (1979) 169-80.

22 F. Cumont, 'Les Mystères de Sabazius et le Judaïsme,' *CRAI* (1906) 67, cf. 63-79.

23 E.R. Goodenough, *Jewish Symbols in the Greco-Roman Period II* (1953) 45-50; M.P. Nilsson, *Geschichte der griechischen Religion II* (Munich, 1961²) 661-63, 667.

the Gnostic "Naassene Sermon,"[24] and in a private cult centre in Philadelphia, Lydia, which appeared to combine Jewish ethics with the worship of a number of pagan deities.[25]

What might originally have been constructed as an hypothesis soon assumed the status of fact. Inscriptions were thought to be particularly good evidence because of their specificity. *Hypsistos*, "the highest," a divine epithet in the Septuagint, occurs also in pagan texts. A few other Anatolian inscriptions, apparently from gentile cult organizations, were thought to refer to a "Sabbath deity", *Sabbasiastes* or *Sabathikos*. But "highest" is a natural epithet for deities in late antiquity, and need not always be Jewish, particularly when pagan deities and concepts are clearly indicated. And the few and scattered "Sabbath deity" texts are too problematic and diverse to form anything like a coherent *corpus* of evidence,[26] normally they would have been left unrelated, had not the other "evidence" of "Jewish syncretism" been at hand to provide a ready explanation.

But if the Jews of this period were engaging in accommodation to the pagan world, one important motivation was thought to be their *missionary zeal* (II). Proper Judaism became contaminated because Jews were too eager to speak the religious language of gentile piety, to make their religion appealing to their neighbours, in order to gain converts or *proselytoi*, proselytes.[27] The most celebrated proselytes were members of the royal family of Adiabene, who converted to Judaism in the first half of the first century C.E. (but without indication of syncretism).[28] Clear and specific examples of successful missionary activity farther west were rare. Some texts from Roman authors often cited in this connection appear to be about Jews concerned with gaining political or social benefits rather than with making converts, see VI below.

Some Jews were expelled from Rome in 19 C.E., ostensibly for proselytizing; but the evidence is equivocal. Tacitus, *Ann.* 2.85.4 (S 284) and Suetonius, *Tib.* 36 (S 306) recorded actions taken against Jews and Egyptians but make no mention of proselytizing as the cause. Philo *Leg.* 159-61, attributed the action against the Jews to slanders fabricated by the emperor's minister Seja-

---

24 Nilsson (*op. cit.*, note 22) 650f.

25 The inscription is SIG^3 985, cf. O. Weinrich, *Stiftungen und Kultsatzungen eines Priva-theiligtums in Philadelpheia in Lydien, AbhHeidelberg* 1919.16, especially 54-66.

26 Nilsson (*op. cit.*, note 22) 665f.; A.T. Kraabel, "*Hypsistos* and the Synagogue at Sardis," *GRBS* 10 (1969) 81-93.

27 Thus in *Beginnings of Christianity I. The Acts of the Apostles*, 5 (London 1933) K. Lake concluded a sound discussion of proselytes and "God-fearers" (74-96) with a section on "syncretistic cults" (88-96) on the assumption that conversion and syncretism were closely related.

28 J. Neusner, 'The Jews East of the Euphrates and the Roman Empire I,' *ANRW* II 9.1 (1976) 52-4.

nus, but Josephus, *Ant.* 18.81-4, and Dio Cassius, 57.18.5a (S 419) connected it to zealous and successful missionary activity.

It is particularly at this point that the New Testament was given inordinate weight and taken far too quickly as solid historical evidence. Mt. 23:15 testified to the great proselytizing zeal displayed "over land and sea" by the Jews of Jesus' time. However, the term *proselytos* occurs in the New Testament only four times, here in Matthew and thrice in Acts; all four texts carry a heavy burden of their authors' theology. Their historical value may be questioned.[29]

Other texts in Acts were understood in such a way as to create a puzzling history-of-religions category, the semi-proselyte or partial convert, found in such older reference works as Juster, Strack-Billerbeck and the earlier editions and original English translation of Schürer.[30] Critical study of the New Testament corrected the earlier understanding of these texts for biblical studies, but the old view remained alive and strong in the handbooks of sister disciplines.

One reason for assuming extensive missionary activity by Diaspora Jews was the further assumption that Jews outside Palestine knew themselves to be *aliens* (III) in the Roman world. To compensate for the great differences between themselves and the gentiles, Jews strove to make some gentiles "Jews."[31] In addition to direct references in the secondary literature to this idea,[32] there are many statements about how difficult it must have been to be a Jew in the Diaspora.[33] To adopt Judaism was to make a clean break with the rest of the world,[34] since Jews were "a people apart, with their own customs and religion which admitted little intermingling with their Greek neighbours"—thus Frend, who documents his claim by citing Josephus on the Jewish community at Sardis.[35]

---

29 A.T. Kraabel, "The Disappearance of the 'God-fearers'," *Numen*, in press. Sevenster (*op. cit.*, note 15) acknowledges that there is almost no *Jewish* evidence for organized missionary activities carried on by Jews, 202.

30 Juster (*op. cit.*, note 1) 274-77; H.L. Strack and P. Billerbeck, *Kommentar zum neuen Testament aus Talmud und Midrasch*, II (Munich, 1924) 715-23. Schürer (*op. cit.*, note 1) 175-77 corrects himself, but the original English translation had already been made from the second edition. Hengel still uses the term, *Judaism and Hellenism* (London, 1974), e.g. I 313f.

31 Festinger's theory of "cognitive dissonance" might fit the traditional view of Diaspora Judaism very well at this point; it has already been applied to early Christianity, cf. J.G. Gager, *Kingdom and Community* (Englewood Cliffs, NJ, 1975) 37-43.

32 According to Sevenster, the "strangeness" of the Jew was "the most fundamental reason for pagan anti-Semitism," (*op. cit.*, note 15) 89.

33 "Was wirklich den (Juden) hass hervorgerufen hat, war die jüdische Diasporaexistenz als solche," A. Schalit, *Gnomon* 50 (1978) 285, in a review of Sevenster, *op. cit.* (note 15).

34 M. Simon, *Verus Israel* (Paris, ²1964) 327.

35 W.H.C. Frend, *Martyrdom and Persecution in the Early Church* (Oxford, 1965) 130 with note 18. The reference there is incorrect; the text is *Ant.* 14.259.

Joining the emphasis on the Jews' zealous missionary activity (III) with the conclusion that these efforts could not often have been successful, led to a third assumption: that while there were relatively few proselytes, there must have been many sympathizers like the semi-proselytes and the God-fearers of Acts. Once again Acts, coupled with Mt. 23:15, was the bedrock of the consensus.

At this point other texts could be brought in, viz., those from classical authors which spoke to the social, economic and intellectual *level* (IV) of Diaspora Jews. Martial, *Epig.* 12.57.13 (S 246) and Juvenal, *Sat.* 3.13f. (S 296) and 6.542-7 (S 299), tell of Jewish beggars, and Cicero describes Jews as *nati servituti* in *Prov. Con.* 5.10 (S 70). Inscriptions from the Jewish catacombs of Rome began to become available from the seventeenth century onward, and some of them were poor indeed, almost illegible scratchings, sometimes in a mixture of languages.[36] These literary and epigraphical data were used as evidence for the assertion that both Diaspora Jews and proselytes were of the lower classes.[37]

Some Jews known to the classical authors were poor, of course; some of them were surely slaves or the offspring of slaves, since a number of Jews had been brought to Rome as prisoners after Pompey's capture of Jerusalem in 63 B.C.E., and after the two later revolts. And it was surely never un-Roman to think of peoples conquered enslaved by the Romans as "born for servitude."[38] But other inscriptions and the Jewish gold glasses showed Roman Jews who were literate and even cultured. This evidence was taken less seriously because of the prior assumption that Jews felt out-of-place and not "at home" in the Diaspora, a self-perception which if true would go along nicely with low social and economic status.

There is a further reason too: Diaspora Jewry was seen to be *monolithic* (V), inter-connected and even directly controlled from Palestine, a kind of "underground" which was feared and alternatively oppressed and appeased by Roman authorities. No matter how long they had lived in the west, Jews were not to be trusted because their overriding loyalty and allegiance remained firmly attached to the Holy Land. The extreme and diabolical form of this view was represented by G. Kittel and his colleagues of the *Forschungen zur*

---

36 H.J. Leon, *The Jews of Ancient Rome* (Philadelphia, 1960) 67-74; A.T. Kraabel, 'Jews in Imperial Rome,' *JJS* 30 (1979) 41-58.

37 On this point, K.G. Kuhn and H. Stegemann, 'Proselyten,' *RE* suppl. IX (1962) 1266f., which also assumes that the "God-fearers" were of a higher social level.Much is made here (1264-67) of the epigraphic evidence, which is statistically inadequate to bear the weight put upon it.

38 See generally, A.N. Sherwin-White, *Racial Prejudice in Imperial Rome* (Cambridge UK, 1967); and J.P.V.D. Balsdon, *Romans and Aliens* (London, 1979).

Judenfrage; they christened the monolith *das antike Weltjudentum*. In their descriptions it was sinister indeed.[39]

More benign reflections of this image are still available however, particularly in the assumption that the western Diaspora was administered or controlled by travelling rabbis, the *apostoloi* of the Patriarch or other agents from Palestine. On occasion rabbis did journey to the west, and the Patriarch did have some representatives or *apostoloi* who travelled in the Diaspora on various errands, but "in order to exert day-to-day authority over Jews from Spain to Afghanistan, the Patriarch would have needed an international political institution of enormous size with vast funds and enjoying widespread recognition. The apostolate we know about was not congruent to such needs."[40]

It is true, of course, that Palestine had been the centre of Jewish religious activity for centuries; but after the destruction of the Temple, the vision of Judaism there began to turn increasingly eastward, with the growing intellectual power of Jews in Babylonia. The issues and agenda of the rabbinic texts were not those of the Diaspora communities farther west; indeed, within that substantial achievement called rabbinic Judaism, there appears to be little concern for the Greek-speaking Jews of western Asia Minor, Greece or Italy, not to mention Spain and North Africa. Such neglect becomes very difficult to understand if the ties between Palestine and the west were as close as the traditional view assumed.

The final element of the old consensus was the most pervasive of all; it was the idea that evidence about the Jews of antiquity is best interpreted in the context of *religion* (VI). Thus relations between Jews and gentiles in the Roman world would be characterized with terms drawn from the vocabulary of religion: mission, persecution, assimilation, propaganda, syncretism, orthodoxy. But it may be suggested that for the Roman government at least, and possibly for most Roman citizens, the single most important thing about the Jews of Palestine was military fact: these Jews were located at a crucial point on the eastern frontier, and their attitude toward Rome had had much to do with the security of the eastern end of the Empire.[41] Similarly, the Jews in Rome itself (where much of the gentile attitude was molded) were first of all a social or sociological datum: they were another of those ethnic groups streaming into the capital from the Greek world in what were for many

---

39 W.F. Albright, 'Gerhard Kittel and tne Jewish Question in Antiquity,' in *Freedom and Reason* (M.R. Cohen Memorial Volume), ed. S.W. Baron et al. (Glencoe IL, 1951) 325-36; F. Werner, 'Das Judentumsbild der Spätjudentumsforschungen im Dritten Reich, Dargestellt anhand der "Forschungen zur Judenfrage" Bd. I-VIII', *Kairos* 13 (1971) 161-94.

40 J. Neusner, *Early Rabbinic Judaism* (Leiden, 1975) 179. On the journeys of Aqiba, see P. Schäfer (*op. cit.* note 8) 114-17.

41 J. Neusner, *op. cit.* (note 28) 46-59.

Romans distressingly large numbers. It is for this reason that they are lumped together with the Egyptians frequently, and also with the Syrians, Lydians and other minorities. In the east or the west, Jews could be volatile and unruly, and on occasion needed tending to; they had strange and sometimes interesting customs and religious practices, but then so did other non-Romans known in Rome.

The uses of *Ioudaioi* and *Judaei* in Greek and Latin literature and inscriptions deserve careful restudy from this standpoint. Clear differences of emphasis can be identified from one example to the next. The terms will be found to denominate a religious group in some instances, but in others to mean something much closer to "inhabitants of Judaea," that is, persons of a particular country, in this case one of great and well-known political and especially military important. Note, for example, *IGRR* IV 1431, line 29-*CII* 742, an inscription from Smyrna dated to the second century. The text mentions *hoi pote Ioudaioi*; translated as "the former Jews", these three words are often used as an example of the public repudiation of their ancestral religion by some Anatolian Jews.[42] But the inscription is the record of donations for public works; the *Ioudaioi* as a group had given a smallish amount. The phrase easily escapes notice, buried as it is in the middle of a long text.[43] This is surely an odd way to record one's apostasy! These are more likely to be "people formerly of Judaea," perhaps immigrants from Palestine, now doing their civic duty as residents of Smyrna.

In other cases *Ioudaioi* or *Judaei* designates first of all members of a particular minority group seeking personal or political advance. The *turba* of Jews in Rome mentioned by Cicero, *Flac* 28.66 (S 68) and Horace, *Sat* 1.4.142f. (S 127) is best understood in this way, as a recent study has shown.[44] Both texts had been widely used as evidence for an aggressive missionary activity by the Jews of Rome (see IV above).

This final and most tenacious element of the old consensus is understandable enough. The chief opposition to Judaism in later centuries was expressed in the language of a religion, Christianity. Most students of the Hebrew Scriptures were Christian, and their interests were primarily theological or apologetic. But their approach to the evidence was taken over without question by many later historians and archaeologists. Thus any pagan's friendly attitude toward Jews was regularly understood as a readiness to convert or, worse, to mix Judaism with paganism. For example, when Julia Severa, a wealthy woman of first-century Acmonia in Phrygia, was proved to have been both a bene-

---

42 Frend, "outright apostasy," in *op. cit.* (note 35) 148 note 47.

43 The inscription may be seen in the Sunken Court of the Ashmolean Museum, Oxford.

44 J. Nolland, 'Proselytism or Politics in Horace *Satires* I.4. 138-43' *VC* 33 (1979) 347-55.

factor of the local synagogue and a high priestess of a pagan cult, the assumption generally was that she had been somehow combining the two religions, even that local Jews had encouraged her to it.[45] But such syncretism is surely inappropriate among Jews associated with synagogues;[46] it is preferable to attribute what she did to philanthropy and a benevolent attitude toward her Jewish neighbours, even though this is a less "religious" explanation of her actions.

What I have called the old consensus provided a tendentious and partial image of ancient Jewry. Many of the flaws in that picture have been a matter of public record for sixty years. In 1921 George Foot Moore published a classic study of Christian writing on Judaism, from the beginnings to his own time.[47] He showed how much of early apologetic, apparently directed to Jews, was written in actuality to edify Christians. Later, Jewish texts were not so much analyzed as totalities, as plundered as sources of ammunition for polemics. Distortions continued even in the "scientific" scholarship of the nineteenth century, with construction of systematic theologies of Judaism on the Protestant model by gentile scholars.

Despite Moore's clear analysis, not much changed in Protestant Europe; Bousset and Schürer remained basic reference works, Strack-Billerbeck was soon added, the whole of it carried along in the immensely influential work of Rudolf Bultmann and his school. Sanders accurately characterizes the fundamental perception of Judaism thus transmitted; it involves "the retrojection of the Protestant-Catholic debate into ancient history, with Judaism taking the role of Catholicism and Christianity the role of Lutheranism."[48] Sanders' assertion that this view prevailed in much, even most, of New Testament study at the time his book was published (1977) was unfair to British New Testament scholarship, which tended to rely more on the guidance of Travers Herford and Moore himself.[49] It also undervalued the influence of the work on post-biblical Jewish texts studied directly (and not as *ancillae* to something else) e.g. by Gershom Scholem, or by the editors of the present volume. For Palestinian Judaism of the Second Temple period, and for rabbinic Judaism,

---

45 Sheppard *op. cit.* (note 21). The crucial inscription is *CII* 766=*MAMA* VI no. 264-B. Lifshitz, *Donateurs et fondateurs dans les synagogues juives* (Paris, 1967) no. 33.

46 This point cannot be emphasized too strongly. There is no lack of evidence, e.g., magical papyri and gems, for individual instances of the conflation of Jewish and pagan pieties by gentiles or Jews about whom nothing else is known. But the *communities* of Jews who have chosen to establish and maintain such buildings as the Ostia, Sardis or Dura synagogues are quite a different matter.

47 Moore, *op. cit.* (note 8).

48 Sanders, *op. cit.* (note 15) 57, cf. 33-59; cf. Klein, *op. cit.* (note 8).

49 Klein, *op. cit.* (note 8) 142-55.

the situation has changed substantially since Moore's article, but for the western Diaspora many of his strictures, and those of Sanders, are still apt.

Of the six elements of the old consensus reviewed above, none has been proved wholly false, although each is seriously undermined by recent reexaminations of the standard literary and epigraphic evidence; some of these are mentioned above, others in the Appendix. But the most substantial corrective to the old view comes from new data from archaeology and palaeography.[50] This evidence has been presented in detail elsewhere; in general what it does is to permit the hypothetical reconstruction of entire Diaspora communities: architecture, iconography, community organization and—perhaps most significant—social situation within the larger gentile city. Frequently this may be done on the basis of excavated evidence alone, this is, from data which are of equal antiquity with the rabbinic literature, but come directly from the western Diaspora, and which are drawn from the Jews themselves, rather than from gentile speculations about them.

The most striking impression from these new data is of the great *diversity* of Diaspora Jewry.[51] In the first century C.E. many Jews in Rome were slaves, products of successful campaigns in Palestine by Roman armies. Jews in Sardis were more prosperous and had a less direct tie with Jerusalem: their community had not come from the Holy Land but had been founded by Jews from Babylonia and Mesopotamia two centuries earlier. In Sardis they controlled their own place of assembly; they had become an influential group within the city. Jews in Dura were living not unhappily under Parthian rule, at this point oriented toward the east more than the west. Jews in Alexandria were locked in yet another conflict with other elements of that multi-national and always explosive population.

Some Jews were well situated in local society, others less so. From the excavated synagogues there is no indication of a ghetto mentality, and only late evidence of local hostility: at Stobi, Jews were "at home" for generations, constructing a series of synagogues for their community; it was only at the end, in the fifth century, that local Christians became strong and hostile enough to raze the building and found a Christian basilica immediately on its pavement. When synagogues are confiscated or destroyed in this fashion, it is

---

50 See *Early Judaism...(op. cit.*, note 5). On the synagogues, Kraabel, *op. cit.* (note 6) and most recently the disappointing *Ancient Synagogues Revealed*, ed. L.I. Levine (Jerusalem, 1981).

51 In his study of the Jewish epitaphs from Rome, Beth She'arim and Egypt, Smith finds that their two most frequent characteristics are "the use of Greek and the identification with the synagogue," but the use of Greek varies from 60% of the Beth She'arim inscriptions to 97% of those from Egypt. And while "in Rome some 54% of the inscriptions are synagogue related, Beth She'-arim has few inscriptions that appear related to the synagogue, Egypt has none." Thus the data in the latter category are an argument for great diversity at least in the kinds of evidence used, and probably also in the Jews who were responsible for it. Quotations from *op. cit.* (note 9), 17.

evidence of the antipathy toward the Jews which develops in some parts of Christianity on new, theological grounds.[52] Archaeological evidence for similar actions by pagans against Jews is very rare.

The assaults which caused the destruction of the Dura synagogue in the middle of the third century fall no less heavily on gentile buildings, including the much less imposing Christian chapel. The Priene and Ostia buildings were not relegated to a "Jewish quarter" nor were they disturbed by their gentile neighbours, to judge from the excavated evidence. At Sardis, where the Jewish community existed for a millennium, the synagogue was located on the main street of the city, at a major intersection; it would have made a spectacular church, but it remained under Jewish control until the entire city was destroyed by Sassanian Persian troops in 616.

There is no evidence from the excavations of attempts to *recruit* gentiles by means of these buildings. In the inscriptions the word "proselyte" is very rare: it appears in but one per cent of the Jewish inscriptions of Italy, the largest sample available; and it does not occur in the synagogue inscriptions at all.[53]

Indications of *assimilation* to pagan piety are also absent from the excavated synagogues. Inscriptions and papyri use Greek chiefly, some Latin in the west, Hebrew and Aramaic very rarely and then usually in formulae; but such linguistic adaptation, sometimes called "Hellenization," is perfectly normal in the Greco-Roman period for immigrant groups and migrant religions, e.g. Christianity, and no sign of syncretism.[54] Jewish use of the symbolic "vocabulary" of the gentile world is a more complicated subject.[55] But here too the evidence from the richest Diaspora sites point in the same direction. At Dura

---

52 I will argue elsewhere that, despite Sevenster (*op. cit.*, note 16) et al., it is only at this point that anything like what the late twentieth century understands by anti-Semitism is present in the Greco-Roman world.

53 The "sociological" conclusions drawn by Kuhn-Stegemann (*op. cit.*, note 36) 1264-67 must be highly tentative in view if the paucity of the evidence. A new inscription from Aphrodisias in Caria is most important in this regard: it was published by J. Reynolds and R.F. Tannenbaum in 1987, cf. M. Mellink, 'Archaeology in Asia Minor,' *AJA* 81 (1977) 306.

54 In any case, any assessment of the degree of assimilation or "Hellenization" in the Diaspora is not be set over against an ideal of "pure" Judaism, but rather compared with the situation in Palestine itself, see E. Shürer, *A History of the Jewish People in the Age of Jesus Christ*, edd. G. Vermes and F. Millar, II (Edinburgh, 1979) 1-84, and Hengel, *op. cit.* (note 30) *passim*.

55 M. Smith, 'Goodenough's *Jewish Symbols* in Retrospect,' *JBL* 86 (1967) 53-68; J. Neusner, *op. cit.* (note 39) 139-215; most recent but not persuasive, P. Maser, 'Irrwege ikonologischer Deutung? Zur Discussion um die spätantik-jüdische Kunst,' *Riv/ArchCrist* 56 (1980) 331-67. Here the old consensus may have had its greatest impact, penetrating even the Jewish reference works of a century ago. cf. 'Art Among the Ancient Hebrews,' *Jewish Encyclopaedia* (1902) II 138-41, especially 141.

and Sardis "pagan symbols" are used with boldness to express biblical themes, not to create some Judaeo-pagan hybrid religion. They and other Diaspora synagogues also provide an indication that devotion to the written scriptures, a core element in ancient Judaism, may have begun earlier and been felt more deeply in the Diaspora than in Palestine, where the Temple while it stood was the obvious focus of popular piety. The evidence for this suggestion is the popularity of the permanent Torah shrine in the Diaspora; such structures were part of the synagogues at Dura, Sardis, Priene, Ostia and possibly Stobi. Only the earliest building, on Delos, gives no indication of this feature.

The traditional picture of post-biblical Jewry is a close relative of the pre-critical understanding of the bible. Both viewed their subject diachronically, looking back into the past through a lens provided by later tradition; it was a narrow field of vision. In both instances, the movement toward a more adequate conception has been slow; pre-critical views were firmly entrenched.

The final irony in the study of the later period may be that each of three main groups of written evidence—the Christian authors, the Jewish authors and the law codes[56]—apparently had its own reasons for representing Jewish life as one of alienation, threatened frequently by attack. Thus a law of Constantine would use insulting language toward the Jews—they are a *feralis ...(et) nefaria secta*—apparently to give the impression to zealous Christians that the law itself had been made more severe, when in fact it merely continued a policy which had been in force for over a century.[57] Christian authors like Jerome and Eusebius would expect the continuing suffering of the Jews as a consequence of "their plot against our Saviour"; and that expectation would express (or fulfil) itself in the colouring and emphasis of the information about the Jews which they offer.[58]

And many Jewish authors, from antiquity nearly to the present, persisted in seeing Jewish history since the Maccabees as a *Leidens- und Gelehrtengeschicfhte* in which suffering and martyrdom on the one hand, and scholars' intellectual pursuits on the other, are the two main themes.[59] Sardis, for one, had little of either. The thesis of this essay has been that other Jewish communi-

---

56 See particularly J. Cohen, 'Roman Imperial Policy Toward the Jews from Constantine until the End of the Palestinian Patriarchate (ca. 429),' *Byzantine Studies* 3 (1976) 1-29; but see also E.M. Smallwood, *From Pagan Protection to Christian Oppression. An Inaugural Lecture... Queen's University of Belfast...1979.*

57 Cohen, *op. cit.* (note 56) 5f.

58 Jerome: Cohen, *op. cit.* (note 56) 17 note 121. Eusebius: see Appendix and R.M. Grant, *Eusebius as Church Historian* (Oxford, 1980), chap. 9.

59 On the "lacrymose conception of Jewish history," see S.W. Baron, 'New Horizons in Jewish History,' in *Freedom and Reason (op. cit.,* note 39) 340-44, cf. 337-353.

16   A.T. Kraabel

ties of the western Diaspora were closer to Sardis than they are to the traditional view.

Appendix

"Christian interest in Jewish literature has always been apologetic or
polemic rather than historical,"[60] but Moore's "Christian writers on Judaism"
were only partially to blame for the distortions mentioned in this article. The
conventional picture of ancient Judaism had a broader development. Many
guides are available to track it; none of them was originally designed to show
how later peoples had come to understand the Jews *of antiquity*, but with
some care they may be turned to this purpose. These are such things as the
surveys of the development of the interpretation of Scripture, or of the growth
of anti-semitism; or the reviews of accounts of Judaism in the west through
the centuries by gentile authors, or of the image of the Jew in western art and
drama.[61] A long book, perhaps several books, would be needed for anything
like a complete examination, but here are a few examples to show that what
earlier generations have said about Jews in antiquity ought not always to be
taken at face value.

In Christian literature the most influential document after the New Testament for this topic is the *Church History* written by Eusebius in the first half
of the fourth century. He clearly states his five chief concerns on the opening
page; third on the list is to record "the calamities that immediately after their
conspiracy against our Saviour overwhelmed the entire Jewish race." For Eusebius, the history of Jewry will be a series of calamities, no balanced account.
Peaceful co-existence is not of interest; conflicts will be stressed, defeats max-
imized. The full story will not be told.[62]

But the distortions began long before Eusebius. As early as the New Testament, Christianity had to deal with two unpleasant facts in the career of
Jesus; the disgraceful manner of his death, and the rejection by nearly all Jews
of the messianic claims made about him. Attempts are made as early as the
Gospel of Luke to exculpate the Roman participants in the Crucifixion, lest

---

60 Moore (*op. cit.*, note 8) 197.

61 The following were particularly useful: *The Cambridge History of the Bible* I. edd. P.R.
Ackroyd and C.F. Evans (Cambridge, 1970) and II. ed. G.W.H. Lampe (1969); J. Parkes, *The
Conflict of the Church and the Synagogue* (London, 1934) and *The Jew in the Medieval Community*
(London, 1938); A. Lukyn Williams, *Adversus Iudaeos* (Cambridge, UK, 1935); R. Blumenkranz,
Les auteurs chrétiens latins due moyen âge sur less juifs et le judaïsme (Paris, 1963) and *Le juif
médiéval au miroir de l'art chrétien* (Paris, 1966); H. Kraus, *The Living Theatre of Medieval Art*
(London, 1967), chap. 7; K. Youong, *The Drama of the Medieval Church*, 2 vols. (Oxford, 1933);
W.S. Seiferth, *Synagogue and Church in the Middle Ages: Two Symbols in Art and Literature* (New
York, 1970); and relevant entries from the *Encyclopaedia Judaica*.

62 Grant, *op. cit.* (note 58), chap. 9.

it appear to gentiles and particularly to the authorities that the new religion was something either disgraceful or subversive. (So successful was this, within Christianity at least, that Roman participants in the story are all but reborn; in the Greek Orthodox tradition the wife of Pontius Pilate was made a saint, and Pilate himself had that status among Coptic Christians.) But then the onus may be shifted to no other group but the Jews; increasingly, the Passion Story was understood in this new way. The pernicious effects of this change are heightened by the fact that in later centuries there were no representatives of "Roman authority" to be used as scapegoats, but often a number of Jews.

Exonerating Rome from responsibility for the Crucifixion thus had an unintended anti-Jewish result. Something similar, and similarly unexpected, took place as Christians confronted the Jews' repudiation of the messianic claims made for Jesus by his followers. This caused a problem of great magnitude which was addressed in many ways from the New Testament on. This is not the place for a full review of this theological *topos*, but some implications for the understanding of the Diaspora should be noted. No matter how benign, Christian attempts to deal with this issue could only have a negative effect on the gentile perception of Jews. The author of Luke-Acts, for example, is concerned to legitimize the existence of Christianity despite Jews' rejection of it; he does this by showing that Christianity is the *replacement* for Judaism within biblical history. Israel had its proper place and responsibilities, but now her time is past, and the next stage of the divine plan must unfold. This created a place for Christianity, and that was Luke's purpose; but it was accomplished by making Judaism redundant, a development to which Luke (unlike Paul) would not have objected, but which was not his main concern.

Other explanations of Jewish refusal to acknowledge Jesus as messiah involve a more direct attack. Jewish "blindness" is a common theme almost from the beginning.In Christian art it produces many images of *Synagoga* as a blindfolded and dejected woman, on occasion holding the lance, sponge and crown of thorns used (by Roman soldiers!) to torment Jesus at his execution. One example from the early twelfth century places The Church, crowned, banners flying, alongside such a representation of The Synagogue, whose legend is as follows: *Synagoga Christum Dei filium abnegans, prophetis incredula, recedens a Deo, corona deposita, vexillo confracto, ad infernum prosperans.*[63]

Not the least of the damage done by these themes of Christian theology was that they led to viewing Diaspora Judaism as little more than a foil for the expansion of Christianity. This development, which is certain to produce distortions as far as the Diaspora is concerned, is helped along by the fact that for biblical thought before the Common Era there was no positive theological symbol for life outside Palestine. The only two kinds of biblical "space" were

---

63 Blumenkranz, *op. cit.* (note 61, of 1966) 107f.

Promised (or Holy) Land and Exile. Diaspora could only be Exile; and no one who read the Hebrew Scriptures carefully could come to any other conclusion than that Exile was punishment. On this point Christians and Jews saw the Old Testament in the same way; on a "biblical" basis, each group could view Jewish life in the western Diaspora only as flawed, and inferior to life in the Holy Land.[64]

The letter of Bishop Hypatios with which this essay began illustrates another part of this story. Very early, such terms as "Jew" and "Judaizer" were used of one Christian by another, with negative connotation. On occasion, the person who used the word fancied that the other had manifested some quality which he associated with the Jews of the bible. In other cases, it was simply that "Jew" had become a powerful negative term, useful in admonition or in attack.

This development within Christianity is important here for three reasons: it suggests that some references to "Jews" in later Christian sources may tell nothing about actual Jews; one example is the "historicizing" of CII 747. It also shows how widespread was the use of the image of the Jews *of the Bible* by later Christians; what the Bible was thought to say about the Jews it describes influenced the way later writers characterized *all* Jews in antiquity, perhaps particularly those about whom direct information was scarce, e.g. the Jews of the Roman Diaspora. Finally, of course, it shows clearly the development of anti-Jewish sentiment among later Christians; those who used "Jew" or "Judaizer" to stigmative their opponents did not have a positive view of the Jews themselves.[65]

Two examples from the fourth century show how the biases which began in the New testament could be extended to issues in a very different context. One controversy which the Council of Nicaea attempted to settle was that over the annual dating of Easter. The major question was whether Easter should always fall on a Sunday, or whether the sequence Last Supper/Cruci-fixion/Easter should be commemorated annually according to the date of the Passover *seder*, which fell on the same date of the month each year. There was no question but that the New Testament Passion Story was directly linked to Passover: in the Synoptics the Last Supper is a Passover Meal, and in the Gospel of John Jesus dies as the Passover Lamb. In the early period the time

---

64 See the comments on "diasporic religion" in the context of the history of religions, in J.Z. Smith, *Map is Not Territory* (Leiden, 1978), e.g. in "Earth and Gods," 104-28.

65 *CII* 747 may illustrate yet another practice: the assumption that what one understands to be true of *later* Jews was also characteristic of Jews in antiquity. If one associates later Jews with avarice (usury, money lending), it becomes easy to see "Jewish greed" in a text from the past, cf. Parkes, *op. cit.* (note 61, of 1938), 269-382. but such retrojection was less common than the first three.

for Easter was fixed in different ways, depending on how the gospel accounts were used; thus the dating was not the same from one area to the other. This was less acceptable as the Church became larger and more centrally organized, and the interest in uniformity became more powerful. The concern grew among some Church leaders to a single date each year. An obvious method was to begin with the fixed date of Passover; calculation was simple enough, and there was ample support in the gospels. But this was thought to give Jews too much control over a major Christian event. When the matter was settled by the council, and the now familiar Thursday-Sunday sequence made mandatory, Constantine himself would stigmatize the other options as "Judaizing" or "following the Jews."[66]

In the Easter Controversy, one position might just possibly be called Judaizing, although this by no means guaranteed that those who held it were on good terms with actual Jews.[67] A connection with the Jews is even more remote in the major controversy of the century, that over Arianism. Here the conflict is wholly intra-Christian. The weapons are New Testament texts and the issues Christological. When Arius was attacked for importing "Jewish" ideas into Christianity, the battle was not with Jews but with "Jewish" Christians and "Judaizers," Christians whose Christology was insufficiently exalted, in that it placed too much emphasis on the *humanity* and thus the "Jewishness" of Jesus, and not enough on the *divinity* of Christ.[68]

Being a "Jew," acting like Jews, Judaizing—such charges would be used regularly by one Christian of another through the history of the western Church. Early in the ninth century, for example, Odo of Cluny attacked fellow Christians who would not agree with him as to the sanctity of Gerald of Aurillac. They were "Judaizers" because they first wanted miracles attested for Gerald; that is, they were like the Jews of the Bible in their unbelief.[69]

Examples could be multiplied from the first 1500 years of the church. Judaeus was driven from Judas, thus every Jew is tied to the betrayal of Jesus. The Jewish Diaspora was understood as God's pre-ordained witness to the gentile world, and thus in aid of the Christian mission; Jews, because they possess the Scriptures, point others to Jesus, even though they cannot see him

---

66 A. Strobel, *Upsprung und Geschichte des fruhchristlichen Osterkalendars* (Berlin,f 1977) 389-92.

67 The Quartodeciman dating of Easter was frequently called "Judaizing" but Melito of Sardis, a Quartodeciman, was no friend of local Jews, see A.T. Kraabel, 'Melito the Bishop and the Synagogue at Sardis: Text and Context,' in *Studies Presented to George M. A. Hanfmann,* edd. D.G. Mitten et al. (Cambridge, MA, 1971) 77-85.

68 R. Lorenz, *Arius Iudaizans?* (Gottingen, 1979); Parkes, *op. cit.* (note 60, of 1934) 300-03.

69 See his *Vita Sancti Geraldi, PL* 133.670, cf. Blumenkranz, *op. cit.* (note 60, of 1963), no. 184a, p. 218.

themselves. They are the Christians' *capsarii*, bearing the Old Testament but blind to its true meaning. But the Diaspora was also punishment for the Jews' rejection of the messiah; they are not in the Holy Land, thus they are exiles.

Such distortion was by no means restricted to exegetical and theological writings. In medieval art it appears in the contrast between Church and Synagogue already mentioned. It also prompted representations of the events of the Passion with Jews replacing Roman soldiers; Jews are seen as the ones who beat Jesus, mock him and then force him to carry the cross.[70] Similar themes occur in medieval drama: the Jews are blind in that they cannot see the witness of their own scriptures to Jesus. Here too they are eager to take part in the events of the Passion.[71]

After the Reformation additional distortions emerge, as Protestants see themselves in the Christians of the New Testament, and in the Jews the Church of Rome. As the polemics between Protestant and Catholic warmed up, each side could call the other "Jew" (or "heretic") with great disregard for consistency.[72] From this point on the story is somewhat better known.

---

70 Blumenkranz, *op. cit.* (note 61, of 1966) 96-104.

71 See note 61.

72 J. Trachtenberg, *The Devil and the Jews* (New Haven, 1945) 1186f.

Unity and Diversity among Diaspora Synagogues[1]

A.T. Kraabel

The purpose of this essay is to sketch an *hypothesis* about the Jewish Diaspora.[2] The intent of the hypothesis is to account for the survival and even the success of synagogue Judaism in the cities of the Greco-Roman world. It goes as far as I am able presently to set this phenomenon in the context of the Greco-Roman world.

Let me state the thesis at the outset: The Judaism of the synagogue communities of the Roman Diaspora is best understood, on the basis of the present evidence, as the grafting of a transformed biblical "exile" ideology onto a Greco-Roman form of social organization. The most important result of that process was not a text or a system of thought, but an architectural and social symbol, the synagogue itself—the building and the community.

With more data one could accomplish the kind of detailed treatment of community life, history, and theology that is regularly done from the texts of rabbinic Judaism or of primitive Christianity. But the evidence is severely limited when such a reconstruction is attempted for the Roman Diaspora and is usually based on the works of Philo and scraps of questionable Christian evidence; the results are not persuasive.

Only the synagogue communities can tell us anything very definitive about this Judaism. There is no lack of evidence, such as magical papyri and gems, for individual instances of the conflation of Jewish and pagan pieties by gentiles or Jews. But with the evidence of a synagogue building at Ostia or Sardis or Dura we have definitive information about the Judaism of a specific community whose members chose to establish and maintain this institution, and thus to define and express their understanding of what it meant to be Jewish in that particular situation.

The primary data for the synagogue Judaism of the Roman Diaspora are scattered and diverse. Substantial new excavations would undoubtedly bring to light new data, but none are likely in the near future. The diversity of current data was evident some years ago in the *Age of Spirituality* exhibition at the Metropolitan Museum of Art.[3] The section on Judaism, under the direction of Professor Narkiss, displayed frescoes from Pompeii and Dura and fragments of a synagogue floor mosaic from Hammam-Lif in Tunisia; Rome

---

1 Editor's note: This article first appeared in Lee I. Levine, editor, *The Synagogue in Late Antiquity*, A Centennial Publication of the Jewish Theological Seminary of America (Philadelphia: ASOR, 1987) 49-60.

2 For the primary evidence, see Kraabel "The Diaspora Synagogue" *ANRW* II.19.1 (1979) 477-510; "the Roman Diaspora: Six Questionable Assumptions" *JJS* 33 (1982) 445-464; *Synagoga Caeca "To See Ourselves as Others See Us"* (1985) 219-246.

3 K. Weitzmann *Age of Spirituality: Late Antique and Early Christian Art, Third to Seventh Century* (New York: Metropolitan Museum of Art, 1979).

supplied a sarcophagus and some of the famous gold glass; from Asia Minor came a seventh-century gold medallion and one of the Noah's Ark coins from third-century Apamea in Phrygia; Egypt provided an oil lamp and an incense burner; both examples of Jewish architecture were from outside the Holy Land—the Roman Diaspora's two most spectacular synagogues at Dura and Sardis. These are precious materials, of course, but insufficient for a persuasive detailed reconstruction of Diaspora existence.

My own evidence is even more restricted, since it is limited to synagogues where the sites are well preserved and excavated enough to convey some impressions of the people who maintained and used the buildings, and the gentile communities in which they lived. The six buildings differ greatly, as do their locations.[4] Following are summary descriptions of these sites:

Sardis in Lydia (Asia Minor) was a metropolis before the Trojan War, an economic power, and a political and cultural center ruled by Croesus in the mid-sixth century, then captured by Cyrus of Persia. It surrendered to Alexander the Great in 334 B.C.E. and was controlled by his successors. In 133 B.C.E. it came under Roman control. Sardis is a powerful representative of the Lydian, the Eastern Greek, and later the Roman world, and was open to the rest of Anatolia and the east. The excavated synagogue is the latest known from that community and dates from the second or third century C.E. It was destroyed in 616 C.E..

Priene on the Aegean coast (Asia Minor) was always relatively small, a Hellenistic "planned city" laid out on a regular grid-pattern. Its major deities are the Greek Zeus, Athena, Demeter, the Egyptian Isis, and the Anatolian Cybele; its culture was strongly Ionian and Greek. The synagogue here dates from the third or fourth century C.E..

Dura in Syria, on the remote eastern rim of the Empire, was a small caravan- and garrison-city that was walled and fortified. Its society was a complex racial and religious mixture where no one tradition dominated. Its existence was often precarious; it was only intermittently under Roman authority, and then continued as a non-Roman community under the control of the Roman army. It was open to non-Roman influence from all directions. While Jews lived in Dura long before the second century c.f., its famous synagogue was established during that time and destroyed in 256 C.E.

---

4 Kraabel "The Diaspora Synagogue" (1979); "Social Syatems" (1981).

Delos, the island birthplace of Apollo, was a crossroads in the Aegean from prehistoric times. Well known in the literature of classical antiquity, it attracted merchants, travelers, and immigrants from the eastern Mediterranean, particularly after it became a free port in the second century B.C.E. By that time a permanent community of Greek-speaking Samaritans had been established on the island,[5] along with several important sanctuaries of a non-Greek type for foreign deities. The Jewish synagogue dates from the first century B.C.E. to the second century C.E.

Ostia was the port of Rome during the great expansion of trade in the early Empire. Excavations reveal a well-planned city, with harbors, large warehouses, a traders' office, guild halls, and blocks of private apartments. The community of Ostia included families from Rome and elsewhere in Italy, along with traders, slaves, and ex-slaves from the Mediterranean area. Non-Roman cults are well documented —Cybele, Bellona, Isis, and especially Mithras existed along with Judaism and Christianity. The earliest synagogue on the site may go back to the first century C.E. The latest and most developed synagogue is from the fourth century.

Stobi in Macedonia was a Roman administrative center. It flourished in the second and third centuries, and grew and prospered in the fourth and fifth centuries when three Christian basilicas were built within the city and at least two more outside of it. The earliest building, the "Synagogue of Polycharmos," dates from the third century C.E.; the later synagogue is from the fourth century

Detailed accounts of these buildings may be found in the published reports of these sites. The immediate task is to examine the larger social context for these Diaspora Jewish communities.

In these six examples, and in other cases, a Jewish community survived and even prospered outside the Homeland in a largely gentile environment. The Diaspora synagogue community was a successful social organization that endured and remains to this day. Some of the reasons for that success and for the shape of this new form of Judaism are reflected in ideas and themes found in postexilic Israelite religion. But they are only half of the explanation, and will be discussed in the next section below. I will begin with that part of the story that comes out of the Greco-Roman world, the "gentile" world outside Palestine. It is of a piece with the profound changes that took place within

---

5 P. Bruneau "Les Israélites de Délos et la juiverie délienne" *Bulletin de Correspondance Hellénique* 106 (1982) 465-504; Kraabel "New Evidence" *BA* 47 (1984) 44-46.

Greco-Roman society itself in the period between Alexander the Great and Augustus: the expansions and movements of peoples that began with Alexander, and continued later when the armies of the Republic gave Rome its empire.

These events at the same time produced or accelerated the disintegration of the social unites of the classical world: the coherence of the *polis* ended and, somewhat later, the Roman idea of *communitas*. The Greco-Roman world responded to the demise of these large social units by creating smaller units, as the *polis* and the small town of Rome had been in their glorious pasts. Nowadays these groups are classified as economic, ethnic, cultural, social, or religious. At that time, they had differing frameworks, although the motivation for forming smaller units was the same: to create a small *cosmos* within the chaos that had replaced the former order, to cope with the sense of loss and powerlessness that most people, particularly immigrants, felt in the new ethnic melting pot. In the Hellenistic period and under the Roman Empire voluntary organization into small social units was most popular.[6]

For along time classicists and ancient historians said little about these groups, since classical authors all but ignored them, for at least two reasons: The associations were usually formed by the less affluent, who are poorly represented in the literary texts; and the associations were in their greatest numbers after the "classical" period of Greek and of Latin literature. Thus, for a long time the associations were not attested to in the evidence customarily used to re-create ancient history and were assumed nonexistent. More recently, inscriptions and papyri have become available in great quantity and, together with the data from excavations, clarify the widespread popularity of voluntary organizations and clubs.

Surprisingly few of these organizations were of a religious nature. Most clubs had a patron deity, but after the time of Alexander the Great very few are attested to whose main purpose was to worship or honor a particular deity. The closest thing to a religious guild would be the *technitai* of Dionysus, found in Athens, Smyrna, and Syracuse from the third century on, whose purpose was the promotion of music and drama. They were customarily given privileged status, including exemption from taxation and military service.

Most associations, however, were more everyday affairs, made up of artisans of a particular skill—such as "the associated spikers of razorfish" at

---

6 See K. Ziegler; W. Sontheimer, H. Gärtner, editors, *Der Kleine Pauly: Lexikon der Antike* (Stuttgart, Munich, Germany: Deutscher Taschenbuch Verlag, 1964-75) under "Vereinswesen" and "Berufsverein"; T. Klausner, editor, *Reallexikon für Antike und Christentum* (Stuttgart, Germany:Anton Hiersemann, 1950-) under "Gemeinschaft"; M. Rostovtzeff, *The Social and Economic History of the Hellenistic World* (Oxford:Clarendon, 1941), in index 1, under "Associations").

Miletus[7]—or merchants or ex-soldiers, "Old Boys" from the same school, interest groups of all sorts, even slaves. Dining societies, mutual aid societies, and burial societies were also common.

Such associations were always ad hoc; there was no larger national or international structure to which they were attached. In a very real sense, they were popular because they were local, because they offered something of what the individual had lost in the advent of the Hellenistic and Roman empires.

The need for community in a bewildering larger world affected people at nearly every level of wealth and education. Among the philosophically trained in this period, "friendship" was a topic commonly discussed. This new emphasis reflected a new kind of social grouping where the ties were not of blood or nationality but of intellectual affinity. Epicureans established a community of philosophical friends, the "garden" of Epicurus, to which men and also women and slaves were admitted. In many ways it was not so much a philosophy as a community of like minds. Communal gatherings were important. Memorial feasts were held regularly on the anniversary of Epicurus's death. Centuries after his death there was still remarkably little change in Epicurean teachings.[8] It is not surprising, then, that in the preserved sayings of Epicurus, friendship is mentioned in strong and positive terms: "The noble soul occupies itself with wisdom and friendship: of these the one is a mortal god, the other immortal."[9]

When immigrants from Egypt or Asia Minor entered Greece, they found the voluntary association useful for religious and social purposes, although it was quite different from what they had been used to in the Homeland. They brought their deities with them: in a sense both the god and his followers were immigrants; the private club served the needs of both. Thus, there were organizations honoring the Egyptian Isis or the Anatolian Cybele. There were societies with initiation rites, or mystery rites, involving Greek deities (like Dionysus) or foreign gods. Unlike the rites of the archaic or classical period, these mysteries served to build a sense of belonging to the single localized group. Those who had been initiated in the same rites formed a kinship, a substitute for the multi-generational natural families of earlier times.

Jews began to form their own communities in the Greco-Roman world early in the Hellenistic period. The oldest inscriptions referring to synagogues come from Egypt and are dated to within a century of the death of Alexander

---

7 W. Dittenberger editor, *Orientis Graeci Inscriptiones Selectae* volume 1 and 2 (Leipzig, Germany: S. Hirzel, 1903-05) number 756.

8 See Klauser (1950-) under "Epikur."

9 C. Bailey editor and translator *Epicurus: The Extant Romains, with Short Critical Apparatus, Translation and Note* (Oxford:Clarendon, 1926) *Vatican Sayings*, number 78.

the Great.[10] The oldest excavated synagogue is not in Palestine; it is on the Greek island of Delos, dating from the first century B.C.E. Far to the west, at the same time, the Jewish community in Rome was of good size,[11] and the synagogue community in Ostia just outside of Rome dates to as early as the first century C.E.

More successfully than any other of Rome's minorities, the Jewish population was able to adapt a Hellenistic gentile social form, the private organization, to its particular social and religious purposes. The remarkable developments that occurred among the Greek-speaking Jews in the cities of the Roman world may be summarized as follows:[12]

> They dispensed with a priesthood, even while the Jerusalem Temple still stood. Everything we know about Diaspora synagogue organization indicates that it was led by laymen from the outset.

> They retained the bible in a Greek translation. Their reverence for the Scripture is manifested architecturally in the Torah shrines in five of the six buildings described above, indicating a strong tie to this element of traditional Judaism. This is striking for two reasons: first, the basic pattern of the godly life found in the Scriptures assumes a very different kind of existence than was available to Diaspora Jews; and, second, although in Palestine and Babylonia influential Jews found it necessary to produce substantial, normative materials to supplement the Bible and adapt it to their times, the Jews of the Mediterranean Diaspora saw no such necessity.

> They developed a new form of community organization which was fairly uniform from one Diaspora city to the next.

> They retained essential cultic practices—food laws, circumcision, Sabbath observance—while adjusting to gentile city life.

> They developed a new architecture, based on the public architecture of the Roman Empire but adapted to liturgical use. It replaced the Temple architecture that had dominated Israelite religion for a thousand years, and it was so successful that it is still in use in Jewish, Christian, and Moslem versions.

---

10 P.J.-B. Frey *Corpus Inscriptionum Iudaicarum*, volume 2 (Rome: Pontificio Instituto di Archeologia Cristiana, 1952) 1440, 1532A.

11 H.J. Leon *The Jews of Ancient Rome* (Philadelphia: Jewish Publication Society of America, 1960).

12 See also J.J. Collins Between Athens and Jerusalem (New York: Crossroad, 1983).

They developed an iconography whose symbolism often derived from the figurative language of the Bible. The use of wall paintings, mosaics, and plastic art to carry those forms was novel in a religion that in earlier periods had had a great antipathy to "graven images." Later some striking examples of this iconography appeared in the Homeland, too—the mosaics of Bêt 'Alpâ', for example—but the idea seems to have begun in the Diaspora, as Jews looked for new vehicles to carry the tradition for them and their descendants.[13]

Their community extended into the next world. If possible, Jews established their own cemeteries, separate from the graves of non-Jews. The epitaphs were usually brief, but the thought expressed was often recognizably biblical. Pagan "tombstone theology" involved a few very well-known ideas, endlessly repeated. These rarely occurred in Jewish inscriptions.

In some sense this was also a world community, the only successful example of a network of Hellenistic voluntary associations that extended beyond national boundaries. The common tie was, of course, the Homeland, not necessarily the Palestine of their own times, but the biblical Israel elevated to mythical status. It is not surprising, then, that the Diaspora synagogues placed the Torah shrine on the wall closest to Jerusalem, thus orienting the building toward the Holy City. While most Diaspora Jews had no wish to return to the Holy Land, except perhaps on a brief pilgrimage, it was and has remained the center of their world.

Despite all these changes the communities continued to see themselves as Jewish. That identification was important, and they boldly made it. Other Jewish immigrants blended into the gentile population and disappeared. These did not.

Nor were the Diaspora Jews unreflective. The changes I have mentioned need not have been accidental or unplanned. In order to survive as immigrants in a pluralistic society, Diaspora Jews expanded and adapted certain themes in their ancestral religion and abandoned others. They had been "prepared" to succeed in the Diaspora chiefly by three "external events," incursions of foreign powers into the Jewish Homeland—which indeed would have been avoided at all costs had it been possible.

The result of these events was the beginning of a worldview or theology that would make Jews ready to handle life outside the Homeland. Perhaps

---

13 J. Neusner "The Symbolism of Ancient Judaism: The Evidence of the Synagogue," In *Ancient Synagogues: The State of Research*, BJS 22 (Chico, CA: Scholars, 1981) 7-17.

because other immigrant groups lacked the first—the formative events—they also lacked the second, the theology. They were not ready for the new situation in any way that would allow them to survive as religious and cultural unities.

A great deal has been written about the impact of gentile culture on Palestine, particularly after Alexander the Great. The events of this period are usually called "the Hellenization of Judaism," with the discussion centering on the rise and fall of the Maccabean kingdom in the second and first centuries B.C.E.[14] Important as these events were in Palestine, their impact was not felt in the Roman Diaspora. The Judaism with which the Diaspora Jews identified was the "Israelite religion" of the Bible and the Temple, and not that shaped and revised under the Maccabees.

Two of the three "external events" are in the bible. The first is the capture of the northern kingdom by the Assyrians in 722 B.C.E.; the second is the Exile, beginning in 587 B.C.E. with the fall of Jerusalem to Babylonian armies under Nebuchadnezzar. In both instances, outside forces profoundly altered Israelite existence, forcing thousands of Israelites to live as captives outside the Holy Land.

After the first deportation, many Jews simply "disappeared," having merged into the gentile population of the Assyrian Empire. The second deportation, the Exile, had profoundly different results. In a very real sense Judaism was born out of that Exile. As a result of these two events, particularly the second, the Exile became a permanent element in the religion of Israel. For Jews the Diaspora became a theological issue. No other Mediterranean people has had a similar experience.

There was little in the thought and imagery of other Eastern immigrant religions that might have formed an ideological justification for life in a Diaspora and for this new kind of social organization. The worship of Cybele and especially of Isis became popular also with those who had not come from the homelands of these goddesses. But out of the large number of devotees no extensive communities were formed. No common code of religious practice nor common homeland held them together.

Judaism was different. With increasing migration in the Hellenistic period, what Israel had learned from the Exile became central to a new and often voluntary "Exile" in the Greco-Roman world. At this point "Diaspora" becomes a more appropriate term than "Exile". Indeed some Jews would never return from the East to the Holy Land, but would move directly into the Mediterranean Diaspora from Babylonia. Those who established the Jewish community at Sardis are the best documented example.

---

14 Compare M. Smith *Palestinian Parties and Politics that Shaped the Old Testament* (New York: Columbia University Press, 1971) 57-81.

In Babylonia, desire to maintain one's Jewishness had led to the formation of cohesive communities for that purpose. Ideologically and sociologically the Babylonian exile was where the synagogue began—in its earliest sense, as a community assembly rather than a building. There is no archaeological evidence from that date, of course, and even the literary references are fragmentary. Nevertheless, it was a major innovation, the shift from a national religion of Holy Land and Temple to that of a minority community. Like many other *nova* in religion, its beginnings have left only faint traces in the historical record.

After the return from Babylonia, what might be called "Exile theology" remained a part of Jewish religious thought. Consequently, the later Diaspora of the Hellenistic and Roman periods had at hand the religious symbols, the theology, and a form of social organization sanctioned by earlier generations that would allow Jews to maintain an existence outside of the Holy Land without forfeiting their cultural and religious heritage. Of all the immigrant groups of the Roman Empire, only the Jews were prepared theologically and sociologically for Diaspora existence.

The third "external event" in Jewish history was the destruction of the Jerusalem Temple by Roman troops under Titus. This was in one sense a surprising event—unexpected, terrible, catastrophic—and yet in a very real sense the Jewish people were ready for it. Judaism had become a "larger" religion; Jews had overflowed Palestine to the point that many more of them lived outside of the Homeland than within it. A religion and ideology centering on the Holy Land and the sacrificial cult in Jerusalem were no longer of sufficient scope for what Judaism had become. The larger conception of Judaism that emerged from the Exile now came to justify and validate life outside of Palestine. It made clear how Jews might exist faithfully in a minority community in the gentile world.

In that process the "Exile theology" would itself be transformed. A more positive "Diaspora theology" began to take its place, at least for some Diaspora Jews, as one of the major themes of the "Exile theology" was transcended. I refer to the idea that somehow the displacement from the Homeland (the "Dispersion") was a punishment from God. That idea had included the presupposition that the great hope of many Jews was to escape the world of the gentile and to return to the Homeland one day.

For some Jews in the Roman world this "punishment" language could still make a great deal of sense, for example, for the prisoners of war who became Roman slaves after Jerusalem was captured. Their situation must have been no better than that of the hostages taken to Babylonia after the earlier destruction of the city.

In addition, and perhaps more important, Exile language was soon adopted by Christians in an attempt to discredit the Jews: For Christians the

Jewish Diaspora was not a worthy religious way of life, but a divine punish-ment, an exile in the worst sense of the word.[15] The Christians used this idea so extensively when rationalizing Judaism that it became the dominant interpretive symbol by which many gentiles and Jews understood Jewish existence in the Roman world outside of Palestine.

But over the centuries many Jews left the Homeland voluntarily, as did other people from peripheral areas of the Mediterranean who sought their fortunes in the centers of power of the Hellenistic and Roman world. These individuals did not understand themselves to be in exile, but rather welcomed and desired immigration as part of a new situation that was also under the control of Providence. Just as the rabbis spiritualized the Temple and its cult, so the Diaspora Jews spiritualized the Homeland. Like many immigrants in more recent times, their transplanted, transformed religion allowed them to believe that their *new* homeland was not alien. They had made the main elements of Judaism portable: the Scriptures, the symbols, and the synagogue community itself. The Diaspora was not Exile; in some sense it became a Holy Land, too.

In summary, the synagogue Judaism of the Roman Diaspora is best understood as the grafting of a biblical diaspora theology onto a Greco-Roman social organization. The shift to minority status in places outside the Homeland led to the abandonment of many elements of the ancestral religion, a new emphasis on others, and the adoption of the new environment's iconography, architecture, and organizational form.

The result could be called a new religion, differing from traditional Palestinian Judaism, "biblical religion," as much as rabbinic Judaism had. Yet at the same time it was self-consciously and sometimes enthusiastically Jewish, prepared to survive within an environment of religious pluralism by relying on resources within the tradition.

It was no accident that this is the conference's only paper to have Diaspora Judaism as its main concern. Among Jewish and gentile scholars alike, the emphasis has always been on the biblical and rabbinic literatures, and on the Holy Land. The data from the Diaspora are less accessible and, more significant, less likely to be considered by students either of history or of religion. Hypothetical reconstructions like the one attempted in this paper are difficult to test because there are so few competing hypotheses against which they might be measured. It is the responsibility of those who are dissatisfied with the story I have related here to come up with a better way of assembling the data into a coherent and meaningful whole.

When G.D. Cohen, the chancellor of the Jewish Theological Seminary in New York, wrote—in a 1973 article significantly titled "The Blessing of

---

15 Kraabel "The Roman Diaspora" (1982) 460-464.

Assimilation in Jewish History"—that "the great ages of Jewish creativity have always been products of the challenge of assimilation and of the response of leaders who were to a certain extent assimilated themselves," he might have been describing the Jews of the Mediterranean synagogues.[16] The evidence for the synagogue Judaism of the Mediterranean Diaspora is sparse and scattered. However, there must have been at one time many more synagogues like the six specific examples I have mentioned. It is inconceivable, I believe, that communities as substantial as these could exist only in a few Roman towns.

However, the fact remains that Diaspora Judaism did not survive. Rabbinic Judaism did. My own judgement is that this does not mean that somehow rabbinic Judaism was inherently "better," "more authentic," or "more Jewish." roman Diaspora Judaism did not survive because it succumbed to outside forces, not to any internal flaw or weakness. But that is another topic and another essay.

---

16 Compare Neusner *The Academic Study of Judaism* (Chico, CA: Scholars, 1982) 35-48.

Bibliography

Bailey, C. editor and translator
1926   *Epicurus: The Extant Remains with Short Critical Apparatus, Translation and Notes*. Oxford: Clarendon.

Bruneau, P.
1982   Les Israélites de Délos et la jiverie délienne. *Bulletin de Correspondance Hellénique* 106: 465-504.

Cohen, G.D.
1973   The Blessing of Assimilation in Jewish Histroy. In *Understanding Jewish Theology*, edited by J. Neusner, pages 251-258. New York: Ktav.

Collins, J.J.
1983   *Between Athens and Jerusalem*, New York: Crossroad.

Dittenberger, W., editor
1903-5 *Orientis Graeci Inscriptiones Selectae,* volumes 1 and 2. Leipzig. W. Ger: S. Hirzel.

Frey, P.J.R., editor
1952   *Corpes Inscriptionum Ivdaicarum*, volume 2. Rome: Pontificio Instituto di Archeologia Cristiana.

Klauser, T., editor
1950-   *Reallexikon für Antike und Christentum*. Stuttgart, W. Ger: Anton Hiersemann.

Kraabel, A.T.
1979   The Diaspora Synagogue In *Aufstieg und Niedergang der römischen Welt*, part 2 volume 19.1 edited by II. Temporini and W. Haase, pages 477-510. Berlin New York: de Gruyter.
1981   Social Systems of Six Diaspora Synagogues. In *Ancient Synagogues: The State of Research*, pages 79-91 and figure 19. Series: Brown Judaic Studies 22. Chico, Calif. Scholars.
1982   The Roman Diaspora: Six Questionable Assumptions. *Journal of Jewish Studies* 33: 445-464.
1984   New Evidence of the Samaritan Diaspora Has Been Found of Delos. *Biblical Archacologist* 47: 44-46.
1985   *Synagoga Caeca*: Systematic Distortion in Gentile Interpretations of Evidence for Judaism in the Early Christian Period. In *"To See Ourselves as Others See Us": Christian Jews, "Others" in Late Antiquity*, edited by J. Neusner and F.S. Frerichs, pages 219-46. Chico, Calif. Scholars.

Leon, H.J.
1960   *The Jews of Ancient Rome*. Philadelphia, Pa. Jewish Publication Society of America.

Neusner, J.
1981   The Symbolism of Ancient Judaism: The Evidence of the Synagogue. In *Ancient Synagogues: The State of Research*, pages 7-17. Series Brown Judaic Studies 22. Chico, Calif. Scholars.
1982   *The Academic Study of Judaism*, Chico, Calif. Scholars.

Nock, A.D.
1972   *Essays on Religion and the Ancient World*. Edited by Z. Steward, Oxford: Clarendon.

Rostovtzeff, M.
1941   *The Social and Economic History of the Hellenistic World*. Oxford: Clarendon.

Smith, M.
1971   *Palestinian Parties and Politics that Shaped the Old Testament*. New York: Columbia University Press.

Weitzmann, K.
1979   *Age of Spirituality: Late Antique and Early Christian Art, Third to Seventh Century*. New York: Metropolitan Museum of Art.

Ziegler K.; Sontheimer, W; and Gartner, H., editors
1964-75 *Der Kleine Pauly: Lexikon der Antike* Stuttgart Munich, W. Ger: Deutscher Taschenbuch Verlag.

Synagoga Caeca: Systematic Distortion in Gentile Interpretations of Evidence for Judaism in the Early Christian Period[1]

A.T. Kraabel

I

The Jews of antiquity were not always what they seem. To those of us who study the Greco-Roman world, that has been clear for a long time. It is also widely understood now in New Testament studies—witness the papers touching on the New Testament at this conference. References to Jews and Jewish practices in these first Christian texts may never be taken at face value. In the earliest Christian accounts, the "Jews" in the story fall into three categories: 1) theological phantoms brought in for inner-church reasons, as one group of Christians battles another; 2) political scapegoats, an all-too-familiar role; 3) if they happen to be *real* Jews, they are often under attack from the Christian side, and the picture is necessarily distorted. These Christian texts were never intended to be historical reference works. They were written for more important and immediate reasons than that. Usually, they served theological purposes. So like the rabbinic literature, they must be approached indirectly if we are to draw historical information from them. This characteristic of the sources requires close attention if we are to come to a clear understanding of how Jews and Christians related to those "outside," and particularly how they defined themselves in relation to the other.

This is particularly true for the Greco-Roman world and Diaspora Judaism, where the evidence is not abundant in the first place, and where it may often be mixed up with pagan concerns as well as with the Christian theological agenda. In a recent article in the Yadin *Festschrift*, I discussed the following six questionable assumptions which are part of the "conventional wisdom" in this area: 1) the Mediterranean Diaspora was *syncretistic*; 2) Diaspora Jews were characterized by a great *missionary zeal*; 3) Jews outside Palestine were *aliens* in the Roman world; 4) their social, economic and intellectual *status* was very low; 5) they were a *monolithic* group, interconnected and even directly controlled from Palestine, a kind of "underground" which was feared and alternatively oppressed and appeased by Roman authorities; 6) their activities and the actions toward them by gentiles are best understood on *religious* terms, since Judaism is a religion first of all.[2] If these assumptions

---

1 Editor's note: This essay was first presented at a conference held at Brown University, August 6, 1984, entitled "To See Ourselves as Others See Us." This paper was later published by Scholars Press and edited by J. Neusner and E.S. Frerichs in *"To See Ourselves as Others See Us:" Christians, Jews, "Others" in Late Anitquity* (1985) 219-246.

2 A.T. Kraabel, "The Roman Diaspora: Six Questionable Assumptions." *JJS* 33 (1982) 445-464.

were in fact correct, they would say a great deal about how Diaspora Jews understood themselves in relation to the non-Jewish majority around them. But the assumptions are questionable, and deserve reexamination.

My purpose here is to continue the theme of that paper in a different way, by giving three particular examples of the distortions which concern me.

II

My first example is neither Jewish nor gentile. It is Samaritan, and comes from the middle of the Hellenistic period. It comprises two Samaritan inscriptions that were recently discovered on the island of Delos, which lies just off the Greek mainland and 150 kilometers southeast of Athens. These two texts are now to be added to the Samaritan papyri from the Wadi Daliyeh and the data from the Shechem excavations led by G.E.Wright.[3] (Shechem was located at the foot of Mount Gerezim, the Samaritan holy mountain;it was the Samaritan center during the Hellenistic period.) All of these discoveries are from the last three decades.

The Samaritans themselves have been studied in their own right, so we have reconstructions of their history and religious thought. In Biblical times they are associated with the Northern Kingdom, Israel, whose capital was Samaria. In 722, that Northern Kingdom was captured by the Assyrians. Then, at some point after the Exile which took place subsequent to the fall of the Southern Kingdom, Judah, and the destruction of Jerusalem in 587,the Samaritans began to take on a separate existence.Without going into the vexed question of "the origins of the Samaritans," it is clear that three later military campaigns had much to do with Samaritan history in Palestine. They are the capture of the area by Alexander the Great in the late fourth century, the conflicts between Judah Maccabee and the forces of Antiochus Epiphanes in the early second century, and the capture of Shechem and the destruction of the Samaritan Temple on Mount Gerezim by John Hyrcanus late in the second century.

The excavation of Shechem showed that the site had been unoccupied during most of the Persian period (fifth-fourth centuries), but that a great number of people lived there in the next two centuries.[4] Archaeologists from the Shechem expedition also excavated the ruins at Tell er-Ras on the top of Mount Gerezim. Under a temple of Zeus Hypsistos (from the second century C.E.) they found a large building complex which include the remains of the Samaritan Temple known from accounts in Josephus.[5]

---

3 G.E. Wright, Shechem: *The Biography of a Biblical City* (New York 1965) 170-184.

4 Wright (1965) 170.

5 R.J. Bull "Gerizim, Mount" *IDBS* (1976) 361.

According to Josephus, the Samaritan Temple was built on the model of the Temple in Jerusalem, and stood for two hundred years (*AJ* 13.256). While they were under the control of Antiochus Epiphanes, the Samaritans sought to adapt themselves to his hellenization program by dedicating the temple to Zeus Xenios.[6] Such accommodation would distinguish them from the Maccabees, who came to power in Palestine soon thereafter. Conflicts arose with the Maccabees, and the temple on Mount Gerezim was finally destroyed by John Hyrcanus in 128 B.C.E. Josephus' two hundred years begins, then, with Alexander the Great or soon thereafter, and ends with John Hyrcanus.

During these two centuries, the Samaritans gradually become a group separate from the Jews.[7] "The other" was coming more clearly into focus. The building of the Gerezim Temple, the Samaritans' differences with the Maccabees, and finally, John Hyrcanus' attack on the temple, each are points where Samaritan group becomes more clearly demarcated than it had been before. In all of this, Mount Gerezim is the central symbol to the Samaritans themselves and to those outside. Jews and Samaritans may have had much in common in their history and their scripture, but this piece of real estate always signaled their particularity; in the south there was Jerusalem with its Temple Mount, but the Samaritans had Gerezim.

As for the two inscriptions discovered in 1979 (published by Pierre Bruneau, the leader of the Delos excavations,[8] the older, dated between 250 and 175 B.C.E., is fragmentary. But some of the lost sections may be conjectured. It states "The Israelites on Delos who make offerings to hallowed, consecrated Mount Gerezim honor Menippos of Heraclea, son of Artemidoros, along with his descendants, who, from his own resources, because of a vow to God, constructed, equipped, and presented it." The text fails us at that point, but then continues: "... and they crown him with a golden crown ... " The other inscription, dating from between 150 and 50 B.C.E., is complete.It reads: "The Israelites on Delos who make offerings to hallowed Mount Gerezim crown with a gold crown Sarapion, son of Jason, of knossos, for his benefactions toward them."

Each inscription is cut into a rectangular shaft of white marble. Above each, a fine wreath is carved in high relief. (Indeed, as a classicist, I was

---

6 On a similar move, to dedicate the Temple in Jerusalem to Zeus Olympios (supported by "the Hellenizing party of the Jerusalem priesthood,") see M. Smith *Palestinian Parties and Politics that Shaped the Old Testament* (New York, 1971), 190, citing 2 Macc 6.

7 Purvis, "Samaritans," *IDBS (1976) 776-777.*

8 P. Bruneau, "Les Iraélites de Delos et la juiverie délienne," *Bulletin de Correspondance Hellénistique* 106 (1982) 465-504; J. and L. Robert, "Bulletin épigraphique," *Revue des études grecques*, (1983) 123-124; Kraabel, "New Evidence of the Samaritan Diaspora has been Found on Delos." *BA* 47 (1984) 44-46 (also in this volume).

struck by how properly Greek both steles are; the same design is found time and again across the Mediterranean world.) So the honor was a double one, comprising both the gold wreath ceremonially bestowed on the benefactor, and the inscription that records the honor in a public and permanent fashion. Further,"The Israelites on Delos who make offerings to hallowed Mount Gerezim" are surely Samaritans, part of the Samaritan Diaspora at a time when the Samaritan homeland is prospering and there is a substantial temple on Mount Gerezim. At about the same time, the Samaritan author we know as Ps-Eupolemos is writing in Greek about "hallowed Mount Gerezim," while using the Biblical text of Diaspora Jews, the LXX.[9]

Previous attempts to understand the Samaritans have seen them pretty much as a Palestine phenomenon and very much in second place to the Palestinian Jews. This is particularly the case in New Testament studies despite the reference in Josephus to Samaritans outside Palestine and some other evidence from the Mediterranean Diaspora. But there is indication in Luke-Acts that there was a Christian mission to the Samaritans before the mission to the Gentiles began. The resulting Samaritan Christianity is thought to have left its mark on the New Testament itself. Stephen's speech in the seventh chapter of Acts, the Gospel of John and the Letter to the Hebrews, are the texts most frequently seen as linked to Samaritan Christianity in some way.[10]

The two Delos inscriptions open this picture up considerably, for they are not what one would expect from reading earlier accounts of the data for the Samaritan Diaspora.[11] Rather, they constitute clear evidence of a long-lived Samaritan community well before Christian times and outside the Holy Land, in one of the political and economic centers of the Greek world. The Delos Samaritans call themselves "Israelites," but qualify the term thus: they are the Gerezim Israelites. Apparently, the break with the Jews is not yet final, but over against other "Israelites," some clear specification is needed as to what kind of "Israelites" these at Delos are.

At the same time, the "Israelites on Delos" are at home in the Greek world. The steles themselves, the form and language of the inscriptions and the honors paid to benefactors all follow the most proper and common Greek style. So do the names: Menippos, son of Artemidoros, and Sarapion, son of Jason. If the benefactors are themselves Samaritans, then they indicate an

---

9 J.J. Collins *Between Athens and Jerusalem* (New York, 1983) 38-39; M. Hengel, *Judaism and Hellenism* (London, 1974) 1.88-92.

10 C.H.H. Scobie "The Origins and Development of Samaritan Christianity," *NTS* 19 (1972) 390-414; R. Pummer "New Evidence for Samaritan Christianity?" *CBQ* 41 (1979) 98-117; R.J. Coggins "the Samaritans and Acts," *NTS* 28 (1982) 423-434.

11 J.A. Montgomery *The Samaritans* (Philadelphia, 1907) 148-153; H.G. Kippenberg *Garizim und Synagoge* (Berlin, 1971) 145-150.

even larger Samaritan diaspora. Heracleia and Knossos are close together on
the north shore of Crete, a much larger island some 250 kilometers south of
Delos. There may have been Samaritan "Israelites" there as well. (The Jewish
community on the island of Rhodes apparently had a similar concern for their
temple on Mount Zion. A recent inscription from Jerusalem commemorates
a gift to the temple there from a Rhodian Jew of the first century B.C.E.[12]

But most important in this whole story is the connection with Mount Gerezim. The split between Jews and Samaritans may not have been complete,
but these "Israelites" knew precisely how to identify themselves. The center of
their world was Gerezim. They must have known well the Samaritan Temple
on the mountain and the flourishing Samaritan community below it. Perhaps,
like Ps-Eupolemos, they knew how major Biblical stories had been linked to
that mountain in the Samaritan tradition.So Gerezim remained central to their
lives, the key to their religious identification even while they lived more than
1000 kilometers away from it in the center of the Greek world.

The "Israelites on Delos" typify one point of this paper. They summarize
my response to the invitation offered by those who organized this conference.
Their inscriptions are a significant example of how new evidence requires review of accepted historical reconstructions not only in the immediately
affected area of scholarship, but also in other fields related to it. In this case
the second field, New Testament and ancient Christianity, is much larger than
the first, Samaritan studies. Such discoveries have a "ripple effect" as they
move from the primary field, the point of impact, to secondary areas. Usually
those secondary areas are touched only very slowly by the new data.
Sometimes they are not reached at all.[13]

Before I move to my next example, let me briefly review the implications
of these inscriptions for the study of Diaspora Judaism. The most obvious
point to make of course is that what can be said for the Samaritan Diaspora
might also be true—even more true—for the Jewish Diaspora in the Mediterranean world.The new Samaritan data indicate, first of all, that the Samaritans
were at home in the Greek world. Since there are four or five generations between the earlier inscription and the later one, the Samaritans were a permanent settlement on Delos. They knew Greek customs and the Greek language,
and the two beneiactors and their fathers bore Greek names. But the Samaritans' tie to the Holy Land is just as obvious, and that is the second point. It
was Mount Gerezim which was the center of community identification.

In the third place, the evidence does not fit the standard reconstructions
of Samaritan religious history. That story always seems to take place in Pales-

---

12 B. Isaac "A Donation for Herod's Temple in Jerusalem," *Israel Exploration Journal* 33
(1983) 86-92.

13 Smith (1983).

tine, and in ancient times in the area west of the Jordan, north of Judah and south of Galilee. The new evidence calls into question the old critical orthodoxy, particularly where that older view has been appropriated for use in other disciplines (in this case, New Testament and ancient Christianity). Topics such as "Samaritan Christianity" or "Samaritan influence on the New Testament" take on a very different perspective if one must factor in relatively early Greek-speaking communities on Greek islands far to the west of Mount Gerezim.

And this is the fourth and final point: it is evidence from the Mediterranean Diaspora that raises new issues and brings the scholarly pot to boiling. Samaritanism, like Judaism, is seen to be in some sense a Hellenistic religion, with all that implies. If Dura and Sardis raise questions for those who study the Jews of late antiquity, the Delos evidence—small as it is—should make a similar difference in Samaritan studies. Further, it suggests that "Samaritan studies" and "Jewish studies" may be related in ways we had not expected, at least in the Greco-Roman world. I say this because the earliest Jewish synagogue found in the Mediterranean Diaspora is also on Delos, only 100 meters away from where these two inscriptions were discovered.[14]

III

My first example dealt with some very new evidence and its implications for a limited area of scholarship. The second is much more complex and much better known. With it, the emphasis shifts from the Hellenistic period of the Delos inscriptions to the time of the early Roman empire, specifically, the first seven or eight decades of the early Christian movement.

What I want to take up now is embedded in the Christianity of those decades. It is part of the following central question in the beginnings of this religion: "how did Christianity move from Palestine to the Mediterranean Diaspora?" While this may seem a historical topic, it is at bottom a theological one. Our answer to that question also reveals our view of the relationship between ancient Christianity and the powerful cultural and religious forces and ideas which surrounded it, both Greco-Roman and Jewish. Our answer to that question also says a great deal about our understanding of the New Testament itself. It reveals much about how we would in fact approach the question of "the other" in Judaism or Christianity in this period.

My subject initially, then, is Christianity. The Jews of the early Roman empire are involved in that story, but in a curious way. They were not of direct Interest either to those who created the historical record in the first place or to most of those who have studied it since. Indeed not only was there

---

14 Kraabel "The Diaspora Synagogue," *ANRW* II.19.1 (1979)491-494.

no concern to create a full and accurate picture of those Jews, there were powerful reasons to falsify the records and to tell a slanted and partial story about them. This biased, ostensibly historical account was essentially theology, or a *piece* of a theology. But it was theology in historical guise it was taken as history almost from the first by Christians writing alter the New Testament was completed and also by later scholars right up to our own day.

However this conference is concerned with Jews, not with Christians, and despite what I have just said about Christianity, Jews are my focus also. I want to look again at the image of Roman Empire Jews which was created by certain very influential New Testament texts. I am particularly interested in the Jews of the Mediterranean Diaspora, since it is with them that the distortion has been most severe. In the New Testament the central texts are Acts and the letters of Paul. The examples with which I wish to make my present point are taken from events and issues which Acts and Paul's letters have in common.[15]

Acts

Acts is the longest book in the New Testament. It begins in Jerusalem with the disciples, and ends with Paul in Rome. That makes it a story of movement. First, the Christians move from Palestine to the Mediterranean Diaspora, and thus, second, from the Jewish world to the gentile one. That is, from being a Jewish sect, they become a Greco-Roman cult. But third, this is also, and most importantly, a theological movement, since the author ("Luke") is chiefly concerned to explain and justify Christianity's departure from Judaism and its transformation into a gentile religion. My purpose is to characterize the implications of all of this for the understanding of Jews and Judaism. To do that in brief compass, I will limit myself to an examination of three terms central to what Acts seems to be saying about Jews.

The first term is "synagogue." This word appears nineteen times in Acts. It is used there chiefly as the place where Christian Diaspora missionary preaching begins, and, with one exception (Apollos, in 18:26), Paul is the preacher. Indeed, alter his conversion (9:1-19) Paul's first act is to preach in a synagogue (9:20). This is striking when one considers Paul's well-deserved reputation as Apostle to the Gentiles. However Paul's mission to the Jews of the Diaspora synagogue soon arouses opposition and is finally all but fruitless; in 19:9 he pulls the disciples out of the synagogue in Ephesus, and after that, no Christian in Acts goes into a synagogue again.

So conflict appeared to be inevitable. Three programmatic statements made by Paul in rejection of Diaspora Jews highlight this situation. First, in

---

15 For the background to what follows, see my more detailed article "The Disappearance of the 'God-Fearers.'" *Numen* 28 (1981) 113-126.

chapter thirteen, after a dispute in the synagogue of Antioch in Pisidia on the southeast coast of Asia Minor, Paul is made to say, "It was necessary that the word of God should be spoken first to you. Since you thrust it from you, and judge yourselves unworthy of eternal life, behold, we turn to the gentiles. For so the Lord has commanded us saying, 'I have set you to be a light for the gentiles, that you may bring salvation to the uttermost parts of the earth'" (verses 46-47, citing Isaiah 49:6).

Then in chapter eighteen, there is a similar dispute farther west, in the Greek City Corinth. As a result, Paul says, "Your blood be upon your heads! I am innocent. From now on I will go to the gentiles" (18:6). Despite this declaration, however, Paul returns to preaching in Diaspora synagogues until 19:9.

The third programmatic statement, as I have termed them, comes in Rome at the end of a rather peaceful discussion between Paul and Jewish leaders there. Paul terminates the conversation surprisingly with two blistering verses from Isaiah followed by this final statement of his own: "Let it be known to you then that this salvation of God has been sent to the gentiles; they will listen" (28:25-28). Two verses later Acts ends.

Obviously, despite his title "Apostle to the Gentiles," Paul in Acts has a great deal to do with Jews. Nearly every time the word synagogue is mentioned, he is involved. And the plot is predictable: time after time he enters the Diaspora synagogue to offer the Christian message, and each time the Jews reject him. As a result, he moves across the Mediterranean world from east to west, from Antioch to Corinth to Rome, having no choice but to disavow the Jews because they first rejected him and his message. But as a reconstruction of the historical situation in Paul's time, this is all highly suspect, as we shall see when we look at the letters of Paul directly.

The second term from Acts is "proselyte." This word occurs three times in Acts, and only once in the rest of the New Testament. It is that fourth occurrence, however, which is by far the best known. It is of course the saying in Matthew 23:15 about the scribes and Pharisees who "traverse sea and land to make a single proselyte, and when he becomes a proselyte, you make him twice as much a child of hell as yourselves." A detailed picture of first-century Judaism as an aggressive missionary religion has been anchored in that obviously polemical saying in Matthew. In view of that, it is remarkable how little Acts makes of the idea. Even more remarkable is that the rest of the New Testament omits the term completely.[16]

The third and last term translates as "God-fearer." It is a term which Luke invented, and it is much more frequent than "proselyte." It occurs in the New Testament only in Acts, where it appears eleven times.[17] The precise word

---

16 On the *crux interpretum* in 13:43, "God-fearing proselytes," see the standard commentaries.

17 Kraabel (1981) 114-115, with notes.

combinations in Acts which are usually translated "God-fearer" do not occur outside the New Testament at all, in Christian or Jewish texts. A related Greek adjective, *theosebes*, is found in Jewish inscriptions. There its status as a technical term is disputed. It is frequently argued, however, that *theosebes* in the inscriptions means the person in question was in fact a God-fearer.

As used in Acts, "God-fearer" is usually taken to designate gentiles interested in Judaism and frequenting the synagogue, but not yet converts. Converts would be "proselytes." The archetypical God-fearer is Cornelius, a Roman officer in Caesaria. Acts spends a chapter and a half telling his story (10:1-11:18). With the exception of Cornelius, all God-fearers in Acts are associated with the Diaspora synagogue and with Paul.

In ten of the eleven instances in Acts, the God-fearers are sympathetic to Christianity—so much so that they often become a key factor in scholars' accounts of the earliest Greek-speaking Church. Indeed Acts is often used to construct a history of the earliest Christian mission in linear fashion, from Jews in the Holy Land to Diaspora Jews to God-fearers to other Gentiles, those without particular interest in Judaism. This progression often serves to explain why the last group is the largest of the four by the middle of the second century.

The chief problem with the progression idea is that the God-fearers so quickly disappear from Acts. They are out of the picture even before the Diaspora Jews. Not only are there no references to God-fearers elsewhere in the New Testament, they disappear in Acts as well after 19:19, when Paul withdraws permanently from the synagogue. They are found only in the middle third of the book, while the progression hypothesis would imply that, just at that point, God-fearers should appear in the narrative in increasing numbers. After the rejection of the Jews, the gentiles closest to Diaspora Judaism should next come into consideration. But during Paul's two year sojourns in Ephesus, Caesaria (the home of Cornelius!) and Rome, subsequent to 19:9, while the new religion is spread in these new gentile cities, the God-fearers never appear.

As I indicated, we would not have the term "God-fearer" if it were not for Luke. It is a tribute to his skill as a story teller that the God-fearers have become so much a part of the traditional story of early Christianity and also a part of many histories of Diaspora Judaism. Michael Avi-Yonah called the God-fearers a "numerous class" of gentiles in the time of the Roman empire.[18] The *Encyclopedia Judaica* states that there were "perhaps millions" of God-fearers by the first century (10:55). Luke's "theology in historical guise"

---

18 M. Avi-Yonah *The Jews of Palestine* (Oxford, 1976) 37.

has become religious history for many historians of Judaism, both Jewish and gentile.[19]

Paul

In Acts, "synagogue" and "God-fearer" are almost always associated with Paul. If we examine Paul's own writings, what more do we learn about the Diaspora Judaism which is supposed to be connected with these terms? The answer is, very little. The terms "synagogue," "proselyte" and "God-fearer" never appear in Paul's letters. This is not because Paul is not interested in fellow Jews; that concern is frequent in his letters, and it is immediate and personal. He is earlier than Luke by a generation, and the issue of the non-Christian Jews is very much alive for him. He cannot understand why they cannot accept the Messiah he has found, and their rejection troubles him greatly. Further, he reveals no knowledge of the Lucan idea that Judaism is only a stage which Christianity passes through on its way to the gentile world, quite the contrary. The climax of his profound letter, Romans, is a section of great passion and great pathos in which he insists almost desperately that sometime, somehow Jews and Christians will be a unity again under a common God.[20]

So while the traditional scholarship would tell us three important things about the Jews of the Diaspora which at the same time are said to be very significant to the ministry of Paul, none of the three has left any trace in Paul's letters! All derive wholly from Acts. They are as follows: 1) Christian missionary work in the Mediterranean world began in the Diaspora synagogue that is the conclusion to be drawn from the story of Paul which is told in Acts. But 2) the Diaspora synagogue had its own missionary activity going. There may not have been many converts, but there were many gentile sympathizers or "God-fearers."

These first two ideas have had great influence on the usual understanding of the Diaspora synagogue and Diaspora Jews. In later centuries, as the Church gains numerical and political power after Constantine, and when the third theme of Luke begins to receive more attention, they become sinister. Luke's third concept is that the rejection of Christianity by the Jews and the movement of Christianity to the gentile world were all part of the plan of God. They were not accidental; they were divinely intended. It became increasingly common to use this piece of Lucan doctrine to justify turning the Jews in the Christian Roman empire into second class citizens wherever possible. Their status could justifiably be held to the lowest level; that was the proper thing to do. Jews had put themselves there by choosing to reject the Christian mes-

19 I borrow this useful phrase from J. Neusner, who uses it in a different but related context. See Neusner, *Ancient Judaism: Debates and Disputes* (Chico, CA, 1984) 251.

20 K. Stendahl *Paul Among Jews and Gentiles* (Philadelphia, 1976) 23-40.

sage when it was first offered them. And there was theological justification for it as well-after all, it was part of what God had planned.

Acts (again)

This view drawn from Acts had a serious negative effect on the relations between Jews and the Christian Roman empire. Jews were the single ethnic group whose low status had a theological warrant.

A review of both the archaeological and literary evidence suggests that this was not at all Luke's intent. He was actually going in a different direction. In fact, the treatment of synagogues and God-fearers in Acts is one more example of theology in historical guise. Luke had two major, related theological issues on his mind which relate directly to the question of "the other." The way he tells his story in Acts allows him to address both.

The first, which we have already alluded to, is this: why the split between the Jews and Christianity? Christianity was, after all, a Jewish sect claiming to have discovered the true Jewish Messiah Luke's answer is on two levels: on the surface, the split involved rejection by the Jews, who had been given full access to the new movement and time and again had spurned it. At a deeper level, of course, this rejection was part of that great divine plan—a plan which in Luke, but not in Paul, leaves non-Christian Jews behind forever.

Less commonly recognized is Luke's other major theological issue, that is: what justifies Christians in going to work among gentiles after having left the Jews behind? In the first century, and for two or three centuries after Luke's time, Christianity continued to be attacked by its enemies as a renegade Jewish sect, one which lost any claim to legitimacy when it repudiated its own origins and went after gentiles.[21] Luke's God-fearers are the first theological response to that charge. Luke says that it was legitimate for Christians to offer their faith to gentiles precisely because of this precedent in Judaism. In Acts, Diaspora Jews are shown to have done exactly the same thing even before Christianity began. The God-fearers were the result. If Jews could make their religion available to gentiles, Christians could as well. The Jewish mission which produced the God-fearers justifies the later Christian mission. This is the part the God-fearers play in Acts. Their theological purpose is to povide a precedent, and thus a justification, for the Christians' gentile mission. The God-fearers are on the stage as needed, off the stage after they have served their purpose in the plot. It is a tribute to Luke's dramatic ability that they have become so alive for the later church, but the evidence from Paul's own letters, and now from archaeology, makes their historicity questionable. Perhaps it cannot be demonstrated conclusively that

---

21 R.L. Wilkens *The Christians as the Romans Saw Them* (New Haven, 1984) 112-117; 184-196.

there was never a circle of God-fearers associated with ancient Judaism. But what I am arguing is rather that, at least for the Roman Diaspora, the evidence presently available is far from convincing proof for the existence of such a class of gentiles.

Further, if we cannot rely on the presence of the God-fearers, then the traditional understanding of the make-up of Diaspora Judaism may need to be reconsidered. I will return to that at the end of this paper.

Excursus: The *Aphrodisias Inscription*

I want to conclude this section of the paper with a reference to another inscription, this one still unpublished.[22] When it appears, the evidence I have just summarized, both Jewish and Christian, will all be reviewed again, so it is appropriate that I say something about it today.

This Greek inscription, discovered in 1976, dates from the second or third century and comes from Aphrodisias in Caria, in southwestern Asia Minor. The memorial, or monument (*mnema*) of some sort, is the longest Jewish inscription ever to come from Asia Minor, and one of the longest anywhere. It is not clear whether it comes directly from a synagogue. It consists chiefly of a list of names and occupations, some eighty lines of them in all. A great number of men are being recognized for some unclear reason.

The name list is in two parts. The first is the longer and contains such "Biblical" names as Samuel, Benjamin, Joseph and Judas, whereas the names in the second part of the list are nearly all Greek. The second part of the list is headed *kai hosoi theosebis* (sic), translating as: "and (the following) who (are) pious." The word *theosebes*, which I have translated as "pious," is the closest the Jewish inscriptions come to one of the terms in Acts which is usually translated "God-fearer." Thus, as soon as it is published, this inscription will become the central piece of epigraphic evidence in the God-fearer discussion.

Is this a list of "gentiles who are sympathetic to Judaism but have not converted"? That is possible. But in literature and inscriptions *theosebes* does not have a single meaning. Sometimes it is used of persons who are clearly Jews. In other texts it just as clearly designates gentiles who have never been in contact with Jews at all; the earliest example in Sardis is Croesus, the sixth

---

22 Editor's note: Since Kraabel wrote this essay (1984) the Aphrodisias materials has been published. See J. Reynolds and R. Tannenbaum *Jews and God-fearers at Aphrodisias: Greek Inscriptions with Commentary*. Proceedings of the Cambridge Philological Society Supplement, vol. 12 (Cambridge, England: University Press, 1987). See also Mellink, "Archaeology in Asia Minor" *AJA* 81 (1977) 306; Kraabel "The Disappearance of the 'God-fearers'" (1981) 125 note 26; T. Rajak "Jews and Christians as Groups in the Pagan World in J. Neusner and E.S. Frerichs, *"To see Ourselves"* (Chico, CA: Scholars Press, 1985) 247-262.

century king of Lydia, the one with all the gold (Herodotos calls him *theosebes* in the first book of his *History* 1.86.2).

Another example, much closer to the date of Acts and of this inscription, is a famous anti-Christian graffito from Rome, from the Paedagogium under the Palatine Hill. It shows a boy kneeling before a crucified figure with the body of a man and the head of a donkey. The legend beneath reads: "Alexamenos worships god," and the vocabulary is precisely that found in Acts.[23] Clearly, we are not dealing with an accepted technical term of one and only one meaning.

Let me suggest an alternative explanation for the Aphrodisias inscription, which at the same time will help to illustrate several issues before this conference. The traditional understanding of Diaspora Judaism appears to assume that to be sympathetic to Jews—to be pro-Jewish—means to be interested in the Jews' religion. From this perspective, for gentiles and Jews in the Greco-Roman world the question of "the other" was a religious one, leading perhaps to an interest in conversion. Yet it is possible simply to be friendly toward Jews as one's neighbors or fellow-townspeople. Such, I believe, was the case at Sardis.[24] The synagogue there suggests Sardis gentiles acknowledged that Jews had a proper place in the city; they belonged there as an ethnic minority. However, persistence in seeing Judaism in antiquity first of all as a religion has made it hard for many people to understand openness towards Jews in anything other than religious terms. But to have Jewish friends or to take a positive toward Jews need not mean—either today or in antiquity—an interest in changing one's religion. If some of Aphrodisias' *theosebeis* are gentiles, as it appears they are, they could be nothing more than gentile "good neighbors" whom the local Jews wanted to honor. That too is a legitimate relationship to "the other."

The inscription is soon to be published by Joyce Reynolds of Cambridge University.[25] One thing is certain: every article written about it thereafter will trot out these eleven texts from Acts, and much of what I have just talked about will be rehearsed again. Indeed, I would predict that most discussions of the Aphrodisias inscription will take Luke's "theology in historical guise" as straight history instead, with predictable results.As Jack Neusner often reminds us, once established, scholarship's critical orthodoxy is very slow to change.

IV

---

23 V. Väänänen *Graffiti del Palatino*, I: *Paedagogium* (Helsinki 1966) 209-21, no. 246.

24 Kraabel "Impact of the Discovery of the Sardis Synagogue" *Sardis*, edited by G. Hanfmann, (Cambridge: Harvard, 1983).

25 See note above.

Pascha in the Greek of the Bible may mean "Passover" or "Easter." It was over *pascha* that Christians had one of the longest of their early battles, from the second century until well into the fifth. The dispute is almost forgotten now, but it was one of the two main causes for the very important Council of Nicaea in 325 (Athanasius *Epistula de Synodis* 5 = PG 26.688B). Although this dispute was wholly within the Church and did not involve non-Christians, it is usually linked to another even larger issue, the relation of Christianity to its parent religion, Judaism. From the details of this dispute, many scholars have drawn significant conclusions about Diaspora Judaism.These I wish to examine—briefly—here.

Socrates, the fifth-century Church historian, introduces a discussion of the *pascha* controversy at the time of Nicaea by making the observance that some eastern Christians "preferred to observe the festival (of Easter) in a more Jewish fashion" than was acceptable to the majority of the Church (Socrates 1.8). If this appears to be something like a rapproachement with Judaism, decisions with reference to *pascha* by the later fourth-century Church Council at Laodicaea have been taken much further, as evidence for "actual religious fellowship" between Jews and Christians; specifically, scholars see Christian participation in Jewish Passover observance. But allusions to Jewish practices and to Jews in the ancient Church are often not what they seem. This is particularly true when the context is some part of the gentile world outside Palestine. Several of the most problematic references to "the Jews" come from two assemblies of bishops in Phrygia, one at Pazos, the other (just mentioned) at Laodicaea. Both occur about a half-century after Nicaea and both have to do with *pascha*.

The synod of Pazos was a local meeting of Novatianist Christian bishops. Bishops of the state church did not attend, nor did Novatianist bishops from the west or from Constantinople. These bishops at Pazos altered their practice in regard to Easter, deciding "to observe the Jews as they are doing the feast of unleavened bread (*ta azyma*), and with them to carry out the festival of Easter (*to pascha*)" (Socrates 4.28).

This is striking for the following three reasons: first, if the decision constitutes a move toward conformity with Judaism, that is a stance very different from Novatian's own as regards the Jews. Novatian was a Roman presbyter, and wrote at least three treatises on things Jewish in the middle of the third century. One concerned the Sabbath, another circumcision (both lost), and one was about Jewish foods. At the beginning of the *de cibis Iudaicis* he calls the Jews *perversi... et ab intellectu suae legis alient*, and attacks their blindness and ignorance. This was apparently the burden of the two lost works, and it surely characterizes *de cibis Iudaicis*, which goes on to interpret the Old Testament in allegorical fashion. (Novatian was no heretic; he and his followers went into schism as the result of what they considered to be lax treatment of *lapsi* after the Decian persecution. Nor was he without intellectual gifts; his *de Trinitate* is a major and wholly orthodox piece of early Latin theology.)

Second, the Pazos decision has been attributed to Montanist Christian influence. Another fifth century church historian, Sozomen, links the two splinter groups and makes it clear that, in Phrygia, Montanists and Novatianists both celebrated Easter on a date different from that of the state church (7.18). But Montanism is an unlikely cause of the Novatianist practice. There was little common in the origins of these two groups beyond an opposition to what both saw as moral laxity among the majority of Christians. A century before Novatian, Montanism had begun as an apocalyptic and charismatic sect within Phrygia itself. It never enjoyed the kind of official acceptance which—as we shall see—the Novatianists briefly gained in the fourth century.

Third, the Pazos decision to "celebrate *pascha* with the Jews" was counter not only to the practice of Novatian himself but also to that of Novatianists elsewhere in the fourth century (Socrates 4.28). In the west and in other parts of the Church—Constantinople, for example—their Easter observances were the same as those of the majority. This becomes clear in the story of the Novatianist bishop of Constantinople, Acesius, whom Constantine, in an irenic gesture, invited to the Council of Nicaea. Acesius strongly reasserted the Novatianist position on *lapsi*, but acknowledged that the majority view on the date of Easter was also his position, one which he considered to have apostolic warrant (Socrates, 1.10).

Some decades later the Pazos decision gained a new champion, a converted Jew named Sabbatios who had been ordained a priest by the Novatianist bishop Marcian.[26] Sabbatios was aggressive (and probably self-serving) in his demand that all Novatianists fall in line with the Pazos decree. In response, another synod of Novatianist bishops was called, not in Phrygia this time, but at Sangarum in Bithynia. There, Sabbatios asserted that it was "mandatory that the festival (i.e. *pascha*) take place when the Jews are holding their observance" (Socrates, 5.21).

The response to Sabbatios by the Novatianist bishops goes a long way toward clarifying just what was at stake. It points the direction toward a correct understanding of what the real issues were. The bishops decided that the matter was an *adiaphoron*, a matter of indifference, for in earlier times Christians had observed Easter in different ways and that had not split the Church. So Novatianist Christians should not divide over the issue now. In observing Easter, then, Christians should follow the practice each preferred. "It ought to make no difference as regards Christian fellowship; those who celebrate in different ways are nevertheless in concord with the Church" (Socrates, 5.21).

---

26 C. Andersen *Die Kirchen der alten Christenheit* (Stuttgart, 1971) 280-282.

Two conclusions may be drawn from the Sangarum decision. The first is that even among the Novatianists the issue was wholly an intra-Christian one about the method for dating Easter. Socrates reference to the strength of the Sabbatios? Jewish preconceptions even alter his ordination should be seen as a diversion (Socrates 5.21). No Novatianist had ever been so innovative as to suggest either a common *pascha* celebration between Christians and Jews or, alternatively, Christian participation in Jewish Passover rites. No group of bishops, Novatianist or not, would have called that an *adiaphoron*.

But the important point to observe is that the Novatianists at Sangarum did not demand an end to that form of Easter observance which Pazos had required. Even though the majority of Novatianist and non-Novatianist Christian leaders would not have supported it, even though as we shall see Constantine himself had opposed any form of celebration which might be associated with "the Jews," the Novatianists did not rule out the kind of Easter which Sabbatios had been demanding.

This tolerance has never been satisfactorily explained. What I am suggesting is that the answer to this question lies not in the character of the Diaspora Jews of this area, but in the strength of a particular aberrant Easter tradition in Phrygia and neighboring areas in the interior of Anatolia I will describe this tradition in a few moments.

The broad-mindedness of the bishops at Pazos would not have been acceptable to earlier Church leaders in the west. Nor would Constantine have permitted it; to him, divergences on the Easter date were a threat to the unity of the Church. In a united church it was a scandal to have Easter celebrated on different dates in different places. After Nicaea, Constantine addressed a letter to the bishops on precisely this matter (preserved in Eusebius, *Vit. Const.* 3.18). So Pazos particularly would appear to be a direct challenge to the wishes of the Christian state.

It is impossible that Constantine's dictum would not have been known to the bishops at Pazos. How is their decision to be explained then? Well, as so often in the fourth century, the reasons appear to be more political than theological and more internal than external to the Church. After Constantine's death the situation had become more difficult for the Novatianists. First, under Constantine's son Constantius (ruled 337-361), Novatianists and orthodox alike suffered at the hands of Arian Christians supported by the emperor. In one instance the bishop of Constantinople was able to have government troups sent against the Novatianists. (Socrates had it from an eye witness that the Novatianists armed themselves with sickles and hatchets and killed most of the soldiers [Socrates 2.38].) Valens, emperor from 364 to 378, also persecuted the Novatianists (Socrates, 4.9). And it was during the reign of Valens that the Pazos decision was taken. The Novatianists, then, were feeling considerable pressure from the Constantinople government. Their need to gain support against the state Church caused the Pazos bishops to move in a Jewish direction. That decision must have strengthened the Novatianists' position in Phrygia and the neighboring parts of inland Anatolia where the "more Jewish" method of Easter dating was favored. For after Pazos, Sabbatios would gain followers particularly in Phrygia and Galatia where his "Jewish" way of observing Easter was the traditional one, according to Sozomen (7.18). Socrates too notes that among Sabbatios' followers were "particularly those who had come from Phrygia and Galatia" (5.21).

Phrygian Novatianists and Montanists must have realized that they could expect only opposition from Constantinople. Both groups, it appears, deliberately underscored the differences between the Constantinople authorities and local Phrygian Christians over Easter practices. Their intent would have been to gain support in the interior of Anatolia by coming out in favor of an ancient and traditional practice which the central authorities, civil and religious, had attacked.[27]

However, Constantine's wishes prevailed in the end. He had assured the eventual collapse of their position, and any similar way of dating Easter, by tying them firmly to an unacceptable dependence on the "blind," "sinful" and "wicked" Jews. Given his concerns for unity, as emperor and as Church leader, there may have been no other position for him to take.

In the fourth century, divergence in Easter dating was no small matter. The pressure for uniformity in the state church had begun even before Nicaea. For instance the first canon of the Council of Arles (314 C.E.) is precisely *ut uno die et tempore pascha celebretur*. According to Athanasius there were two chief issues at Nicaea: the Arian controversy and the fact that Christians in Syria, Cilicia and Mesopotamia "customarily observed *pascha* with the Jews" (*Epistula de Synodis* 5 = PC 26.688B). Eusebius, who sided with Constantine on this issue, nevertheless noted that a quarter of the bishops at Nicaea did not (*De solemnitate paschali* 8 = PG 24:701). Nor did the Council settle the matter; six times in the two decades following, Rome and Alexandria celebrated the festival on different dates[28] While the lack of uniformity between these two major Christian centers was a scandal to those concerned with unity, neither position could be stigmatized as "keeping *pascha* with the Jews." Despite the attack by Constantine, "keeping *pascha* with the Jews would continue to be popular in the Anatolian interior into the fifth century.

After Sanganim, Sabbatios continued to press for his understanding of Easter. He and his followers began to meet apart from other Novatianists. Finally, at a meeting held in a place called Xerolophos, he tried to insert his position into scripture itself. While reading aloud from a gospel text which

---

27 Andersen (1971) 275; 280.

28 K.J. Hefele and H. Leclercq *Historie des conciles* I.1 (Paris, 1907) 419.

referred to Passover, he interpolated, "cursed be the one who celebrates the *pascha* outside (the days of) unleavened bread" (Socrates, 7.5). This put considerable distance between him and the majority of Novatianists. The "followers of Sabbatios" soon became a distinct group, recognized as such by other Christians. Our earliest sure reference to this separation is from the early 390's (Didymus the Blind, *de Trinitate* = PC 39:420A). In a civil law of 413, "deserters and fugitives from the company of the Novatianists" are directly condemned (*CTh* 16.6.6). Other attacks on Sabbatianoi and Novatianists occur in laws of 423 C.E. (*CTh* 16.5.59) and C.E. 435 (*CTh* 1.6.5.65).

My thesis in this part of the paper is that these condemnations are the proper background for understanding the puzzling references to the Jews in the decrees of the Council of Laodicaea, the later fourth-century meeting mentioned earlier. Marcel Simon has called them "among the most particularly anti-Jewish canons in the entire conciliar literature."[29] James Parke saw them as strong evidence of an "actual religious fellowship" between Christians and Jews which the bishops at Laodicaea intended to bring to an end.[30] But the bishops' concern may have been over Christian issues, not with Jews at all. Neither Simon nor Parkes could have known of the strength of Judaism in this part of Asia Minor. The bulk of that evidence has appeared since they wrote; it comes chiefly from Aphrodisias (already discussed) and from Sardis in nearby Lydia. The excavations at Sardis yielded remains of the largest ancient synagogue ever found, and more Jewish inscriptions than had been known from all of Asia Minor previously.[31] These discoveries prompted a reexamination of all the evidence for the Judaism of western Asia Minor. For Sardis at least, the impression is of self-confident Jews, at home in the gentile world while at the same time quite concerned for the maintenance of their ancestral traditions and piety. The Jewish evidence now suggests much more contact with pagans than with Christians at least until after the reign of Julian (361-363). Since the great majority of Christians in Asia Minor after the second century were gentiles, not converted Jews, there is no reason on the Jewish side for any kind of rapprochement with Christians. This is a point worth emphasizing, since the earlier understanding of the Laodicaea canons assumes in local Jews a propensity, and even an eagerness, for religious interaction with their Christian neighbors.

Here is how the Anatolian "Easter controversy" began. Lydia and Phrygia had been a center of controversy over Easter since the middle of the second century. This was because they were the home of Quartodecimanism, the

---

29 Simon (1964) 382.

30 J. Parkes *The Conflict Between Church and Synagogue.* (Cleveland and Philadelphia, 1934) 176.

31 Kraabel (1983).

ancient practice of dating the *pascha* by the Jewish date for Passover, a custom which could correctly be described "keeping *pascha* with the Jews." Because Passover falls on a fixed date in the first Jewish (lunar) month Nisan, any weekday might be designated for Passover—and for the Quartodeciman Easter which depended on it. Ultimately this practice goes back to the gospel of John.[32]

The first "council" of Laodicaea occurred about 164 C.E.; the only issue had been the dating of Easter, and the big dispute (*zetesis polle*) had been between two kinds of Quartodecimans—what would become the orthodox position in the fiourth century and later was not even represented.[33] Most of the early leaders of the church in this area were Quartodecimans, and the tradition endured into the fifth century (see Socrates, 7.29 about events at Sardis). But being a Quartodeciman most assuredly did not mean being sympathetic to Judaism or to one's Jewish neighbors. Perhaps the best known Quartodeciman of all, the late second-century bishop of Sardis, Melito, is also the author of a decidedly anti-Jewish paschal sermon.[34] Eric Werner once called him "the first poet of deicide."[35]

In the fourth century, before the Council of Laodicaea, the synod of Pazos and the subsequent successes of Sabbatios suggest that the "Jewish" method of dating Easter remained strong in the area around Laodicaea well after Nicaea. The bishops at Laodicaea, who took a general position against a number of heresies, may have felt the need for caution when it came to the condemnation of traditional local practices. In order to assert the position of the majority in the Church in regard to the *pascha* a position not popular around Laodicaea—they worked indirectly, attacking "Jewish" practices within the Church. What they were implying, without stating it directly, is that the Quartodeciman Easter must be seen to be wrong despite its antiquity and its support in Phrygia, e.g. at Pazos. It was wrong because it was "Jewish"; it depended on the Jews.

The details in Socrates accounts lead to this conclusion. Despite a positive attitude toward the Novatianists generally, Socrates had no sympathy for the kind of Novatianists represented by the Pazos bishops arid Sabbatios, and he

---

32 J.A. Fisher "Die Synoden im Osterfeststreit des 2. Jahrhunderts." *Annurium Historiae Conciliorum* 8 (1976); R.T. Beckwith "The Origin of the Festivals Easter and Whitsun." *Studia Liturgica* 13 (1979).

33 Eusebius 4.26; Fischer (1976) 19-21.

34 Kraabel "Melito the Bishop and the Synagogue of Sardis: Text and Context" *Studies Presented to George M.A. Hanfmann*, edited by D.G. Mitten, J.G. Pedley and J.A. Scott (Cambridge, MA, 1971).

35 E. Werner "Melito of Sardis, the First Poet of Deicide." *Hebrew Union College Annual* 37 (1966).

was persistent in his efforts to blacken them by linking them to Judaism. As Socrates describes it, the decision at Pazos was "to celebrate the festival of *pascha* with them," i.e. the Jews (Socrates, 4.28). His concern to tie "Sabbatianism" to Judaism is introduced when he first describes Sabbatios as a convert still dominated by "Jewish preconceptions" (Socrates, 5.21). Immediately before he recounts the events at Xerolophos which will divide the followers of Sabbatios from the rest of the Novatiainists, he spends a page telling of a crippled Jew whom Atticus, bishop of Constantinople, had healed in baptism; while this miracle converted pagans, it could not convince other Jews to accept the faith. The point Socrates wishes to make is clear enough.

The language of Socrates probably reflects the usual way these practices were described by their opponents in the fourth century and later. According to Socrates, many Christians in the east favored observing Easter "more Jewishly" (Socrates, 1.8). What they were doing could be described as "following the Jews" or "celebrating the festival with the Jews" (Socrates 5.21 and 5.22). Their partisans were "those who wholeheartedly favored following the Jews now" (5.22). Sabbatios' followers are "those who separated from the Novatians over the Jewish *pascha*" (7.25). It is this issue, then, rather than any accommodation between gentile Christians and non-Christian Jews, which appears to lie behind the rulings of the Council of Laodicaea. Let me conclude this section of the paper by turning to that Council.

Simon identified seven canons of the Council as being concerned with this issue: 7, 16, 29, 35-38; only the last two referred explicitly to Jews.[36] Canon 7 gives the procedures by which Novatianists, Photinians and Quartodecimans may be received into the Church. Simon holds that these are "Judaizing"-groups; but "Judaizing" need not imply interaction with Jews or participation with them in Jewish rites. Canon 16 requires that "gospels with other scriptures" be read on the sabbath, Saturday. Those who presupposed Christian participation in Jewish rites in the Phrygia of this period suggested that Christians and Jews were holding religious observances on Saturdays at which only the Old Testament was read; this canon then would have forced the use of Christian texts at those meetings, and presumably made it impossible for Jews to participate. But Saturday and Sunday were the two days of the week recognized by the Council for Christian religious observance (see canons 49 and 51); so this canon is more likely to be concerned to assure a service with scripture readings on Saturday as well as on Sunday. The canons closest to it are also concerned with the proper conduct of services.

Canon 29 goes on to attack "Judaizing," specifically, refraining from work on Saturday. The bishops hold that Christians should observe Sundays as a

---

36 Simon (1964) 382-383.

rest day "if possible," but should work on Saturday in any case. Again, their target is a "Jewish" practice, not association with Jews.

Then canon 35 forbids, as "secret idolatry," the cult of angels. This had been a problem in the area around Laodicaea since the first century—witness the New Testament letter *Colossians* 2:18.[37] (Colossae is some ten miles east of Laodicaea.) The pagan cult of angels is well attested in Phrygia; it developed into the cult of Saint Michael the Archangel, which has its beginning in this area in the fourth century and then moves west.[38]

As for canon 36, it prohibits the making of *phylakteria* by priests; nor are they to be *magoi*, enchanters, *mathematikoi* or astrologers. While *phylakteria* recalls the "phylacteries" worn by Jews in the New Testament, it here has its more common meaning of "amulet." Again, no mention is made of Jews.

Canon 37-39 appear to go together, though Simon did not include the lasi one on his list. Their general theme is the avoidance of contact with three groups of unacceptable persons: pagans, heretics and Jews. Forbidden are "holding festivals together with" Jews or heretics (canon 37) or pagans (canon 39), and "participating in" Jewish impieties (conon 38) or pagan atheism (canon 39). More particularly Christians are not to receive "festival gifts" from Jews or pagans (canon 37). specifically, in what appears to be an extension of this canon, they are not to accept "unleavened bread" from Jews (canon 38).

It is canon 38, of course, which has been used to suggest that Christians had been joining in Passover observances with Jews. But this now seems unlikely for at least three reasons: 1) from what we know now about Phrygian and Lydian Jewish communities, it is improbable that such an invitation would come from the Jewish side; 2) the chief concern of the Council is not with pagans (mentioned once) or Jews (mentioned twice) but with heretics (canons 7, 8, 9, 31, 32, 33, 34 and 37). This is the situation generally in the church after Nicaea: the enemy is not outside but within. 3) In the heavily gentile Christianity of fourth-century Asia Minor, something as bizarre as Christian participation in the Jewish Passover would surely have occasioned a much more explicit and elaborate protest than the half-dozen words in canon 39. Constantine's dictum on the Easter controversy indicates how devastating it could be to be associated with the Jews merely in the dating of a purely Christian festival. Joining in a Passover observance would have gone far beyond that, and surely called for a thunderous response from the Council of Laodicaea and beyond.

If this reconstruction is correct, then the bishops at Laodicaea were not facing the issue of Jewish and Christian joint rites, or of Christian participa-

---

37 Simon (1971) 126-128.

38 J.P. Rohland *Der Erzengel Michael, Artz und Feldherr* (Leiden, 1977) 69-73; A.R.R. Shepherd "Pagan Cults of Angels in Roman Asia Minor" *Talanta* 12-13 (1982).

tion in Jewish Passover ceremonies. There is no evidence here for Christian relations with non-Christian Jews. Something which we thought we knew about Anatolian Judaism turns out to be without documentation; a significant point in the old hypothetical reconstruction of Diaspora Judaism needs to be corrected. The problem at the Council was rather to assert the orthodox position on the dating of Easter in a part of Anatolia where an alternative method was quite deeply embedded. Montanists and Novatianists had appropriated local Easter customs as their own, and had gained temporary support thereby. Sabbatios would continue the same line in a decade or two at Sangarum, and take it much farther at Xerolophos.

In Phrygia in the late fourth century it is highly unlikely that Christians would be treated so obliquely if they were in "actual religious fellowship" with the local Jews, as Parkes thought. What the Council of Laodicaea did was to tie Jews, pagans and heretics together in a joint condemnation in order to undercut a Jewish practice regarding Easter. This way of dating Easter had to be attacked because it was at variance with the State church and thus divisive. But the attack had to be made indirectly; the practice itself was old and deeply embedded in local Christianity. The subject was a volatile one, and worse, it was open to exploitation by non-orthodox groups. Pazos had already shown that, and before long Sabbatios would do it again.

V

Let me draw some conclusions quickly. The *pascha* controversy in the fourth century illustrates four things. 1) It indicates how "Jews" in older reconstructions of the history of that period in the Mediterranean Diaspora are often phantoms, fictional characters in disputes taking place between Christian groups. The archaeological evidence for western Asia Minor shows substantial Jewish communities there, but they did not always conduct themselves in the way later historians had assumed. The *pascha* controversy also illustrates (2) that references to Jewish practices do not necessarily indicate the presence either of Jews or of non-Jews sympathetic to Judaism. The "others" are not what they seem.

References to Jews occur in many places in the Christian literature of this period: in the sermons and theological treatises of course, but also in the martyr-acts and in that genre called *adversus Judaeos* literature.[39] Yet there was little interest on the part of non-Jews in studying these Jews dispassionately or in portraying them objectively. This leads to two further conclusions: 3) the information which we thought we had about these Jews and their Juda-

---

39 A more detailed study of this literature, against the background of new methods and data for ancient Judaism, has been prepared by Robert S. MacLennan, *Early Christian Texts on Jews and Judaism* Brown Judaica Series 194 (Atlanta, GA: Scholars Press, 1990).

ism must now be viewed with great skepticism, for from the Christian sources at least, we really know less than we think we know; 4) but that also requires taking a second look at what is sometimes called the "anti-Semitism" of this period.[40] The tensions between Jews and gentiles may have been greater or less than they appear. There was no uniformity of treatment, and it would be misleading to assume that what held for one period or location was true necessarily for another. There is no way to tell until each source has been tested first for its inner biases.

It was somewhere between the time of Luke and the time of the historian Socrates that the general racism of the Roman empire became refined into the theological anti-Judaism well known in later Christian history.[41] Such events as the *pascha* controversy help it along even though "real Jews" were not involved in that battle between Christians. That is a point of some significance for a proper understanding of this period in the history of Judaism!

In the texts from the New Testament, however, the Jews are real enough. They are a matter of great concern, to Paul in one way, to Luke in another. Here it is possible to see the beginnings of the theological manipulation of the story of the Jews from the Christian standpoint.[42] Paul has a personal concern for Jews which is also theological. Luke, on the other hand, presents stylized Jews, characters in a story which has already moved some distance away from him and into the past. Neither author is concerned to present a full and unbiased picture, and perhaps no one expects that. But Luke's God-fearers are just one more example of how quickly the Christian movement could begin to embellish and transform its image of the Jews of the recent past even when there were still eyewitnesses alive who—had they been so minded—could have set the story straight.

I included the Samaritan evidence from Delos first because it was so recently discovered. More important, it is an example of how one piece of new information can help to shift an entire field to new level of complexity and clarity. In this case the evidence comes from the Mediterranean Diaspora, a circumstance which gives it a larger place in the historical record. For Samaritans as well as for Jews, it is the happenings in Palestine which are the better known. Because the Diaspora is much less well attested, the historical reconstructions of it which are commonly used must often be highly hypotheti-

---

40 S. Sandmel *Anti-Semitism in the New Testament?* (Philadelphia, 1978); J. Gager *The Origins of Anti-Semitism* (Oxford, 1983).

41 A.N. Sherwin-White *Racial Prejudice in Imperial Rome* (Cambridge UK, 1970); J.P.V.D. Balsdon *Romans and Aliens* (Chapel Hill, 1979).

42 A study of the history of interpretation of Acts in this regard has been prepared by Dr. Paul Stuehrenberg, in Ancient Studies, University of Minnesota.

cal. Any new evidence from that direction must receive particularly careful scrutiny because of its potential for rearranging the entire construct. That occurred with Dura and it is happening with Sardis in relation to the Jewish Diaspora. The Delos discoveries will have a comparable impact on Samaritan studies.

One of the best known images of Judaism for the medieval church was a figure of a blindfolded woman, *synagoga caeca*, the "unseeing synagogue" unable to perceive the truth of the Christian message. But if the synagogue was "unseeing," it was just as much *unseen*, unclear and obscured to those outside.[43] The Diaspora synagogue is still unclear in many ways. Diaspora Judaism plays all too small a part in the history of Judaism in late antiquity. In the first and second centuries, the situation must have looked very different. The best pattern for success would have been someone like Josephus. He attached himself to one of the most powerful of Romans, was removed from Palestine, and began writing in Rome in Greek for a Diaspora audience of gentiles and Greek-speaking Jews.

In this period many more Jews lived outside the Holy Land than within it. If you were a young Jew living, say, in the time of Akiba, wondering where your future would be the brightest, the cities of the Mediterranean Diaspora would have been much more desirable than anything in Palestine. Indeed they were more promising, and remained so for several centuries thereafter. For the reasons I have illustrated, the story of these millions of Jews has not been well told in the sources available. That record was compiled almost exclusively by non-Jews. Not only was it incomplete, it was also completely overshadowed by the abundance of rabbinic literature from farther east, much of it indeed from outside the Roman world completely. Now there are new sources—from archaeology primarily—and, more important, new methods and a clearer view of the problem. They must have their impact on the conventional view of the subject.[44]

I polished the conclusions of this paper while on an extended vacation trip through the west coast of the United States by train. My other companion was Eberhard Busch's 1976 biography of the Swiss theologian Karl Barth. As I got

---

43 See Klein (1978) and Kraabel (1982) 460-464, and also recent summaries of the anti-Jewish bias in the most influential of ancient church historians, Eusebius, by R.M. Grant *Eusebius as Church Historian* (1980) 97-113, and T.D. Barnes *Constantine and Eusebius* (Cambridge, 1981) 169-172, 181-186.

44 To give just one example: in the Mediterranean Diaspora, at least, it seems likely that the major "Jewish symbol" was not any particular form, such as the *menorah* or the lion, but the building itself and the Torah (shrine) within it. On the general subject, and especially on the work of Erwin R. Goodenough, see Smith (1967), Neusner (1981), and Neusner (1984), 143-180. See also Kraabel *Goodenough on the Beginning of Christianity* Brown Judaic Studies 212 (Atlanta: Scholars Press, 1990).

the last form of these sentences ready for the word processor, I also observed my fellow passengers-nearly all of them non-Jews—and I read about Barth's career in Germany, and then in Switzerland after his dismissal by the Nazis. I could not help wondering what Europeans between the Wars and Americans in the 1980's—and the hosts of other gentiles before them—would have thought "a Jew" to be if the Mediterranean Diaspora had had its fair share of coverage in the historical record along with Babylonia and Palestine in late antiquity. When the Diaspora synagogue of late antiquity became invisible to the non-Jewish world in the West, the negative effects went far beyond the realm of scholarship. Correction of those distortions, even as late as this, can have unusually broad salutary effects.

Bibliography

Andresen, C.
1971   *Die Kirchlien der alten Christenheit.* Stuttgart.
Avi-Yonah, M.
1976   *The Jews of Palestine.* Oxford.
Balsdon, J.P.V.D.
1979   *Romans and Aliens.* Chapel Hill.
Barnes, T.D.
1981   *Constantine and Eusebius.* Cambridge MA.
Beckwith, R.T.
1979   "The Origin of the Festivals Easter and Whitsun." *Studia Liturgica* 13: 1-20.
Bruneau, P.
1982   "Les Israelites de Delos et la juiverie délienne." *Bulletin de Correspondance Hellénistique* 106: 465-504.
Bull, R.J.
1976   "Gerizim, Mount." *IDBS* 361.
Busch, E.
1976   *Karl Barth.* Philadelphia.
Coggins, R. J.
1975   *Samaritan's and Jews.* Atlanta
1982   "The Samairitans and Acts." *New Testament Studies* 28:423-434.
Collins, J.J.
1983   *Between Athens and Jerusalem.* New York. *Encyclopedia Judaica.* Jerusalem, 1971.
Fischer, J.A.
1976   "Die Synoden im Osterfeststreit des 2. Jahrhunderts." *Annuarium Historiae Concilioum* 8: 15-29.
Gager, J.G.
1983   *The Origins of Anti-Semitism.* Oxford.
Grant, R.M.
1980   *Eusebius as Church Historian.* Oxford.
Hefele, K.J. and Leclercq, H.
1907   *Histoire des conciles.* I. 1. Paris.
Hengel, M.
1974   *Judaism and Hellenism.* London.
Isaac, B.
1983   "A Donation for Herod's Temple in Jerusalem." *Israel Exploration Journal* 33: 86-92.
Kippenberg, H.G.
1971   *Gerezim und Synagoge.* Berlin.

Klein, C.
1978   *Anti-Judaism in Christian Theology*. Philadelphia.

Kraabel, A.T.
1971   "Melito the Bishop and the Synagogue at Sardis: Text and Context." *Studies Presented to George M.A. Hanfmann*. Edited by D.G. Mitten, J.G. Pedley and J.A. Scott. Cambridge MA. Pages 77-85.
1979   "The Diaspora Synagogue." *Aufstieg und Niedergang der römischen Welt: Geschichte und Kultur Roms im Spiegel der neueren Forschung*, II. 19.1: 477-510.
1981   "The Disappearance of the 'God-fearers'." *Numen* 28: 113-126.
1982   "The Roman Diaspora: Six Questionable Assumptions." *Journal of Jewish Studies* 33:444-64 (special number in honor of Yigael Yadin).
1983   "Impact of the Discovery of the Sardis Synagogue." *Sardis from Prehistoric to Roman Times*. Edited by G.M.A. Hanfmann. Cambridge MA. Pages 178-190.
1984   "New Evidence of the Samaritan Diaspora has been Found on Delos." Biblical Archaeologist 47: 44-46.

Mellink, M.
1977   "Archaeology in Asia Minor." *American Journal of Archaeology* 81: 306 (on the Aphrodisias inscription).

Montgomery, J.A.
1907   *The Samaritans*. Philadelphia.

Neusner, J.
1981   "The Symbolism of Ancient Judaism: The Evidence of the Synagogue." *Ancient Synagogues: The State of Research*. Edited by J. Gutmann. Chico CA. Pages 7-17.
1984   *Ancient Judaism: Debates and Disputes*. Chico CA.

Pummer, R.
1979   "New Evidence for Samaritan Christianity?" *Catholic Biblical Quarterly* 41: 98-117.

Purvis, J.D.
1976   "Samaritans." *IDBS* 776-777.

Robert, J. and L.
1983   "Bulletin épigraphique." *Revue des études grecques*, pages 123-124, no. 281 (on Bruneau 1982).

Rohland, 7. P.
1977   *Der Erzengel Michael, Arzt und Feldherr*. Leiden.

Sandmel, S.
1978   *Anti-Simitlsm in the New Testament?* Philadelphia.

Scobie, C.H.H.
1972   "The Origins and Development of Samaritan Christianity." *New Testament Studies* 19; 390-414.

Sheppard, A.R.R.
1982   "Pagan Cults of Angels in Roman Asia Minor." *Talanta* 12-13:77-101.
Sherwin-White, A.N.
1970   *Racial Prejudice in Imperial Rome*. Cambridge UK.
Simon, M.
1964   *Verus Israel*. Paris.
1971   "Remarques sur l'Angélolatrie Juive au Début de l'Ere Chrétienne."
       Comptes rendus de l'Académie des Inscriptions & Belles-Lettres. Pages
       120-134.
Smith, M.
1967   "Goodenough's Jewish Symbols in Retrospect." *Journal of Biblical
       Literature* 86: 53-68.
1971   *Palestinian Parties and Politics that Shaped the Old Testament*. New
       York.
1983   "Terminological Boobytraps and Real Problems in Second Temple
       Judaeo-Christian Studies." *Traditions in Contact and Change...Proceed-
       ings of the XIV Congress IAHR*. Edited by P. Slater and D. Wiebe.
       Winnipeg. Pages 295-306.
Stendahl, K.
1976   *Paul among Jews and Gentiles*. Philadelphia.
Väänänen, V.
1966   *Graffiti del Palatino*, I: *Paedagogium*. Helsinki. No. 246, pages 209-212
       (the Alexamenos inscription).
Werner, E.
1966   "Melito of Sardis, the First Poet of Deicide." *Hebrew Union College
       Annual* 37: 191-210.
Wilken, R.L.
1984   *The Christians as the Romans Saw Them*. New Haven.
Wright, G.E.
1965   *Shechem: The Biography of a Biblical City*. New York.

The Diaspora in the Modern Study of Ancient Judaism

J. Andrew Overman

For over twenty years A.T. Kraabel has drawn attention to the vitality and strength of Jewish diaspora communities in the Roman period. He has sought to demonstrate the importance of these communities in the larger history of Judaism in antiquity, and cautioned against treating these Jews, and the Judaisms they represented as second cousins to an implicit normative Judaism. The opposition of diaspora and homeland, so often employed in discussions on diaspora Judaism, has frequently served as a thinly veiled code for the older opposition of "Hellenistic" and "Palestinian" Judaism. Kraabel himself has consistently stressed the need to revise this "old consensus" concerning the life and nature of Jews living outside Palestine in the Roman period.[1] He has correctly maintained that neglect, and in some cases distortion of Jewish communities in the diaspora by scholars has helped to reinforce an implicit normative Judaism, the understood definition of which tended to exclude the Jews of the Greco-Roman diaspora.[2] This essay is an attempt to build on Kraabel's work by taking seriously his own suggestion to examine diaspora Judaism within the broader context of ancient Judaism. In particular I would like to call into question, in light of important advances in the study of ancient Judaism generally, the analytical value of the category "diaspora Judaism" for the study of these communities outside of Palestine in the Roman period.

The eighties saw the passing of the notion of a normative Judaism. The tremendous diversity within and among groups understanding themselves as Jews shattered what might have remained of any notion of "Judaism" as a monolith. The recognition of the impact of Hellenism throughout the Roman world played an important role in the shift in perception about Judaism in this period. Greek culture, art, language and religion was ubiquitous throughout Palestine, even, perhaps especially, in Galilee, home to both the early stages of the Jesus movement and nascent rabbinic Judaism.[3] This insight did away

---

1 A.T. Kraabel, "The Impact of the Discovery of the Sardis Synagogue," which originally appeared in *Sardis From Prehistoric to Roman Times: Results from the Archaeological Exploration of Sardis 1958-1975,* edited by G. Hanfmann, (Cambridge, MA: Harvard, 1983), 178.

2 See especially Kraabel's, "*Synagoga Caeca*: Systematic Distortion in Gentile Interpretations of Evidence for Judaism in the Early Christian Period," which appeared first in, "*To See Ourselves as Others See Us": Christians, Jews, and Others in Late Antiquity,* edited by J. Neusner and E. Frerichs, (Atlanta: Scholars Press, 1985), 219-246. See also by Kraabel, "Unity and Diversity Among Diaspora Synagogues," in L.I. Levine, *The Synagogue in Late Antiquity,* (Philadelphia: *ASOR,* 1987), p.60, where Kraabel notes the focus on biblical and rabbinic literatures by both Jewish and gentile scholars.

3 See S. Liebermann, *Hellenism in Jewish Palestine,* (New York: *JTS,* 1950), M. Hengel, *Judaism and Hellenism: Studies in Their Encounter in Palestine During the Early Hellenistic Period,* trans. by J. Bowden, (Philadelphia: Fortress, 1974) and, for Galilee see, J.A. Overman, "Who
(continued...)

with the old distinction between "Palestinian" and "Hellenistic" Judaism. The evidence for Jewish religion throughout Palestine, Syria and north Africa exhibits such stunning diversity that scholars now speak of Judaisms,[4] in order to emphasize a range of religious forms among the Jews of the Roman period.

In an essay published in 1987 A.T. Kraabel hypothesized that diaspora Jews in the Roman period developed their own religion. In his view four features distinguish the religion of diaspora Jews from the Jewish religion in Palestine.[5] The Jews of the Greco-Roman diaspora emphasized and drew heavily from the Greek scriptures and scriptural traditions; they worshipped without a priesthood; they modelled their social a religious collectivities on the Greco-Roman voluntary associations; and their life-world was not shaped by historical events specific to Palestine, (the Maccadean revolt, the Roman administration of Palestine from the time of Pompey and Gabinius, and the two revolts against Rome). In time, diaspora Jews developed art, iconography, and architecture; their own liturgical modes and traditions; and a place where all these developments were represented or enacted, the synagogue.

Kraabel has significantly advanced our understanding of diaspora Jews and Judaism. His advocacy of the strength and contribution of Jewish communities in the Greco-Roman diaspora, his caution against Christian biases in the

---

3(...continued)
Were the First Urban Christians? Urbanization in First Century Galilee," *Society of Biblical Literature Seminar Papers*, edited by D. Lull, (Atlanta: Scholars Press, 1988), 160-168. Also the degree of hellenization in Galilee at the height of the rabbinic period is demonstrated in the recent excavations at Sepphoris in Galilee. See, E. Meyers, E. Netzer, and C. Meyers, "Sepphoris: Ornament of Galilee," *BA* 49 (1986) 153-167.

I concur with the claim made by Feldman, Millar and others that what passes for "hellenism" can often times be traced to the Persian period and Persian influences. Feldman's interest in showing that "hellenism" had not made the in-roads into Jewish Palestine *by the Maccabean revolt* that Hengel claims it has seems strained, but is not directly relevant to our thesis. (In contrast to Feldman see E. Bickerman, *The God of the Maccabees: Studies in the Meaning and Origin of the Maccabean Revolt*, (Leiden: Brill, 1979) 76-92). See L. Feldman, "How Much Hellenism in Jewish Palestine," *HUCA* 57 (1986) 83-111, and F. Millar, "The Background to the Maccabean Revolution: Reflections on Martin Hengel's 'Judaism and Hellenism,'" *JJS* 22 (1978) 1-21.

4 Due largely to the work of J. Neusner. *Rabbinic Traditions About the Pharisees Before 70*: 3 vols., (Leiden: Brill, 1973), *Method and Meaning in Ancient Judaism*: Vol.2, (Chico, CA: Scholars Press, 1981), et al.

5 In his suggestive article, "Unity and Diversity among Diaspora Synagogues," Kraabel sketches this thesis about the nature of diaspora Jewish communities and religion. After listing the distinctive traits of diaspora communities, which I have just summarized, Kraabel writes, "the synagogue Judaism of the Roman Diaspora is best understood as the grafting of a biblical diaspora theology onto a Greco-Roman social organization." Jews in the Roman diaspora had to shift from a national religion of Holy Land and Temple to that of a minority community. Kraabel suggests that there is a "diaspora theology," and that the cumulative result of the distinctive features, history and theology of diaspora Judaism could be called a new religion.

study of these Jews, and his placing the study of Jews in the Greco-Roman diaspora within the larger context of ancient Judaism generally all represent important advances. However, as this is a volume which both honors and engages the work of A.T. Kraabel, I would like to ask if distinctions between the religion of Jews at "home" and "abroad" can be sustained. While Kraabel has helped to do away with a number of artificial categories in the study of ancient Judaism, he has suggested another set of criteria by which diaspora and native Judaisms can be distinguished. But does the geographical location of a type of Judaism shape its religion? Can the religion of Jews in the Roman period be distinguished in any sense between "home" and "abroad"?

Let us take Kraabel's four traits of the religion of diaspora Jews in order. The now widely recognized penetration of Greek language and texts in Palestine from the Ptolemaic period dramatically changes assumptions about linguistic differences between the diaspora and Palestine.[6] Hellenistic culture, which includes of course Greek language in particular, was deeply rooted in Palestine by the turn of the eras. The epigraphical evidence from Palestine reveals a far greater number of Greek inscriptions than Aramaic ones. Indeed Palestine was polyglot. However, Greek seems to have pervaded Palestinian society.[7] Coins from Palestine bear predominantly Greek terms or slogans.[8]

---

6 Works which highlight the influence of Greek language and culture in Palestine include M. Hengel, *Judaism and Hellenism: Studies in Their Encounter in Palestine During the Hellenistic Period*, S. Lieberman, *Hellenism in Jewish Palestine*.

7 See S. Applebaum, "Romanization and Indigenism in Judea," in *Judea in Hellenistic and Roman Times*, (Leiden: Brill, 1989), 155-165. The epigraphical evidence places the burden of proof on those who would claim aramaic was the lingua franca. Concerning the Greek inscriptions from Scythopolis see G. Fuks, "The Jews of Scythopolis," *JJS* 33 (1982) 409. 30 of the ossuaries found north of Scythopolis contain only Greek inscriptions. See also, M. Avi-Yonah, "Scythopolis," *IEJ* 12 (1962) 131. N. Avigad, "A Depository of Inscribed Ossuaries in the Kidron Valley," *IEJ* 12 (1962) 1-12, discusses the unadorned Greek inscriptions from the Kidron valley. Also, J. Strange, "Late Hellenistic and Herodian Ossuary Tombs at French Hill, Jerusalem," *BASOR* 219 (1975) 39-70, and D. Edwards, "First Century Urban/Rural Relations in Lower Galilee," *SBLSP*, ed. D. Lull (Atlanta: Scholars Press, 1988) 179-182. For Greek influence and presence in Upper Galilee see, E. and C. Meyers, "Digging the Talmud in Ancient Meiron," *BAR* 4 (1978) 42. More directed at lower Galilee is E. Meyers' article, "Galilean Regionalism as a Factor in Historical Reconstruction," *BASOR* 221 (1976) 93ff., and his judicious critique of S. Freyne's *Galilee* in "Galilean Regionalism: A Reappraisal," in *Approaches to Ancient Judaism V*, Brown Judaic Studies 32, ed. by W.S. Green, (Atlanta: Scholars Press, 1985) 115-132. And above all for the rather conclusive evidence from Bet She'arim see, "M. Schwabe and B. Lifshitz, *Bet She'arim: The Greek Inscriptions*, Vol. II, (New Brunswick, NJ: Rutgers University, 1974) especially 217-222.

8 See for example, Y. Meshorer, *Jewish Coins of the Second Temple Period*, (Tel Aviv, 1967), "Sepphoris and Rome," in O. Morkholm and N. Waggoner eds., *Greek Numismatics and Archaeology: Essays in Honor of Margaret Thompson*, (Belgium: Cultura Press, 1979) 159-171. In the same volume see L. Mildenberg, "Yehud: A Preliminary Study of the Provinicial Coinage of
(continued...)

Synagogues from the period when synagogue worship, and the synagogue as an institution were more fully developed also bear Greek inscriptions and allusions to scripture.[9]

Several significant religious texts from Palestine in this period were written in Greek. The original language of the book of Judith seems to have been Greek. The Gospel of Matthew is now viewed by more and more scholars as being of Palestinian provenance.[10] Certain of the Bar Kochba letters are written in Greek so everyone would be able to understand them.[11] The use of the LXX by these putative Palestinian authors, which is Kraabel's hypothesis about diaspora Jews, is a tougher issue. It would stand to reason that these Greek texts would employ the Greek version of Israel's scriptures. However, given the language milieu of Palestine it would not be surprising to find someone using both Hebrew or Greek, or translating one into the other. Yet even here dependence upon, or use of the LXX by Palestinian, or what we would call southern Syrian, authors is not hard to find. Matthew's Gospel is dependent on the LXX for its use of scripture. Judith 9.2 provides a citation from Genesis 34.7, as does Testament of Levi 2.1-2, 5-7.[12] The influence of the LXX Psalms in the Prayer of Manasseh has been noted by Charlesworth[13], and the surviving Greek manuscripts of Tobit preserve a number of LXX citations.[14]

8(...continued)
Judea," 183-196. G.F. Hill, *Catalogue of the Greek Coins of Palestine*, (London: British Museum, 1965).

9 E. Bickerman, "Sur la theologie de l'art figuratif. A propos de l'ouvrage de E.R. Goodenough," Syria 44 (1967) reprinted in *Studies in Jewish and Christian History*, Part III, (Leiden: Brill, 1986) 245-269. Noteworthy of course are the images and inscriptions from Hammat-Tiberias and Dura-Europos, to name just two. The latter worked out in great detail by E.R. Goodenough and the former by M. Dothan.

10 J.A. Overman, *Matthew's Gospel and Formative Judaism: The Social World of the Matthean Community*, (Minneapolis: Fortress, 1990) 158-59. D. Harrington, "Matthew and Judaism," *Canadian Catholic Review* (April, 1989) 136-138.

11 *The Documents from the Bar-Kochba Period in the Cave of Letters: Greek Papyri*, ed. N. Lewis, (Jerusalem: Israel Exploration Society/Hebrew University, 1989). All but 10 of the 37 documents discovered by Y. Yadin in the early sixties are in Greek. Similarly, see *Masada II: The Greek and Latin Documents* eds. H. Cotton and J. Geiger.

12 A Palestinian provenance, with the original language being Greek has been suggested by J. Becker, *Die Testamente der zwoelf Patriarchen*, (Guetersloh: Mohn, 1980), 23-27. H.C. Kee argues for a provenance of Palestine or southern Syria for the Testament of the Twelve Patriarchs in J. Charlesworth ed., *The Old Testament Pseudepigrapha* I, 775-780.

13 *The Old Testament Pseudepigrapha* II, 630-31.

14 The original language of Tobit is more problematic. The text only survives however in Greek. See the citations in 2.6//Amos 8.10; 8.6//Gen.2.18. For a discussion of the use of scrip-
(continued...)

Josephus is an interesting case in point regarding the use of scripture and scriptural traditions. In his preface to the *Antiquities* Josephus celebrates the LXX as the precedent for his work.[15] Apparently Thackery noted that of the thirteen times he clearly found Josephus citing the LXX, ten followed the manuscript Alexandrinus, while three followed Vaticanus.[16] Feldman has attempted to demonstrate the use of Hebrew, Greek and Aramaic scriptural traditions on the part of Josephus, but this has received at best a mixed reaction from scholars. E.C. Ulrich has shown, and has been followed by others, that Josephus used a proto-Lucianic form of the LXX for some of his material.[17]

In the relatively rare instance Josephus cites scripture there is clear evidence he uses some form of the LXX. In his reinterpretation of biblical history which guides the *Antiquities* Josephus' use of his version of the LXX is also very much in evidence. But do we think of Josephus as someone representing a form of "diaspora Jewish religion" or "Palestinian Jewish religion?" Is the sort of Judaism he represents, and which he portrays to his audience based on his experience in Palestine or the diaspora? Certainly there are complicating factors in answering this question. In the main however, Josephus speaks about Judaism in Palestine and environs, as he understood it. The Judaism he explicates for his audience, however tendentious this portrayal may

---

14(...continued)
ture by various apocryphal and pseudepigraphical books see D. Dimant, "Use and Interpretation of Mikra in the Apocrypha and Pseudepigrapha," in *Compendia Rerum Iudaicarum ad Novum Testamentum*, II, entitled, *Mikra: Text, Translation, Reading and Interpretation of the Hebrew Bible in Ancient Judaism and Early Christianity*, edited by M.J. Mulder, (Van Gorcum/Fortress: Assen/Philadelphia, 1985), 379-420.

15 H. Attridge, *The Interpretation of Biblical History in the Antiquitates Judaicae of Flavius Josephus*, HDR 7, (Scholars Press: Missoula, 1976), 41.

16 See L. Feldman in his, "Use, Authority and Exegesis of Mikra in the Writings of Josephus," in *Mikra*, (note 14 above), p. 458. See the more balanced discussion of Josephus, and others use of the LXX by B.M. Metzger, "The Lucianic Recension of the Greek Bible," in *Studies in the Septuagint: Origins, Recensions, and Interpretations*, ed. S. Jellicoe, (New York: KTAV, 1974), 270-291. Thackery, *Josephus, the Man and the Historian*, (New York: KTAV, 1967), and A. Mez, *Die Bibel des Josephus untersucht fuer Buch V-VII der Archaeologie*, (Basel: Jaeger, 1895), were less cautious about clear dependence on a Lucianic version of the LXX. However, there is clear dependence on such a Lucianic recension in Josephus' use of Kings and Samuel. See A. Rahlfs, *Septuaginta-studien*, (Goettingen: Vandenhoeck und Ruprecht, 1904-1911).

17 *The Qumran Text of Samuel and Josephus*, HSM 19, (Scholars Press: Missoula, 1978). See also the comments by D. Harrington, "Palestinian Adaptations of Biblical Narratives and Prophecies," and H. Attridge, "Jewish Historiography," in R.A. Kraft and G.W.E. Nickelsburg, *Early Judaism and Its Modern Interpreters*, Scholars/Fortress Press: Atlanta/Philadelphia, 1986). Josephus is not alone in using this earlier Lucianic recension of the LXX. Justin Martyr also demonstrates dependence on such text as noted some time ago by W. Bousset, *Die Evangeliencitate Justins des Maertyrers in ihrem Wert fuer die Evangelienkritik*, (Goetttingen: Vandenhoeck und Ruprecht, 1891).

be, is Palestinian. The political and religious life and struggles Josephus describes belong to Palestine in the years leading up to the first revolt against Rome. His characterization of Jewish beliefs, piety, tradition, and life under Roman rule is based on his own life and experience in Palestine. Josephus describes a Judaism based on and shaped in the homeland. This is often overlooked. Josephus may be that figure who brings together of forms and practices we usually have thought of only as diaspora-like, or only as Palestinian-like. In his work Josephus captures the artificial nature of the scholarly distinction between the religions of the Jewish diaspora and the homeland.

Josephus was not alone among Jewish historiographers in Palestine to write in Greek and rely upon some version of the LXX. The second century B.C.E. historian Eupolemus wrote in Greek, and in his work, *Concerning the Judean Kings*, demonstrates dependence on both the LXX and MT.[18] His work appears to draw heavily from Greek version of Chronicles and Kings. Of course Josephus' contemporary and nemesis Justus of Tiberias, was by Josephus' own admission well versed in Greek language and culture. His *Chronicle of the Jewish Kings*, and *A History of the Jewish War* were written in Greek in Palestine. Jerome attributes another work to Justus, a scriptural commentary, but its existence is doubted by many.[19]

If Greek was ubiquitous throughout Palestine, and several significant Palestinian Jewish authors, as we might suspect, use some version of the LXX and rely on scriptural traditions and personae in their stories, then use of the Greek scriptures and scriptural traditions cannot be a distinguishing feature of diaspora Jewish religion.

But what though of the Temple and its priesthood? Is this not a difference in religion between diaspora and homeland? Did the diaspora communities live and worship without a priesthood, (because there was no temple and therefore no sacrifice), and was this a distinguishing feature between diaspora and Palestinian religious life for Jews?

Despite Deuteronomy's stricture that Yahweh has only one valid sanctuary, "the place God will choose as a dwelling for God's name," Jewish sacrifice was carried out in Egypt. A temple was built at Leontopolis by Onias sometime in the second c. B.C.E., and was closed by the Romans in 74 C.E. Josephus says it functioned for 343 years.[20] The temple at Leontopolis may have

---

18 C.R. Holladay, *Fragments from Hellenistic Jewish Authors*, Vol.I: Historians, (Chico, CA: Scholars, 1983) 93-104. Feldman attempts to raise some question about the provenance of Eupolemus. "How Much Hellensim in Jewish Palestine?," 96-97.

19 Ibid., 371-389.

20 See Jos. *B.J.* 7.436. J.A. Overman and W.S. Green, "Judaism in the Greco-Roman Period," in *The Anchor Bible Dictionary*, (Doubleday: Garden City, forthcoming). R. Hayward, "The Jewish Temple at Leontopolis," *JJS* 33, (1982) 429-44.

influenced the author of the Third Sibyl.[21] It is instructive to recall that a
temple existed in Egypt long before the one at Leontopolis. This of course
was the temple at Elephantine. There was indeed an "altar to the Lord in the
midst of the land of Egypt," (Is. 19.19), and there had been from about the 7th
century B.C.E.

In the post exilic and Greco-Roman period the Samaritans loom large as
a Jewish community who, like the cult in Jerusalem, held the priesthood and
sacrifice at the Temple to be a central feature of their version of Judaism. The
Samaritan's temple on Mt. Gerizim was built around the time of Alexander
the Great (*Ant.*11.302ff.). The tension between Samaritan Judaism and the
Judaism centered on and represented by the Jerusalem cult increased during
the time of John Hyrcanus (c.128 B.C.E.). Under this Hasmonean leader the
Gerizim Temple was destroyed. Excavations have shown that the temple was
built again during the reign of Hadrian.[22]

Two inscriptions from Delos discussed by Kraabel speak of "the Israelites
on Delos who make offerings to hallowed Mt. Gerizim."[23]

Yet there was another Samaritan tradition which seemed to resist the emphases on cult and priesthood; the so-called Dositheans. What needs to be stressed here in terms of Samaritan history and development is that Temple sacrifice and priesthood on the one hand, and a non priestly form of Samaritanism
on the other, did not divide within Samaritan Judaism between homeland and
diaspora. The inscription from Delos gives the impression that the Samaritan
diaspora still sacrificed, but only on Mt. Gerizim. This may have been the case
for the Samaritans on Delos, or in Thessalonica for that matter. But at home
there was emerging a form of Samaritanism which marginalized the Samaritan
priesthood. The more lay centered Dositheans took a view that was more or
less dismissive of the notion and function of a priesthood. This was, according
to Purvis and others, a lay movement which required no priesthood. They
waited for a prophet like Moses, believed in a resurrection, and functioned
without, if not altogether abandoned, the priesthood. These Dositheans did
not have to be located in the "Samaritan diaspora" in order to hold this position which so challenged the more priestly and cultic centered Samaritanism.[24]

---

21 J.J. Collins, *Between Athens and Jerusalem*, (New York: Crossroads, 1983) 63, 71, 95.

22 See J. Purvis, "The Samaritans and Judaism," in Kraft and Nickelsburg, *Early Judaism and
Its Modern Interpreters*, 81-98. Also, Overman and Green, "Judaism in the Greco-Roman Period."

23 A.T. Kraabel, "New Evidence of the Samaritan Diaspora has been Found on Delos," *BA*
47, (1984) 44-46.

24 J.D. Purvis, "The Samaritans and Judaism," in Kraft and Nickelsburg, *Early Judaism and
Its Modern Interpreters*, 81-95. S.J. Isser, *The Dositheans: A Samaritan Sect in Late Antiquity*, (Lei-
(continued...)

Dositheus is thought to have lived between the first century B.C.E. and first century C.E. It was during the period when the Samaritan Temple lay in ruin that this movement within Samaritanism developed. Dositheus is known by Hegesippus, Origen, Eusebius, Epiphanius, and others. In his commentary on John (4.25), and again in Matthew (24.4ff.) Origen says that Dositheus was thought to be the prophesied Messiah, or the predicted prophet like Moses (*C.Celsus* 1.57). Eusebius states essentially the same thing about Dositheus (*Theophany* 4.35). There was a tradition that Dositheus did not die, and wrote books which continue to be used by his adherents.[25]

Epiphanius (*Panarion* 9-14), recognizes that Samaritanism is not monolithic. There are four Samaritan sects he says which differ primarily in smaller things. The Dositheans however differ from these others in big things.[26] They believe in a resurrection, have their own communities, do not eat animals, observe circumcision and Sabbath, and are concerned about the distinction between pure and impure. The Dositheans were a prophetic-messianic movement which arose within Samaritanism around the turn of the eras. This movement would have filled a void resulting from the Temple's destruction, or, more to the point, constituted simply a rival to the Samaritan Temple-priest structure. Dositheus was a figure thought by his followers to be a prophet like Moses who fulfilled the traditions derived from Dt.18. Based particularly on the material from Epiphanius the Dositheans have been described as a "Pharisaizing Samaritanism."[27] Their beliefs can in some fashion be traced to the Temple, but they carried on their beliefs without need of an actual Temple, and it appears without a Priesthood.

Not all of the Judaisms in Roman Palestine required a Temple, much less possessed a priesthood. We cannot assume that simply because the Temple in Jerusalem was in Palestine that all forms of "Palestinian Judaism" required a Temple or a priesthood, or felt an allegiance to the Temple. From what little we can surmise about the Pharisees, it seems that they had no need for the actual Temple in Jerusalem, and were themselves in a certain respect a lay movement.[28] It is clear from Josephus that the Pharisees periodically enjoyed

24(...continued)
den: Brill, 1976). See also Isser's, "Dositheus, Jesus, and a Moses Aretology," in *Christianity, Judaism, and Other Greco-Roman Cults. Studies for Morton Smith at Sixty*, ed. J. Neusner, (Leiden: Brill, 1975) 167-189.

25 S.J. Isser, *The Dositheans*, p.33, 164.

26 Ibid. p.40.

27 Isser, *The Dositheans*, p.107. Also, J. Bowman, "The Importance of Samaritan Researches," *Annual of Leeds University Oriental Society*, 1 (1958-59) 43-54, who asserts the Dositheans developed a synagogue like model, rather than an emphasis on the holy place at Gerizim.

28 Two places where this view is expressed by Neusner are, *From Politics to Piety: The*
(continued...)

power with those in Jerusalem. They have been likened in their political function to *retainers* who through the patronage of the political leader(s) are granted power, but can just as quickly loose it.[29]

In B.J. 1.108-112 the story is told of the Pharisees working their way into
the favor of Alexandra, the successor of her husband Alexander Jannai (c.76
B.C.E.). The Pharisees, Josephus says, were a certain body who appear more
pious than others and interpret the laws more accurately. Under Alexandra
the Pharisees became the real administrators of the state, enjoying "royal
authority." *Antiquities* 13.405 describes Alexandra's power sharing arrangement
with the Pharisees. She restored the practices and traditions of the Pharisees
which had been previously abrogated by her father-in-law Hyrcanus (*Ant.* 13.
409), and gave them the authority to "banish and recall, to bind and to loose."

Earlier in *Antiquities* the down side of the fate of the retainer class is captured by Josephus when he tells the story of Hyrcanus' displeasure with the
Pharisees, his withdrawal of support, and choosing instead to work with the
Sadducees in governing the kingdom (*Ant.*13.288). So the Pharisees were no
strangers to the power of the elite in Palestinian society, and would have been
associated with the Temple only when they worked for those priests and high
priests who were in charge politically, and chose to use the Pharisees in imple-
menting their rule.

Yet as far as we can reconstruct what the Pharisees might have believed
and how they behaved, there is no indication that the actual Temple, or the
priesthood figured prominently, if at all. If Neusner is correct and the Pharisees did seek in some sense to replicate the Temple in a more domestic setting, and thereby make all the participants in effect priests, this is still not
Temple-centered. Such a program need not have been necessarily anti-Temple, but it could easily have been construed as anti-priest. In fact, if indeed
Pharisaism played a large role in the synthesis of various Judaisms in the post
70 period, it was because they did not need a Temple for their piety and the
execution of their religious program. The Pharisees were well positioned in
the post 70 period because they did not require, and never focused on either
the Temple in Jerusalem, or the priesthood. In fact, their concern to see the
ritual purity heretofore associated with the Temple applied to the local, if not
domestic setting, is *de facto* a supercession of the Priests' function.

The influence of the Pharisees, and their popularity with the people is
due, according to Josephus, because they are *akribeis tou nomou*, or "the most

---

28(...continued)
Emergence of Pharisaic Judaism, (Englewood Cliffs: Prentice-Hall, 1973), and, "Two Pictures of
the Pharisees: Philosophical Circle and Eating Club," *ATR* 64 (1982) 525-38.

29 See the recent illuminating work by A.J. Saldarini, *Pharisees, Scribes and Sadducees in
Palestinian Society: A Sociological Approach,,* (Wilmington: Michael Glazier, 1988).

accurate interpreters of the law" (*B.J.*1.110; 2.162; *Vita* 38.191). They advocate
certain traditions which are not in the law of Moses (*Ant.*13.297).[30] Their use
of these traditions and the popularity their expertise with the law brought
them with the people made the Pharisees occasionally useful for those who in
fact held political power. These aspects of Pharisaism gave the Pharisees some
measure of influence and position in Roman Palestine. But this had little or
nothing to do with the Temple and less to do with the priesthood. To the extent that the Pharisees obtained influence they did so through Torah interpretation and not the Temple system.[31]

Another form of Judaism in Palestine which did not advocate a priesthood, and functioned without one, is represented by the so-called popular
movements which sprang up in Palestine under the pressure of Roman imperial rule. In the period of Roman domination in Palestine the Temple served
as an instrument of imperial legitimation. Tithes, taxes and debt were all collected and recorded in the Jerusalem Temple (*Ant.*14.203).[32] One such group,
the so-called Fourth Philosophy, appears in Josephus as primarily a tax-resis-
tance movement. It was lead by Judas the Galilean who reproached others for
paying taxes to Rome and tolerating human masters (*B.J.*2.118). In *Antiquities*
18 Josephus writes that Judas was in league with Zadok the Pharisee, and that
the beliefs and behavior of the Fourth Philosophy closely resemble those of
the Pharisees, except for their unusual commitment to freedom. The role of
the priesthood in taxation of the people and their complicity with Rome would
have pushed the Fourth Philosophy even further into a stance which stood in
opposition to the priesthood. Their "zeal for liberty" would have simply exacer-
bated this distance. Despite Josephus' political loyalties, even his description
of these groups suggests a tension in this period between the Temple elite and
the people's traditional beliefs in Israel's theocracy (*B.J.*2.433; *C.Ap.*2.164-165;
*Ant.*4.223). As we now recognize there were a host of other, similar rebel
groups who fought, so they believed, for the God of the people of Israel, and

30 See A.I. Baumgarten, "The Pharisaic *Paradosis*," *HTR* 80 (1987) 63-78. Such a dispute over
the *"paradosis ton presbuteron"* takes place in Mark chapter 7 and Matthew chapter 15. See J.
Neusner, "First Cleanse the Inside," *NTS* 22 (1975-76) 486-495. Also, Overman, *Matthew's Gospel
and Formative Judaism*, 78-86.

31 See S. Isenberg, "Power Through Temple and Torah in Greco-Roman Palestine," in
Christianity, Judaism, and Other Greco-Roman Cults, ed. J. Neusner, (Leiden: Brill, 1975) 2:42.
See also J.A. Overman, "Consolidation and Legitimation in Formative Judaism," in *Matthew's
Gospel and Formative Judaism*, 65-72.

32 R. Horsley, *Jesus and the Spiral of Violence*, (San Francisco: Harper & Row, 1987) 285-
318.

in many cases against the Priesthood which had emerged in the eyes of some rebels as pawns of the Romans.[33]

The stance of Jesus movement concerning the Temple and its priesthood is a subject which has garnered much attention. Jesus pronounced numerous oracles against the ruling institutions of Palestine including of course the priesthood and the Temple. In the earliest Gospel it is Jesus' threat against the Temple which finally condemns him.[34] The response of followers of Jesus to the Temple seems to have varied somewhat. It has been suggested that there is an absence of Temple polemic in Matthew's Gospel, while Jesus' opposition to the Temple, as noted above, is more pronounced in Mark.[35] It is clear from the Gospels that some of the followers of Jesus were concerned about the perception that Jesus was anti-Temple. Though Jesus' charge against and hostility toward the Temple are clear in Mark, in a narrative aside in Mk.14.56 the author claims it is false witnesses who say Jesus said he was going to destroy the Temple. Matthew follows Mark in the passages concerning false witnesses (Matt.26.59ff.), and in the call of the people at the foot of the cross who recall that Jesus said he would destroy the Temple (Mk.15.29 //Matt.27.40). John 2.19ff. carefully tries to explain this widespread tradition about Jesus' stance to the Temple in Jerusalem. The tradition that Jesus threatened the Temple is deeply embedded within the Gospel tradition. Some subsequent redactional activity by the Evangelists are attempts to explain this hostility. In the wake of the destruction of the Jerusalem Temple in 70 Palestinian Jews who were followers of Jesus were most likely divided over the role of the Temple, and Jesus' stance toward it. Some of the earliest followers of Jesus clearly understood him as opposed to the Temple,[36] while certain, subsequent followers sought to correct this perception.

Temples and priesthood could arise in the diaspora, and, it is clear, certain Judaisms in the land of Palestine did not require either Temple or priest, and some outright rejected one or both.

The application of the broad model of the Greco-Roman associations to diaspora communities would seem to fit also for Jewish communities in Pale-

---

33 See the review of such movements in R. Horsley and J. Hanson, *Bandits, Prophets and Messiahs: Popular Movements in the Time of Jesus*, (Minneapolis: Winston, 1985). Also now the recent treatment by F. Murphy in *The Religious World of Jesus*, (Nashville: Abingdon, 1991) 277-310.

34 See for example D. Juel, *Messiah and Temple*, *SBLDS* 31, (Missoula, MT: Scholars Press, 1977).

35 For the discussion of the absence of a Temple polemic in Matthew see, R. Hummel, *Die Auseinandersetzung Zwischen Kirche und Judentum im Matthaeusevangelium*, (Muenich: Kaiser, 1963).

36 Horsley, *Jesus and the Spiral of Violence*, p.300.

stine. Philo likens the Jews' synagogues to the Roman *collegia*.[37] Josephus, presummably for the sake of his Greco-Roman audience, likens the Jewish *haireseis* in Palestine to well known Greco-Roman groups (*Ant.*13.171-73).[38] Here, as in *Vita* (9-12), Josephus remains consistent in his attempt to portray Jewish collectivities or bodies, and ways of thought, as being as respectable as Greek philosophies, and not "rabble," or revolutionaries.[39] Josephus seems to believe he can establish with his audience sufficient knowledge of the three major Jewish groups by simply likening them to well known Greek *haireseis* of the Greco-Roman period. Josephus claims these Jewish Palestinian groups are roughly analagous to the Greek Epicureans, Cynics and Stoics.

The material culture of Palestine yields some interesting evidence in this regard. The modest first century structures in Palestine which have been called synagogues are viewed now architecturally as similar to the common associations of the broader Greco-Roman world. A so-called *Domus Ecclesia*, a "synagogue," or hall where a guild or association might meet are all similar, and sometimes identical in structure, lay-out and development.[40] Halls in Gamla, Herodium, Masada or perhaps Magdala have all been offered as first century examples of these simple communal gathering places.[41] Gathering places in the broader Greco-Roman world for popular assemblies, legislative or religious activities, such as the *ecclesiastrion* at Priene or the *bouleterion* at Herakleia, served as models for the so-called Galilean synagogues.[42] These

---

37 M. Smallwood, claims a similar assumption was made in Roman law generally. "Philo and Josephus as Historians of the Same Events," in *Josephus, Judaism, and Christianity*, ed. L. Feldman and G. Hata, (Detroit: Wayne State University, 1987) 114-132.

38 The classic treatment is G.F. Moore's, "Fate and Free Will in the Jewish Philosophies According to Josephus," *HTR* 22 (1929) 371-389. It has been noted that here Josephus may well have relied on a "non-Jewish ethnographic source" for this comparison between Jewish philosophies and Greek schools. A.J. Saldarini, *Pharisees, Scribes and Sadducees*, 109, Attridge, *Interpretation*, 178-79, n.4. M. Smith, "The Description of the Essenes in Josephus and the Philosophumena," *HUCA* 29 (1958) 273-313.

39 Saldarini, *Pharisees, Scribes and Sadducees*, 114-115. In *Life* Josephus says that he finally decided to "govern his life according to the *hairesis* of the Pharisees, a *hairesis* having points of resemblance to that which the Greeks call the Stoic *hairesis*.

40 See L.M. White's, *Building God's House in the Roman World: Architectural Adaptation Among Pagans, Jews, and Christians*, (Baltimore: Johns Hopkins, 1990).

41 The hall at Gamla is a site which is still debated in terms of synagogue with small or capitol "s." The orientation of the building, and the main entrance, even the rosette stone on the lintel are all factors in this debate about the nature and function of the Gamla building. See S. Gutman, "The Synagogue at Gamla," and Z. Ma'oz, "The Synagogue at Gamla and the Typology of Second-Temple Synagogues in *Ancient Synagogues Revealed*, ed. L. Levine, (Jerusalem: Israel Exploration Society, 1981).

42 G. Foerster, "Architectural Models of the Greco-Roman Period and the Origin of the
(continued...)

common first century buildings in Palestine have been referred to as "Hellenistic prototypes" for the later Palestinian synagogues of the 3rd and subsequent centuries.[43] In the case of Tell Hum, and perhaps the Roman port of Ostia, the latter develops, and is even literally founded on, the former.[44]

These first century structures should be thought of as synagogues with a small "s." They date from a period prior to the development of synagogue-based Judaism. Later, when the Judaism which operated from the synagogues was more developed, a structure emerged replete with officials or personnel, a more sophisticated liturgical life, and above all more expansive, ornate and developed buildings. The synagogues at Tell Hum/Capernaum or Hammat-Tiberias are fine examples of just such a stage in the development of synagogue-based Judaism.[45] Prior to these developments however, these structures are *synagogues*, but in the literal and generic sense of this Greek term. They were "gathering places" that doubtless provided for a host of activities. Arguably this sort of common, communal gathering place is analagous to, and may have indeed been modelled on, the common Greco-Roman associations.

Finally, Kraabel has pointed out the historical events and circumstances that are distinct to Palestine and not part of the experience or life-world of diaspora Jews in the Roman period. This is an important point for any discussion about differences or similarities between diaspora and homeland Juda-

---

42(...continued)
'Galilean' Synagogue," in *Ancient Synagogues Revealed*, ed. L. Levine, (Jerusalem: Israel Exploration Society, 1981) 45-48. This is a precis of a chapter in the Foerster's *Galilean Synagogues and Their Relation to Hellenistic and Roman Art and Architecture* (in Hebrew), (Jerusalem: Hebrew University, 1972).

43 N. Avigad, "The 'Galilean' Synagogue and Its Predecessor," in Levine, *Ancient Synagogues Revealed*, 44. Also Ma'oz, "The Synagogue of Gamla and the Typology of the Second-Temple Synagogues," *Ancient Synagogues Revealed*, p.41, who notes that Gamla, Masada and other Palestinian halls "display a typical hellenistic appearance," and that they are derived from the hellenistic halls of assembly.

44 E. Meyers, J. Strange, *Archaeology, the Rabbis, and Early Christianity: The Social and Historical Setting of Palestinian Judaism and Christianity*, (Nashville: Abingdon, 1981) 58-60. R. Meiggs, *Roman Ostia*, 2nd Edition, (Oxford: Claredon, 1973), 587-88. The Ostia synagogue, discovered in 1959, is a first century structure inhanced in the second century and is developed further in the late Roman period. A menorah and inscription noting the benefaction of the building, and a Pro salute Augusti inscription have all been uncovered. Also L.M. White, *Building God's House in the Roman World*, 69-71.

45 For Tell-Hum see Loffredo... and J. Strange, "Review Article: The Capernaum and Herodium Publications," *BASOR* 226 (1977) 65-73. For Hammat-Tiberias, M. Dothan, ... For a brief discussion of the so-called early synagogues in Palestine and the Golan see E. Meyers and A.T. Kraabel, "Archaeology, Iconography, and Nonliterary Written Remains," in Kraft and Nickelsburg, *Early Judaism and Its Modern Interpreters*, 175-210. And J. Strange, "Archaeology and the Religion of Judaism in Palestine," in W. Haase ed., *Aufstieg und Niedergang der Roemischen Welt* II.19.1 646-85.

isms. The significant events between 165 B.C.E. and 135 C.E. in Palestine were not a part of the experience of Jews in Rome, Alexandria or Sardis. Kraabel is quite right. Here one may recall that according to II Maccabees Jews in Alexandria must be told of Hannakuh, and what it represents, and are enjoined to celebrate this holy day which was important to many Jews in and around Jerusalem. Similarly, it is instructive to note that very few documents purported to be from the diaspora reflect upon the destruction of the Temple in 70 C.E.[46] On the other hand post 70 Palestinian documents such as II Baruch, IV Ezra, the Apocalypse of Abraham or the post Mishnaic document The Fathers According to Rabbi Nathan are engaged with this event and its repercussions.

Yet even within Palestine these significant events lent themselves to a range of interpretations. The Maccabean revolt would have been understood differently within the collective memory of communities who faired differently under the rule of the Hasmoneans. Communities to the west and north of Jerusalem shortly after the reclamation of the Temple, or part of it, by Judas and his children would have started to view the Maccabean revolt and Hasmonean rule with, at best, mixed emotions.[47] There are indications that the Hasmonean expansion northward through Alexander Jannai was met with resistance in the Galilee and Golan.[48] Also, there is little evidence of the Bar Kochba revolt making any headway or developing a following in the north. So, within Palestine itself there is a range of attitudes and reactions to the significant historical events between 165 B.C.E. and 133 C.E. These events were neither uniformly nor consistently fundamental to the self-understanding of all the Judaisms in Palestine. These events could be viewed positively or negatively, depending on the group in question.

---

46 The Gospel of Luke is one document, which is almost certainly from outside Palestine, which reflects to a considerable extent, for clear theological reasons, on the Temple's destruction. See L. Gaston, *No Stone on Another: Studies in the Significance of the Fall of Jerusalem in the Synoptic Gospels. NOVTSUP* 23 (Leiden: Brill, 1970).

47 Due to the expansion and colonialization under Simon and Jonathan, certainly some Jews in Palestine shared what J. Goldstein claims is the view of the Letter of Aristeas that "Judea was better off under the Ptolemies than under the Seleucids and Hasmoneans." J.A. Goldstein, "The Message of Aristeas to Philokrates: In the Second Century BCE, Obey the Torah, Venerate the Temple of Jerusalem, but Speak Greek, and Put Your Hopes in the Ptolemaic Dynasty," in *Eretz Israel, Israel and the Jewish Diaspora Mutual Relations*, ed. M. Mor, Studies in Jewish Civilization I, (Lanham, Md: University Press of America, 1991) 12.

48 I Maccabees itself is clear about the struggles with the "heathens" in Galilee. Judas tells Simon and Jonathan to choose men and march into Galilee to "rescue" their countrymen (I Macc. 5.14ff.). They relocate people from the north in Judea. Resistance in the form of "the godless renegades" led by Alcimus, who aspired to be high priest emerges in I Macc.7.1ff. Subsequently Jonathan leaves an occupying force of 2000 men in Galilee.

On the other hand, Jewish communities in the diaspora had their own historical events which, naturally, would have had special significance for them. Jews in Palestine did not experience the Claudian edict of 48 in anyway similar to those Jews in Rome who were expelled. Jews in Alexandria around 38 C.E. experienced distinctive persecutions as Philo's *In Flaccum* and the slightly later *Legatio ad Gaium* make very clear. Similarly, living in Sardis in the second half of the second century of this era would have been very difficult for Jews if the sermons of Melito were obtaining any audience at all. Conversely, there were no *adversus Judaeos* preachers in Palestine in the first two centuries.

Indeed events help to shape the world of the authors and the texts they produce, whether in the diaspora or Palestine. Kraabel has helped to draw attention to something many students of Judaism in this period have tended to overlook. We must begin to study these tremendously diverse Judaisms according to their locale and region, not according to the broad, and now effectively empty categories of diaspora and homeland. Within a very small geographical area a range of Judaisms, a spectrum of interpretations of and opinion about the traditions and history of Israel, the scriptures, who should govern, and what of Israel's future, can all be present. Events could effect people differently in the same area. Competing groups from the same locale interpreted events in contrasting ways. All Judaisms were effected differently by the various historical events that took place in and around their setting. Greater attention to this fact, and a nuancing of how these events were interpreted and the kind of impact these events had, are part of paying attention to the local setting and environment of each and all of these Judaisms, in or outside of Palestine. The address of these Jewish groups will not signal in anyway how certain events are interpreted, and if indeed they were at all significant for a given Judaism. The broad categories of diaspora and homeland do not help us to understand, or even anticipate, how various Judaisms interpreted scripture or Israel's mythic past, or how they regarded the Temple or priesthood. These categories do not help in trying to understand how certain significant events would have been understood by Jews at "home" or "abroad."

The realization that the evidence from antiquity offers no indication of a normative, much less a monolithic, Judaism has altered the modern study of all ancient Judaisms for good. Diaspora Judaisms reflect all the diversity that Judaisms anywhere else exhibit. As modifiers for a kind of Judaism, the categories "native" and "diaspora" have scant analytical value. The terms signal no clear difference in kind or nature between types of Judaisms. The language, religion, modes of communion, and self-understanding vary immensely among the Judaisms of the Roman period. The differences among Judaisms do not break down along the lines of diaspora and homeland.[49] Rather, the difference and diversity is exhibited across geographical boundaries, and, even, within a rather small region. As far as their religion is concerned, Jews in Palestine can have much in common with certain Jews outside Palestine. On the other hand Jewish groups in Palestine can have much less in common with one another than any given diaspora group. While the diversity within Judaism in the Roman period can be staggering, this difference is not explained through recourse to geography. The phrase diaspora Judaism is little more than a mailing address as far as an analytical category is concerned. Its function as a mailing address is only to tell us where these Jews do *not* live. It is a descriptive category as far as the natives are concerned. We are unable to predict anything substantive about diaspora Jews' life or religion because of this address. The Jews in question may have had quite a lot in common with other Jews in Palestine, more perhaps than the competitors of certain Palestinian Jews who may have been living across town.

With the passing of the notion of *a* Judaism, the category diaspora is of little value analytically or historically. We should now be able to see that as far as the Roman period is concerned, this distinction in kind between diaspora and Palestinian Judaism cannot be sustained. The religions of these various Jewish groups, whether in Palestine or beyond, were quite disparate. These differences did not at all breakdown between 'here and there.' We would not be able to see this development in the nature and diversity of Judaism, whether in Palestine or not, were it not for important advances in the study of ancient Judaism generally. And we would not be able to see this development were it not for Tom Kraabel and a few others who pushed us to place and view so-called diaspora Jews in the broader context of Judaism in late antiquity.

---

49 In the case of the Mishna, here and there, in the sense of 'in the land/out of the land', is of course an important issue. A classic location for this discussion is M. Kelim 1:6ff. The question of land in this context pertains to the issue of tithing. Just what is important about being 'in the land' and 'out of the land', however, is debated, even within the Mishna. Is it the land, or the produce of the land which is holy? This question persists in subsequent rabbinic literature. See the discussion in Sifre Numbers 110 in J. Neusner, *Sifre to Numbers: An American Translation and Explanation*, II, Brown Judaic Studies 119, (Atlanta: Scholars Press, 1986) 151ff. Yet land itself does not constitute a *distinctive* feature of any one Judaism in this period. Land, and sacred cities and places figure in many of the Judaisms in the Roman period. Land, as an analytical category for distinguishing Judaisms then, is no different than scripture or scriptural traditions, the Temple, or the treatment of significant historical events. This category, like these others, can be located in sources for Judaism in all ages. And like these other categories, it is used in different circumstances for different purposes. See C. Primus, "The Borders of Judaism: The Land of Israel in Early Rabbinic Judaism," in *The Land of Israel: Jewish Perspectives*, ed. L. Hoffman (Notre Dame: The University of Notre Dame, 1986) 97-108. Also in the same volume R. Sarason, "The Significance of the Land of Israel in the Mishna," 109-138.

The Two Vocabularies of Symbolic Discourse in Ancient Judaism[1]

Jacob Neusner

Among the many excellent students of Erwin R. Goodenough, Thomas Kraabel stands out. He not only loyally preserved the master's legacy, he extended it. His own work made his own his master's, with the result that learning in the area of the study of the symbolic system of ancient Judaism was enriched through continuing access to Goodenough as well as original thinking of Kraabel. My contribution to this exercise in honoring a distinguished scholar is to undertake the comparison between the vocabulary of symbolic discourse in iconic form and that of the same mode of discourse carried on in verbal form.

In some of the canonical writings of the Judaism of the dual Torah we find lists of different things joined with the words, "another matter." These different things cohere in two ways. First, all of them address the same verse of Scripture. Second, each of these other matters in its way proves to make the same statement as all the others. Appeal is made to what we shall see is a standard and fixed repertoire of things—events, named persons, objects or actions or attitudes. As these things combine and recombine, a thing appearing here next to one thing, there next to another, they appear to serve, as words serve, to make statements. Strung out in one selection of the larger vocabulary of symbols, they then say this, and in another set of choices made out of the same larger repertoire, they say that. How do people know which things to choose for which statement? Why combine this with that? These are the questions I bring to the examination of the numerous sets of "another matter" composites, scattered throughout the canonical literature. Along these same lines a restricted repertoire of persons, events, and objects is portrayed in synagogue art, mosaics, frescoes, carvings, and the like. Were we to compose a list of things that might have been chosen, it would prove many times longer than the list of things that in fact were selected and represented by the synagogue artists. Do these too make a statement, and if they do, how are we to discern what it is?[2]

II. One symbolic Language or Two?

In asking the literary and artistic evidence to tell us about shared convictions of a common Judaism attested for late antiquity in both written

---

1 Editor's note: Our thanks to Jacob Neusner who has generously supported the inclusion of this volume in the South Florida Judaic Studies series. We appreciate Dr. Neusner's support and enthusiasm for this collection of essays by Tom Kraabel and other scholars.

2 I review the findings of my *Symbol and Theology in Judaism* (Minneapolis, 1991: Fortress Press).

and iconic representation, how are we to proceed? It is, first, by identifying the sort of evidence that serves. We limit our analysis to this public and official evidence: in literature, what anonymous, therefore genuine, authorities accepted as the implicit message of canonical and normative writings, on the one hand, in art, what synagogue communities accepted as the tacit message of the symbols in the presence of which they addressed God, on the other. Excluded then are expressions deriving from individuals, e.g., letters or private writings, ossuaries and sarcophagi, which can have spoken for everyone, but assuredly spoke only for one person.

Second, within public evidence, what do we identify as potential evidence for a shared vocabulary, common to evidence in both media, written and iconic, and shared among all sponsors—artists and patrons, authors, authorships, and authorities of canonical collections alike? The answer must be, the evidence provided by symbolic discourse, which is the only kind of discourse that can be shared between iconic and literary expressions. By definition, iconic evidence does not utilize the verbal medium, and, it goes without saying, our documents are not illustrated and never were. But the two bodies of publicly accepted and therefore authoritative evidence on the symbolic structure of Judaism deliver their messages in the same way. So constant reference to a set of what we must classify as not facts but symbols will turn up evidence for a shared vocabulary.

We wish to bring the restricted iconic vocabulary of the synagogue into juxtaposition, for purposes of comparison and contrast, with that of the canonical books. What we want to know is first, whether the same symbols occur in both media of expression, literary and artistic. Second, we ask whether the same messages are set forth in the two media, or whether the one medium bears one message, the other a different message. If, as I claim, symbolic discourse in the fifth and sixth centuries took place in Judaic expression in both synagogues and among sages, the one in iconic, the other in written form, we naturally wonder whether the symbols were the same, and whether the discourse was uniform. To frame the question in simple terms: were the same people saying the same things in different media, verbal and iconic, or were different people saying different things in different media? At the present, elementary stage in our reading of the symbolic discourse, we cannot expect to reach a final answer to that question. But the outlines of an answer even now will emerge when we compare the symbolic language of synagogue iconography with the symbolic language framed in verbal terms in the rabbinic Midrash-compilations.

Effecting that comparison of course requires us to frame in the same medium the two sets of symbols. But which medium—the visual (in our imagination at least) or the verbal? If it is to be the verbal, then we have to put into words the symbolic discourse portrayed for us on the walls and floors of synagogues. That is to say, we have to set forth in a manner parallel to symbolic discourse in words the symbols of the *etrog* and *lulab, shofar*, and *menorah*. And we have to do so in accord with the rhetoric forms that sustain symbolic discourse in verbal media. But by definition that cannot be done. First, symbolic discourse in verbal form requires us to identify and parse a verse of Scripture. But which verse for the items at hand? Second, we should require a clear notion of the meanings of the iconic symbols. But among the possible meanings, e.g., for the *shofar*—the New Year and Day of Atonement, Abraham binding Isaac on the altar, the coming of the Messiah, Moriah and the Temple—which are we to choose? And, third, since the symbolic discourse in iconic form obviously joins the *etrog* and *lulab, shofar,* and *menorah*, translating the three (or four) into words demands a theory about what those symbols mean when they are joined in order, arrangement, and context. What do symbols mean together that they do not mean apart? The key is why certain combinations yield meaning, others, gibberish (Moses and Sennacherib on the same list, for example). Since we do not have that key for symbolic discourse in iconic form, we had best consider the alternative.

Since we cannot meet any one of those three conditions, we take the other road, which is open. That is, we must proceed to translate into visual images (in our imagination) the symbols in verbal form that we have. Here, by definition, we have access to the context defined by a parsed verse of Scripture. We have a fairly explicit statement of the meanings imputed to the symbols, that is, the use in communication that is made of them. And, finally, the combinations of symbols for symbolic discourse are defined for us by our documents—again by definition. So we can turn to written evidence and ask whether, in verbal form, sumbolic discourse seems to converge with the counterpart discourse in the iconic medium.

III. Connections, Iconic and Verbal

To repeat: the key to a symbolic code must explain what connects with one thing but not with another, and how correct connections bear meaning, incorrect ones, gibberish. Now to carry forward that notion, we ask whether a single key will serve to decipher the code of symbolic discourse that governs symbols in both verbal and iconic form. The answer to that lies on the surface, in the connections in both verbal and literary sumbolic discourse, we may not know what message (if any) is supposed to be communicated, but we have solid grounds for thinking that a single code governs discourse in both media. On the other hand, if we find no combinations of the same symbols in both media of symbolic discourse, then we have no reason to supposed that a single key will explain what connects one thing with some other, or why one thing connects with this other, but not with that other. So the first test of whether or not we have a single discourse in two media or two distinct discourses, symbolic in both cases, but differentiated by media, is whether or not we find the same combination of symbols in both writing and iconography. We take as our test-case symbols we now know are very commonly connected, the *etrog* and *lulab, shofar,* and *menorah.* Our question is simple: when in writing people refer to the *lulab* or to the *shofar,* do they forthwith think also of the *menorah* and *shofar* along with the *lulab,* or the *lulab* and menorah, along with the *shofar*? Or do they think of other things—or of nothing? As a matter of fact, they think of other things, but not, in the case of the *lulab,* of the *menorah* and *shofar* and not, in the case of the *shofar,* of the *lulab* and *menorah.* So the combinations that people make in writing are not of the same symbols as the combinations that people make iconically. In combination with these things that in iconic form clearly connect with one thing and not some other, they think of other things.[3]

To satisfy ourselves that the distinctive combination of symbols—the *etrog* and *lulab, shofar,* and *menorah*—does not occur in the literary form of discourse (whether symbolic or otherwise) I present a brief account of how the Midrash-compilations treat two of the three items, the first and second. Here we shall see that the persistent manipulation of the three symbols as a group finds no counterpart in writing. The connections are different.

We begin with the *lulab* and ask whether representation of that symbol provokes discourse pertinent, also, to the symbols of the *shofar* and of the *menorah,* or even only of the *menorah.* The answer is negative. Other matters, but not those matters, are invoked. Leviticus Rabbah Parashah XXX treats the festival of Tabernacles (*Sukkot*), the sole point in the liturgical calendar at which the *etrog* and *lulab* pertain. The base-verse that is treated is Lev. 23: 39-40: "You shall take on the first day the fruit of goodly trees, branches of palm trees and boughs of leafy trees and willows of the brook," and that statement is taken to refer, specifically, to the *lulab.* When sages read that verse, they are provoked to introduce the consideration of Torah-study; the opening and closing units of the pertinent unit tell us what is important:

Leviticus Rabbah XXX:I

I. A. "[On the fifteenth day of the seventh month, when you have gathered In the produce of the land, you shall keep the feast of the Lord seven days . . .] And you shall take on the first day [the fruit of goodly trees, branches of palm trees and boughs of leafy trees and willows of the brook, and you shall rejoice before the Lord your God for seven days]" (Lev. 23:39-40).

B. R. Abba bar Kahana commenced [discourse by citing the follow-ing verse]: "Take my instruction instead of silver, [and knowledge rather than choice gold]" (Prov. 8:10).

C. Said R. Abba bar Kahana, "Take the instruction of the Torah instead of silver.

D. "Why do you weigh out money? Because there is no bread' (Is. 55:2).

E. "Why do you weigh out money to the sons of Esau [Rome]? [It is because] "there is no bread," because you did not sate your-selves with the bread of the Torah.

F. "And [why] do you labor? Because there is no satisfaction" [Is. 55:2].

G. "Why do you labor while the nations of the world enjoy plenty? 'Because there is no satisfaction,' that is, because you have not sated yourselves with the wine of the Torah.

H. "For it is written, 'Come, eat of my bread, and drink of the wine I have mixed'" (Prov. 9:5).

6. A. Said R. Abba bar Kahana, "On the basis of the reward paid for one act of 'takIng,' you may assess the reward for [taking] the palm branch [on the festival of Tabernacles].

B. "There was an act of taking In Egypt: 'You will take a bunch of hyssop' [Ex. 12:22].

C. "And how much was it worth? Four *manehs*.

D. "Yet that act of taking is what made Israel inherit the spoil at the sea, the spoil of Sion and Og, and the spoil of the thirty-one Kings.

E. "Now the palm-branch, which costs a person such a high price, and which involves so many religious duties—how much the more so [will a great reward be forthcoming on its account]!"

F. Therefore Moses admonished Israel, saying to them, "And you shall take on the first day. . . " (Lev. 23:40).

Whatever the sense of *lulab* to synagogue artists and their patrons, the combination with the *etrog: menorah*, and *shofar* was critical; nothing in these words invokes any of those other symbols. What would have led us to suppose some sort of interchange between iconic and verbal symbols? If we had an association, in iconic combinations, of the Torah-shrine and the *etrog* and *lulab*, we might have grounds on which to frame the hypothesis that some sort of association—comparison, contrast for instance—between the symbols of the festival of Tabernacles and Torah-study was contemplated. Here there is no basis for treating the iconic symbols as convergent with the manipulation of those same symbols in propositional discourse. It suffices to say that nowhere in Leviticus Rabbah Parashah Thirty do we find reason to introduce the other iconic symbols.

What about the *shofar*? If we speak of that object, do we routinely introduce the *etrog, lulab, menorah*? The answer is negative. We introduce other things, but not those things. Pesiqta deRab Kahana *pisqa* 23 addresses the New Year as described at Lev. 23:24: "In the seventh month on the first day of the month you shall observe a day of solemn rest, a memorial proclaimed with blast of trumpets." The combination of judgment and the end of days is evoked in the following. I give two distinct statements of the same point, to show that it is in context an important motif.

Pesiqta de Rab Kahana XXIII:II

2. A. *For I will make a full end of all the nations* (Jer. 30:1 1): As to the nations of the world, because they make a full end (when they harvest even the corner of) their field, concerning them Scripture states: *I will make a full end of all the nations among whom I scattered you.*

    B. But as to Israel, because they do not make a full end (when they harvest, for they leave the corner of) their field, therefore: *But of you I will not make a full end* (Jer. 30:11).

    C. *I will chasten you in just measure, and I will by no means leave you unpunished* (Jer. 30:11). I shall chasten you through suffering in this world, so as to leave you unpunished In the world to come.

    D. When?

    E. *In the seventh month, [on the first day of the month]* (Lev. 23:24).

Pesiqta de Rab Kahana XXIII:V

1. A. R. Jeremiah commenced [discourse by citing the following verse]: *"The wise mans path of life leads upward that he may avoid Sheol beneath* (Prov. 15:24).

    B. *"The path of life:* The path of life refers only to the words of the Torah, for it is written, as it is written, *It is a tree of life* (Prov. 3:18).

    C. *"Another matter: The path of life*: The path of life refers only to suffering, as it is written, *The way of life is through rebuke and correction* (Prov. 6:23).

    D. *"[The wiseman's path]* . . . *leads upward* refers to one who looks deeply into the Torah's religious duties, [leaning how to carry them out properly].

E. "What then is written just prior to this same matter (of the New Year)?

F. *"When you harvest your crop of your land, you will not make a full end of the corner of your field* (23:22).

G. "The nations of the world, because they make a full end when they harvest even the corner of their field, [and the rest of the matter is as is given above: *I will make a full end of all the nations among whom I have driven you* (Jer. 30:11). But Israel, because they do not make a full end when they harvest, for they leave the corner of their field, therefore, *But of you I will not make a full end* (Jer. 30:11). *I will chasten you in just measure, and I will by no means leave you unpunished* (Jer. 30:11)." When? *In the seventh month, on the first day of the month, [you shall observe a day of solemn rest, a memorial proclaimed with blast of trumpets* (Lev. 23:24)].

What is now linked is Israel's leaving the corner of the field for the poor, Lev. 23:22, the connection between that verse and the base-verse here is what is expounded. Then there is no evocation of the *menorah* or the *lulab* and *etrog*—to state the obvious. We can explain what is combined, and we also can see clearly that the combination is deliberate. That means what joined elsewhere but not here bears another message but not this one. An elaborate investigation of the role of *lulab* and *etrog, shofar* and *menorah* in the literary evidence of the Midrash-compilations hardly is required to demonstrate what we now know: we find no evidence of interest in the combination of those items in literary evidence.

IV. One Version of a Symbolic Structure of Judaism: Symbols in Verbal Form

Now that we have identified the iconic representations that form, if not a system, at least a structure—items that occur together in a given manner—let me set forth one example of what I conceive to be a fine statement of the symbolic structure of Judaism as symbols in verbal form set forth such a structure. This will serve as an example of the kinds of symbols we find in general in symbolic discourse in verbal form.[4] Our further experiments will then draw on the symbolic repertoire that a single passage—counterpart to a single synagogue—has supplied. The character of the passage will explain why have chosen it as representative:

---

4 A reference to the materials gathered in *Symbol and Theology in Judaism*, Chapters Four through Seven will suffice to show that what follows is reasonably proposed as representative.

Genesis Rabbah LXX:VIII

2. A. "As he looked, he saw a well in the field:"
   B. R. Hama bar Hanina interpreted the verse in six ways [that is, he divides the verse into six clauses and systematically reads each of the clauses in light of the others and in line with an overriding theme:
   C. "'As he looked, he saw a well In the field:' tells refers to the well [of water in the wilderness, Num. 21:17].
   D. "' . . . and lo, three flocks of sheep lying beside it:' speclfically, Moses, Aaron, and Miriam.
   E. "'. . . for out of that well the flocks were watered:' from there each one drew water for his standard, tribe, and family."
   F. "And the stone upon the well's mouth was great:"
   G. Said R. Hanina, "It was only the size of a little sieve.
   H. [Reverting to Hama's statement:] "'. . . and put the stone back in its place upon the mouth of the well:' for the coming journeys. [Thus the first interpretation applies the passage at hand to the life of Israel in the wilderness.]
3. A. "As he looked, he saw a well In the field:' refers to Zion.
   B. "' . . . and lo, three flocks of sheep lying beside it:' refers to the three festivals.
   C. "'. . . for out of that well the flocks were watered:' from there they drank of the holy spirit.
   D. "' . . . The stone on the well's mouth was large:' this refers to the rejoicing of the house of the water-drawing."
   E. Said R. Hoshaiah, "Why is it called 'the house of the water drawing'? Because from there they drink of the Holy Spirit."
   F. [Resuming Hama b. Hanina's discourse: and when all the flocks were gathered there:' coming from 'the entrance of Hamath to the brook of Egypt' (I Kgs. 8:66).
   G. "' . . . the shepherds would roll the stone from the mouth of the well and water the sheep:' for from there they would drink of the Holy Spirit.
   H. "' . . . and put the stone back in its place upon the mouth of the well:' leaving it in place until the coming festival. [Thus the second interpretation reads the verse in light of the Temple celebration of the Festival of Tabernacles.]
4. A. "' . . . As he looked, he saw a well in the field:' this refers in Zion.
   B. "' . . . and lo, three flocks of sheep lying beside it:' this refers to the three courts, concerning which we have learned in the Mishnah: **There were three courts there, one at the gateway of**

the Temple mount, one at the gateway of the courtyard, and one in the chamber of the hewn stones [M. San. 11:2].

C. " '. . . for out of that well the flocks were watered:' for from there they would hear the ruling.

D. 'The stone on the well's mouth was large:' this refers to the high court that was in the chamber of the hewn stones.

E. " '. . . and when all the flocks were gathered there:' this refers to the courts at session in the Land of Israel.

F. " '. . . the shepherds would roll the stone from the mouth of the well and water the sheep:' for from there they would hear the ruling.

G. " '. . . and put the stone back in its place upon the mouth of the well:' for they would give and take until they had produced the ruling in all the required clarity." [The third interpretation reads the verse in light of the Israelite institution of justice and administration.]

5. A. "'As he looked, he saw a well in the field:' this refers to Zion.

B. " '. . . and lo, three flocks of sheep lying aide it:' this refers to the forst three kingdoms [Babylonia, Media, Greece].

C. " '. . . for out of that well the flocks were watered:' for they enriched the treasures that were laid upon up in the chambers of the Temple.

D. " '. . . The stone on the well's mouth was large:' this refers to the merit attained by the patriarchs.

E. " '. . . and when all the flocks were gathered there:' this refers to the wicked kingdom, which collects troops through levies over all the nations of the world.

F. " '. . . the shepherds would roll the stone from the mouth of the well and water the sheep:' for they enriched the treasures that were laid upon up in the chambers of the Temple.

G. " '. . . and put the stone back in its place upon the mouth of the well:' In the age to come the merit attained by the patriarchs will stand [in defense of Israel].' [So the fourth interpretation interweaves the themes of the Temple cult and the domination of the four monarchies.]

6. A. "'As he looked, be saw a well in the field:' this refers to the sanhedrin.

B. " '. . . and lo, three flocks of sheep lying beside it:' this alludes to the three rows of disciples of sages that would go into session in their presence.

C. "for out of that well the flocks were watered:' for from there they would listen to the ruling of the law.

D. "'. . . The stone on the well's mouth was large:' this refers to the most distinguished member of the court, who determines the law-decision.

E. "'. . . and when all the flocks were gathered there:' this refers to disciples of the sages in the Land of Israel.

F. "'. . . the shepherds would roll the stone from the mouth of the well and water the sheep:' for from there they would listen to the ruling of the law.

G. "'. . . and put the stone back in its place upon the mouth of the well:' for they would give and take until they had produced the ruling In all the required clarity." [The fifth interpretition again reads the verse in light of the Israelite institution of legal education and justice.]

7. A. As he looked, he saw a well in the field:' this refers to the synagogue.

B. "'. . . and lo, three flocks of sheep lying beside it:' this refers to the three who are called to the reading of the Torah on week-days.

C. "'. . . for out of that well the flocks were watered:' for from there they hear the reading of the Torah.

D. "'. . . The stone on the well's mouth was large:' this refers to the impulse to do evil.

E. "'. . . and when all the flocks were gathered there:' this refers to the congregation.

F. "'. . . the shepherds would roll the stone from the mouth of the well and water the sheep:' for from there they hear the reading of the Torah.

G. "'. . . and put the stone back in its place upon the mouth of the well:' for once they go forth [from the hearing of the reading of the Torah] the impulse to do evil reverts to its place. [The sixth and last interpretation turns to the twin themes of the reading of the Torah in the synagogue and the evil impulse, temporarily driven off through the hearing of the Torah.]

Genesis Rabbah LXX:IX

1. A. R. Yohanan interpreted the statement in terms of Sinai:

B. "'As he looked, he saw a well in the field:' this refers to Sinai.

C. "'. . . and lo, three flocks of sheep lying beside it:' these stand for the priests, Levites, and Israelites.

D. "'. . . for out of that well the flocks were watered:' for from there they heard the Ten Commandments.

E. "'... The stone on the well's mouth was large:' this refers to the
   Presence of God."

F. "... and when all the flocks were gathered there:"

G. R. Simeon b. Judah of Kefar Akum in the name of R. Simeon:
   "All of the flocks of Israel had to be present, for if any one of
   them had been lacking, they would not have been worthy of
   receiving the Torah."

H. [Returning to Yohanan's exposition:] "'the shepherds would roll
   the stone from the mouth of the well and water the sheep:' for
   from there they heard the Ten Commandments.

I. "'...and put the stone back in its place upon the mouth of the
   well:' 'You yourselves have seen that I have talked with you from
   heaven' (Ex. 20:19)."

The six themes read in response to the verse cover (1) Israel in the wilderness, (2) the Temple cult on festivals with special reference to Tabernacles,
(3) the judiciary and government, (4) the history of Israel under the four kingdoms, (5) the life of sages, and (6) the ordinary folk and the synagogue. The
whole is an astonishing repertoire of fundamental themes of the life of the
nation, Israel: at its origins in the wilderness, in its cult, in its institutions
based on the cult, in the history of the nations, and, finally, in the twin social
estates of sages and ordinary folk, matched by the institutions of the master-
disciple circle and the synagogue. The vision of Jacob at the well thus encom-
passed the whole of the social reality of Jacob's people, Israel. Yohanan's
exposition adds what was left out, namely, reference to the revelation of the
Torah at Sinai. The reason I have offered the present passage as a fine
instance of symbolic discourse is now clear. If we wished a catalogue of the
kinds of topics addressed in passages of symbolic, as distinct from propositional, discourse, the present catalogue proves compendious and complete. Our
next experiment is now possible.

V. Symbolic Discourse in Iconic and in Verbal Form: Convergence or
   Divergence?

A simple set of indicators will now permit us to compare the character of
symbolic discourse in verbal form with that in iconic form. The question is
now a simple one. Let us represent the Judaism—way of life, world view,
theory of who or what is "Israel"?—set forth by symbolic discourse in iconic
form effected by the *lulab* and *etrog, shofar* and *menorah*. Let us further
represent the Judaism set forth by symbolic discourse in verbal form, treating
as exemplary a discourse that will appeal to visual images appropriate to the
themes of Israel in the wilderness, the Temple cult, the judiciary and govern-

ment, Israel under the four kingdoms and at the end of time, the life of sages, ordinary folk and the synagogue. How do these statements relate?

The shared program will cover the standard topics that any symbolic structure of representing a religion should treat: holy day, holy space, holy word, holy man (or: person), and holy time or the division of time.

	ICONIC SYMBOLS	VERBAL SYMBOLS
Holy day	New Year/Tabernacles	Tabernacles/Pentecost/Passover/Hanukkah
Holy space	Temple	Temple/Zion
Holy man/person	No evidence	the sage and disciple
Holy time	Messiali (shofar)	Four kingdoms/Israel's rule
Holy event	Not clear	Exodus from Egypt

The important point of convergence is unmistakable: holy space for both symbolic structures is defined as the Temple and Mount Zion. That is hardly surprising; no Judaic structure beyond 70 ignored the Temple, and all Judaisms, both before and after 70, found it necessary to deal in some way with, to situate themselves in relationship to, that paramount subject. So the convergence proves systemically inert, indeed trivial.

Whether or not we classify the treatment of holy time as convergent or divergent is not equally obvious to me. Both structures point toward the end of time; but they speak of it differently. So far as the *shofar* means to refer to the coming of the Messiah the gathering of the exiles, and the restoration of the Temple, as, in the synagogue liturgy, it does, then the iconic representation of the messianic topic and the verbal representation of the same topic diverge. For the latter, we see in our case and in much of the evidence surveyed earlier, frames the messianic topic in terms of Israel's relationship with the nations, and the principal interest is in Israel's rule over the world as the fifth and final monarchy. That theme is repeated in symbolic discourse in verbal form, and, if the *shofar* stands in synagogue iconography for what the synagogue liturgy says, then the message, if not an utterly different one, is not identical with that delivered by symbols in verbal form. So here matters are ambiguous.

The unambiguous points of divergence are equally striking. The most important comes first. Symbolic discourse in verbal form privileges the three festivals equally and utterly ignores Hanukkah. So far as the menorali stands for Hanukkah—and in the literary evidence, the association is firm—we may suppose that, just as the *lulab* and *etrog* mean to evoke Tabernacles, and the *shofar*, the New Year and Day of Atonement, so the *menorah* speaks of Hanukkah. Then we find a clear and striking divergence. That the *menorah* serves, also, as an astral symbol, is well established, and if that is the fact, then another point of divergence is registered. In symbolic discourse in verbal form I find not one allusion to an astral ascent accessible to an Israelite, e. g. through worship or Torah-study. A survey of the cited passages yields not a trace of the theme of the astral ascent.

The second point of divergence seems similarly unambiguous. Critical to the symbolic vocabulary of the rabbinic Midrash-compilations is study of the Torah, on the one side, and the figure of the sage and disciple, on the other. I do not find in the extant literary sources a medium for identifying the figure of the sage and the act of Torah study with the symbols of the *lulab*, *etrog*, *shofar* or *menorah*. Quite to the contrary, the example given above from Leviticus Rabbah counterpoises the *lulab* with words of Torah. The fact that these are deemed opposites, with the former not invoking, but provoking, the latter, by iiself means little. But it does not sustain the proposition that the combined symbols before us, the *lulab, etrog shofar* and *menorah*, somehow mean to speak of Torah-study and the sage.

Thus far we see marks of convergence and also of divergence. What happens if we present a sizable repertoire of the combinations of symbols in verbal form that we find in Song of Songs Rabbah? We wonder whether a sizable sample of combinations of symbols in verbal form intersects, or even coincides, with the simple vocabulary, in combination, paramount in iconic representations of symbolic discourse in synagogues. A list drawn from combinations of symbols in verbal form found in Song of Songs Rabbah must include the following items:

Joseph, righteous men, Moses, and Solomon;

patriarchs as against princes, offerings as against merit, and Israel as against the nations; those who love the king, proselytes, martyrs, penitents;

first, Israel at Sinai; then Israel's loss of God's presence on account of the golden calf; then God's favoring Israel by treating Israel not in accord with the requirements of justice but with mercy;

Dathan and Abiram, the spies, Jeroboam, Solomon's marriage to Pharaoh's daughter, Ahab, Jezebel, Zedekiah;

Israel is feminine, the enemy (Egypt) masculine, but God the father saves Israel the daughter;

Moses and Aaron, the Sanhedrin, the teachers of Scripture and Mishnah, the rabbis;

the disciples; the relationship among disciples, public recitation of teachings of the Torah In the right order; lections of the Torah;

the spoil at the Sea = the Exodus, the Torah, the Tabernacle, the ark;

the patriarchs, Abraham, Isaac, Jacob, then Israel In Egypt, Israel's atonement and God's forgiveness;

the Temple where God and Israel are joined, the Temple is God's resting place, the Temple is the source of Israel's fecundity;

Israel in Egypt, at the Sea, at Sinai, and subjugated by the gentile kingdoms, and how the redemption will come;

Rebecca, those who came forth from Egypt, Israel at Sinai, acts of loving kindness, the kingdoms who now rule Israel, the coming redemption;

fire above, fire below, meaning heavenly and altar fires; Torah in writing, Torah in memory; fire of Abraham, Moriah, bush, Elijah, Hananiah, Mishael, and Azariah;

the Ten Commandments, show-fringes and phylacteries, recitation of the *Shema* and the Prayer, the tabernacle and the cloud of the Presence of God, and the *mezuzah*;

the timing of redemption, the moral condition of those to be redeemed, and the past religious misdeeds of those to be redeemed;

Israel at the sea, Sinai, the Ten Commandments; then the synagogues and school houses; then the redeemer;

the Exodus, the conquest of the and, the redemption and restoration of Israel to Zion after the destruction of the first Temple, and the final and ultimate salvation;

the Egyptians, Esau and his generals, and, finally, the four kingdoms;

Moses's redemption, the first, to the second redemption in the time of the Babylonians and Daniel;

the litter of Solomon: the priestly blessing, the priestly watches, the sanhedrin and the Israelites coming out of Egypt;

Israel at the sea and forgiveness for sins effected through their passing through the sea; Israel at Sinai; the war with Midian; the crossing of the Jordan and entry into the Land; the house of the sanctuary; the priestly watches; the offerings in the Temple; the sanhedrin; the Day of Atonement;

God redeemed Israel without preparation; the nations of the world will be punished, after Israel is punished; the nations of the world will present Israel as gifts to the royal messiah, and here the base-verse refers to Abraham, Isaac, Jacob, Sihon, Og, Canaanites;

the return to Zion in the time of Ezra, the Exodus from Egypt in the time of Moses;

the patriarchs and with Israel in Egypt, at the Sea, and then before Sinai;

Abraham, Jacob, Moses;

Isaac, Jacob, Esau, Jacob, Joseph, the brothers, Jonathan, David,
Saul, man, wife, paramour;
Abraham in the fiery furnace and Shadrach Meshach and Abednego,
the Exile in Babylonia, now with reference to the return to Zion

Now let us ask ourselves some very simple questions: is there a single
combination of symbols in verbal form in this catalogue that joins the same
symbols as are combined in the symbolic vocabulary in iconic form that we
have identified? No, not a single combination coincides. Is there a paramount
role assigned to Tabernacles at all? No, in this catalogue the principal holy
day must be Passover, commemorating the Exodus, which occurs throughout,
and not Tabernacles, commemorating the life in the wilderness, which occurs
not at all. Is there a single set of symbols in verbal form that can be served
by the *shofar*? No, not one. Whatever the sense or meaning that we assign to
the *shofar*, if the *shofar* stands for Isaac on the altar with Abraham ready to
give him up, if it stands for the New Year and Day of Atonement, or if it
stands for the coming of the Messiah and the ingathering of the exiles, makes
no difference.

On the list before us, I see no point at which the *shofar* in any of these
senses will have served uniquely well or even served at all. Whatever the sense
of the *menorah*, whether invoking Hanukkah or an astral ascent, makes no
difference; it is not a useful symbol, in verbal form, for any of the combinations before us; it cannot have served in a single recombinant statement. The
lulab and *etrog* so far as I can see can have claimed no place, in verbal form,
in any of our combinations. While, therefore, at certain points the symbolic
discourse in verbal form surely intersects with the same mode of discourse in
iconic form, in the aggregate, symbolic discourse represented in one medium
bears one set of symbols—singly or in combination!—and symbolic discourse
in another medium appeals to a quite different set of symbols altogether.

VI. What is at Stake in Analyzing Symbolic Discourse?

The divergent vocabularies utilized for symbolic discourse point toward
divergent symbolic structures: two Judaisms, one of them represented by the
symbolic discourse in verbal form of the rabbinic Midrash-compilations, the
other by symbolic discourse iniconic form represented by the synagogue
ornamentation. That conclusion[5] calls into question the possibility of describ-

---

5 Goodenough's work led to precisely the same conclusion. But the proposition that "Judaism" was diverse, meaning that there was more than a single normative Judaism, has been implicit, if not entirely conventional, even from the late 1940's. The most effective and important
statement of the divergence of literary and iconic evidence in general emerged in the earliest
(continued...)

ing, on the basis of the written and archaeological evidence, a Judaism that is attested, in one way or another, by all data equally; a Judaism to which all data point; a Judaism that is implicit in or presupposed by, all data. If there were such a uniform and encompassing Judaic structure, sufficiently commodious to make a place for diverse Judaisms, then it is at the level of symbolic discourse that we should find evidence for its description. For in the preverbal evidence of symbols should emerge messages, at least significations, that can be expressed in the diverse ways that verbal discourse makes possible (and may even require). But, as we have now seen, when we compare the symbols that reach us in two distinct forms, the verbal and the iconic, we find ourselves at an impasse. The verbal symbols serve in one way, the iconic in another, and while they occasionally converge, the points of convergence are few, those of divergence, overwhelming.

At stake in these observations is whether we can locate evidence that, beyond any text or artifact, a body of thought—a religious system, encompassing a world view, way of life, and theory of the social group that held the one and realized the other—circulated. What is this "Judaism" to which my hypothesis make reference? It is, as a matter of working hypothesis, that set of conceptions and convictions that the generality of Jews took for granted, but that no particular group of Jews made distinctively its own. It is the Judaism that all writings, all art, presupposes. And at stake in this analysis of the repertoire of symbols is, can we claim that a single such structure served to sustain all Judaisms? Is there such a unitary, single, and harmonious "symbolic structure of Judaism" at all? That body of thought, that Judaism— perhaps formed of one Judaism out of many, perhaps identified as what is essential throughout, perhaps defined as the least common denominator among all evidence, is then alleged to be presupposed in all documents and by all artifacts. The answer to that question is simple. No evidence permits us to describe that one Judaism. So far as we are limited to the demonstration made possible by evidence, e.g. sources whether in writing or in iconic or other material form, the kind of evidence that is most general, fundamental, and susceptible of homogenization, the picture is clear and one-sided.

Now some who posit a "Judaism" of which we are informed appeal not to evidence (e.g. of a given period) but to an *a priori*: they maintain that there is one Judaism by definition and without demonstration informs all Judaisms, or to which all Judaisms refer or give testimony. Some scholars just now claim that there is a "Judaism out there," beyond any one document, to which in

---

5(...continued)
volumes of Goodenough's *Jewish Symbols in the Greco-Roman Period*. The recognition that that divergence pointed toward more than a single Judaic system or Judaism, and the specification of the meaning of that fact, derive principally from my *oeuvre*.

some way or other all documents in various ways and proportions are supposed to attest.[6] They even know how to describe that Judaism even though

---

6 One statement of the matter derives from the British medievalist, Hyam Maccoby. Writing
in the symposium, "The Mishnah: Methods of Interpretation," *Midstream*, October, 1986, p. 41,
he states:

> Neusner argues that since the Mishnah has its own style and program, nothing
> outside it is relevant to explaining it. This is an obvious fallacy. The Mishnah, as a
> digest, in the main, of the legal . . . aspect of rabbiaic Judaism, necessarily has its own
> style and program. But to treat it as something intended to be a comprehensive
> compendium of the Oral Torah is simply to beg the question. Neusner does not
> answer the point, put to him by E. P. Sanders and myself, that the liturgy being
> presupposed by the Mishnah, is surely relevant to the Mishnah's exegesis. Nor does
> he answer the charge that he ignores the aggadic material within the Mishnah itself,
> e.g., Avot; or explain why the copious aggadic material found in roughly contem-
> poraneous works should be regarded as irrelevant. Instead he insists that he is right
> to carry out the highly artificial project of deliberately closing his eyes to all aggadic
> material, and trying to explain the Mishnah without it.

Maccoby exhibits a somewhat infirm grasp upon the nature of the inquiry before us. If one starts
with the question, "What does the authorship of this book mean to say, when read by itself and
not in light of other, *later* writings?" then it would be improper to import into the description
of the system of the Mishnah in particular (its "Judaism"——hence "Judaism: The evidence of
the Mishnah") conceptions not contained within its pages. Tractate Avot, for one instance, cites
a range of authorities who lived a generation beyond the closure of the (rest of the) Mishnah
and so is ordinarily dated to about 250, with the Mishnah dated to about 200. On that basis how
one can impute to the Mishnah's system conceptions first attaining closure half a century later
I do not know. To describe the Mishnah, for example, as a part of "rabbinic Judaism" Is to
invoke the premise that we know, more or less on its own, just what this rabbinic Judaism" is and
says. But what we cannot show we do not know. And, as a matter of established fact, many
conceptions dominant in the final statements of Rabbinic Judaism to emerge from late antiquity
play no material role whatsoever in the system of the Mishnah, or, for that matter, of Tosefta
and Abot. No one who has looked for the conception of "the Oral Torah" in the Mishnah or in
the documents that succeeded it, for the next two hundred years, will understand why Maccoby
is so certain that the category of Oral Torah, or the myth of the dual Torah, applies at all. For
the mythic category of "Oral Torah" makes its appearance, so far as I can discern, only with the
Yerushalmi and not in any document closed prior to that time, although a notion of a revelation
over and above Scripture——not called "oral Torah" to be sure——comes to expression in Avot.
Implicitiy, moreover, certain sayings of the Mishnah itself, e.g., concerning rulings of the Torah
and rulings of sages, may contain the notion of a secondary tradition, beyond revelation. But that
tradition is not called "the oral Torah, and I was disappointed to find that even in the
Yerushalmi the mythic statement of the matter, so far as I can see, is lacking. It is only in the
Bavli, e.g., in the famous story of Hillel and Shammai and the convert at b. Shab. 30b-31a, that
the matter is fully explicit. Now, if Maccoby maintains that the conception circulated in the form
in which we know it, e.g., in the Yerushalmi in truncated form or in the Bavli in complete form,
he should supply us with the evidence for his position. As I said, what we cannot show we do not
know. And most secular and academic scholarship concurs that we have no historical knowledge
a priori, though in writing Maccoby has indeed in so may words maintained that we do. In fact
the documents of formative Judaism do yield histories of ideas, and not every idea can be shown

(continued...)

no document and no artifact on its own attests to its character. And that Judaism—which I label, the "Judaism out there," that is, prior to, encompassing all documents, each with its own distinctive representation of a Judaic system, which I label a "Judaism in here" is readily defined. Indeed, that Judaism beyond, or beside, all evidences and data is such as to impose its judgment upon our reading of every sentence, every paragraph, every book.[7] Now if such evidence is to be located, then non-verbal data such as we have examined should have provided it, for here, by definition, in symbols, we should have been able to demonstrate that, whatever verbal explanations people attached

---

6(...continued)
to have taken part in the statement of each, let alone all, of the documents. But those who appeal to a Judaism out there, before and beyond all of the documents, ignore that fact.

7 Commenting on this debate with Maccoby and Sanders, William Scott Green says, Sanders "reads rabbinic texts by peering through them for the ideas (presumably ones Jews or rabbis believed) that lie beneath them." This runs parallel to Maccoby's criticism of my "ignoring" a variety of conceptions I do not find in the Mishnah. Both Macooby and Sanders, in my view, wish to discuss what they think important and therefore to ignore what the texts themselves actually talk about, as Green says, "the materials that attracted the attention and interest of the writers" (Personal letter, January 17, 1985). In my original review I pointed out that Sanders' categories ignore what the texts actually say and impose categories the Judaic-rabbinic texts do not know. Sanders, in Green's judgment, introduces a distinct premise:

> For Sanders, the religion of Mishnah lies unspoken beneath its surface; for Neusner it is manifest in Mishnah's own language and preoccupations (William Scott Green in his Introduction, Approaches to Ancient Judaism (Chicago, 1980: Scholars Press for Brown Judaic Studies) II, p. xxi.).

Generalizing on this case, Green further comments in those more general terms that bring us into a debate on the nature of religion and culture, and that larger discourse lends importance to what, In other circumstances, looks to be a mere academic argument. Green writes as follows:

> The basic attitude of mind characteristic of the study of religion holds that religion is certainly in your soul, likely in your heart, perhaps In your mind, but never in your body. That attitude encourages us in construe religion cerebrally and individually, to think in terms of beliefs and the believer, rather than in terms of behavior and community. The lens provided by this prejudice draws our attention to the intense and obsessive belief called "faith," so religion is understood as a state of mind, the object of intellectual or emotional commitment, the result of decisions to believe or to have faith. According to this model, people have religion but they do not do their religion. Thus we tend to devalue behavior and performance, to make it epiphenomenal, and of course to emphasize thinking and reflecting, the practice of theology, as a primary activity of religious people . . . The famous slogan that "ritual recapitulates myth" follows this model by assigning priority to the story and to peoples' believing the story, and makes behavior simply an imitation, an aping, a mere acting out.

Now as we reflect on Green's observations, we of course recognize what is at stake. It is the definition of religion, or, rather, what matters in or about religion, emerging from one reading of Protestant theology and Protestant religious experience. But in these pages, only a limited aspect of the larger debate is at issue.

to symbols, a fundamentally uniform symbolic structure served all Judaisms that our evidence attests.

Now to test the proposition that there was one Judaism nourishing all Judaisms, I have proposed to find out whether we may discern *the* symbolic system or structure upon which all Judaic systems relied, with which every system contended (each in its own way to be sure), and, above all, to which all Jews responded. If we had been able to show that a single symbolic vocabulary and a single syntax and grammar of symbolic discourse served in all extant testimonies to all Judaisms—iconic, literary evidence alike, then we should have begun to pursue the problem of defining that Judaism through the principles of symbolic discourse.

Why choose the symbolic data? Because, it seems to me, it is through the study of what is inchoate and intuitive, a matter of attitude and sentiment and emotion rather than of proposition and syllogism, therefore through the analysis of symbolic structure, that we should be able to discern and set forth the things on which everyone agreed. As a matter of hypothesis, that is the repertoire of conventions and accepted facts that made possible the character-istic disagreements, small and fundamental alike, that until now have required us in studying the formation of Judaism in the first seven centuries of the Common Era [=A.D.] to describe diverse Judaisms and not a single Judaism. All our evidence derives from Judaisms, however, which is to say, every piece of writing speaks for a particular authorship, every work of art met the specifications of a single artist and patron. True, the writings resort to conventions, for instance, the entirety of the Scriptures of ancient Israel known as the Old Testament (for Christianity) or the written Torah (for Judaism). Admittedly, the artists and their patrons implicitly accepted whatever restrictions they recognized, made their selections, as to both themes and representational conventions, from whatever repertoire they deemed self-evident.

Why give privilege to symbolic discourse rather than the propositional kind? Consider the alternative. Were we to have compiled a list of facts we must suppose everyone knew, the truths everyone affirmed, we should still not have an answer to the question of the character of normative theological statements which all known parties affirmed. True, in the canonical literature of the Judaism of the dual Torah, for one example, we are able to list matters of fact, bearing profound meaning, that all authorships of all documents affirm, but that serve to deliver the particular message of none of them in particular. Beyond that important, indeed paramount, corpus of literary evidence for Judaism, moreover, we may take note of beliefs and practices implicit in buildings set aside for cultic purposes—Temple and synagogue before 70, synagogue afterward—and take for granted that, whatever charac-terized as special one place or group, all Jews everywhere came to synagogues to do pretty much the same thing, such as say prayers and read the Torah. But our task is not only or mainly to outline the range of agreement, the consensus of practice and belief, that characterized all those Jews represented by the evidence now in our hands. For much that people affirmed was commonplace, and facts, by themselves, do not give us the outlines of a vivid religious system. We saw a case in point when we found that both symbolic vocabularies appealed to the Temple in one way or another. But that proved art inert fact, when we proceeded to see the symbolic vocabulary of Song of Songs Rabbah, which proved to have nothing in common with the symbolic vocabulary that dominated in the provenance of synagogue life.

That observation draws us to another initiative in the description of this single prior Judaism, of which we are informed *a priori*: What are the facts that mattered to everybody, that delivered the same message in behalf of everybody? That is a different question, since it introduces the consideration of consequence. We hardly need to demonstrate that all Jews took as fact the miraculous exodus from Egypt or the giving of the Torah by God to Moses at Sinai. But any supposition that those facts meant the same thing to everybody, that all Judaic systems through the same facts made the same statement, not only is unfounded, but also is unlikely. Facts that serve a particular system in a particular way—the revelation of the Torah at Sinai to convey the systemically-emblematic myth of the dual Torah, for instance, in the Judaism of the dual Torah we call rabbinic—by definition do not serve any other system in that same way. So when we want to know about consequence, we inquire into facts that mattered in all systems in the same way; those are the facts that tell us about the religious and cultural system as a whole that we call Judaism, not a Judaic system or the aggregate of Judaic systems, but simply Judaism encompassing, ubiquitous, universal, and, as a matter of fact, particular also to every circumstance and system.

A shared symbolic vocabulary can have overcome a further difficulty, namely, the very particular context to which the evidence in hand attests. The evidence we have, deriving as it does from particular synagogues or distinct books or sets of books, by its nature tells us about not the general but the specific: this place, for synagogues, that authorship, for compilers of books, that authority, for decisors of canonical composites. One authorship then makes the points important to it in its context, for its purpose—by nature, therefore, not merely informative but polemical. And another authorship will speak of what matters in its setting. Drawing two or more documents together not uncommonly yields the impression of different people talking about different things to different people. So too with the art of synagogues: it is by definition local and particular, because a given synagogue, however it may conform to conventions of architecture and decoration we discern throughout, still attests only to what its community—the people who paid for the building, directed its construction and decoration, and contentedly worshipped within it for centuries—desired. If we were to collect all the statements of all the books and homogenize them, we should produce a hodgepodge of contradictions and—more to the point—non-sequiturs. And if we were to combine all the representations on all the walls and floors of all the synagogues of late antiquity, what we should have would be a list of everything everywhere. In both cases, the labor of collecting and arranging everything about everything from everywhere yields uninterpretable, indeed, unintelligible facts.

Our task—to define the kind of evidence that forms the *lingua franca* of all documents and all iconic evidence alike—then demanded attention to symbolic discourse. By definition, then, documentary evidence read propositionally will not serve, since that kind of evidence excludes the mute but eloquent message of art, such as we have in abundance. The artistic evidence by itself cannot be read at all, since in its nature it communicates other than propositions and through other than syllogistic media. Arrangements of figures to be sure tell stories, and narrative art can be read as to its tale. But the sense and meaning the tale is meant to convey appeals to representation, and that, by definition, forms a distinctive medium for communication in other than verbal ways.

VII. The Way Forward: Symbolic Discourse and the Description of the Theology of the Dual Torah

The theology of the Judaism of the dual Torah that took shape in late antiquity comes to expression in not only in propositional but also in symbolic discourse.[8] The "another-matter"-construction, constitutes a play on what I have been calling theological "things,"—names, places, events, actions deemed to bear theological weight and to affect attitude and action. The play is worked out by a reprise of available materials, composed in some fresh and interesting combination. When three or more such theological "things" are combined, they form a theological structure, and, viewed all together, all of the theological "things" in a given document constitute the components of the entire theological structure that the document affords. The propositions portrayed visually, through metaphors of sight, or dramatically, through

---

8 At this point I cannot claim that the principal or the preferred medium is symbolic discourse, but my instinct tells me that that is the case. However, what is required is the analysis of theological discourse in a given, important document and the comparison of what is said in propositional discourse, what in analytical, what in symbolic, and what in narrative. When we have classified and compared the media for theological expression in a given document in which theology forms a principal theme or topic, we shall be able to proceed with this discussion, which is tangential to the argument of this book.

metaphors of action and relationship, or in attitude and emotion, through metaphors that convey or provoke feeling and sentiment, when translated into language prove familiar and commonplace. The work of the theologian in this context is not to say something new or even persuasive, for the former is unthinkable by definition, the latter unnecessary in context. It is rather to display theological "things" in a fresh and interesting way, to accomplish a fresh exegesis of the canon of theological "things."

Until now, in my judgment, we have had no method of description of theology in the canonical writings of the Judaism of the dual Torah that is both coherent with the character of the documents and also cogent with the tasks of theological description. By theological description I mean the account of the principles and ideas concerning God's relationship with Israel (for we speak of a Judaism) that form the foundation and substrate of the thought that comes to expression in a variety of canonical writings. The problem has been the character of the documents and their mode of theological discourse. It is not that the writers speak only in concrete terms; we could readily move from their detail to our abstraction and speak in general terms about the coherence of prevailing principles of a theological order.

The problem has been much more profound. We face a set of writings that clearly mean to tell us about God and God's relationship to Israel and Israel and Israel's relationship to God. The authorships *a priori* exhibit the conviction that the thoughts of the whole are cogent and coherent, since they prove deeply concerned to identify contradiction, disharmony, and incoherence, and remove it.[9] But we have not known how to find the connections between what they have written and the structure or system of thought that leads them to say, in detail, the things that they say. In working out a theory of the symbolic discourse, I hope to make possible the description of the symbolic structure set forth by that discourse, and, thereby, I further mean to open the way to the description of the theology.

The reason that I think we must begin with the elementary analysis of how discourse proceeds is simple. The kind of evidence before us offers little alternative. When we propose to describe the theological system to which a piece of well-crafted writing testifies, our task is easy when the writing to begin with discusses in syllogistic logic and within an appropriate program of propositions what we conceive to be theological themes or problems. Hence—it is generally conceded—we may legitimately translate the topically-theological writings of Paul, Augustine, or Luther into the systematic and coherent theologies of those three figures, respectively: finding order and structure in materials of a cogent theological character. But what about a

---

9 To prove that proposition, I need merely to point to the Talmud of Babylonia, the triumph of the Judaism of the dual Torah and its definitive and complete statement.

literature that to begin with does not set forth theological propositions in philosophical form, even while using profoundly religious language for self-evidently religious purposes? And how shall we deal with a literature that conducts theological thought without engaging in analytical inquiry in the way in which the philosophers and theologians of Christianity have done, and did in that period?

Surely the canonical literature of this Judaism testifies to an orderly structure or system of thought, for the alternative is to impute to the contents of those writings the status of mere episodic and unsystematic observations about this and that. True, profound expressions of piety may exhibit the traits of intellectual chaos and disorder, and holy simplicity may mask confusion. But, as I have already stressed, such a description of the rabbinic literature of late antiquity, which I call the canon of the Judaism of the dual Torah, defies the most definitive and indicative traits of the writings. These are order, system, cogency, coherence, proportion, fine and well-crafted thought.

To begin with, we have to justify the theological inquiry, through analysis of symbolism, into literature that self-evidently does not conform to the conventions of theological discourse to which Western civilization in its Greco-Roman heritage and Christian (and, as a matter of fact, Muslim) civilization in its philosophical formulation has made us accustomed. The Muslim and Christian theological heritage, formulated within the conventions of philosophical argument, joined by a much smaller Judaic theological corpus to be sure, does not allow us to read as a theological statement a single canonical writing of the Judaism of the dual Torah of late antiquity. So if the literary canons of Western theology are to govern, then to begin with the literature of Judaism in its formative age by definition can present no theological order and system at all.

But that proposition on the face of it hardly proves compelling. For it is difficult for us to imagine a mental universe so lacking in structure, form, and order as to permit everything and its opposite to be said about God, to imagine a God so confused and self-contradictory as to yield a revelation lacking all cogency and truly unintelligible.[10] The very premises of all theol-

---

10 As a matter of fact, the great Zoroastrian theologians of the ninth century criticized Judaism (and other religions) on just this point, see my "Zoroastrian Critique of Judaism," reprinted in my *History of the Jews in Babylonia* (Leiden: E.J. Brill, 1969) 4:403-423. But not a single Judaic thinker, whether a philosopher or a theologian, whether in the Islamic philosophical tradition or the Western theological and philosophical tradition, has ever entertained the proposition that the God who gave the Torah is confused and arbitrary; and why should anyone have thought so, when, after all, the entire dynamic of Judaic thought embodied within the great halakhic tradition from the Yerushalmi and Bavli forward has aimed at the systematization, harmonization and ordering of confusing, but never confused, facts of the Torah. There is, therefore, no possibility
(continued...)

ogy—that there is order, structure, and composition, proportion, and form, in God's mind, which in fact is intelligible to us through the medium of revelation properly construed—*a priori* render improbable the hypothesis that the canonical writings of the Judaism of the dual Torah violate every rule of intelligible discourse concerning the principal and foundation of all being. If, after all, we really cannot speak intelligibly about God, the Torah, holy Israel, and what God wants of us, then why write all those books to begin with?

While theology may comprise propositions well-crafted into a cogent structure, about fundamental questions of God and revelation, the social entity that realizes that revelation, the attitudes and deeds that God, through revelation, requires of humanity, there is another way entirely. Theology—the structure and system, the perception of order and meaning of God, in God, through God—these may make themselves known otherwise than through the media of thought and expression that yield belief that; theology can deliver its message to and through sentiment and emotion, heart as much as mind; it can be conviction as much as position, and conviction for its part also is orderly, proportioned, compelling of mind and intellect by reason of right attitude, rather than right proposition or position. That is to say, theology may set forth a system of thought in syllogistic arguments concerning the normative truths of the world-view, social entity, and way of life of a religious system. But theology may speak in other than dynamic and compelling argument, and theologians may accomplish their goal of speaking truth about God through other than the statements made by language and in conformity with the syntax of reasoned thought.

Theology may also address vision and speak in tactile ways; it may utilize a vocabulary of not proposition but opaque symbol (whether conveyed in visual or verbal media), and through portraying symbol, theology may affect attitude and emotion, speak its truth through other media than those of philosophy and proposition. From the time of Martin Buber's *Two Types of Faith*, now nearly four decades ago, people have understood that this other type of theology, the one that lives in attitude and sentiment and that evokes

---

10(...continued)
of finding in the Judaism of the dual Torah the slightest hint of an unsystematic system, an a-theological corpus of thought. True, a fixed truth of the theological system known as *die Wissenschaft des Judentums* has maintained that "Judaism has no theology," but that system knew precisely what it meant by "Judaism," even while never explaining what it might mean by the "theology" that that "Judaism" did not have. But that is a problem of description, analysis, and interpretation for those who take an interest in the system of thought that underpins "Jewish scholarship" and Reform Judaism in particular, that is, specialists in the history of ideas in the nineteenth century, and of the nineteenth century in the twentieth century. These are not statements of fact that must be taken into account in describing, analyzing, and interpreting documents of the Judaism of the dual Torah.

and demands trust, may coexist, or even compete, with the philosophical type to the discourse of which, in general, we are accustomed. Since, as a matter of fact, in the canonical writings of the Judaism of the dual Torah we do not have a single sustained theological treatise, while we do have a monument to a faith that is choate and subject to fully-accessible expression, we must teach ourselves how to describe the theology of the Judaism of the dual Torah out of its fully-exposed and complete, systemic documents, and, as we shall see, one way of doing so lies in the analysis of symbolism. Some documents utilize certain forms to make theological statements in symbolic discourse, the recombinant symbolic ones such as that which we have now examined. These documents communicate through symbolic discourse. They, therefore point toward the symbolic structure that, for the Judaism of the dual Torah, constitutes the theological statement and message.

Now that we recognize the mode of discourse that serve as one principal medium of theological speech, understanding that at stake was the portrayal of God in relationship to Israel, and Israel in relationship to God, rather than dialectical analysis of propositions concerning that relationship and the demonstration thereof, we may begin the task of the description of the theology of the Judaism of the dual Torah—and even contemplate the further task,the theological description of the Judaism of the dual Torah. Each thing will take place in its turn—God willing.

Diaspora as Metaphor:
Bodies and Boundaries in the Book of Tobit

Amy-Jill Levine

Although the Book of Tobit has been mined with folklorist-formalist, historical-critical, and textual-comparative tools, previous studies have not extracted the pivotal role played by boundary definition and transgression. Such analytic categories, often employed by anthropology and critical theory, provide substantial insight into the diaspora setting of the novella. Where families are scattered and where the law of the land is not the law of Moses, the covenant community requires precise means of self-definition. As Mary Douglas puts it, "It is only by exaggerating the difference between within and without, above and below, male and female, with and against, that a semblance of order is created."[1] Emphasizing the acute threat to identity posed by the exilic collapse of boundaries and then diffusing that threat by reinscribing distinctions, the Book of Tobit brings stability to the unstable world.

William Soll correctly observes that the "instances of 'villainy' in Tobit can be seen as acute manifestations of the chronic condition of exile."[2] In exile, dead bodies lie in the streets and those who inter them are punished; demons fall in love with women and kill their husbands; even righteousness is no guarantee of stability, as both Tobit and his nephew Ahikar (cf. 14:10) realize. In the diaspora, no immediately clear solid ground for self-definition exists. To alleviate these problems, the text makes three moves. First it emphasizes imaginary geographical and historical references; these indicate that the spatial and temporal coordinates of exilic life do not determine Israel's identity. Next, it creates a series of boundary-breaking events—eating, defecating, inseminating, interring—to institute, transgress, and then reinforce distinctions. Finally, it delineates Israel by means of genealogy rather than geography. In order to distinguish the Israelite from the Gentile, the Book of Tobit advances a program centered on endogamy. Women properly domiciled in an endogamous relationship become the means by which the threat of the diaspora is eliminated. That territorial relations are displaced onto gender relations is reinforced by the manner in which hierarchical, value-laden gender differences structure the novella.

---

1 *Purity and Danger: An Analysis of the Concepts of Pollution and Taboo* (London: Routledge and Kegan Paul, 1966), 4.

2 "Tobit and Folklore Studies, with Emphasis on Propp's Morphology," in David J. Lull, ed., *SBL Seminar Papers* (Atlanta: Scholars Press, 1988), 51. He also notes, p. 50, that the explicit setting distinguishes Tobit from most fairy tales. The exile "imparts to the community a lingering background of shame, an abnormal dislocation which renders the time 'out of joint' so long as it endures."

References to Nineveh frame the text[3] and so metonymically situate the story in the diaspora. But the historical map generated by this geographical figure is both imaginary and unstable. The first chapter (1:2) claims that Naphtali and Zebulun were exiled from the Galilee under Shalmaneser, not Tiglath-Pilesar III (2 Kings 15:29).[4] Tobit states that Shalmaneser, not Sennacherib, was Sargon's son; he claims that Assueres and Nebuchadnezzar, not Cyaxares and Nabopolassar, took Nineveh.[5] Rages is described as only a two-day journey from Ecbatana (5:6S).[6] Further, Raphael situates Rages at the mountains and Ecbatana out on the plateau" (5:6,10S), but Ecbatana is in fact 2,500 feet higher than Rages.[7] The disjunction between the real and the recounted indicates the problem of diaspora existence: things are not as they should be.

Jerusalem represents the real. But the community is in exile, so Jerusalem is of little help. Indeed, the only references to cultic matters appear in the prologue and the epilogue, in the context of references to the unstable Gentile nations (1:4; 13:10-18; 14:5 on the Temple; 1:6-8 on tithing). Rather than provide permanence to Assyria or Media, Jerusalem's mention so contextualized demonstrates the hope for return as well as the need for stability of those in exile.

The unreality of diaspora existence also complicates both travel and the home. As in apocalyptic, only supernatural intervention brings meaning to movement and security to stasis. Before the deportation, travel was a religious act: Tobit emphasizes that he alone (1:6a, 9, κάγὼ μονώτατος, but cf. 5:14) fulfilled pilgrimage regulations (Deut 12:11-14; 16:16-17; 2 Chron 11:16). But because of the community's sin, even the possibility of occasional travel, let alone pilgrimage, becomes problematic. Exile at first means perpetual movement: Tobit made the frequent trek between Rages in Media and his home in Nineveh (1:14); he fled to escape Sennacherib (1:19); he returned upon the accession of Ahikar (1:22); and prior to his blindness he moved frequently

---

3 See Irene Nowell, "The Narrator in the Book of Tobit," in David J. Lull, ed., *SBL Seminar Papers* (Atlanta: Scholars Press, 1988), 33.

4 Irene Nowell, "The Book of Tobit: Narrative Technique and Theology," Ph.D. Dissertation, Catholic University of America (Washington, D.C., 1983), 45, suggests that the author might have drawn the reference to Shalmaneser from 2 Kings 17:1-6 and 18:9-13.

5 Details and discussion in A. Wikgren, "Tobit," *IDB* 4: 660; J.C. Dancy, *The Shorter Books of the Apocrypha*, Cambridge Bible Commentary (Cambridge: University Press, 1972), 35; Frank Zimmermann, *The Book of Tobit*, Dropsie College Series (New York: Harper and Brothers, 1958), 15-16.

6 Wikgren, *IDB*, 660. Nowell, "Book of Tobit," 151 n. 69. Dancy, *Shorter Books*, 15, marks the confusing and unknown geographical references in both Sinaiticus and Vaticanus.

7 Nowell, "Book of Tobit," 151 n. 69. Dancy, *Shorter Books*, 10, suggests that Tobit's "ignorance of the geography of Babylonia and Media" indicates a non-Diasporan origin.

between the streets and his home. This mobility is even part of Tobit's legacy: Tobias also traverses street and home, as well as moves between Nineveh and Ecbatana in Media. In his testamentary speech, Tobit commands his son not to remain in Nineveh (14:8), and Tobias complies by moving to Ecbatana (14:12). However, even this mobile marker of existence is undermined by affects of the diaspora setting: Tobit is immobilized when he is blinded. Tobias does "not even know which roads to take for the journey into Media" (5:2) and, since he cannot leave Ecbatana, he sends Raphael to Rages for Tobit's money (8:19-10:17). Only the angel can navigate foreign territories and survive unsafe roads (cf. 1:15). With his aid, Tobias is able to replace the pilgrimage his father made to Jerusalem with a pilgrimage to find a bride.[8] Thus a genealogical focus replaces a geographical one.

The lack of stable place and so of both secure movement and a secure home is directly connected to kinship ties. On the structural level, kinship remains literally outside the diasporan frame: the opening line of the book, "This is the story of Tobit, son of Tobiel, son of Hananiel...of the family of Asiel, of the tribe of Naphtali," precedes the mention of the exile (1:2). The family remains untouched although threatened by the deportation. Similarly, when Tobit is punished for transgressing Sennacherib's law, he observes: "Nothing was left to me but Anna my wife and my son Tobias" (καὶ οὐ κατελείφθη μοι οὐδὲν πλὴν Αννας τῆς γυναικός μου καὶ Τωβιου τοῦ υἱοῦ μου, 1:20BA). Such stable kinship is, again, immediately contrasted with the instability of the diaspora. While families unite and define the Israelite community, the Assyrian king is murdered by two of his sons (1:21).

Concern for kinship also pervades Tobit's tribal identification. Written during the Hellenistic period but backdated to the eighth century, the apocryphon concerns the preservation of one Naphtalite family. The choice of tribes is not accidental. Naphtali was geographically separated from the other Rachel tribes even in Palestine by the apportionment of land to Issachar and Zebulun (Josh 19:32-39); it was also closely connected with the local population, as Judges 1:33 makes clear: "Naphtali dwelt among the Canaanites, the inhabitants of the land." While the tribe showed community solidarity in battle (Judg 5:18; 6:35; 7:23), it was not secure even in Palestinian borders. Because of the Assyrian exile, Naphtali, like the rest of the Northern tribes, permanently lost both its connection to the land and its self-identity.[9] The shift from a geographical to a genealogical definition is therefore appropriate as well as poignant.

---

8 I thank Jay Geller for this observation.

9 Tobit is thus consistent with if not the origin of other notices that the so-called "ten lost tribes" were thriving in Media and its environs. For brief discussion, see Yehoshua M. Grintz, "Tobit," *EncJud* 15: 1186.

Since identity is maintained through kinship ties and not the land, Tobit emphasizes endogamy. He and Anna are from the same family (1:9), and he strongly urges his son to follow suit (4:12-13).[10] In turn, Sarah (incorrectly) notes she has no relative left to marry (3:15). And Raphael observes that Tobias, as Sarah's only eligible relation, is her destined spouse (6:11; cf. 7:10, 12). Because these familial contacts transcend geographic borders—Tobit's family follows him to Media; Tobias must travel to Rages to find his bride and must return with her to Media; even Tobias's inheritance is *movable* property (cf. 10:10)[11]—the family is both the most threatened and the most stable institution in the narrative world.

George Nickelsburg suggests that the concern for endogamy is less a matter of ethnic purity than it is an argument against any "arrogant disdaining of one's own people," which then could lead to the loss of self-identity.[12] However, when in-group and out-group are problematic categories, ethnic purity would not be an unexpected agendum. On the transcendent level, the transgression of human/supernatural borders by Asmodeus leads to lack of conception and to death. The demon's love for Sarah (6:15BA) cannot be requited, and it cannot lead to reproduction. So it follows that, on the domestic level, exogamy would lead to sterility and death for Tobit's family. This factor is suggested by the deaths of Sarah's first seven husbands, who are not explicitly described as members of her family or tribe. The concern for genealogical distinction even has a teleological focus. In the universalistic prophecies of the final chapter, ethnic categories are maintained. "All the Gentiles will turn to fear the Lord God in truth, and will bury their idols; all the Gentiles will praise the Lord" (14:6-7). The point is that they will do so *as Gentiles*. Finally, endogamy is also a necessary element in Israel's eschatology. As Tobit advises: "Above all, marry a woman of the lineage of your forefathers. Do not marry a stranger who is not of your father's tribe, because we are sons of the prophets. My boy, keep in mind Noah, Abraham, Isaac and Jacob...all of them took wives from among their own kinsmen and were blessed in their children. Remember that their posterity shall inherit the land" (4:12; cf. 14: 10BA). The telos of endogamy is thus the ingathering of the exiles. By identity-determining kinship ties the land is reobtained; the land is now the result, rather than the

---

10 On kinship ties, see Nowell, "Book of Tobit," 121 n. 42 and, on kinship terms, Paul Deselaers, *Das Buch Tobit*, Orbis Biblicus et Orientalis 43 (Göttingen: Vandenhoeck and Ruprecht, 1982), 309-15. The concern for endogamy is noted in particular by Dancy, *Shorter Books*, 8, who observes that the motif "is not present in the original folk-tale, and is not necessary even to the story of Tobit." See, most recently, Mordechai A. Friedman, "Tamar, a Symbol of Life: The 'Killer Wife' Superstition in the Bible and Jewish Tradition," *AJS Review* 15.1 (1990), 33-35.

11 Nowell, "Book of Tobit," 272. See further discussion below.

12 "Tobit," in James L. Mays, ed., *Harper's Bible Commentary* (New York: Harper and Row, 1988), 796.

origin, of community self-definition. And women are both the means of salvation and the threat to it: exogamy and entry of women into the public sphere destroys the community; endogamy and an attendant restriction of women to the home saves it.

But the acute conditions of exile both make appropriate marriage partners difficult to find and displace the stability of the Israelite household. The obstacles which exile places before identity formation are played out in the plights of the central characters of the narrative. Although they all suffer, the significance of their tragedies is gender-coded. While Tobit's suffering makes his character paradigmatic of the displaced community, the sufferings of women—of Sarah and Edna and Anna—do not. Women instead represent the loss of identity produced by dislocation.

Because the attack on Sarah's ability to consummate her marriage and so produce children parallels the attack on Tobit's sight, the two scenes can be compared to show that more is going on than simply that the deity "works even in cruel and evidently arbitrary circumstances."[13] The circumstances may be cruel, but they are by no means arbitrary. Rather, they indicate an exaggerated concern for boundaries between not only man and woman, but also life and death, clean and unclean, human and nonhuman. The diaspora problematizes these distinctions by muddying the boundaries; Soll even proposes that "the author of Tobit thought that exile made Jewish maidens more vulnerable to evils" such as interference by local demons.[14] The role of male characters is, then, to reinstate those boundaries.

Sarah, the woman, is threatened by the mixing of the human and the supernatural. The demon Asmodeus has killed her seven grooms and thereby prevented her from producing an heir. She consequently cannot fulfill her duty to either her father or her family line; the Vaticanus text suggests that daughters may not inherit (3:15 cf. 8:21; 14: 13).[15] Since her situation is recounted five times,[16] Sarah literally cannot escape associations of childlessness. Ironi-

---

13 So Nickelsburg, "Tobit," 794, citing Sir 38:1-7.

14 Soll, "Tobit and Folklore Studies," 51.

15 R.H. Pfeiffer, *History of New Testament Times With an Introduction to the Apocrypha* (New York: Harper and Brothers, 1949), 266: "The prescription that daughters who must inherit their father's estate because they have no brothers must marry within their tribe (Num 7:1-11; 36) seems to be understood in 6:12 (Gk 6:13), in the sense that a father who fails to give his daughter (who will inherit from him) to her next of kin is guilty of a capital offense." See also B. Bow and G.W.E. Nickelsburg, "Patriarchy with a Twist: Men and Women in Tobit," in Amy-Jill Levine (ed.), *"Women Like This." New Perspectives on Jewish Women in the Greco-Roman World.* EJL 1 (Atlanta: Scholars Press, 1991) 141.

16 In 3:8 by the narrator; 3:8-9, by the maids; 3:15 in Sarah's prayer; 6:14-15 in Tobias's comments; and 7:11 in Raguel's note. This list, with commentary, appears in Nowell, "Book of Tobit," 100-1.

cally, because of the demon's sexual interest, her body remains untouched and therefore incapable of fulfilling its role.

By desiring Sarah, Asmodeus creates category confusion whose disastrous implications are well known to those familiar with the Fall of the Watchers. Raphael apparently had such familiarity. He never speaks with women, and he appears to avoid their company. Returning to Nineveh, he urges Tobias: "You know how we left your father [not mother]. Let us hurry on ahead of your wife" (11:2-3). Similarly, to convey his parting instructions, Raphael "called the two men aside privately" (κρυπτῶς, 12:6). Tobit receives from the angel the explanation that the deity had been testing him (12:13S); Sarah receives no such commentary.

Sarah's position is further marginalized by her ignorance and her silence. Although her parents know of Tobit (7:2), and Tobias knows of her (6:14), she is so far removed from contact with others that she is unaware of her spouse-to-be (3:15).[17] Nor, apparently, is she aware of Asmodeus. This lack of connection translates into lack of communication. She does not respond to her maids' taunts (3:8-9); is mute at her wedding ceremony (7:12-13); fails to address her mother's words of comfort (7:17); and does not react to Tobit's effusive welcome (11:17).[18] Her first word is "no,"[19] and "Amen" is the only word she speaks in another's presence (8:8).[20]

Like other women in the text as well, Sarah is object rather than subject. She is her father's property, "and her chief function is marriage to the appropriate kinsman" (cf. 3:8ff.; 7:11-13; 10:10).[21] Tobias actually inherits her (6:12; cf. 7:10). Similarly, her value and her fate are determined by her reproductive capacities: thus, Tobit advises his son to care for his mother because "of all the dangers she faced for your sake while you were in her womb" (4:4). Woman is, in effect, in a perpetual diaspora; her location is never her own, but is contingent on that of her father, husband, or sons. Labels applied to women confirm this subordinated, objectified role. For example, Tobit refers to Sarah as his daughter (cf. 11:17) and so keeps her in a dependent position; Edna elevates Tobias by addressing him as "dear brother" (10:12).[22]

Complementing Sarah's exaggerated marginalization is Anna's exaggerated entry into the public sphere. According to this apocryphon as well as texts

---

17 Nowell, "Book of Tobit," 46, in a list of several inconsistencies.

18 Ibid., 191.

19 Ibid., 182.

20 See the more extended discussion in Bow and Nickelsburg, "Patriarchy."

21 Nowell, "Book of Tobit," 145; cf. Bow and Nickelsburg, "Patriarchy," 135: "Like a piece of property, Sarah is given to Tobias (7:13), just as Raguel gave her to her seven previous husbands (7:11).

22 See Bow and Nickelsburg, "Patriarchy," 141.

such as the *Testament of Job,* Judith, and Ecclesiasticus, when women leave the safety of the home, category confusion and marital disharmony result.[23] Anna's engagement in "women's work"[24] gives rise to the first of her three extended conversations with Tobit (2:11-14; 5:17-19; 10:1-7), and none is a model of domestic harmony. In 2:11-15, Tobit accuses Anna of stealing the goat her employers had given her: "Give it back to its owners; we have no right to eat anything stolen." Although Anna is innocent, the accusation connects women with the transgression of both social and dietary codes.

This breakdown of domestic peace contrasts with Tobit's prayer for his future daughter-in-law. To his hope that, like Eve to Adam, she will be a helper, Tobit has added "and support" (8:5-7). Bow and Nickelsburg suggest the addition represents the father's concern that, should Tobias also become disabled, Sarah will support the family.[25] However, given the marital problems Anna encounters after her venture into the public sphere, this hypothesis requires an addendum: Tobit wants both to profit from his wife's work and to demean her for doing it. Thus he does not allow her an identity through her labor. Further, her entry into the public sphere is a threat to his honor, and to hers.

The woman's role—demonstrated by Edna—is to be in the house; there she performs her duties of caring for her husband and comforting her children. Her public or religious duties emerge only in men's absence. When Tobit is blinded, Anna enters the work force; when Tobit is orphaned, his grandmother Deborah assumes responsibility for his religious training (1:8).

The content of the angel's instructions confirms this division of labor. Raphael states (12:6-7, 17-18) that the proper response to divine beneficence is public praise (cf. 13:11; 14:6-7). If so, then women, only unnaturally placed in the public arena, are removed from the instruction as well as its fulfillment.

This removal of women from divine contact is supported even by the symbolic value of their names: Nowell observes that all four male characters—Tobit, Tobias, Raguel, and Raphael/Azariah—have theophanic names.[26] The

---

23 Such may be a recurring theme in one set of Jewish-Hellenistic documents: because of her husband's unexplained illness, Job's wife in *T. Job* finds herself in the same position as Anna. See Nowell, "Book of Tobit," 114 n. 20 and Deselaers, *Tobit,* 378. On Ben Sira, see Claudia V. Camp, "Understanding a Patriarchy: Women in Second Century Jerusalem Through the Eyes of Ben Sira," in Levine (ed.), "*Women,*" esp. 26-33.

24 On the connection with *T. Job,* see Nickelsburg, "Tobit and Enoch," 54.

25 Patriarchy," 138.

26 Nowell, "Book of Tobit," 108-9 and n. 5. Tobit and Tobias derive from טוביה or טוביהו, meaning "the Lord is my good"; Raguel is from רגואל, "friend of God" (the name is shared with Moses' father-in-law [Exod 2:18; Num 10:29] and is the name of an archangel in I En 20:4, cf. 23:4); Raphael is from רפאל, "God heals"; and Azariah is from עזריה, "God has helped."

women—Sarah, Anna, and Edna—do not. Rather, these three names are all connected with procreation. Sarah shares her name with Abraham's barren wife. Edna's name, from the Hebrew עדנה, occurs only once in the Masoretic text: in Sarah's comment in Gen 18:12: "Am I still to have pleasure."[27] For the apocryphon, the roles of mother and daughter are shared: each wishes for the consummation of the marriage and the birth of a child. Anna's name evokes the biblical Hannah, whose existence is defined by her relationship to her son as well as, notably, to the priority she places on conceiving him.[28]

Without the anchors of husband and home, women become either shrewish or despondent. Sarah's relationship with her maids shows that her unmarried and childless states both injure her and cause her to injure others. Like her matriarchal namesake, this Sarah is reproached by social inferiors: her maids accuse her of murder.[29] Moreover, like her biblical counterpart, Sarah's relationship to her maids is morally strained. Just as the menopausal wife tormented Hagar, so the Israelite virgin abuses her servants. The maids say to her: "Why do you beat us? If they [your husbands] are dead, go with them! May we never see a son or daughter of yours!" (3:8). Like Anna, Sarah's maids suffer because one higher on the social scale suffers. Like Tobit, upon female rebuke, Sarah is lead to pray for her own death.

Sarah's prayer confirms her objectified state. In 3:13-15, she gives the choice of her fate to heaven. As Nowell observes: "She is a woman and so used to having her life decided for her by others."[30] While Israel too is in a position determined by others, a qualitative distinction remains between the woman and the people. Israel determined its own fate: "All the tribes that joined in apostasy used to sacrifice to the calf Baal, and so did the house of Naphtali my forefather" (1:5). Sarah has done nothing. As a woman, as unaware, as unable to interact, as impeded from conceiving, Sarah cannot represent the covenant community. Instead, unless she is redeemed by the community's pure, male representatives, Sarah represents what could be its fate in the diaspora: ignorant, childless, and in the undesired embrace of idolatry represented by the demon. Because she, like the other women in the novella, is defined by marital relationships, her identity only assumes meaning when she becomes a wife. On the symbolic level, she reveals that exiled Israel is only

---

27 Nowell, "Book of Tobit," 109.

28 See the extended comparison in ibid., 109-10.

29 Like the matriarch as well, she requires supernatural intervention to achieve her wish, and she is removed from direct contact with both the deity and those outside her own family. See Bow and Nickelsburg, "Patriarchy," 139, and Nowell, "Book of Tobit," 109, on additional connections to the matriarch.

30 Nowell, "Book of Tobit," 145; Bow and Nickelsburg, "Patriarchy," 129-30, offer an extended comparison of the prayers of Sarah and Tobit.

redeemed through the restoration of the genealogical continuity lost along with her first seven husbands.

Unlike Sarah, Tobit is, as George Nickelsburg puts it, "paradigmatic for the exiled nation."[31] More precisely, Tobit represents the nation in temporary exile; he forms the bridge between the diaspora and the return home. The distinctions in the sufferings of Tobit and Sarah reveal additional, gender-coded emphases. For example, both characters deal with the borders between life and death: Sarah wishes to produce an heir for her father and so continue the community; inversely, Tobit wishes to bury the dead and so bring closure to that same community. But Tobit can carry out his duties independently; Sarah requires the help of a man.

Second, Tobit's blindness recapitulates a conventional description of the unfaithful community. Refusing to acknowledge the workings of their deity, Israel became spiritually blind and then removed from the sight of Jerusalem's glory. The metaphoric connections of Israel with blindness are themselves gender exclusive. While Raphael explicitly associates demonic difficulties with both men and women, only men get cataracts (6:8-9).[32]

Third, Tobit is, much like Job, afflicted by the deity: the angel informs him that "[W]hen you did not hesitate to get up and leave your dinner in order to bury the dead, I was sent to put you to the test" (12:13-14S). Sarah is not afflicted by the deity, she is afflicted by a demon. Further, Tobit is blinded because he fulfills a man's duty; Sarah is tormented for being a woman.

Finally, Tobit's burials are of unidentified members of the community who die outside the home. The concern for burial indicates an anxiety of having a stable resting place. By interring his coreligionists, Tobit stakes out the land as a parcel of sacred—that is, Israelite—space. Conversely, corpses are piling up at Sarah's house, and she is the direct occasion of them. While Tobit lays the corpse to rest and thus places the dead body in its appropriate locale, Sarah causes her suitors to die and so brings about category confusion: dead men in the bedroom. Nor is the disposing of corpses at Sarah's house depicted with solemnity or sacrality. We are left with the macabre picture of Raguel's arranging for a grave to be dug even as the wedding feast is underway (8:8-9).

Tobit's burial of a corpse is a mitzvah, but it is one that breaks boundaries and creates a triple transgression. Burying brings the living in contact with the nonliving, and so the distinction that needs to be maintained between the

---

31 "Tobit," 791; cf. "Tobit and Enoch," 60; Nowell, "Book of Tobit," 116: "He accepts responsibility for corporate guilt (Tob 3:3-5). He sees his own suffering and deliverance as model for that of the nation (Tob 11:15; 13:2, 5, 9).... He is at one and the same time an individual and a symbol of the Jewish people"; and 123. Dancy, *Shorter Books*, 5, suggests that Tobit and Tobias, as split-heroes, share this paradigmatic role.

32 Nowell, "Book of Tobit," 151 n. 71.

two for society to exist is temporarily compromised. As Numbers 19:11 states: "Whoever touches a corpse shall be ritually unclean for seven days." Second, burying means opening the earth, but not, as in agricultural endeavors, to create new life. And third, interment transgresses political regulations: the act takes precedence over the commands of the king (1:18).

Because the corpse mediates between life and death, it is shrouded in ritual taboos. Kristeva states: "connected with excrement and impure on that account [cf. Deut 24:1], the corpse is to an even greater degree that by means of which the notion of impurity slips into that of abomination and/or prohibition.... [The corpse] is above all the opposite of the spiritual, of the symbolic, and of divine law."[33] That the exilic state forces Tobit to come into frequent contact with corpses shows the chaos of the diaspora. Indeed, Tobit finds Israelite corpses "thrown outside the wall"(ἐρριμμένον ὀπίσω τοῦ τείχους Νινευη) and so on the town garbage dump (1:17).[34] The situation is one of both boundary transgression and "decomposition." And this state is emphasized. Nowell observes that "[i]n a book of 244 verses, 53 verses, or almost 22 per cent, contain one or more words referring to death or burial."[35]

The chaos of the muddied boundary between life and death directly impacts on Tobit, since the connection between corpse and excrement is directly played out on his body. As Douglas notes, "The body is a model which can stand for any bounded system. Its boundaries can represent any boundaries which are threatened or precarious."[36] Here anthropological categories confirm Tobit's paradigmatic function. His body represents the borders Israel should have maintained: "all my kindred (ἀδελφοί) and nation (γένους) ate gentile food (ἐκ τῶν ἄρτων τῶν ἐθνῶν); but I myself scrupulously avoided doing so" (1:10). That is, he did not eat what was unclean. Additionally, he attempts to establish appropriate borders: he stayed outside after the burial in self-imposed exile from his house "because I was unclean" (μεμιασμένος, 2:9BA). In a nice example of structural irony, Tobit leaves the good food, and his body is invaded by digested waste product (2:4-8).

---

33 J. Kristeva, *Powers of Horror: An Essay on Abjection* (trans. L.S. Roudiez; New York: Columbia University, 1982), 109, cf. her comments on p. 3: "If dung signifies the other side of the border, the place where I am not and which permits me to be, the corpse, the most sickening of wastes, is a border that has encroached upon everything."

34 So Dancy, *Shorter Books*, 19.

35 Nowell, "Book of Tobit," 203, using Sinaiticus.

36 Douglas, *Purity and Danger*, 115. On page 124 Douglas notes that "when rituals express anxiety about the body's orifices the sociological counterpart of this anxiety is a care to protect the political and cultural unity of a minority group." Tobit connects the body, eating, and death in 1:16.

Parallels between Tobit and his son confirm the problematic relationship between commandments and pollution. Both the father's duty to bury and the son's duty to marry and reproduce involve crossing boundaries. On the one hand, Tobit's actions connect him to his ancestors, and Tobias's role is directed toward his descendants. On the other hand, burial involves corpse-pollution, and marriage involves sexual relations and so emissions, which are themselves ritually unclean (Lev 15:16-18). Leviticus 22:4 connects death and emission directly: "Whoever touches anything that is unclean through contact with the dead or a man who has had an emission of semen...." Given the cause of Tobit's predicament (i.e., corpses and excrement) and the threat to Tobias (i.e., a demon who prevents the consummation of a marriage) it is appropriate that the cures recuperate both the threatening and the polluting.

The cures conform to the type of evil in question. And each form originates in the bizarre tale of a ravenous fish that threatened to devour Tobias as he was washing in the Tigris (6:1-8).[37] The fish conforms to the trope of eating which is so significant to the structure of this narrative. Also revealing its structural cohesion, the fish transgresses two borders: it leaves its natural habitat (it "leaped up from the river" [ἀνεπήδησεν ἰχθὺς ἀπὸ τοῦ ποταμοῦ]); and it seeks to become the consumer rather than the consumed ("It would have swallowed the young man" [6:2]). This fish, which transgresses the natural relationship between human and animal, will be used to eliminate the demon who also seeks to muddy human/non-human borders. Finally, the fish cements the connection between Tobit and Tobias: both are unexpectedly attacked by unlikely animals; both are rescued through angelic intervention.

Following Raphael's direction, Tobias catches the fish, removes its gall, heart, and liver, and eats part of the rest. Sinaiticus notes that the remainder was salted, which at least suggests that the detritus was not quite so malodorous. The organs of the dead fish are then used to heal the living. Raphael tells Tobias: "You must therefore anoint [your father's] eyes with the gall; and when they smart he will rub them, and will cause the white films to fall away, and he will see you" (11:8). Tobit's problem arises from his intense interaction with problematic categories: corpses and excrement. He is therefore apotropaically healed with the gall (χολή). The term in the Septuagint translates the Hebrew,מררה, which runs the semantic gamut from "bitterness" to "poison" (cf. Job 13:26; 16:13; 20:14, 25). The same Greek word is also used for a poisonous herb which may be hemlock, ראש, in Deut 29:17; Ps 68:22, and to לענה, wormwood (Prov 5:4; Lam 3:5). The use of poison or bitterness to bring life

---

37 According to A and B, the fish threatened to devour him; in S, it threatens to devour his foot. Structurally, in Sinaiticus the foot offers a parallel to Tobit's head. Sinaiticus also adds that it was a large (μέγας) fish.

and sight exaggerates and so reestablishes the boundaries between clean and unclean, life and death.[38]

To release Sarah from her tormenter, Tobias "took the live ashes of incense and put the heart and liver of the fish upon them and made a smoke" (8:3). There may be an apotropaic connection here as well between problem and cure. Sarah's plight is that she cannot produce an heir: she prays for death at the point her maids state: "May we never see a son or daughter of yours!" (3:8). The heart and liver, especially when inflamed, are more than centers of cognition and volition, they are also loci for reproduction.[39] In conventions that may have been known to the author of Tobit, the heart and the liver[40] are both involved in the production of semen. In addition, the heat applied to the heart, liver, and the incense may be connected to the common cultural and medical view that heat generates sperm.[41] Both blood and semen are, in turn, interpreted as "residues of the concoction of food."[42]

"When the demon smelled the odor he fled to the remotest part of Egypt, and the angel bound him" (8:3). Here the sacrificial elements, incense and animal parts, are used to banish supernatural forces rather than to summon or to thank them. This inverse recapitulation of the cult sends the demon into

---

38 These anthropological observations neither confirm nor deny the efficacy of the treatment. Dancy, *Shorter Books*, 39, observes that fish gall was regularly recommended in ancient medical texts to treat leucoma.

39 A. Neubauer's Aramaic ms. and the Münster text or HM (cf. also *Shabb.* 110a) declare that the heart and liver are to be burned under Sarah's clothes; see Zimmermann, *Book of Tobit*, 85. This reading strengthens the connections among the organs, the heat, and fertility/insemination. On the ancient use of fumigation (of various materials) of the vagina either to insure or to prevent conception, see O.S. Wintermute, "A Survey of Ancient Egyptian Medical Texts: Gynecological Concerns" (I thank Prof. Wintermute for his permission to cite this unpublished essay). The *Oneirocritica* of Artemidorus connects the heart with marriage and the liver with the productions of male/female relationships: "The heart signifies the wife of the dreamer or, if the dreamer is a woman, her husband, since he exercises control and authority over her body.... The liver signifies a child, one's life, and anxieties" (I.44), *The Interpretation of Dreams,* trans. and comm. by Robert J. White (Park Ridge, NJ: Noyes Press, 1975), 38. I thank Derek Krueger for this reference.

40 Zimmermann, *Book of Tobit*, 9-11, 80, suggests that the heart and liver once served separate functions and notes that several versions drop the reference to the liver.

41 See, for example, Aristotle, *Generation of Animals* 717b24 and 717a5: the emission of semen in men is due "to the penis being heated by its movement"; further, the final concoction or "maturation" of semen occurs through the heating of copulation. Citation from *The Complete Works of Aristotle,* ed. J. Barnes, 2 vols. (Princeton, 1984), in Thomas Laqueur, "Orgasm, Generation, and the Politics of Reproductive Biology," in *The Making of the Modern Body,* eds. C. Gallagher and T. Laqueur (Berkeley: University of California Press, 1987), 36. Laqueur notes similar ideas in the works of Galen. For Plato, *Timaeus* 69c-72d, 86c, the liver is responsible for the baser emotions; an overproduction of semen also involves liver functions.

42 Laqueur, "Politics," 37.

exile. Just as improper respect for the Temple caused the exile of Naphtali, so manipulation of the sacrificial elements will allow the tribe to increase. Exaggeration of the profane—of the false sacrifice, of the expulsion of the demon—defines and reestablishes those elements that delineate the covenant community.

With Asmodeus in exile, the relationship between Tobias and Sarah can be consummated. Their marriage indicates the ideal gender roles for the future of Israel. Passive, dependent, and silent, Sarah emerges as the perfect wife. Her husband insists that their relationship is based on "sincerity" or "singleness of heart" as opposed to lust (οὐ διὰ πορνείαν ἐγὼ λαμβάνω τὴν ἀδελφήν μου ταύτην, ἀλλ' ἐπ' ἀληθείας, 8:7); the opposition suggests that Tobias is concerned not with sexuality (the domain of the demon), but with procreation.[43]

By constraining women's roles, by using women as tokens of exchange to preserve kinship and economic ties, by depicting them as the cause as well as the locus of despair, and by removing them from direct contact with heaven, the Jewish male has brought order to his diaspora existence. In captivity, he can assert his freedom and his self-identity by depicting the other as in captivity to him. With boundaries redefined in relation to as well as upon bodies, Tobit's family is more stable than the world of the exile, even given such peculiar phenomena as blinding through bird excrement, a carnivorous fish, an angel in disguise, and a demon with unrequited love for a nice Jewish girl.

---

43 Friedman, "'Killer Wife,'" 34.

The Disappearance of the 'God-Fearers'[1]

A.T. Kraabel

It is notoriously difficult to comprehend what happens when one religious tradition comes in contact with another. The problem arises first of all from the fact that we approach such a confluence either from one tradition or from the other. In the West, at least, we usually lack a paradigm which may equally and fairly include both. When the examples come from the ancient world, the problems are compounded; not only are the sources incomplete, but modern prejudices and presuppositions often get in the way. Such misreadings may distort our perception of the ancient traditions themselves, as well as of the effects of their meeting. This paper explores one instance in which such a serious misreading of the evidence has taken place.[2]

For many years we have had an image of those Gentiles who stood at the intersection of *Judaism* and *Greco-Roman* piety in the classical world; they are called the "God-fearers." In 1962 the classicists' primary reference work, *Pauly-Wissowa*, distinguished God-fearers from proselytes (= converts). The God-fearers are more numerous: "they frequent the services of the synagogue, they are monotheists in the biblical sense, and they participate in some of the ceremonial requirements of the Law, but they have not moved to full conversion to Judaism through circumcision. They are called ... *sebomenoi* or *phoboumenoi ton theon.*"[3] The *Encyclopedia Judaica* in 1971 stated that "in the Diaspora there was an increasing number, perhaps millions by the first century, of *sobomenoi* (... God-fearers), gentiles who had not gone the whole route towards conversion."[4]

For Michael Avi-Yonah these God-fearers were a "numerous class" of Gentiles under the Empire; "although most of them did not feel able to shoulder the whole burden of the Law, they sympathized with Judaism ... They were to be found in the provinces as well as in Italy, even at Rome ... As they often belonged to the upper classes, their mere presence added in the eyes of the authorities to the weight of Jewish influence ..."[5] (1976).

---

1 Editor's note: This article in the above form appeared in *Numen* 28.2 (1981) 113-126.

2 Earlier versions of this paper were presented in Oxford at the *Sixth International Congress on Biblical Studies* in April, 1978, and to Prof. George Caird's seminar on Acts in May, 1978; at the University of Kansas in April 1980, and at the annual meetings of the *Society of Biblical Literature* in Dallas in November, 1980. Earlier drafts were read by Caird, P.J. Cuff, T.R.W. Longstaff, Dennis Nineham, Jerome Quinn and David Tiede; though none of these is responsible for the conclusions reached here, this essay is much the better for their help.

3 K.G. Kuhn and H. Stegemann, "Proselyten," *RE*, suppl. ix (1962), 1260.

4 *Encyclopedia Judaica* 10:55, s.v. "Jewish Identity."

5 M. Avi-Yonah, *The Jews of Palestine* (Oxford, 1976) 37.

David Flusser wrote in 1976 that the existence of these "many God-fearers" reveals that "Hellenistic Judaism had almost succeeded in making Judaism a world religion in the literal sense of the words."[6] Martin Hengel agrees with Flusser on the number and influence of the God-fearers, but draws different conclusions: "the large number of [God-fearers] standing between Judaism and paganism in the New Testament period...shows the indissoluble dilemma of the Jewish religion in ancient times. As it could not break free from its nationalist roots among the people, it had to stoop to constant and ultimately untenable compromises" (1975).[7]

The reference to New Testament times is not out of place, because the best-known God-fearer is a Roman soldier who eventually becomes a Christian, the centurion Cornelius of chapter 10 of the *Acts of the Apostles* in the New Testament. Indeed, it is Acts which has always provided the canonical picture of the God-fearer; the authors cited above rely on these eleven verses in Acts: 10: 2, 22, 35; 13:16, 26 (where the operative word is *phoboumenos/oi*) and 13:43, 50; 16:14; 17:4, 17; 18:7 (which have some form of *sebomenos*). No other clear references are found in the rest of the New Testament.[8]

In the traditional reconstruction of the historical situation, the characteristics of the God-fearer are as follows:

1) They are gentiles interested in Judaism, but not converts—proselytes; the men are not circumcised.

2) They are found in some numbers in the synagogues of the Diaspora, from Asia Minor to Rome.

3) The God-fearer as traditionally understood is particularly significant for students of the New Testament and early Christianity; it was from the ranks of the God-fearers that Christianity supposedly had recruited a great number of its first members.

---

6 D. Flusser, "Paganism in Palestine," in *Compendia Rurum Iudaicarum ad Novum Testamentum* 1.2, edd. S. Safrai and M. Stern (Assen, 1976) 1097.

7 M. Hengel, *Judaism and Hellenism* (Philadelphia, 1975), vol. 1, p. 313.

8 In the past half-century the most influential treatments of this issue have been K. Lake's "Proselytes and God-fearers" in F. Foakes Jackson and K. Lake, *The Beginnings of Christianity I. The Acts of the Apostles*, vol. 5 (London, 1933) 74-96, and the extended note to Acts 13:16 in H.L. Strack and P. Billerbeck, *Kommentar zum neun Testament aus Talmud und Midrasch*, vol. 2 (Munich, 1924), 715-723. More recent studies: L.H. Feldman, "Jewish 'Sympathizers' in Classical Literature and Inscriptions," *TAPA* 81 (1950) 200-208. R. Markus, "The Sebomenoi in Josephus," *JSS* 14 (1952) 247-250. Kuhn and Stegemann, "Proselyten" 1248-1283. K. Romaniuk, "Die 'Gottesfürchtigen' im Neuen Testament," *Aegyptus* 44 (1964) 66-91. H. Bellen, *Sunagogè ton Ioudaion kai Theosebon ... JAuC* 8/9 (1965/6), 171-176. B. Lifshitz, "*Du nouveau sur les 'Sympathisants*,'" *JSJ* 1 (1970) 77-84. F. Siegert, "Gottesfürchtige und Sympathisanten," *JSJ* 4 (1973) 109-164. H. Hommel, "Juden und Christen im kaiserzeitlichen Milet ... ," *Istanb. Mitt.* 25 (1975) 167-195. M. Wilcox, "The 'God-fearers' in Acts: A Reconsideration," *Journal for the Study of the N.T.* 13 (Oct. 1981) 102-22.

The evidence which produced this picture of the God-fearer was overwhelmingly literary; Acts provided the initial description, and to it were added isolated references from classical literature and Greek and Latin inscriptions. Always the *technical terms* were drawn from Luke, the author of the Gospel and of Acts. These are *phoboumenos* and *sebomenos*, which appear in Acts, and *theosebes*, which was thought to be a variant of the latter term. (The last is an adjective, common in the inscriptions, which occurs only once in the New Testament, in John 9:31.) The other scattered evidence for Diaspora God-fearers, in Greek and Latin literature and inscriptions, is all held together by the *locus classicus*, Acts. It was argued that literary texts and inscriptions in which any of these words (or the Latin equivalent) was found were in fact using them in a technical sense, = God-fearer. Finally, rabbinic discussions of sympathizers and proselytes, and of conversion, were brought in. That completed a picture which most scholars adopted, particularly on the Continent, less so in Britain.[9]

II

But another part of the picture has recently materialized; since the Second World War the archaeological evidence for Diaspora Judaism under the Roman Empire has increased substantially. Well-preserved ancient synagogues were discovered at Ostia, the port of Rome, in 1961 and at Sardis in western Asia Minor in 1962. Substantial collections of Jewish inscriptions, papyri and artifacts are now in print, along with detailed studies of Jews in the Roman east at Dura Europus, in North Africa, in Alexandria and in Rome itself. Excavation continues on the synagogue of Stobi in Yugoslavia.[10]

By now enough information has become available to permit fairly detailed reconstructions of Jewish life in the Diaspora which are based *entirely* on archaeological evidence.

This new evidence broadens the older picture considerably. For earlier reconstructions of the Judaism of the Roman Empire, archaeological data

9 See the commentaries to Acts and the standard histories of the New Testament period. Translations of Acts which conflated the two Greek terms appear to be one source of the problem, to judge from the research presently being conducted by Paul F. Stuehrenberg (Ancient Studies, University of Minnesota) into the medieval and later understanding of the God-fearer.

10 A.T. Kraabel, "The Diaspora Synagogue: Archaeological and Epigraphic Evidence since Sukenik," *Aufstieg und Niedergang der römischen Welt* II.19 (1979) 477-510; and "Social Systems of Six Diaspora Synagogues, in J. Gutmann, ed. *Ancient Synagogues: The Current State of Research*, Brown Judaic Studies 22 (Chico CA: Scholars Press, 1981); A.T. Kraabel and E.M. Meyers, "Archaeology, Iconography and Non-Literary Written Remains," chapter 9 of *Early Judaism and its Modern Interpreters* edd. R.A. Kraft and G.W.E. Nickelsburg, vol. II of *The Bible and its Modern Interpreters* ed. D.A. Knight, (Atlanta: Scholars Press/Philadelphia:Fortress Press, 1986).

were very limited; historians and exegetes were forced to rely almost entirely on literary evidence, the bulk of it rabbinic. But the direct relevance of rabbinic sources to western Diaspora Judaism is questionable; at the least, they needed to be filled out with other information as it becomes available. The archaeological evidence is particularly useful for this purpose, since it is of equal antiquity with the rabbinic literature and has the added advantage of coming directly from Diaspora sites. Further, it comes from the Jews themselves, rather than from Gentile comments about them; Stern's recent re-editing of the relevant Greek and Latin texts from pagan authors offers many examples of how partial and distorted that "outside" evidence could be.[11] And as we shall see, the use of Christian literature,. particularly Acts, as direct evidence for Diaspora Jewish history is also plagued with difficulty.

The archaeological evidence I have drawn upon comes from six excavated synagogues of the Roman Diaspora; ordered from east to west, the ancient cities which contained them are as follows:

Dura Europos in Syria: the building is second century C.E. to 256.

Sardis in Asia Minor: second or third century C.E. to 616.

Priene in Asia Minor: third or fourth century?

Delos, on an island in the Aegean Sea: first century B.C.E. to second century C.E.

Stobi in Macedonia: fourth century. Earlier synagogues third century or before?

Ostia in Italy: fourth century. Earlier synagogue first century?

The dates are approximate except for those indicating the fall of Dura (256) and of Sardis (616). The Dura and Sardis buildings were extensively remodelled during their history. The earlier synagogues at Stobi and Ostia are attested in the excavated evidence; they were supplanted by the later buildings.

Much more evidence from Diaspora Judaism is available, of course, from random epitaphs to papyri to gems. But recall that the God-fearers are associated with *synagogues*, with organized Diaspora Jewish communities. They are substantial groups of people, not isolated individuals.[12] They are found at the

---

11 M. Stern, *Greek and Latin Authors on Jews and Judaism* I (Jerusalem, 1974). See also E.N. Lane, "Sabazius and the Jews in Valerius Maximus: A Reexamination," *JRS* 69 (1979) 35-38, cf. A.T. Kraabel, "Paganism and Judaism: The Sardis Evidence," in *Paganisme, Judaïsme, Christanisme ... Mélanges offerts à Marcel Simon,* edd. A. Benoit, M. Philonenko, C. Vogel (Strasbourg 1978) 25-31.

12 This point cannot be emphasized too strongly. There is no lack of evidence, e.g. magical papyri and gems, for individual instances of the conflation of Jewish and pagan pieties by gentiles or Jews about whom nothing else is known. But in the standard reconstructions, the God-fearers are a substantial social sub-class; the existence of such a group cannot be proved with scattered

(continued...)

center of Judaism, not at the fringe. If they are to be identified archaeologically anywhere, it would be in association with the excavated buildings.

I have reviewed the evidence from these six buildings and for related sites in a recent survey article, and refer the reader to it and its bibliography for details.[13] What is presented in this paper is chiefly conclusions. A thorough study of this evidence reveals:

1) The synagogue inscriptions—over 100 of them—never use the term *phoboumenos* or *sebomenos*. *Theosebes* appears perhaps 10 times, but as an adjective describing Jews, usually Jewish donors. (The God-fearers, for all their interest in Judaism, are not Jews.)[14]

2) There are no other references in the inscriptions which would suggest the presence of interested but non-converted Gentiles in the buildings in which the inscriptions were placed. If we had only the synagogue inscriptions as evidence, there would be nothing to suggest that such a thing as a God-fearer had ever existed.

3) The symbolism used in the buildings is directed toward the Jewish community, with no apparent attempt to communicate with persons who come from outside this tradition. The evidence from Dura is best known in this regard, but other sites make the same impression.

4) The functions of the synagogues need also to be considered. Each is probably the only building owned by the city's Jewish community, and is the center of its religious and social life; as such it is more significant for its community than any synagogue in Palestine might have been.It is not accidental that at least four of these six were dominated by a Torah Shrine; their importance as *Jewish* centers is paramount.

5) Contact with Christians is rare, though such contact is assumed to be common from the accounts in Acts. To judge from the material remains, the gentile world is which these Diaspora Jews lived is considerably more pagan than Christian. In third-century Dura the synagogue is much more elaborate than the Christian building. The Stobi synagogue is displaced by a church building, but not before the fifth century; and two synagogues had been erected in Stobi before that. And at Sardis there is no archaeological evidence for a significant impact by Christianity on Jews at any point in Late Antiquity.

12(...continued)
gems or charms, rarely if ever associated with excavated synagogues, indeed usually lacking any clear social context whatever.

13 Kraabel, "Diaspora Synagogue" (see above, note 10).

14 Generally B. Lifshitz, *Donateurs et fondateurs dans les synagogues juives* (Cahiers de la RB 7; Paris, 1967).

To summarize: the terms in question do not occur in the synagogue inscriptions. There is nothing in the excavated buildings to suggest the presence of a kind of Gentile "pnumbra" around the Diaspora synagogue communities. There is no hint in these data that these Jews are reaching toward their Gentile neighbors with any sort of religious message.

If interested Gentiles in some numbers had been an accepted part of the Diaspora synagogue life, something should have shown up in the excavations. To this date, nothing has.

III

These results from archaeology prompt a re-investigation of the older literary evidence. It quickly becomes apparent that Acts is the key. The most vivid descriptions of God-fearers are based on this book. We would not know the term "God-fearer" if it were not for Acts. The other evidence commonly used—epigraphy, and literature both classical and rabbinic—is almost always "explained" with reference to Acts.[15]

But recent studies of Acts are revealing the extent to which it is first of all a literary composition-or, perhaps, theology in narrative form-rather than an historical record.[16] Luke's concern is to tell an edifying story of the way Christianity began. His revisionist treatment of Paul is the best known example of this element in his writing; neither the theology[17] of Paul nor the chronology[18] of his career, as found in Acts, can be made to line up with the Pauline epistles.

New Testament redaction criticism has provided many other examples of Luke' alteration and amplification of his sources, in the service of the story he wishes to tell. His way of presenting Christianity is narrative. For too long he has been taken as an historian in the modern sense; a distorted picture of the religious situation of the first century has heen the result.

---

15 And arguments for the historical value of these elements in Acts may become circular, for example: "The picture which Acts gives of Paul's visiting synagogues and preaching there has been rejected as unhistorical on the ground that, by Paul's own account, his apostleship was specifically to the Gentiles, not to the Jews (Gal. 1:16, 2:7-9; Rom 9:13f.). But the apostle to the Gentiles was a sufficiently good strategist to know that he could find an excellent bridgehead for the discharge of his commission in the God-fearing Gentiles who attended synagogue worship in the cities of the Diaspora," F.F. Bruce, "Is the Paul of Acts the Real Paul?" *BJRL* 58 (1975-76) 293 note 2.

16 For an introduction, and further bibliography, see N. Peterson, *Literary Criticism for New Testament Critics* (Philadelphia, 1978) 81-92.

17 E. Haenchen, *The Acts of the Apostles: A Commentary* (Philadelphia, 1971) 112-116.

18 R. Jewett, *A Chronology of Paul's Life* (Philadelphia, 1979) 7-24.

Luke's literary creativity served the best of purposes; but at the same time it requires us to be cautious in attempts to use Acts as an historical source, *especially* when conclusions from Acts are not independently supported by other evidence.[19]

Put the suggestions of the literary critics together with the archaeological data, and the function of some major elements in the plot of Acts becomes immediately apparent:

1) The theme of "missionary preaching in the Diaspora synagogues"—The word *synagoge* is used in Acts chiefly to designate the place where Diaspora Christian missionary preaching begins; with one exception (Apollos, 18:26) Paul is the synagogue preacher. After his conversion (9:1-19) Paul's first act (as the "Apostle to the Gentiles"!) is to preach in a synagogue (9:20). This is particularly striking in view of the fact that the term *synagoge* is not used once in the letters written by Paul. Luke's point is clear: Christianity's path to the Gentiles was through the Jews.

2) The hero "Cornelius the God-fearer"—Cornelius, whose story is told in 10:1-11:18, is the first God-fearer met in Acts; three of the eleven references to God-fearers in Acts are found in this story. And Cornelius is the best kind of Gentile! He is a Roman citizen and an army officer.He prays to God *dia pantos*. He is pious, and so is the soldier who assists him. He has the full approval of the Jews. Most important, his conversion is accomplished at the direct command of God through a vision to Cornelius himself and a triple vision to Peter. A chapter and a half of Acts is devoted to the story of Cornelius. After him, no other God-fearer in Acts is given as much as a single sentence of description. Only two others are even named: one is Titius Justus (18:7), the other—in line with another of Luke's emphases—is a woman, Lydia (16:14). But Cornelius is the archetype; he *defines* the God-fearer for Acts. When other God-fearers are brought in after chapter 10, we know about them already; they are like Cornelius. The Lukan pattern has been clarified further: the path to the

---

19 In a chapter titled "Narrative World and Real World in Luke-Acts," Peterson argues that "the rejection of God's agents by God's people in connection with God's sanctuaries (synagogues and temple) is the plot device by which the movement of the narrative as a whole is motivated," *Literary Criticism* 83. Drawing on the parallels between Luke and Acts already identified by earlier commentators, he shows that the "narrative world" of Luke-Acts is constructed in such a way that Jesus, Peter and John, Stephen, and Paul all have the same "experience": expulsion from Temple or synagogue at the hands of "God's people," the Jews. Thus for Peterson, at least, themes 1 and 3 below are not peculiar to Acts but reflect major plot-lines running through the entirety of the two-volume work, Luke-Acts. Acts' picture of Paul as synagogue-preacher is central to Peterson's analysis, cf. his summary of the discrepancies between Acts and Paul's letters on this point, 82f.

Gentiles through the Jews was also through that *tertium quid*, the God-fearer.

3) "The three programmatic renunciations of the Jews"—When Paul, the Apostle to the Gentiles, becomes a Christian missionary, he immediately begins his work in a synagogue. Then the Cornelius story makes Paul's work legitimate via Peter. But almost immediately there is a strain on this procedure, and it is caused by the Diaspora Jews. Luke's Paul is provoked into three formal and programmatic renunciations of (Diaspora) Jews in favor of a mission to the Gentiles. These statements are set in three major zones of the Gentile world, in progression toward the west: 13:46 in Asia Minor, 18:6 in Greece and 28:28 in Rome.[20]

The first Renunciation (13:46)[21] takes place in the synagogue of Antioch in Pisidia, among Jews and God-fearers. The final break with the Diaspora synagogue is at 19:9 in Ephesus, when Paul withdraws from the most Jewish of teaching sites, the synagogue, to the most Gentile, the *scholé*. But this break is anticipated in Corinth in the second Renunciation (18:6),[22] which is followed immediately by the last reference in Acts to a God-fearer (18:7). After nine more chapters in which no God-fearers are mentioned and no one enters a synagogue, the third formal Renunciation of the Jews occurs at 28: 28;[23] two verses later, Acts ends.

4) "The disappearance of the God-fearers"—the God-fearers disappear altogether, rather than coming to the fore, when Paul withdraws from the synagogue. After 19:9 Paul spends two years each in Ephesus, Caesaria (Cornelius!?) and Rome, but they never appear again as the faith is spread in these Gentile cities. It is no accident that we have no more God-fearers after 18:7 and no more "going into the synagogues" after 19:8; these two themes go together, and after 19:9 neither one has any further use.

The God-fearers are on the stage as needed, off the stage after they have served their purpose in the plot.[24] Acts cannot be used as evidence that there ever were such groups in the synagogues of the Roman Empire.

---

20 The renunciations and the artificality with which they are introduced into the story have been noted by many commentators, e.g. M. Dibelius, *Studies in the Acts of the Apostles* (London, 1956) 149f.

21 "It was necessary that the word of God should be spoken first to you. Since you thrust it from you...behold, we turn to the Gentiles" (+ Isa 49:6).

22 "Your blood be upon your heads...From now on I will go to the Gentiles."

23 (Isa 6:9f. +) " . . . this salvation has been sent to the Gentiles; they will listen."

24 With the exception of the third renunciation (28:28), all texts relevant to these four themes, and all references to the God-fearers, are found in the central third of Acts, between 9:20 and 19:9. A study of the terms for God-fearer, in connection with the other words associated closely with them in this section of Acts, will be published elsewhere.

It is a tribute to Luke's dramatic ability that they have become so alive for the later Church, but the evidence from Paul's own letters and now from archaeology makes their historicity questionable in the extreme.[25]

But since I have questioned the historical value of this part of Acts, I have the obligation to say what more important point Luke was trying to make with this theme. I suspect that with his references to *synagogues* and *God-fearers* Luke is trying to tell both good news and bad news. The bad news is that most Jews in Palestine and the Diaspora have rejected Christianity despite the missionaries' repeated efforts; this is part of the point of the three formal renunciations in 13:46, 18:6, and 28:28 with their Old Testament proof-texts. Luke has concluded that the time has passed when Jews in some numbers might be expected to come into the new religion.

The good news is symbolized by the God-fearers, the Gentiles whom the Jews had begun to attract before Christianity came on the scene. Thanks to Peter and especially to Paul, these Gentiles came *into Christianity* in far greater numbers. Christianity is becoming more and more a Gentile religion; that outreach to the Gentiles is legitimated by the "existence" of the God-fearers, examples of an earlier outreach to Gentiles by the Jews.

The God-fearers are a symbol to help Luke show how Christianity had become a Gentile religion lgitimately and without losing its Old Testament roots. The Jewish mission to Gentiles recalled in the God-fearers is ample precedent for the far more extensive mission to Gentiles which Christianity had in fact undertaken with such success. Once that point has been made, Luke can let the God-fearers disappear from his story.[26] That is just what they do, and that is why there is no further reference to them in the New Testament and no clear independent record of them in the material evidence from the classical world.

---

25 Luke's freedom to rewrite a part of early Christian history in this fashion surely says something about his distance from the events, that is, about the date of the writing of Acts.

26 The abruptness with which they vanish is difficult to account for if the historicity of the circle of God-fearers is assumed, and even more difficult if Luke himself is thought to be a former God-fearer, as is held by M. Hengel, *Acts and the History of Earliest Christianity* (Philadelphia, 1980) 107.

IV

Perhaps it can not be demonstrated conclusively that there never was a circle of God-fearers associated with ancient Judaism. The hypothesis of this paper is rather that, at least for the Roman Diaspora, the evidence presently available is far from convincing proof for the existence of such a class of Gentiles as traditionally defined by the assumptions of the secondary literature.

The new evidence required to falsify this hypothesis would have to be substantial; one clear inscription using the term *phoboumenos* or *sebomenos* precisely as in Acts would be helpful, but not sufficient, since at most it might prove God-fearers for that particular synagogue community.[27]

Consider a parallel example, the Christian Gnostics: they are a slippery group; despite a substantial amount of ancient evidence,the social location and the various forms of this piety remain difficult to define. They were self-admittedly, perhaps by choice, a small fraction of that tiny minority of the first- and second-century world called Christians.[28] By some accounts cited here, e.g. the *Encyclopaedia Judaica*, the population of God-fearers in the Roman world at that time would have been higher than the number of Christian Gnostics. It does not seem unreasonable to expect something comparable in substance to the kind of evidence which was available for Christian Gnostics before the Nag Hammadi discoveries, before we place some faith in the existence of another social group of perhaps comparable size.

There are important implications of the hypothesis of this paper for the history of Christianity and of Judaism; to begin with Christianity:

1) The distance between Palestinian Jewish Christianity and Diaspora Jewish Christianity has probably been over-stressed by earlier scholarship, for the first century at least. They did not exist in sealed compartments. Movement back and forth between Diaspora and Holy Land was not difficult. Christianity could reach the Diaspora directly via Jewish Christian missionaries; the God-fearer is not needed as a go-between.

2) The percentage of Jews in the Christianity of the late first and early second centuries may have been higher than is usually assumed. But these

---

27 The closest yet to such a text is the inscription from Aphrodisias in Caria published by J. Reynolds and R.F. Tannenbaum, *Jews and God-fearers at Aphrodisias* (Cambridge, England, 1987), cf. M. Mellink, "Archaeology in Asia Minor," *AJA* 81 (1977) 306; the term it uses is *theosebes*. At the least, this text is evidence for (from?) a Jewish community in Aphrodisias, one which probably had a place of meeting, i.e. a synagogue. More tantalizing but much less helpful for reconstructing the life of Diaspora Jews are inscriptions such as *IG* III (2) 13209, 13210 = *SIG* 1239 (from Athens) and *SIG* 1240 (from Chalcis in Euboea), in which curses resembling those in Deut 28:22, 28 are used to protect the graves of well-to-do sophists of the second century; for a recent study of the possible connections, see L. Robert, "Malédictions funéraires grecques," *CRAI* (1978) 241-289, especially 241-252.

28 Irenaeus, *adv. Haer.* I.24.6 on Basileides, cf. *Gospel of Thomas*, logion 23.

Jewish Christians spoke the religious language of the Diaspora well because more and more they were *Diaspora* Jews, e.g. Paul of Tarsus; the first expansion of Christianity in the Gentile world is perhaps due more to them, and less to *Gentile* Christians than we usually admit.

3) Acts' straight-line picture of the expansion of Christianity runs: Jew—God-fearer—Gentile. But that is a simplified version, for the purposes of Luke's story. Rather, Christianity expanded over a broad front; it used several religious "languages" at the same time—with inevitable internal conflicts, attested as early as Paul's letters.

For the History of Judaism

1) The figure of the God-fearer has often been used to demonstrate the inadequacy of Judaism in the Greco-Roman period, what Hengel termed its stooping "to constant and ultimately untenable compromises" in order to make a place for itself in an alien world. But the New Testament provides no evidence for such failure, if the God-fearer texts are properly understood.[29]

2) When this understanding of Acts is coupled with the new evidence from excavations, we conclude that the Jews of these synagogue communities need not have felt alien to the Diaspora; we need not assume that they were never really "at home" there. At Stobi Jews were "at home" for generations, constructing a series of synagogues for their community; it was only at the end that Christianity became strong enough to change things for the worse. The assaults which destroyed the Dura synagogue in the middle of the third century fell no less heavily on Gentile buildings. The Ostia evidence is incomplete but nothing suggests either a ghetto there, or a ghetto-mentality.

But the clearest example of a Jewish minority "at home" in a Gentile world is Sardis. This community was a very old one. Generations of Sardis Jews were native Anatolians, not refugees, immigrants or slaves from the troubled lands farther east. By the time the synagogue and the city were sacked by the Persians in the seventh century the Jews had lived there for nearly a millennium, perhaps more; and almost from the beginning they apparently enjoyed some standing with the various Gentile authorities.[30]

---

29 If Paul's contemporary, Philo of Alexandria, had been previously unknown and the *de Vita Mosis* or the *Legum Allegoria* were suddenly to be discovered in 1980, their author would inevitably be called a God-fearer; the traditional understanding of Diaspora Judaism would have no place for such a Jew.

30 On Sardis: Kraabel, "Diaspora Synagogue," 483-488; C. Foss, *Byzantine and Turkish Sardis* (Archaeological Exploration of Sardis, Monograph 4; Cambridge, 1976), both with further bibliography.

3) Missionary activity conducted from these synagogues[31] may have been much less extensive than was once thought to be the case. The only reference to a proselyte in the New Testament outside Acts[32] is Mt 23:15: the scribes and Pharisees "traverse sea and land to make a single proselyte, and when he becomes one [they] make him twice as much a child of hell as" themselves. The polemic of the verse is obvious (nothing similar appears in the parallel texts of the other two Synoptic gospels); in the absence of other evidence from the Roman Diaspora, it is of little or no value for the reconstruction of the historical situation.

4) In the past we have surely exaggerated the control of one segment of ancient world-Judaism over another. Almost as soon as there was a "diaspora," Judaism in the west began to develop in parallel with the older communities of Syria-Palestine and farther east;[33] each had its local alliances, its own social organization and to some degree its own theology.

5) But at the same time this does not mean that those in Diaspora synagogue communities were Jews any less. They acted as though their form of Judaism was authentic; the burden of proof is on those who would argue that is was otherwise.

---

31 See D. Georgi, *Die Gegner des Paulus im 2. Korintherbrief: Studien zur religiösen Propaganda in den Spätantike* (WMANT 11; Neukirchen-Vluyn, 1964) 83-187, especially 83-137.

32 In Acts the term occurs three times, at 2:11 and 6:5, and in a notorious *crux interpretum* at 13:43. Logical inconsistencies resulting from the use of the New Testament to define Diaspora Judaism are of course not new; that striking history-of-religions category, the "semi-proselyte," was also the product of an uncritical reliance on the God-fearer texts in Acts, cf. Strack-Billerbeck (note 8 above) *ad* Acts 13:16.

33 Thanks to the work of Jacob Neusner and his students the particularity of the rabbinic world view has taken on a new vividness and detail in the last two decades; see e.g. his "The History of Earlier Rabbinic Judaism: Some New Approaches," *HR* 16 (1977) 216-236.

The God-Fearers—A Literary and Theological Invention

R.S. MacLennan and A.T. Kraabel

New Testament scholars, both Jewish and Christian, have for years accepted the existence of a group of gentiles known as God-fearers.[1] They were thought to be closely associated with the synagogue in the Book of Acts. Although they did not convert to Judaism, they were an integral part of the synagogue and provided fertile ground for early Christian missionary activity. As pious gentiles, the God-fearers stood somewhere between Greco-Roman piety and Jewish piety in the synagogue.

In his classic but now somewhat outdated study titled *Judaism in the First Centuries of the Christian Era*, Harvard scholar George Foot Moore argued that the existence of the God-fearers provides evidence for the synagogue's own missionary work outside of Palestine during the first century C.E. The God-fearers were the result of this Jewish missionary movement. Although Jews may not have been actually sending out missionaries to proselytize the heathen, the influence of Jewish outreach was nevertheless felt in a world hungry for something more than mere empty religious forms.

Recent scholarship adds authority to Moore's conclusions. The critical Greek words are *phoboumenos* (plural: *phoboumenoi*), meaning "fearing one," and *sebomenos* (plural: *sebomenoi*), meaning "worshipping one."

In 1962, a standard German reference work drew a distinction between God-fearers, on the one hand, and proselytes or converts, on the other. The God-fearers, we are told, were more numerous. "They frequent the services of the synagogue, they are monotheists in the biblical sense, and they participate in some of the ceremonial requirements of the Law, but they have not moved to full conversion through circumcision. They are called . . . *sebomenoi or phoboumenoi ton theon.*"[2]

The *Encyclopaedia Judaica*, published in 1971, tells us that "in the Diaspora there was an increasing number, perhaps millions the first century, of *sebomenoi,* gentiles who had not gone the whole route towards conversion."[3]

Other scholars describe the God-fearers with equal confidence. For the late Israeli scholar Michael Avi-Yonah, these God-fearers were a "numerous class" of gentiles under the empire; "although most of them did not feel able to shoulder the whole burden of the Law, they sympathized with Judaism . . .

---

1 Editor's note: This essay first appeared as an article in *Biblical Archaeology Review* 12 no. 5 (September/October 1986) 47-53 and includes references to the recent work done by J. Reynolds and R.F. Tannenbaum at Aphrodisias (see note 15 below) which were not available when Tom Kraabel wrote his "The Disappearance of the 'God-Fearers'," in *Numen* 28, 2 (1981) 113-126.

2 K.G. Kuhn and H. Stegemann, "Proselytes," in Pauly-Wissowa, *Realenzyklopädie der klassischen Altertumswissenschaft* (Stuttgart, 1893-) suppl. ix (1962), p. 1260, cf. pp. 1248-1283.

3 *Encyclopaedia Judaica*, vol. 10 s.v. "Jewish Identity," p. 55.

They were to be found in the provinces as well as in Italy, even at Rome . . .
As they often belonged to the upper classes, their mere presence added in the
eyes of the authorities to the weight of Jewish influence . . .[4]

David Flusser, another distinguished Israeli scholar, wrote in 1976 that the
existence of these "many God-fearers" reveals that "Hellenistic Judaism had
almost succeeded in making Judaism a world religion in the literal sense of
the words."[5] Martin Hengel, a prominent German scholar, agrees with Flusser
as to the number and influence of the God-fearers, although Hergel draws
different conclusions: "The large number of [God-fearers] standing between
Judaism and paganism in the New Testament . . . shows the indissoluble dilemma of the Jewish religion in ancient times. As it could not break free from
its nationalistic roots among the people, it had to stoop to constant and ultimately untenable compromises" (1975).[6] This comment by Hergel is doubly
unfortunate, in that it moves from what may be a misinterpretation of Acts to
what is surely an anti-Jewish statement. Hengel's conclusion may derive from
the theology of the Protestant Reformation and its understanding of Judaism.[7]
But, as we shall see, there is theology at work in Luke himself as he composes
Acts; indeed, Acts is best described as "theological history," a term applied to
it by Robert Maddox, or even as "theology in narrative form."[8] As we will
spell out at the end of this essay, we see the God-fearers as theological characters, an integral part of Luke's understanding of the Church in its relation
to pagans and Jews.

It is in the New Testament that we find the principal evidence for the
God-fearers.[9] Indeed, the best-known God-fearer is a Roman soldier who

---

4 Michael Avi-Yonah, *The Jews of Palestine* (Oxford, 1976), p. 37.

5 David Flusser, "Paganism in Palestine," in *Compendia Rerum Judaicarum ad Novum Testamentum* I.2, ed. S. Safrai and M. Stern (Arsen, 1976), p. 1097.

6 Martin Hengel, *Judaism and Hellenism* (Philadelphia, 1975), vol. 1, p. 313.

7 A.T. Kraabel, "Greeks, Jews and Lutherans in the Middle Half of Acts," in Christians
Among Jews and Gentiles: Essays in Honor of Krister Stendahl, ed. G.W.E. Nickelsberg (Philadelphia: Fortress, 1986).

8 Robert Maddox, *The Purpose of Luke-Acts* (Edinburgh: T&T Clark, 1982), p. 16; Kraabel,
"The Disappearance of the 'God-Fearers,'" *Numen* 28 (1981).

9 In the past half-century some of the most influential treatments of this issue have been K.
Lake's "Proselytes and God Fearers" in Foakes Jackson and Lake, *The Beginning of Christianity
I. The Acts of the Apostles,* vol. 5 (London, 1933), pp. 74-96 and the extended note to Acts 13:16
in H.L. Strack and P. Billerbeck, *Kommentar zum neuen Testament aus Talmud und Midrash,* vol.
2 (Munich, 1924), pp. 715-723. More recent studies include: Louis H. Feldman, "Jewish Sympathizers in Classical Literature and Inscriptions," Transactions of the American Philological Association 81 (1950), pp. 200-208. R. Markus, "The *Sebomenoi* in Josephus," *Journal of Semitic Studies* 14 (1952), pp. 247-250. M. Wilcox, "The God fearers in Acts: A Reconsideration," *Journal*

(continued...)

eventually became a Christian. His name was Cornelius; he was a centurion stationed in Caesarea. Cornelius, we are told in chapter 10 of the Acts of the Apostles, was a "devout man who feared God," as did his household (Acts 10:2, Revised Standard Version). He prayed "constantly." In a vision Cornelius is told to send to Joppa in Judea for Simon Peter. He does so; Simon Peter comes and tells him that "God shows no partiality . . . Everyone who believes in [Jesus] receives forgiveness of sins through his name." The Holy Spirit had poured out-apparently for the first time-"even on the Gentiles" (Acts 10:45).

In the Jerusalem Bible, the critical part of Acts 10:2 states that Cornelius "and the whole of his household were devout and God-fearing." A note tells us that "the expressions 'fearing God,' 10:2, 22, 35; 13:16, 26, and 'worshipping God,' 13:43, 50; 16:14; 11:4, 17; 18:7, are technical terms for admirers and followers of the Jewish nation who stop short of circumcision" (*JB*, 1966, NT 217).

As already mentioned, the important Greek words are *phoboumenos* and *sebomenos*. They are used several times in Acts, in chapter 10 and elsewhere. (In chapter 10, see verses 22 and 35.) In chapter 13, Paul addresses the Sabbath crowd at the synagogue in Antioch: "Men of Israel and you that fear God" (Acts 13:16). The phrase is sometimes translated as "fearers of God" or "God Fearers." (See also verse 26.)

In chapter 17, we read that in Athens Paul "argued in the synagogue with the Jews and the devout persons" (Acts 17:17). (See also Acts 16:14; 17:4 and 18:7.)

Apart from these eleven references containing some form of *phoboumenos* (fearing one) and *sebomenos* (worshipping one), the New Testament is silent as to any alleged God-fearers.

In the traditional reconstruction, the God-fearers may be described as follows:

1. They are gentiles interested in Judaism, but not converts or proselytes; the men are not circumcised.
2. They are found in significant numbers in the synagogues of the Diaspora, from Asia Minor to Rome.
3. As a group, they are particularly significant for students of the New Testament and early Christianity because Christianity supposedly recruited from them a great number of its earliest members.

9(...continued)
for the Study of the N.T. 13 (1981), pp. 102-122; Kraabel, "The Disappearance of the 'God-Fearers,'"pp. 113-126; Thomas M. Finn, "The God Fearers Reconsidered," *Catholic Biblical Quarterly* 47.1 (1985) pp. 75-84.

While Acts provides the only New Testament support for the existence of the God-fearers, scholars have also found isolated and oblique references to them in classical literature, as well as in Greek and Latin inscriptions, although the technical terms *phoboumenos* and *sebomenos* appear only in Acts. The other scattered evidence for Diaspora[10] God-fearers in Greek and Latin literature and inscriptions is all held together by the references in Acts; the argument is that the various terms in the Greek and Latin literary texts and inscriptions are in fact being used in a technical sense, that is, as God-fearers. Additional evidence for the existence of God-fearers is also drawn from rabbinic discussions of sympathizers, proselytes and converts.

We strongly doubt that there ever was a large and broadly based group of gentiles known as God-fearers. The archaeological evidence first pointed us in the direction of this conclusion. This led us to reexamine the literary evidence, including Acts, and our reexamination simply confirmed our doubts. We've concluded that the God-fearers were never as significant among Diaspora Jews as most scholars suggest. If they existed at all, they were isolated and did not have the effect that many suppose. In a sense they were a figment of the scholarly imagination, based on a literary and theological expansion of what Luke says in Acts. We would like to share with you the evidence that has led us to this conclusion.

The archaeological evidence for Diaspora Judaism under the Roman Empire has recently increased substantially. In the 1960's, well-preserved ancient synagogues were discovered at Ostia, the port of Rome, and at Sardis in western Turkey. Another important Diaspora synagogue is being excavated at Stobi in Yugoslavia.[11] Substantial collections of Jewish inscriptions, papyri and artifacts have provided the basis for detailed studies of Jews all over the Roman empire in the east at Dura-Europos, in North Africa, in Alexandria and in Rome itself.

We now have enough information to permit a fairly detailed reconstruction of Jewish life in the Diaspora based entirely on archaeological evidence.

The archaeological evidence is of equal antiquity with the rabbinic literature and Greek and Latin literary texts, and has the added advantage of coming directly from Diaspora sites. Moreover, the archaeological evidence comes from the Jews themselves, rather than from gentile comments about them in

---

10 Diaspora is the term used for Jews dispersed outside the land of Israel. The word is used for both the people and their communities.

11 Kraabel, "The Diaspora Synagogue: Archaeological and Epipgraphic Evidence Since Sukenik," *Aufsteig und Niedergang der romischen Welt* II.19 (1979), pp. 477-510; and "Social Systems of Six Diaspora Synagogues," in J. Gutmann, ed., *Ancient Synagogues: The Current State of Research* (Chico, CA, 1981), pp. 79-91. Kraabel and Eric M. Meyers, "Archaeology, Iconography and Non-Literary Written Remains," Chapter 7 of *Early Judaism and Its Modern Interpreters*, edd. R.A. Kraft and G.W.E. Nickelsburg, vol. II, (1986) *175-210.*

Greek and Latin literature. An examination of Greek and Latin texts will produce many examples of how partial and distorted that "outside" evidence can be.[12] And as we shall see, Christian literature, and particularly Acts, also provides an uncertain basis for reconstructing Jewish life in the Diaspora.

The archaeological evidence on which we rely comes mainly from excavated synagogues. This is because the God-fearers are supposedly associated with synagogues, that is, with organized Diaspora Jewish communities.

These synagogues[13] date from the first century B.C.E. to the early seventh century C.E.

A study of these excavations reveals the following:

1. Over 100 synagogue inscriptions have been uncovered. Not a single one uses the term *phoboumenos* (fearing one) or *sebomenos* (devout one). *Theosebes* (plural: *Theosebeis*) (God worshipper) appears apparently ten times, but as an adjective describing Jews, usually Jewish donors. We include a reference to it here because it too is often taken as meaning "God-fearers."

2. There is nothing in these inscriptions to suggest the existence of an interested, but unconverted group of gentiles who frequented the synagogue. If our only evidence were synagogue inscriptions, there would be nothing to suggest that God-fearers had ever existed.

3. The symbolism used in the synagogue buildings is directed toward the Jewish community, with no apparent attempt to communicate with persons who come from outside this tradition. For example, in the Dura-Europos synagogue (c. 245 C.E.), the paintings display Biblical themes and characters like David, Moses and Abraham, relevant to Jewish community life.[14]

4. In the Diaspora, the synagogue was probably the only building owned by the Jewish community; it served as the center of the community's social as well as religious life. It thus played a far more significant role than a synagogue in Palestine. It is not accidental that at least four of the six Diaspora synagogues listed in footnote 13 were dominated by Torah shrine that marks the

---

12 Texts are assembled in M. Stern, *Greek and Latin Authors on Jews and Judaism*, I-III (Jerusalem, 1974-1984).

13 Delos, on that island in the Aegean Sea (first century B.C.E. to second century C.E.); Ostia, in Italy (fourth century C.E.; the earliest synagogue may be as early as the first century C.E.); Dura-Europos, in Syria (the building is second century C.E. to 616 C.E.); Stobi, in Macedonia (fourth century C.E.; earlier synagogues at the site date to the third century C.E. or earlier); Priene, in Asia Minor (third or fourth century C.E.).

14 M. Rostovtzeff, *Dura-Europos and its Art* (Oxford, 1938).

impotence of the Diaspora synagogue as a distinctively Jewish center.

5. Diaspora synagogue contact with Christians was rare, despite the fact that the accounts in Acts assume such contact was common. To judge from the material remains, the gentile world in which these Diaspora Jews lived was considerably more pagan than Christian. In third century Dura-Europos, the synagogue was much more elaborate than the Christian building. The Stobi synagogue was rebuilt twice before it was finally displaced by a church building, and that did not occur before the fifth century. At Sardis, excavations have established the prominent position of the Jews in the life of the larger community, but there is nothing in the archaeological evidence to suggest any significant impact of Christianity or Christians on Jewish life in Sardis before the city fell to a Persian invasion in 616 C.E.

In short, none of the supposedly technical terms for God-fearers appear in any of the synagogue inscriptions. Nothing in the excavated buildings suggests the presence of religious life. It thus played a far more significant role of a kind of gentile "penumbra" around the Diaspora synagogue communities. Nor is there any hint in the data that these Diaspora Jews were reaching out toward their gentile neighbors with some kind of religious message.

If interested gentile—"millions by the first century," as one source cited earlier suggested—had been accepted as part of Diaspora synagogue life, something should have shown up in the excavations of these synagogues. To date, nothing has!

There is one possible exception: In 1976, a Greek inscription was discovered at ancient Aphrodisias in Asia Minor that some scholars have argued now provides solid archaeological evidence for the existence of God-fearers. Unfortunately, the inscription is still unpublished.[15] Its publication has been assigned by the excavator, Kenan T. Erim of New York University, to Joyce Reynolds of Cambridge University. Miss Reynolds hopes to publish the inscription soon. But until she does, we must base our discussion on a brief prepublication notice Reynolds provided to *Biblical Archaeology Review* and to the authors of this essay.

The inscription appears on a stone that perhaps once served as a doorjamb. Each side of the stone is inscribed. Miss Reynolds dates at least one and perhaps both inscriptions to the third century C.E. One side lists 18 names of a group devoted to learning, who contributed a memorial to the con-

---

15 Editor's note: It has recently been published as J. Reynolds and R.F. Tannenbaum, *Jews and God-fearers at Aphrodisias: Greek Inscriptions with Commentary*, Proceedings of the Cambridge Philological Society Supplement, vol. 12, (Cambridge, England: University Press, 1987).

gregation. Three of the men are described as proselytes and two as *theosebeis* meaning "God worshipper" or "pious" but sometimes translated "God-fearers." The second side of the stone contains two lists of names divided by a blank space. The heading of the upper list has not survived; 55 apparently Jewish names survive in whole or in part in the upper list. The lower list contains 52 names and is headed "And those who are *theosebeis*."

The *theosebeis* bear non-Biblical names, according to Reynolds (with perhaps one exception). The upper list contains mostly recognizably Jewish names.

Miss Reynolds suggests that these names listed on a monument with Jewish names reflects "a solid core of men" who "set a high value upon Judaic tradition, piety and the cooperative virtues, and it appears that their interest in Judaic tradition was on the increase."[16] According to Reynolds, "Here we have *theosebeis* involved in what must be the study of the law, a category of *theosebeis* closely associated with Jewish congregations." Dr. Reynolds concludes in her notice, "To me, it seems that there is a good case for regarding them as what are conventionally called 'God-fearers,' gentiles attracted to Judaism, but stopping short of becoming proselytes."

Does this inscription now prove the existence of a group conventionally called "God-fearers." Or, are we faced with an inscription that, despite Reynolds's cautionary notice, other scholars will use to interpret *theosebeis* as it has been conventionally conceived? Reynolds is not at the point of concluding that *theosebeis* should carry such theological baggage. She is interested in providing basic information about the inscription, which was found in an area not associated with any building. Reynolds is not trying to prove the existence of a large group of God-fearers in the Diaspora; rather she is describing a connection between one Jewish community and some pious gentiles.

Other texts just as clearly designate gentiles who have never been in contact with Jews at all as *theosebeies*. In literature and inscriptions *theosebeis* does not have a single meaning. In the late second century, Melito, bishop of Sardis, uses *theosebes* to refer to Christians in general.[17] Sometimes *theosebes* is used to describe persons who are clearly Jews. In other texts, it just as clearly designates gentiles who were never in contact with Jews. For example, in the first book of his History (1.86.2) Herodotus calls Croesus (the sixth century B.C.E. king of Lydia, who had all the gold) *theosebes*.

Another example, much closer to the language and date of Acts, is the famous anti-Christian graffiti from Rome—from the *paedagogium* under the Palatine Hill. It shows a boy kneeling before a crucified figure with the body

---

16 Joyce Reynolds, letter to Hershel Shanks, *Editor* of BAR.

17 In Eusebius, *Historia Ecclesiastica* 4.26.5, 7.

of a man and the head of a donkey. The legend beneath reads: "Alexamenos worships God [*sebete theon*]." *Sebete theon*—"worships God—is precisely the vocabulary found in Acts, but Alexamenos is neither Jewish nor pagan but clearly Christian.[18] We are not dealing with an accepted "technical term of one and only one meaning."

Behind these discussions of technical or quasi-technical terminology in Judaism is often the erroneous assumption that Judaism in the Roman empire was monolithic and everywhere the same,[19] and thus that wherever a term appears its meaning will be the same.

The exceedingly important Aphrodisias inscription, offers an opportunity for a full exploration of the term, perhaps the first in which all the affected disciplines might participate.

What is behind this reading of this ancient evidence? We see at least two broad misconceptions, one about the Jews of antiquity and their friends and associates, the other about the New Testament.

Many scholars seem to assume that in Diaspora Judaism whenever someone is sympathetic to Jews or is pro-Jewish, that means he or she is interested in the Jewish religion. But that is not necessarily true. It is quite possible that gentiles were friendly toward Jews simply as neighbors or fellow-townspeople. This was no doubt the case at Sardis, where excavations have uncovered a synagogue in the heart of the city and inscriptions that reflect Jewish involvement in the gentile life of the city (but not gentile involvement in the religious life of the synagogue).[20] The synagogue at Sardis suggests that gentiles acknowledged that Jews had a proper place in the city; they belonged there as an ethnic minority.

If we persist in seeing Judaism in antiquity first of all as a religion, it will be difficult to understand the openness of many non-Jews toward Jews in anything other than religious terms. But to have Jewish friends or to take a positive stand toward Jews need not mean—either today or in antiquity—an interest in converting.

The other misconception has to do with the nature of the evidence that the New Testament provides.

Now that we have placed the archaeological evidence in context, we can come back to Acts to determine whether it should be used as a foundation to argue for the widespread existence of God-fearers.

---

18 V. Vaananen, *Graffiti del Palatino, I: Paedagogium*, no. 246 (Helsinki, 1966), pp. 81-92.

19 Kraabel, "The Roman Diaspora: Six Questionable Assumptions," *JJS* 33 (1982) particularly pp. 453-454.

20 Kraabel, "Impact of the Discovery of the Sardis Synagogue," in *Sardis from Prehistoric to Roman Times*, ed. G.M.A. Hanfmann, (Cambridge, MA, 1983), pp.178-190.

In order to understand this literary evidence, we must understand the purpose of the text, in which the supposed references to God-fearers are found.

New Testament writers were not trying to tell their readers what they already knew, namely, the facts surrounding the events of the early Church. These writers were not trying to describe the events that had occurred. They were interested rather in *interpreting* the meaning of those events. They wanted to tell why the church existed, what the Cross meant, why Jesus was the Messiah, why there was a split between the Jewish Christian movement and the Jews. Their concern was not simply to give an account of what happened, but rather to provide an interpretive portrait in words of the events surrounding the origin of the Church. The New Testament is not so much a history book, in a modern sense, as a collection of early Christian sermons and letters.

Modern preachers and commentaries often give Luke credit for describing in Acts how Christianity moved from the Jews to the gentiles. But this is a historical question that was never really at the center of Luke's concerns. Recent studies of Acts have shown the extent to which it is a literary composition—or, perhaps, more accurately, theology in narrative form—rather than a historical record. In Acts, Luke wants to provide an edifying story of the way Christianity began.

To appreciate how non-historical Luke can be in Acts, we need only compare an event described by him with the same event described by Paul—for example, the Jerusalem Council, which considered whether one must be a Jew to be a Christian. Compare Paul's account of the Jerusalem Council in Galatians 2 with Luke's account of it in Acts 15. An objective reader must conclude that either Luke and Paul are talking about two different events or they are describing the same event from entirely different viewpoints for different audiences. Paul was probably more nearly correct historically, but both writers had a story to tell, each from his own point of view in order to make his own case. It is doubtful that we can fully reconstruct what actually happened from either text. Neither account was concerned with providing data for such a reconstruction. Both were far more interested in defending their view of the need for, and the results of, the Jerusalem Council.

Acts is essentially an argument for the early Church's mission to the gentiles, not a description of that mission. Searching the text for historical details is a frustrating endeavor because Luke is constantly interpreting events instead of merely describing them.

Similarly with Paul: His letters are proclamation rather than description. Neither Paul nor Luke was concerned with recounting history. Each had a passion for his message. As a result, it is impossible to reconcile Paul's theology or the chronology of his career, as found in Acts, with the description of those same elements in the Pauline epistles.

At first glance, the God-fearers referred to in Acts may appear to be a group of real people who "sympathized with Judaism and enjoyed a recognized status upon the fringes," as Salo Baron has described them.[21] We must question the use of these references as historical data. New Testament scholars have provided many examples of Luke's alteration and amplification of his sources in the service of the story he wishes to tell. His way of presenting Christianity is narrative. For too long he has been taken as a historian in the modern sense; the result has been a distorted picture of the religious situation of the first century.

Luke's literary creativity served the best of purposes; but at the same time it requires us to be cautious in attempts to use Acts as a historical source, especially when conclusions from Acts are not independently supported by other evidence.

Here there is no independent evidence. The other evidence, such as it is —inscriptions and classical and rabbinic texts—is almost always "explained" with reference to Acts. Indeed, if it were not for the references in Acts, we would not have the term "God-fearer" at all.

The point Luke is making is clear: Christianity's path to the gentiles was —had been—through the Jews, in contrast to Paul, who wished to appeal directly to the gentiles.

Luke's narrative serves his viewpoint. He is telling us good news and bad news. The bad news is that Christianity has been rejected by most Jews in Palestine and the Diaspora. The new religion must move beyond them. Luke has therefore concluded that the time has passed when Jews in considerable numbers might be expected to become Christians.

The good news is symbolized by the God-fearers, the gentiles whom the Jews had begun to attract before Christianity came onto the scene. In Luke's view in Acts, these gentiles, thanks to Peter and especially to Paul, inherited the Christian message. Christianity is becoming more and more a gentile religion; Christianity's outreach to the gentiles is legitimized by the broad based "existence" of the God-fearers surrounding the synagogues of the Diaspora Jews, representing an earlier outreach to gentiles by the Jews. This Jewish outreach to these gentiles justifies Christianity's outreach to them, in Luke's view.

Luke uses the God-fearers as a device to show how Christianity had legitimately become a gentile religion, without losing its roots in the traditions of Israel. The Jewish mission to the gentiles represented by the Godfearers was intended to be ample precedent for Christianity's far more extensive mission to the gentiles, a mission that had in fact enjoyed considerable success.

---

21 Michael Grant, *The Jews in the Roman World* (London, 1973), p. 61.

It is significant that the word synagogue is not used at all in Paul's letters. In Acts, on the other hand, the term is used frequently, almost always as the place where Diaspora Christian missionary preaching begins. Paul's first act as the "Apostle to the gentiles" is to preach in a synagogue (Acts 9:20). Luke's point is clear: only when the Jews rejected the Christian message did the Diaspora mission turn to gentiles.

When Paul in Acts withdraws from the synagogue, angered by Jewish rejection of his message, we might expect to hear more about the God-fearers as the focus of Paul's mission. But the fact is that they then disappear from the story. We never hear of them again. It is no accident that we have no more God-fearers after Acts 18:7 and no more "going into the synagogues" after Acts 19:8. These two themes go together, and after Acts 19:9 neither God-fearers nor synagogues have any further function.

The God-fearers are on-stage as needed, offstage after they have served their purpose in the plot. Once his point has been made, Luke can let the God-fearers disappear from the story. The abruptness with which they vanish would surely be difficult to account for, if, as Martin Hengel suggests, Luke was himself a God-fearer.[22] But they simply disappear; there is no further reference to them in the New Testament and no clear independent record of them in the material evidence from the Classical world. Thus, Acts cannot be used as evidence that there ever were such groups in the synagogues of the Roman empire.

It is a tribute to Luke's dramatic ability that the God-fearers have become so alive for the later church. But the evidence from Paul's own letters and now the negative evidence from archaeology makes their historicity, as conventionally defined, questionable in the extreme.

If we are right that "the evidence presently available is far from convincing proof for the existence of such a class of gentiles as traditionally defined by the assumptions of the secondary literature,"[23] this has some important implications for both Christian and Jewish history.

The straight-line picture of the expansion of Christianity given in Acts runs from the Jews to the God-fearers, to the gentiles. That, however, is a simplified version for the purpose of Luke's story; rather, Christianity expanded over a broad front, and in doing so, used several religious "languages" at the same time—with inevitable internal conflicts, attested as early as Paul's letters.

This means that Christianity must be seen as much more varied in the first two centuries after its birth. The New Testament itself is a record of the

---

22 Hengel, *Acts and the History of Earliest Christianity*, (Philadelphia, 1980), p. 107.

23 See Kraabel, "The Disappearance of the 'God-Fearers,'" p. 120.

diversity of Christianity in the first century. The seeds of a multifarious church were sown in the early years of the Christian mission.

The God-fearers have often been used to demonstrate the inadequacy of Judaism in the Greco-Roman period—what Martin Hengel has termed the Jewish religion's "stoop[ing] to constant and ultimately untenable compromises" in order to make a place for itself in an alien world. But the New Testament provides no evidence for such a failure, if the God-fearer texts are properly understood. In fact, quite the opposite is the case. The vitality of first-century Judaism, especially after the Roman destruction of the Jerusalem Temple in 70 C.E., is reflected in Judaism's powerful impact on the Greco-Roman world. The vehemence of the church's polemic against the Jews almost certainly suggests that the synagogues of the Diaspora made no compromises with the Christian mission.

A proper understanding of Acts, coupled with the new evidence from excavations, indicates that many Diaspora Jews did not feel like aliens. This is perhaps most clearly shown from the excavations at Sardis. The Jewish community there was a very old one. Generations of Sardis Jews were natives of Anatolia (modern Turkey); they were not refugees, immigrants or slaves from troubled lands farther east. By the time the synagogue and the city were sacked by the Persians in the seventh century C.E., Jews had lived there for nearly a millennium, perhaps more; and almost from the beginning, they apparently enjoyed considerable standing with the various gentile authorities.[24] It would not be unreasonable to assume that an established and respected Jewish community had a profound religious, philosophical and social effect on the city in which it lived. The values expressed in the synagogue would certainly have influenced the values of the community, just as they do today..

Finally, Jewish missionary activity conducted from these synagogues may have been much less extensive than was once thought to be the case. The only reference to a proselyte in the New Testament outside Acts 2:11, 6:5 and 13:43, is Matthew 23:15, where Matthew rebukes the scribes and Pharisees saying "you traverse sea and land to make a single proselyte, and when he becomes one you make him twice as much a child of hell as yourselves." The polemic of the verse is obvious. (Nothing similar appears in the parallel texts of the other two Synoptic Gospels, Mark and Luke.) In the absence of other evidence of Jewish missionary activity from the Roman Diaspora we can base no sound historical conclusions on the New Testament references.

Understanding "the disappearance of the God-fearers" enables us to reconstruct more accurately several aspects of Christian and Jewish history.

---

24 On Sardis see Kraabel, "Diaspora Synagogue," pp. 483-488; Kraabel, "Impact of the Discovery," pp.77ff.; C. Foss, *Byzantine and Turkish Sardis* (Archaeological Exploration of Sardis, Monograph 4; Cambridge, MA, 1976), with further bibliography.

The following note was provided by the Editor at the end of this essay: Obviously there will be a continuing discussion of the fascinating issues raised in this and the following two articles. Scholars, including our co-author, A. Thomas Kraabel, will next be pursuing the subject in late November (1986) in Atlanta at the Hellenistic Judaism section of the annual meeting of the Society of Biblical Literature. In addition, one or more of the scholars here may make a response in a forthcoming issue of *BAR*, it should be noted that MacLennan and Kraabel did not see the Tannenbaum or Feldman articles that appear in this issue until shortly before publication when it was not possible to revise their article to make direct reference to the other two articles. -Ed.[25]

---

25 Editor's note: The "other two articles" referred to by the Editor of *BAR* are: R.F. Tannenbaum: "Jews and God-Fearers in the Holy City of Aphrodite" and L.H. Feldman, "The Omnipresence of the God-Fearers," in *BAR* 12.5 (1986) pp. 54-57 and 58-63. Also a recent discussion of God-fearers which argues against A.T. Kraabel's position may be found in A.F. Segal, *Paul the Convert*, (New Haven, Yale University Press, 1990): 93-96 and 330 n. 47.

The God-Fearers: Some Neglected Features[1]

J. Andrew Overman

The composition of first century Judaism has received considerable attention over the last fifty years.[2] A significant aspect of this discussion has involved Jewish 'sympathizers' from the Gentile community. This group was in some way involved in the life of the synagogue and Jewish community.[3]

An important element in this continuing discussion has been the *phoboumenoi/sebomenoi ton theon* who appear in the New Testament, but only in the Acts of the Apostles.[4] Those who 'fear God', or those who 'revere God', are such a group of Gentiles interested in and sympathetic to the Jewish religion. While these 'God-Fearers' apparently were not full members of these diaspora Jewish communities through circumcision, they did subscribe to certain aspects of the Jewish religion, and appeared to enjoy a degree of respect and honor from the Jewish community.

The discussion of the so-called God-fearers in Acts took on renewed vitality with the appearance of A.T. Kraabel's 1981 article, "The Disappearance of the God-Fearers,"[5] and a series of articles that followed Kraabel's essay.[6] Kraabel put forth the thesis that "at least for the Roman diaspora, the evidence presently available is far from convincing proof for the existence of such a class of Gentiles as traditionally defined by the assumptions of secondary literature."[7]

Kraabel arrived at his conclusion by using two types of data: archaeological and literary evidence from Acts. The archaeological evidence largely constitutes an argument from silence. That is, in the six Roman diaspora syna-

---

1 Editor's note: This article originally appeared in the *Journal for the Study of the New Testament*, 32 (1988) 17-26.

2 Earlier drafts of this paper were read by the late Robert Guelich and David Tiede. They are not of course responsible for the content and conclusions, but the essay is far better for their help. In the early summer of 1991, my friend Bob Guelich died of sudden heart failure. I am deeply sadden by this loss.

3 Some of the more influential discussions have been L. Feldman, "Jewish 'Sympathizers' in Classical Literature and Inscriptions," *TAPA* 81 (1950) 200-208; F. Siegert, "Die Gottes-fuechtige und Sympathisanten," *JSJ* 4 (1973) 109-164; B. Lifshitz, "Du nouveau sur les 'Sympathisants," *JSJ* 1 (1970) 77-84. K. Lake, "Proselytes and God-Fearers," in F. Foakes-Jackson and K. Lake, *The Beginnings of Christianity* I. *The Acts of the Apostles,* vol.V (Grand Rapids:Baker, 1979) 74-96.

4 The passages are Acts 10.1, 22, 35; 13.16, 26, 43, 50; 16.14; 17.4, 17; 18.7.

5 *Numen* 28 (1981) 113-26.

6 Ensuing articles are: M. Wilcox, "The 'God-Fearers' in Acts: A Reconsideration," *JSNT* 13 (1981) 102-22; T. Finn, "The God-Fearers Reconsidered," *CBQ* 47 (1985) 75-84; A.T. Kraabel, "Greeks, Jews, and Lutherans in the Middle Half of Acts," in *Christians Among Jews and Gentiles,* ed. G. Nickelsburg and G. MacRae, (Philadelphia: Fortress, 1986); and in the same volume, J. Gager, "Jews, Gentiles, and Synagogues in the Book of Acts."

7 Kraabel, "Disappearance," 121.

gogues he examines, Kraabel cannot find a single inscription that would indicate the presence of such a group of Gentile adherents known as God-fearers. From a literary-critical viewpoint, the God-fearers play an important role in Luke's stylized and creative history of the early Church. Kraabel points out the strategic places at which the God-fearers appear and disappear in Acts and concludes that these players are essentially a literary tool employed by the author. "The God-fearers are on the stage as needed, and off the stage after they have served their purpose in the plot.[8]

Accordingly, the 'God-fearers' represent a bridge over which the Christian faith is carried from the Jewish community to the Gentile world. Kraabel believes Acts has so informed and defined our picture of the God-fearers that we "would not know the term 'God-fearer' if it were not for Acts."[9] The purpose of this article is to question some of Kraabel's conclusions concerning the God-fearers. What is being challenged is the conclusion that we lack sufficient evidence for a class, or group of Gentiles involved in and attracted to the life of the Jewish community in the Roman diaspora. This will be done by drawing attention to some neglected features of this discussion as it has developed recently.

The first point concerns the term proselutos. Over fifty years ago K. Lake raised the question of the proper rendering of the term *proselutos* in the LXX and New Testament.[10] He warned against imposing an anachronistic meaning on this term in both the LXX and New Testament.

In the LXX, *proselutos* is consistently used for the Hebrew *GER*, usually rendered 'foreigner' or 'alien'. The Hebrew scriptures use two expressions for the 'stranger' or 'foreigner'.[11] One is *NOKRIM,* which refers to the foreigners who were only in the land temporarily, often for the purposes of trade (cf. e.g. Deut 29.212-23; I kgs 8.41-43). The other term for 'foreigner' is *GER.* The *GERIM* are distinguished from the *NOKRIM* in that, though often non-Israelites, they have in some way become a part of the life of the Jewish community. The *GERIM* eventually work their way into the Pentateuchal regulations. Exod.22.21 and 23.9 reflect legislation involving the *GER.* The *GERIM* were sufficiently part of the community as to deserve protection, as Exod.22.21 and 23.9 make clear. Deut.10.18 and 24.19 group the *GERIM* with the widow and the orphan and further express the legislation and protection afforded them. Eventually the *GERIM* became a part of Israelite worship and were expected

---

8 Ibid., 120.

9 Ibid., 120.

10 K. Lake, "Proselytes and God-fearers," 83.

11 M. Guttman, "The Term 'Foreigner' Historically Considered," *HUCA* 3 (1926) 1.

to follow certain religious observances (cf. Exod.20.10; 23.12; Num.15.13-16).[12] It is clear that *GERIM*, while being foreigners, enjoyed a special relationship with Israel. They were incorporated in some way into her life and worship.

Proselutos renders *GER* seventy-seven times in the LXX. *Paroikos* renders *GER* eleven times. Yet a consistent distinction exists between these two terms in the LXX. When *Paroikos* renders *GER*, it refers to an Israelite, or Israel herself as the 'alien' or 'sojourner'(cf. Gen. 15.13; I Chron. 29.15; Ps. 39.12). When Proselutos renders *GER*, it refers to a non-Israelite as the 'alien' or 'foreigner' (cf. Deut. 10.18; 26.13; Mal. 3.5).[13]

Since in the LXX *Proselutos* stands for the resident alien of the Hebrew scriptures, there is no reason to understand it as a technical term referring to a convert to Judaism. Rather, in the LXX it consistently refers to a non-Israelite who is in some way involved in the Jewish community and sympathetic to Jewish religious worship and practice.

Philo confirms this understanding of *Proselutos* in his description of *GERIM* in Exod. 22.20ff.; 23.9.[14] As Feldman pointed out, if the more technical meaning of *Proselutos* was widely in vogue at this time, Philo has used it in an erroneous and confused manner.[15] Wolfson writes that the use of this term by Philo "reflects the actual existence at his time of a class of Gentiles who, while uncircumcised, had renounced idolatry and otherwise led a virtuous life.[16] Philo uses *Proselutos* here in the same manner as the LXX to translate *GER*. These are the resident aliens, friendly or allied with Jews, but in no technical sense are they converts to Judaism.[17]

In later rabbinic literature the term GER takes on the more technical meaning of a full convert to Judaism (cf. e.g. *Mekhilta Mishpatim 18; Sifre Deut. 307; b. Shabbat 31A)*. Here *GER* is usually rendered 'proselyte', which accounts for the confusion of this term in both the LXX and Acts. It has been the mistaken assumption of many commentators, despite Lake's warning, to read this later rabbinic meaning into the term *Proselutos* in Acts.

With the exception of Mt. 23.15, Acts is the only New Testament document to use the term *Proselutos*. A close examination of these passages in

---

12 Kuhn, *"PROSELUTOS,"* TDNT, VI (1968) 727-44.

13 The four exceptions to this noted by Allen do not conflict in this regard. See W.C. Allen, "On the Meaning of *Proselutos* in the LXX," *The Expositor* 4 (1894) 269.

14 Philo, Virt., 102-103; *Quaestiones in Exodum* 2.2. See R.D. Hecht, "Scripture and Commentary in Philo, " *SBL Seminar Papers*, 1981, 146-47.

15 Feldman, "Sympathizers," 205-6.

16 H. Wolfson, *Philo*, (Cambridge: Harvard, 1948) II, 372-73.

17 S. Belkin, *Philo and the Oral Law*, (Cambridge: Harvard, 1948) 47-8.

Acts reveals that Luke employs the term with the same general meaning that one finds in the LXX and Philo. Acts 2.10 and 13.43 mention *Proselutoi* together with *Ioudaioi*. Though together, each forms a distinct group. If one were to understand *Proselutoi* here in the technical sense of a convert to Judaism, Luke would be speaking nonsense, because, according to this meaning, 'proselytes' are Jews.[18] But Luke does not employ the term in this technical manner in any one of the passages. In Acts *Proselutoi* are Gentiles closely allied with the synagogue and the Jewish people, yet are a group distinct from the *Ioudaioi*.

That Luke's usage of *Proselutos* corresponds with that of the LXX and Philo is not at all surprising. One would assume Luke to be aware of this meaning of the term, given his extensive use and familiarity with the LXX.[19] Further, *Proselutoi* in Acts emerge as a group strikingly similar to the *phoboumenoi/sebomenoi ton theon* as they have been classically understood. In other words, the *Proselutoi* in Acts are distinct from the *Ioudaioi*, yet closely related to the synagogue and the Jewish community.[20]

By contrast, *Proselutos* in Mt.23.15 seems to carry the more technical meaning as understood in later rabbinic literature: "Woe to you, scribes and Pharisees, hypocrites, because you travel about on sea and land to make one *Proseluton*; and when he becomes one you make him twice the son of Gehenna as yourselves." Therefore, it would appear that there were at least two different understandings of the term *Proselutos* operative at the time of Luke and Matthew. One meaning, as reflected in Matthew, resembles the more technical reference to a convert to Judaism. The other meaning has its roots in the LXX and refers to a non-Israelite who is sympathetic to Jewish beliefs and is involved in the life of the Jewish community. This meaning is reflected in Luke's use of the term.

A second neglected feature is the use of the phrase *oi phoboumenoi* in the LXX. There are at least five instances where such a group appears in the LXX (II Chron.5.6; Pss.115.9-11; 118.2-4; 135.19-20; Mal.3.16). In the Psalms and Malachi this group is *oi phoboumenoi ton kurion*, a title with obvious parallels with the God-fearers of Acts. In the Psalms they are mentioned together

---

18 Rather than reevaluating their understanding of this term, some scholars have accused Luke of misunderstanding this term. See Haenchen, *Acts of the Apostles*, (Philadelphia: Westminster, 1971, 413.

19 Concerning Luke's use of the LXX, see H. Cadbury, *The Style and Literary Method of Luke*, (Cambridge: Harvard, 1920), and C.H. Dodd, "The Fall of Jerusalem and the 'Abomination of Desolation'," *JRS* 37 (1947) 47-54.

20 The parallel between the God-fearers and the *Proselutoi* is further highlighted in Acts 13.43, where the *Proselutoi* are described as *sebomenon Proseluton*.

with the house of Israel, and the house of Aaron, the house of Levi, and "those who fear the Lord."

In Malachi these 'Lord-fearers' are distinguished from those Israelites who do not serve God but "test God." The *phoboumenoi tov kurion* refers to a group that remains faithful to the God of Israel and "esteem his name." These 'Lord-fearers' are "the righteous," and the ones "who serve God."

In II Chron. *ton kurion* is absent. The group is simply *oi phoboumenoi*. The passage is significant for two reasons. First, this group does not appear in the Hebrew text. We find them only in the LXX. Second, the group appears to be distinct from the Israelites. The phrase in 5.6 reads, "*pasa synagoge Israel kai oi phoboumenoi.*" A second group was added to the assembly formerly described as "the synagogue of Israel," by the LXX translators; that is the *oi phoboumenoi*.

Unfortunately the evidence is too limited to know the precise identity of the *oi phoboumenoi ton kurion* in the LXX. However, two observations can be made. First, Kraabel's statement that "we would not know the term 'God-fearer' were it not for Acts," is not entirely correct.[21] *Oi phoboumenoi ton kurion* is essentially the same as *oi phoboumenoi ton theon* in Acts. Since for Luke and his audience *kurios* referred specifically to Jesus, the writer would have needed to select a word that meant 'God' for his audience when borrowing this phrase from the LXX. *Kurios* meant for the LXX what *theos* meant for Luke.

Second, the phrase 'God-fearer' would be familiar to the person, like Luke, steeped in the LXX. One cannot say that Luke necessarily understood the *oi phoboumenoi ton kurion* of the LXX to refer specifically to a group distinct from, yet allied with the synagogue. But in light of the passages noted above this conclusion is certainly plausible. What is clear is that Luke took over from his tradition a term to describe a group of Gentiles in Acts who were associated with the synagogue and sympathetic to Jewish life and religious expression.

Finally, recent discussions concerning the God-fearers have tended to focus too narrowly on the phrase *oi phoboumenoi/sebomenoi ton theon*. This is particularly true in Kraabel's article where he is concerned simply with the terms *phoboumenoi* or *sebomenoi* in his study of more than 100 synagogue inscriptions. The specific name or title of a group of Gentile 'sympathizers' is far less important than the question concerning the evidence from this period which might indicate that Jewish communities of the diaspora had included such a group of Gentiles in their life and worship.

Literature from the period in which Acts was written suggests the involvement of non-Jews in the life and worship of the Jewish community. For exam-

---

21 "Disappearance," 118.

ple, Josephus mentions Greeks who respect and emulate the religion of the Jews.[22] Speaking of the Jews of Antioch he writes: "They were constantly attracting to their religious ceremonies multitudes of Greeks, and these they had in some measure incorporated with themselves."[23] Collins notes correctly that this report accords well with the book of Acts and Paul's encounter in the synagogue with the God-fearers.[24]

Juvenal's *Satire* 14, c.130, tells of those who have 'sabbath-fearing' fathers who revere certain Jewish customs. Their sons fully embrace the Jewish religion. They abstain from pork, follow the law of Moses and "get themselves circumcised."[25] This seems to assume a situation familiar to Juvenal and his readers.

Kraabel's own work on Judaism in western Asia Minor reveals that some of the Jewish communities of the diaspora were closely related to the predominantly Gentile environment around them. The Jews of Sardis, for example, were part of the economic and social life of that city and seemed to have influenced religious practices there. Sardis, Kraabel suggests, was a logical place for Jewish missionary activity, given the age and status of that Jewish community.[26] Acmonea emerges in Kraabel's study as a Jewish community closely related to the Gentile community around it. The patroness of the synagogue was Julia Severa, a Gentile benefactor of whom Kraabel writes, "She was probably a Gentile sympathizer like her contemporary Poppaea, the mistress of Nero; she is proof of the attractiveness of Acmonian Judaism to Gentiles in the first century."[27] Both Acmonea and Sardis provide evidence for the involvement of sympathetic Gentiles in the life and worship of the Jewish communities of the late first and early second century.

The account from Juvenal, the passages from Josephus and Kraabel's own description of the Jewish communities of Sardis and Acmonea concur in one respect. All indicate the presence of Gentile sympathizers or adherents in the synagogues and communities of late first and early second century diaspora Judaism.

The aim of this essay has been to question the thesis of Kraabel's paper that we lack convincing proof from the Roman diaspora for the existence of

---

22 *C.Ap.* 2.282.39.

23 *B.J.* 7.3.3

24 J.J. Collins, *Between Athens and Jerusalem: Jewish Identity in the Hellensitic Diaspora*, (New York: Crossroads, 1983) 163.

25 Juvenal, *The Sixteen Satires* (ET and introduction by Peter Green; London, 1967) 266.

26 A.T. Kraabel, *Judaism in Western Asia Minor under the Roman Empire*, (Th.D. Dissertation, Harvard University, 1968) 201ff., 242.

27 Ibid., 78. Acmonea is of particular interest because of the late first century date Kraabel assigns it.

a class of Gentiles associated with the synagogue and sympathetic to Jewish beliefs.[28] The term *Proselutos*, properly understood, in the both the LXX and Acts represents just such a class of people. The *Proselutos* of the LXX and Acts was a Gentile related to the synagogue and viewed as sympathetic to the beliefs and practices of the Jewish religion. The rich background of this term in the Hebrew scriptures (*GERIM*), and the numerous references to such a class in the LXX, demonstrate that the *Proselutoi* were not a rare breed, but formed a class of considerable size. Just such a group is represented in Acts.

We have seen that the literature from this period also supports the same phenomenon. Philo, Josephus and Juvenal all report the attraction of the Jewish religion to both Greeks and Romans. These Gentiles were apparently drawn to Judaism in significant numbers and on occasion, according to Juvenal, fully participated in Jewish worship and practice.

Kraabel's own account of the Jewish communities of Sardis and Acmonea is consistent with this picture in that these communities attracted Gentiles to their religion. Kraabel identifies the benefactor in Acmonea, Julia Severa, as a 'gentile sympathizer' and proof of the attraction of Judaism in this area to some Gentiles.

Since we have found ample evidence for the existence of such a class of Gentiles associated with the synagogues of the diaspora, the absence of the particular phrase *oi phoboumenoi/sebomenoi ton theon* in synagogue inscriptions poses no real problem.[29] Luke may well have taken this term, or one approximating it, in the LXX and used it to describe a class of Gentiles regularly found in and around the synagogue. Indeed, Luke may have understood *oi phoboumenoi ton kurion* as a group similar in piety and composition to the oi phoboumenoi ton theon.

The recognition of such a class of Gentile 'God-fearers' or sympathizers is important for the reconstruction of late first century Judaism and Christianity because this group illustrates the grey area that existed between Jew and Gentile in this period. The presence of such a group of Gentiles in the life of the synagogue indicates that the boundary between these two groups was vague.[30] Luke may be writing 'theological history',[31] but there is no reason to assume he has manufactured the picture of the synagogues and their sur-

---

28 "Disappearance," 121.

29 The discovery of the inscription under the heading *Theosebes* at Aphrodisias, however, bears upon this discussion. See Gager, "Jews, Gentiles, and synagogues in the Book of Acts," M.J. Mellink, "Archaeology in Asia Minor," *AJA* 81 (1977) 306, and J. Reynolds and R. Tannenbaum, *Jews and Godfearers at Aphrodisias*, Cambridge Philological Society Supplementary Series 12, (Cambridge: Cambridge University, 1987).

30 J.J. Collins, *Between Athens and Jerusalem*, 245.

31 Kraabel, "Greeks, Jews, and Lutherans in the Middle Half of Acts," 149.

rounding communities in Acts. On the contrary, in light of this evidence there is every reason to assume the presence of a class of Gentiles associated with the synagogue is an authentic reflection of the diverse composition of diaspora Judaism in the late first century.

Christians and Jews in Colossians

Daniel J. Harrington, S.J.

Tom Kraabel's research on the archaeological and epigraphical evidence for synagogues in the Diaspora has sharpened the way we look at Judaism in the first century. Kraabel has taught us to be sensitive to the local character of Diaspora Judaisms and the varieties of Judaisms in various places. He has emphasized the importance of the synagogue in the cultural, political, educational, and religious life of Jews in the Greco-Roman world. He has shown that Diaspora Jews lived in full and open contact with their Gentile neighbors, not in ghettoes cut off from others. He has also warned us against easy appeals to "syncretism" by insisting on the integrity of the Judaisms promoted in Diaspora synagogues, however strange they might seem to those who see through rabbinic spectacles.

This paper tests out and develops some of Kraabel's ideas with reference to the letter to the Colossians. It takes its starting point from Kraabel's article entitled "Impact of the Discovery of the Sardis Synagogue."[1] The Sardis synagogue, of course, is the linchpin of his research on the Diaspora synagogues. In his presentation Kraabel remarks: "The New Testament contains letters written to Christian groups in Ephesus and Colossae, both on the Roman highway which runs south of Sardis..."[2] Shortly thereafter he describes the conflict in early Christian circles regarding the "Judaizers": "apparently Jewish or Jewish-Christian practices were brought to the attention of some Anatolian Gentiles when they became Christians, and they adopted them to the dismay of the Christian leadership."[3]

The letter to the Colossians addressed Gentile Christians in western Asia Minor. It warned these Gentile Christians against the attractions of a form of Judaism, one that may seem exotic to us but may well have been the "normal" Judaism of the Colossians. In warning these Gentile Christians the author used the language of the Hellenistic synagogue. He knew and used that language preemptively in order to suggest that the Christian community offered everything (and more) that the synagogue did.

The Origin of Colossians

In covering a story reporters are trained to ask basic questions: Who? When? Where? What? Why? How? The first three questions pertain to the

---

1 See G.M.A. Hanfmann, *Sardis from Prehistoric to Roman Times: Results of the Archaeological Exploration of Sardis 1958-1975* (Cambridge, MA: Harvard University Press, 1983) 178-90, 284-85.

2 Kraabel, "Impact...," 186.

3 Ibid., 186.

origin of the letter to the Colossians. The last three will be taken up in the remaining sections.

Who is speaking to whom? That the addressees were Gentile Christians is clear from several passages. According to Col 1:21 they "once were estranged and hostile in mind, doing evil deeds." These terms describe the addressees' former condition apart from Christ and function as part of the "once/then" and "now" pattern common in the New Testament (Rom 6:17-22; 7:5-6; 11:30; Gal 4:8-9; Eph 2:1-22; 1 Pet 1:14-25; 2:10).[4] In Col 1:26-27 the "mystery hidden for ages and generations" is defined as the preaching of the good news of Jesus the Messiah among the Gentiles. The goal of this proclamation is that every person might be presented as "perfect" (teleios) in Christ (1:28). In calling Paul to be apostle to the Gentiles (1:25) God has revealed the "mystery" as "Christ among you (Gentiles)" (1:27). The Gentile origin of the addressees is underlined by another use of the "once/then" and "now" pattern in Col 2:13: "you who were dead in trespasses and the uncircumcision of your flesh, God made alive together with him [Christ]."

If we can put any stock in the concluding messages and greetings in Col 4:7-18, these Gentile Christians experienced church membership along the lines laid down in the letter to Philemon. They gathered for meetings and worship at the homes of those members with houses large enough to accommodate them (see Rom 16:5; 1 Cor 16:9; Phlm 1:2; Col 4:15). But the Christians at Colossae seem also to have been an open sect; they sought to bring "outsiders" around to their viewpoint. In 4:5-6 ("conduct yourselves wisely toward outsiders") they are urged to have contact with non-Christians and to carry out their encounters in a gracious, witty or charming ("seasoned with salt"), and sensitive manner. There is no indication that these Gentile Christians knew much about Judaism before becoming Christians. There is no debate about the proper interpretation of biblical texts. As the second part of this paper will show, it appears that they had come to know about Judaism after their conversion to Christianity and were attracted to it.

The other part of the "Who?" question is the author. The letter purports to be written by Paul and Timothy (1:1). Though part of the Pauline corpus from earliest times, the Pauline authorship of Colossians is rendered doubtful by its language and style as well as its theology (Christ as "head" of the body, the presence of salvation, the universal church, etc.).[5] Nevertheless, the situation presupposed by the letter seems real, not fictive. Thus an admirer or student of Paul has used the form and authority of the Pauline letter to

---

4 P. Tachau, "Einst" und "Jetzt" in Neuen Testament (FRLANT 105; Göttingen: Vandenhoeck & Ruprecht, 1972).

5 For a full discussion, see E. Lohse, Colossians and Philemon (Hermeneia; Philadelphia: Fortress, 1971) 84-91 (on language and style), 177-83 (on theology).

address an issue that had developed in a community founded as part of the Pauline mission (through Epaphras, see 1:7; 4:12-13), though not by Paul himself.

The questions about "When?" and "Where?" are related closely to the authorship of the letter. It has become a commonplace in NT studies to express the question of date and place in the following way: If by Paul, as late as possible; if by another, as early as possible. If Colossians was composed by Paul, it could be placed with Philemon and assigned to Paul's imprisonment at Caesarea Maritima or Rome shortly before his death. An earlier imprisonment at Ephesus is not out of the question. If it was composed by an admirer of Paul, then Ephesus as a center of the Pauline mission or Rome are the most likely places.[6]

The letter purports to be written to Christians at Colossae, a city in western Asia Minor located in the upper Lycus River Valley, about 110 miles east of Ephesus. Colossae lay ten miles east of Laodicea and twelve miles southeast of Hierapolis. A large Jewish population lived in the area according to Cicero in Pro Flacco 68. According to Tacitus in Annales 14.27 the area was hit by an earthquake in A.D. 60-61, though it is not clear to what extent Colossae was struck by this earthquake. Lindemann[7] argues that the community actually addressed was the church at Laodicea about A.D. 70-80. His argument is based on the letter's many references to Laodicea (Col 2:1; 4:13, 15-16), the personal data in 4:7-17, historical information about Colossae and Laodicea, and the description of the Laodicean church in Rev 3:14-22. But the general geographical area and the reality of the situation are not questioned by this alternative hypothesis.

The approach to Colossians adopted by most critical scholars is summarized neatly by Meeks: "Whoever the author, the situation is real. There is no reason to doubt the address to Colossae, with attention to other congregations in the Lycus Valley cities (4:13, 15f), nor the actuality of the specific conflict that occasioned the letter."[8]

Who? An admirer or student of Paul speaks to Gentile Christians. When? Probably after Paul's death, around A.D. 70-80. Where? From Ephesus or Rome to the church at Colossae in particular and probably also to the other churches in the Lycus Valley.

---

6   E. Schweizer, *The Letter to The Colossians* (Minneapolis; Augsburg, 1982) solves the problem by attributing authorship to Timothy.

7   A. Lindemann, "Die Gemeinde von 'Kolossä.' Erwägungen zum 'Sitz im Leben' eines pseudopaulinischen Briefes," *Wort und Dienst* 16 (1981) 111-34.

8   W.A. Meeks, *The First Urban Christians: The Social World of the Apostle Paul* (New Haven—London: Yale University Press, 1983) 125-26.

The Warning (Col 2:6-23)

What the problem addressed by the letter was and why it was a problem become clear especially in Col 2:6-23. When I say "become clear," I do not pretend that no questions remain. Indeed, the nature of the so-called Colossian heresy is among the most controversial issues in biblical scholarship.[9] But reading Colossians in its historical setting can help make some things clearer and at the same time contribute to our knowledge of Christian-Jewish relations in Western Asia minor.

The warning against the false "philosophy" can be divided in two parts (2:6-15; 2:16-23). The warning begins (2:6-7) by reminding the Colossians that the gospel they received ("Christ Jesus is Lord") demands an appropriate response by way of action ("in him walk"). The warning proper (2:8) calls the "philosophy" a vain delusion built on human tradition and the "elements of the world." The reason why this philosophy can be ignored safely is that genuine "fullness" can be found only in Christ (2:9-10). The genuine circumcision is baptism into Christ's death and resurrection (2:11-12), which the Colossians have experienced as a coming to life out of death in sin (2:13a). The argument is sealed by an appeal to a fragment of an early Christian hymn (2:13b-15), which explains what has happened to these Gentile Christians through the death of Christ.

The first section of the second part (2:16-19) features two warnings: "Therefore let no one judge you" (2:16); "Let no one disqualify you" (2:18). The first warning characterizes the food laws and festivals as mere "shadow" in comparison with Christ as the substance (2:17). The second warning criticizes fasting and angels' worship as puffery precisely because they ignore Christ the head from whom all divine growth comes (2:18b-19). The second section (2:20-23) appeals to baptism as death with Christ (2:20) and uses it as the ground for refusing to submit to human regulations about perishable things (2:20b-22) that lead only to indulgence of the flesh (2:23) despite the claims made for them.

We learn about the "philosophy" menacing the Colossian Christians only indirectly, by means of the letter's refutation of it. What is most obvious are the elements that pertain to Judaism: circumcision (2:11), observance of Sabbaths and other festivals (2:16), and ritual purity regarding food (2:16, 20-22).

In 2:11 there is a contrast between physical/human circumcision and spiritual/divine circumcision ("without hands"), which is identified with baptism in 2:12. Whereas physical circumcision strips away merely the prepuce of the

---

9 F.O. Francis and W.A. Meeks (eds.), *Conflict at Colossae: A Problem in the Interpretation of Early Christianity Illustrated by Selected Modern Studies* (SBLSBS 4; Missoula: Scholars, 1974).

male, spiritual circumcision in Christ (baptism) removes that aspect of the person ("the flesh") that is hostile and opposed to God.

The list of holydays in Col 2:16 ("a festival or a new moon or a Sabbath") appears also in the Septuagint (1 Chr 23:31; 2 Chr 2:3; 31:3; Ezek 45:17; Hos 2:13) and indicates a clear connection with Judaism. Given the context of the warning about letting others pass judgment concerning "food or drink" (2:16) alongside this clearly Jewish list, there is likely here a reference to Jewish ritual purity regulations pertaining to foods and vessels. This impression is strengthened by the apodictic statements in Col 2:21: "Do not handle, Do not taste, Do not touch." The parenthetical comment in 2:22 ("according to human precepts and doctrines") alludes to Isa 29:13, a text used in Mark 7:7 and Matt 15:9 in connection with Jesus' attitude toward the food laws and ritual purity.

So what is clearest about the "philosophy" are the Jewish elements. The work of Kraabel and other scholars caution against speaking too quickly about syncretism; indeed, most of the other elements can be fitted within a form of Judaism. The term "philosophy" (2:8) had a wide scope in antiquity and could include Judaism, as many Jewish texts show (see 4 Macc 5:11; Josephus' *War* 2:119 and Ant. 18:11; Philo's Legatio and Gaium 156 and De mutatione nominum 223). The "elements" (stoicheia) of the world (2:8, 20) were most likely the basic building blocks of creation: earth, air, water, and fire. Interpretations of the stoicheia as mythic beings or demons go beyond the text of Colossians. The term tapeinophrosyne in 2:18, 23 may be translated "self-abasement." But it can just as well be taken as the Greek rendering of the Hebrew term *ta anit* which can mean both "affliction" and "fasting." Fasting was frequently part of the preparation for receiving visions; this fits with what follows in 2:18 about "angels' worship." The idea of *threskeia ton angelon* is that of entering by vision the sphere where the angels worship God, not making angels the object of worship.

The chief objection to identifying the Colossian "philosophy" with the Judaism current in western Asia Minor is the absence of a polemic in Colossians against the Torah. One can answer that the criticisms of the regulations in 2:16, 21 constitute such an attack, at least on certain interpretations ("human precepts and doctrines," see 2:22). Perhaps the author did not want to go as far as Paul did in Galatians and Romans in his comments on the Torah's inability to bring about right relationship with God. And the somewhat obscure reference to "legal demands" in 2:14 may allude to the Torah.

So what is clearest about the "philosophy" at Colossae are its Jewish elements: circumcision, Sabbaths and other festivals, and ritual purity regulations about food. These elements were precisely what set Jews apart in the ancient world and were the target of Paul's criticisms against those who sought to impose Judaism on Gentile Christians.[10] This being so, a careful analysis of the remaining features indicates that practically everything can be understood within the framework of Judaism.

As noted previously, there was a large Jewish population in southwestern Asia Minor—the general area comprising both Ephesus and Colossae, Hierapolis, and Laodicea. There Judaism may well have developed and carried on in relative independence from Palestinian Judaism. According to L.H. Feldman,[11] Judaism was attractive to non-Jews in southwestern Asia Minor for various reasons: Judaism's reputation for wisdom and high ethical standards, the attractiveness of the Jewish synagogue services, the festivity associated with Sabbaths and holydays, and the esoteric knowledge (healing, magic, astrology, etc.) ascribed to Jews.

Did the Gentile Christians addressed in Colossians have a thorough knowledge of Judaism before they became Christians? In other words, were they "God-fearers?" Though Kraabel has not made the "God-fearers" disappear from modern scholarship,[12] he has introduced a healthy caution into the use of that term. In fact, nothing in Colossians indicates that these Gentiles had been frequenting the synagogue and learning the Scriptures before they became Christians.

The more likely scenario was that the addressees first accepted the gospel and then learned about the Judaism from which it derived. Since it is assumed that these Christians were open to dialogue with outsiders (see 4:5-6), it is natural that they would meet up with Jews and be challenged by them to go all the way into Judaism after their initial exposure to Christianity. Their desire to learn more about Judaism and to have fuller contacts with the synagogue may well have alarmed their Christian teachers of the Pauline gospel. There is no need to talk about a Jewish "mission" to Christians or a Christian "mission" to Jews. What happened came about through the informal contacts made among people of a fairly cosmopolitan city.

The Pauline response was "Christ alone." Christ is not only sufficient to bring Gentiles into right relationship with God, but he also renders any other way unnecessary. In him the fullness of divinity resides (2:9), and through him the Colossians have been filled (2:10). Baptism is the better circumcision willed by God (2:11), for in baptism "you were also raised with him" (2:12). Those who insist on Jewish holydays and ritual purity are mistaken because they are "not holding fast to the head" (2:19), who is Christ, and therefore remain "in the flesh" (2:23). Their festivals and food laws are human com-

---

10 J.D.G. Dunn, "The New Perspective on Paul," *BJRULM* 65 (1983) 95-122.

11 "Proselytes and 'Sympathizers' in the Light of the New Inscriptions from Aphrodisias," *REJ* 148 (1989) 265-305.

12 "The Disappearance of the 'God-Fearers,'" *Numen* 28 (1981) 113-26.

mands and teachings (2:22)—at best "a shadow of what is to come" (2:17), at worst "indulgence of the flesh" (2:23).

Why Colossian Judaism was perceived to be a problem was that it was attracting Pauline Christians into what it probably presented as a fuller form of Judaism. Indeed, the term "fullness" (pleroma) may have been part of its appeal. To the Pauline Christian who wrote the letter to the Colossians this was a dangerous development. He responded by putting forward Christ as the Wisdom of God (1:15-20) and insisted that apart from Christ the head Gentiles cannot find the fullness of salvation.

What was the problem? It was the attractiveness of Judaism to Gentile Christians at Colossae. Why was this a problem? Because it threatened the basic principle of the Pauline gospel: "Here there cannot be Greek and Jew, circumcised and uncircumcised...but Christ is all, and in all" (3:11).

The Use of "Qumran" Language

How the Pauline author responded to this problem is interesting in its own right. He used the conventions of the Pauline letter and the persona of Paul himself. He used part of an early Christian hymn about Christ as the Wisdom of God (1:15-20), which may have been the adaptation of a Jewish original. He used the language of early Christian paraenesis, including the so-called household code (3:18-4:1), derived from Hellenistic philosophy, specially Stoicism. But a particularly interesting feature of the author's response was his use of what some might call "Qumran language." As Lohse noted, "a list of noteworthy parallels to the vocabulary and style of the Qumran texts can be uncovered in Colossians."[13] Indeed, long before the discovery of the Qumran scrolls J. B. Lightfoot wrote about the "Essene" character of the opponents in Colossians.[14]

A full catalogue of parallels is far beyond the scope of this article.[15] But a few examples from the Qumran Manual of Discipline will at least indicate the shape of the phenomenon. The keywords in Col 1:9-11 ("knowledge...wisdom...understanding...walk worthily...all good pleasure...his glorious might") are prominent not only throughout Manual of Discipline but also in War Scroll, Thanksgiving Hymns, and Damascus Document. The idea of two spheres or "lots"—light and darkness—underlying Col 1:12-14 is spelled out in the "Instruction on the Two Spirits" in Manual of Discipline 3-4: Christ has delivered us

---

13 E. Lohse, *Colossians and Philemon*, 181.

14 *St. Paul's Epistles to the Colossians and to Philemon* (London: Macmillan, 1875).

15 See Lohse, *Colossians and Philemon*. See also N. Kehl, "Erniedrigung und Erhöhung in Qumran und Kolossä," *ZKT* 91 (1969) 364-94; M.P. Horgan, "Colossians," in *New Jerome Biblical Commentary* (Englewood Cliffs: Prentice-Hall, 1990) 876-82.

from the dominion of darkness and transferred us to the kingdom of light. Just as the Qumran community referred to its own members as "near" to God (1QS 6:16; 19, 22; 7:21; 8:18; 11:13), so Col 1:21-23 describes the former lives of the Gentile Christians as "estranged and hostile" and implies that now they are near to God through Christ. The catalogues of vices to be avoided (Col 3:5-11) and virtues to be pursued (3:12-17) parallel the lists in 1QS 4:9-11 and 4:3-6, respectively.

What are we to make of the fact that in warning Gentile Christians against the attractions of Judaism the author uses so much "Qumran" language? Theories of direct dependence—that the author had been an Essene, or that the recipients had been Essenes, or that the opponents were Essenes —are unlikely. It is more likely that in the Qumran scrolls and Colossians we have the Hebrew and Greek versions of a theological language that had developed among first-century Jews and was adapted by early Christians. The phenomenon of "Qumran" language suggests some contact between Palestinian Judaism and Diaspora Judaism. As Lohse put it, "the Hellenistic synagogue could represent the connecting link both for the adoption of certain ideas...and for the influence that is visible in comparable features of language and style."[16]

Thus the Pauline author may have been using some of the language used by Jews in Colossae. Some of it can be attributed to a preemptive use of the opponents' vocabulary of Christians through Paul and his contemporaries. Its prominence in Colossians suggests that the Gentile Christians have little new to gain by continuing in their infatuation with Judaism.

Conclusion

This reading of Colossians in light of archaeological and epigraphical research on Diaspora synagogues neither proves nor disproves Tom Kraabel's theories. It does, however, add to the plausibility of those theories and illumine our reading of Colossians. What is striking is the nice fit between Colossians and the archaeological and epigraphical evidence.

When Colossians is read against the background of Kraabel's theories, it emerges as a warning by a Pauline author to Gentile Christians against the attractions of the local version of Judaism. To those accustomed to looking at Judaism through Palestinian and/or rabbinic spectacles, that Judaism seems somewhat strange and even exotic. The Jewish community at Colossae appears to have been in contact with Gentile Christians. Some of its religious vocabulary shows contacts with Palestinian Judaism, though there is no evidence for authoritative direction from Palestine. Kraabel's research warns us against too

---

16 Lohse, *Colossians and Philemon*, 181.

quickly characterizing this Judaism as "syncretistic" or assuming that the Gentile Christians had been "God-fearers" and knew Judaism well before they became Christians.

This reading of Colossians also offers a neat snapshot of Christianity in the Lycus Valley ca. A.D. 70-80. The Pauline mission succeeded in attracting Gentiles to Christianity. Some Gentile Christians in turn became infatuated with the local form of Judaism. The Pauline writer sought to break that infatuation by arguing that "fullness" resides in Christ, for to him "Christ is all, and in all" (3:11).

Oikoumene and the Limits of Pluralism in Alexandrian Judaism and Paul[1]

Calvin J. Roetzel

Once in a blue moon an essay appears that reshapes the discipline and permanently alters the way we think about Judaism in the ancient world. Such an essay by Nils Dahl showed how the convenient universalistic-particularistic dichotomy used to distinguish late Judaism from early Christianity was false.[2] Dahl showed first century Judaism to be more universalistic than usually allowed and early Christianity to be more particularistic than normally recognized. While Dahl's position has become a scholarly consensus, more work is needed on the tensions between universalistic and particularistic tendencies in Diaspora Judaism and their possible influence on Paul. While Paul did not borrow directly from the Alexandrian community, that community provides a useful model, nevertheless, for understanding how Diaspora Jews balanced loyalty to the Jewish Torah, the temple and the land with attraction to the Hellenistic culture. By sampling literature from that community this discussion will deal with the tension between accommodation to and rejection of the Hellenistic culture within Alexandrian Jewry. We shall see how the community turned the symbols and rhetoric of the dominant culture to its own defense, and how the community embraced ecumenical tendencies while guarding its own particularity. By studying the ways the Diaspora community appropriated the Hellenistic vision of *oikoumene* to lay claim to their status as God's elect we may better understand how a Diaspora Jew like Paul could combine a universalistic gentile mission with an appeal to a rather narrow slice of Jewish tradition.[3] An important assumption of this essay is that pluralism affects the way a community interprets its texts, and those texts then provide a lens through which the pluralistic setting is viewed. A clear grasp of this hermeneutical loop should give us a better understanding of the way Paul employed texts to develop a protocol for engaging the Hellenistic world.

The LXX

A primary force shaping both the outlook of Paul and that of Alexandrian Judaism was the Septuagint. It provided the language, many of the models and most of the sacred texts for Jewish writers from the third century to the first.

---

1 I am grateful to the Trial Balloon Society for its critique of this paper, and I am proud to contribute to a volume honoring A.T. Kraabel, one of the charter members of the Trial Balloon Society, whose scholarship on Diaspora Judaism has placed biblical scholarship in his debt.

2 Nils Dahl, "The One God of Jews and Gentiles (Romans 3:29-30)," in his *Studies in Paul, Theology for the Early Christian Mission* (Minneapolis: Augsburg, 1977), pp. 178-191.

3 This essay is a response to the work of David Tracy, *Plurality and Ambiguity*, (San Francisco: Harper & Row, 1987), and the recent concerns of Martin Marty.

Legends formed supporting its authoritative claim (e.g. The Letter of Aristeas).[4] Festivals arose celebrating its genesis and reinforcing its religious value. A vast body of commentary grew up linking it to the changing circumstances of the Jewish community in the Greco-Roman world. Aside from the works of figures like Artapanus, Aristobulus, and Pseudo-Aristeas, most of the voluminous works of Philo either served as commentary on the LXX or appealed to it in the development of its argument.[5] These works show that among the vehicles of revelation Philo assigned the preeminent place to the Septuagint.[6]

More than a text generating interpretation, however, the text itself WAS the interpretation. Coming from different periods from many hands and written in the Hellenistic vernacular of the day,[7] the Septuagint was devoted to

---

4 The LXX hardly received universal endorsement as the defense of its accuracy and authority by both Pseudo-Aristeas and Philo shows. Some shadow was cast on the Septuagint by Jesus ben Sirach (ca 132 b.c.e.) for "what was originally expressed in Hebrew does not have exactly the same sense when translated into another language." Emil Schürer, *The History of the Jewish People of the Age of Jesus Christ*, revised and edited by Geza Vermes, Fergus Millar, and Martin Goodman (Edinburgh: T.& T. Clark, 1986), p. 477.

5 Works not serving as direct commentary on the LXX are Quod Omnis Probus Liber sit, De Vita Contemplativa, De Aeternitate Mundi, In Flaccum, Hypothetica, De Providentia, and De Legatione ad Gaium. Volumes I-VIII of the Loeb series all serve as commentary on the Pentateuch of the LXX.

6 A substantial bibliography of secondary literature on the Septuagint is available. For a survey of the literature see: E. Tob, "Die griechischen Bibelübersetzung," ANRW 20.1, pp. 121-189, and his "Jewish Greek Scriptures," in *Early Judaism and Its Modern Interpreters*, eds. Robert A. Kraft and George W.E. Nickelsburg (Philadelphia: Fortress and Atlanta: Scholars Press, 1986), pp. 223-237. See also S.P. Brock, C.T. Fritsch, S. Jellicoe, eds. A *Classified Bibliography of the Septuagint* (Leiden: Brill, 1973); D.W. Gooding, "A Sketch of Current Septuagint Studies," in *Proceedings of the Irish Biblical Associations* 5(1981), 1-13 offers a good survey of the issues. For current literature see *Elenchus. Die International Zeitschrift für Bibelwissenschaft* and the *Bulletin of the International Organization for Septuagint and Cognate Studies*. See also the Congress volume in *Supplements to Vetus Testament*, ed. J.A. Emerton, LX (Leiden: Brill, 1988) and Klaus Berger, *Die Gesetzauslegung Jesu, Ihr historischer Hintergrund im Judentum und im Alten Testament*. Teil I: *Markus und Parallelen* (Neukirchen-Vluyn: Neukirchener Verlag, 1972), esp. pp. 100-136; 137-147 and 258-277. Also of value are Peter Katz, *Philo's Bible, The Aberrant Text of Bible Quotations in Some Philonic Writings* (Cambridge, 1950) and Sidney Jellicoe, *The Septuagint and Modern Study* (Oxford: Oxford University Press, 1968). More recently we have Schürer, revised and edited, *The History of the Jewish People in the Age of Jesus Christ*, III.1, pp. 474-493. Marguerite Harl, et al *La Bible Grecque des Septante, du Judaisme Hellenistique au Christianisme Ancien* (Cerf: Editions du Cerf, 1988).

7 J.A.L. Lee, *A Lexical Study of the Septuagint Version of the Pentateuch* (Chico: Scholars Press, 1983) has proven that the Greek of the Septuagint was the Greek of the time. The peculiarities found there were caused by the translation process. This same view is shared by Marguerite Harl ed., *La Bible d'Alexandrie. La Genese* (Paris: Editions du Cerf, 1986), who argues

(continued...)

the exegesis of the "Old Testament" text as well as to its preservation in Greek.[8] While Georg Bertram noticed this tendency as early as 1936, no systematic study yet exists of the theological tendencies of the various books of the Septuagint.[9] Granting that the Septuagint was the Bible of Paul's Diaspora community and that it was in the blood of Paul himself,[10] such studies are a *sine qua non* for deciphering Paul's world view. While a comprehensive treatment of the theological tendencies in the Septuagint is outside the scope of this paper, a consideration of the Septuagint of Isaiah is germane for our study of *oikoumene* and the limits of pluralism.

Because of its ecumenical emphasis and its importance to Paul, our study must give Isaiah attention. Far from showing "obvious signs of incompetence," as Swete charged,[11] the translation of Isaiah reflects a skillfully developed theological agenda. That agenda advocated the inclusion of gentiles in the people of God and encouraged an expansion of *nomos* to include the language and ethos popular in circles of Hellenistic piety. The translator steered a middle course between strict and liberal interpretations and sought to moderate tensions between traditions in conflict. Translated in the second century B.C.E. when relationships between the Seleucids and Palestinian Jewry were explosive, the translator(s) of Isaiah emphasized the importance of constructive interaction with gentiles. The translators' concern for the proselytes is evident in their emphasis on the universal reach of the Jewish religion. While

---

7(...continued)
in the preface that the Greek of the LXX was not a Jewish-Greek dialect but the ordinary language of the time which despite its Hebraisms was fully intelligible.

8 Georg Bertram, "Das Problem der Umschrift und die religionsgeschichtyliche Erforschung der Septuaginta," BZAW 66 (1936), 109, already noted, "Die Septuaginta gehört mehr in die Geschichte der Auslegung des Alten Testaments als in des altestamentlichen Textes." Bertram's statement may be a bit extreme, but it is valid, nevertheless, in some sense.

9 Notable exceptions, however, do exist. See I. L. Seeligmann, *The Septuagint Version of Isaiah, A Discussion of its Problems* (Leiden: Brill, 1948); Georg Rosen, *Juden und Phoenizier. Das Jüdischen Diaspora*, revised by Friedrich Rosen and D. Georg Bertram (Tübingen: J.C.B. Mohr, 1929); Georg Bertram, "Zur Bedeutung der Religion der Septuaginta in der hellenistischen Welt," *TLZ* 92 (1967), 245-250; G. Bertram, "Vom Wesen der Septuaginta-Frömmigkeit," in *Die Welt des Orients*, 3(1956), 274-284; John W. Olley, *Righteousness in the Septuagint of Isaiah; A Contextual Study* (Missoula, Montana: Scholars Press, 1978); H.M. Erwin, "Theological Aspects of the LXX of the Book of Psalms," (Unpublished Dissertation, Princeton, 1962).

10 After the work of Dietrich-Alexander Koch, *Die Schrift als Zeuge des Evangeliums, Untersuchung zur Verwendung und zum Verständnis der Schrift bei Paulus* (Tübingen: J.C.B. Mohr [Paul Siebeck], 1986) there should be little doubt that the Septuagint was the Bible of Paul. Over a half century ago Adolf Deissmann, *Paulus* (Tübingen: J.C.B. Mohr, 1925, p. 69 anticipated Koch with his description of Paul as a Septuagint Jew.

11 Henry Barclay Swete, *Introduction to the Old Testament in Greek* (Cambridge: At the University Press, 1934), I, p. 314.

the translators affirmed the importance of their Jewish tradition, they left open the possibility of a fruitful encounter with representatives of the Hellenistic world. The importance of this encounter is evident in their use of *oikoumene* in the LXX of Isaiah.

Thirty-three of the 54 references to *oikoumene* in the Old Testament appear in Isaiah and the Psalms (16 and 17 respectively). Only one anomalous reference appears in the entire Pentateuch (Exodus 16:35). Commonly used to refer to the whole inhabited world, *oikoumene* usually renders the Hebrew words *tevel* and *eretz* but sometimes appears without warrant in the Hebrew text. Whereas Herodotus and Democritus used *oikoumene* to refer to the civilized GREEK world as opposed to the lands of the barbarians, Philo (using the term 57 times) like the Stoics and Cynics expanded the scope of the term to embrace both Greeks and barbarians in the whole inhabited world.

While the LXX of Isaiah gives *oikoumene* a dark as well as sunny side, announcing the Lord's stern judgment on all peoples (10:13; 13:9; 13:11), this divine condemnation was balanced by the promise of salvation for the *oikoumene*. In 23:14-24:1, for example, the translator introduces salvation for peoples of the world into a Hebrew text. The MT promises humiliation for Tyre: "The Lord will visit Tyre and she will return to her hire and will play the harlot with all the kingdoms of the world upon the face of the ground." This text universalizes sin and suffering rather than promise and consolation. The LXX, however, instead of this condemnation of Tyre for its historic association with the Canaanite fertility cult, promises redemption to Tyre: "The God of Tyre shall make a visitation and she will turn again to the old ways and shall be a port of merchandise for all the kingdoms of the world (*pasais tais basileiais tes oikoumenes*) and her merchandise and HER HIRE SHALL BE HOLY UNTO THE LORD." Thus the LXX reverses the indictment of Tyre appearing in the MT, and instead recognizes Tyre as the gateway through which eschatological benefits will flow from all the kingdoms of the world to Israel. Thus, the passage exchanges the humiliation predicted in the MT for a "holy" offering by the kingdoms of the world.

More dramatic, however, is the adaptation the LXX makes in the famous Zion poem in Isaiah 62. With an invocation of intensely personal if not erotic imagery the MT places Zion securely at the center of Yahweh's affection:
You shall no more be called "*Azuvah* (abandoned),"
And your land shall no more be called "*Shemamah* (wasteland),"
But you shall be called "*Hephsi Bah* (my delight is in her)"
And your land "*Be'ulah* (mistress)."(62:4)
This personal language is carried forward into v. 5b where God as the bridegroom "rejoices over the bride."

In the LXX, however, the deeply personal or perhaps erotic nuances drop away, replaced by a Jewish piety that made Zion a symbol of habitation resonating with a wider meaning:

And no longer shall you be called "*Kataleleimmene* (dismissed),"
And your land shall no longer be called "*Eremos* (desert),"
For you shall be called "*Thelema Emon* (my will),"
And your land "*OIKOUMENE*."

One could read *OIKOUMENE* as a synonym of *ge* (land or "domesticated region"). Standing as an antithetical parallel to "*Eremos*" (desert), *oikoumene* might follow the Hebrew text promising human habitation for desolation. There are resonances, however, in the text itself that subvert that meaning. Two verses earlier in the LXX of 62:2, the *ethne*, or peoples of the world, witness Zion's vindication and are joined by the kings of the world who give independent confirmation of Yahweh's righteous action. In the subtext, therefore, the Judaism of the text is able to read itself into the witness of the gentiles. Were it not possible for the Jews of Alexandria to see themselves in the *anomic* world, Judaism would exist in total alienation. The terms with which the subtext embraces the "kings of the world" are quite clear. No longer will they dominate and exploit Zion. No longer will they feed themselves on her grain, nor slake their thirst with her wine (62:8). Stripped of their status as superordinates they will be discerning witnesses to the truth. Consequently, the text and subtext promise what Zion as *oikoumene* will do, namely provide an environment and a future in which tensions that dominate the relationship between Zion and the "nations," will be relaxed.

Those same tensions surely characterized the life of Diaspora Jews in Alexandria. Jews there sought direction for life in a setting in which they lived by gentiles, traded with gentiles attended the games and theater with gentiles, received education with and sometimes married gentiles. The language, concepts, customs, practices and piety which were inevitably absorbed from those associations were reconstructed by Jewish thinkers and refracted back onto the biblical text itself. Even when Jewish interests collided with those of their gentile neighbors, the Hellenistic idiom remained integral to the Jewish identity. One such Hellenistic concept was *oikoumene*.

There are signs within the LXX that these accommodations with Hellenistic universalism met resistance. The alarm expressed in 24:16 that Jews were abandoning *nomos* points to this conflict. Working off a Hebrew text which read, "Woe is me! For the treacherous deal treacherously; woe is me, for the treacherous deal treacherously," the translators made several alterations to address elements in the community whose attitudes toward the law were too liberal. Changing the object of the woe from "me" in the MT to "those" the translators gave the redundant Hebrew a sharp twist: "Woe to THOSE setting aside. Those setting aside THE LAW." This simple change made the text condemn those who were too casual about the specific requirements of *nomos* and the traditions it upheld.

Over forty years ago Seeligmann noticed a condemnation of an anti-dogmatic faction in 8:12-16.[12] He suggested that 8:ll-14 lists the rhetoric and slogans of those who were indifferent to the study or observance of *nomos*. They accuse other Jews of being hard (*skleron*, v. l2) and oppressive, and of requiring obedience to harsh, restrictive laws which ensnare their victims in a crippling bondage. This liberated faction urges other Jews to free themselves from superstitious allegiance to these laws and to worship the Lord in holiness and fear. By the clever addition of a conjunction, *dia touto* ("because" or "on account of this"), and a prepositional phrase, *en autois* ("among them") in 8:15, the translator links the divine warning to ignore the errorists ("Do not call *skleron* [hard, harsh, austere] everything that this people calls *skleron*, and do not fear what they fear, nor be in dread....") with the preceding threat ("ON ACCOUNT OF THIS (*dia touto*) many AMONG THEM (*en autois*) will be powerless and will fall and be crushed; and those who are safe will draw near and be taken." Now the translator added *tote*, "then," linking this warning and prediction of judgment with 8:16: "THEN (*tote*) those being sealed who DO NOT TEACH THE LAW WILL BE MANIFEST" (*tote phaneroi esontai hooi sphragizomenoi ton nomontou memathein*). The Greek of this passage bears little resemblance to the Hebrew command to "Bind up the testimony, seal the teaching among my disciples (*sor te'udah hathom torah belimudai*)." With these changes the LXX had changed the warning of the MT against the strategy of political expediency invoked in the face of the Assyrian threat into an indictment of Jews who not only do not teach the Law but actively oppose those observing the austere teachings of Torah. Conservatives and liberals were quarreling over the correct reading of the text. One faction called the other rigorist; the "rigorists" found their accusers guilty of apostasy for "setting aside" *nomos*. The disagreement was over the level of accommodation Jews could make with the Hellenistic environment and still remain Jews.

In some cases the Septuagint was made to condemn the materialism of the dominant culture. The Hebrew of Isaiah 24:8, for example, responds to the exile as one of the darkest periods in Israel's history. The MT laments the despoiling of the land by the Babylonians, and blames lawlessness and covenant violation for this catastrophe (24:5). The description of the land's desolation is filled with pathos: "The wine mourns, the vine languishes," and "the roar of the jubilant has ceased." The LXX, however, rejects this political judgment in favor of other concerns: "the STUBBORNNESS and RICHNESS of the IMPIOUS has ceased" (*pepautai authadia kai ploutos asebon*) appears in place of "the roar of the jubilant has ceased." By substituting two words for

---

12 Seeligmann, work cited, p. l06.

one (*authadia* and *ploutos* [stubbornness and richness] for one (*sheon* [Heb. roar]) and identifying the offenders no longer as inhabitants in general but as *asebon* (impious) in particular, the translator recast the Hebrew to condemn behavior which Stoics and Cynics also found repugnant. This condemnation of atavistic greed only makes sense as a rejection of a very tempting option for Jews as well as gentiles.

In spite of its obvious debt to Hellenistic culture, the Diaspora community often viewed itself as an island in a sea of *anomia*. Necessary for the definition of the Jewish community in Alexandria *anomia* provided something for the community to push against. A devotion to *nomos* required its opposite to establish identity and to define piety.

In his study of the Psalms, Flashar demonstrated how *anomia* expanded to refer to over twenty forbidden acts denounced in Hebrew.[13] He found *anomia* used for Hebrew terms like *awon* (sin), *pasha'* (apostasy), *zad* (arrogance), *halal* (boastfulness), *rasha'* (wickedness), *hamas* (brutality), *hawah* (crime), and *awal* (unrighteousness). Reflecting this same tendency the LXX of Isaiah uses anomia for *pasha'* (rebellion) six times,[14] *awon* (iniquity) five times,[15] *hata* (sin) two times,[16] *awen* (wickedness, trouble, sorrow) two times.[17] In single instances *anomia* stands for a number of Hebrew words: *sarah* (rebellion, 1:4); *mispach* (bloodshed, 5:7); *rasha'* (wickedness, 55:7); *ma'shakoth* (fraudulent gain, 33:15), and *hamas* (violence, 53:9). In 3:8 and 43:24 *anomia* appears in the text without justification from the Hebrew. Enjoying such a broad application *anomia* was no anemic generalization but a canopy under which hovered a very broad range of misconduct not specifically condemned by the 613 commandments.

This identification of conduct outside the traditions of Israel as *anomia* and its condemnation contradicts the tendency, perhaps unconscious, to surrender to the allure of a powerful Hellenistic culture. On the one hand we have seen how both Hellenistic language and values intruded into the Jewish experience in Alexandria, yet on the other hand we recognize that the community viewed itself as an island in a sea of *anomia*. At one level the Jews were aware of being influenced and yet at another level they repressed that awareness. So in this particular case the tension operated at a very deep level, and the tension operating at this unconscious level restrained pluralistic tendencies

---

13 Martin Flashar, "Exegetische Studien zum Septuaginta-Psalter," *ZAW* 32 (1912), 161-189, especially pp. 169f.

14 See 24:20; 43:25; 44:22; 53:5; 59:12a; and 59:12b.

15 See 6:7; 27:9; 50:1; 59:3; and 64:5.

16 Present in 55:7b and 58:1.

17 See 59:4 and 59:6.

fostered by the spirit of *oikoumene*. So a simple retrieval of the tradition was insufficient to maintain a sense of Jewish identity in Alexandria. The pluralism manifest in the Hellenestic world and the manifest ambiguity that created for the Jewish response could not be papered over with a simple division of the world into spheres of *anomia* and *nomos*. A new and more complex response was required from a community in which a metamorphosis was taking place.

In summary then, the alterations surveyed here, some of them delicately nuanced and highly sophisticated, refute Swete's judgment that the LXX translation of Isaiah shows "obvious signs of incompetence."[18] Instead with sophistication and subtlety the LXX of Isaiah altered the MT to stress theological issues of importance for the Alexandrian Jewish community. The universal emphasis admonished the community to be diligent about the inclusion and nurture of the *ethne*. Along with this stress on inclusiveness went a *nomos* spirituality that absorbed into itself ideal elements of Hellenistic piety while simultaneously guarding against reckless compromises with the Hellenistic milieu. The mythic or symbolic interpretation of *nomos* not only offered protective benefits to the faithful but also provided a sacred connection with the heavenly realm and a prophylactic against excessive accommodation or *anomia* —a synonym of chaos and dislocation. So *oikoumene* was informed by an understanding of *nomos* that allowed for the absorption of language, concepts, practices and piety that were essentially Hellenistic yet guarded against absorption into the dominant culture. *Nomos* thus provided a way not only for penetrating and ordering chaos but also for balancing accommodation with the Hellenistic emphasis on *oikoumene* with devotion to the ancestral religion. No mere legalistic system securing boundaries between Jew and gentile, as Schoeps held was the case in Diaspora Judaism, *nomos* provided a protocol for crossing boundaries and interacting with neighbors who had become their cultural cohorts. Yet in this pluralistic setting, *nomos* did guard against extreme accommodations with the dominant culture without defining those accommodations precisely or in some cases without even bringing them to consciousness. And while the pluralism of the Diaspora affected the texts and the way they were read, the texts provided the lens through which the dominant Hellenistic culture was viewed, ordered and subordinated. The stable ingredient in this strategy was tension between the affirmation of one's own tradition and a fruitful encounter with the dominant Hellenistic culture.

The *Letter of Aristeas*

Noting the way Pseudo-Aristeas reaches out to the Hellenistic culture while clinging to his ancestral Jewish traditions, Victor Tcherikover concluded

---

18 See above.

that Aristeas sought to be a citizen of two worlds and succeeded in belonging to neither. That Pseudo-Aristeas embraced the universalism of the Hellenistic world is generally recognized. The implied author shared the cosmopolitanism of King Ptolemy whose love of the cultures of the world inspired his efforts to collect "all the books of the world (*oikoumenen*)."(9). Our author notes that the tranquility of his kingdom and the esteem it enjoyed "throughout the inhabited world (*holen ten oikoumenen*)" prompted the King to dedicate "a thankoffering to God the Most High."(39) This Jewish commentator notes that the responses of the Jewish translators mirror this same cosmopolitanism. In responding to the King's question about piety, a Jew is made to say: "God is the benefactor of the whole world....(*holon kosmon*)"(210) Another Jew advised the King to "practice benevolence to all men" (*pantas anthropous*). (225) And while looking to Jerusalem as an idealized source of Israel's scriptures and worship, Eleazar, the high priest, appears as a believer in God's universal rule "EVERY PLACE being filled with his sovereignty" (*peplerwmenou pantos topou*).(132) And even while condemning the "wisest of the Greeks" for their fabrication of images of wood and stone which they worship and the "very foolish...Egyptians" who worship beasts, serpents and monsters (134-138), Pseudo-Aristeas encouraged tolerance as the *modus vivendi:* "Our law forbids harming anyone (*medena*) in thought or in deed," adding that the law encourages the extension of justice "to ALL humanity" (*pros pantas anthrwpous*, 168).

This cosmopolitanism carried with it a special piety and anthropology. We hear in Pseudo-Aristeas that the God of Israel is the same God all people worship, as the gentiles say, "except that we have a different name. This name for him is Zeus and Jove. The primitive [peoples] consistently with this, demonstrated that the one by whom ALL live and are created is the master and Lord of all"(16). All humanity, we are told, respects the legislation of the Jews "concerning meat and drink" (128). The "letter" has King Ptolemy Philadelphus recognize and worship Israel's God and aims to promote "justice and piety in all things" (24). Moreover, the cultural ideal held up for all Jews to emulate comes from the Greek *paideia*. Their basic moral qualities are to include prudence (*swphrosune*), justice (*dikaiosune*), temperance (*egkrateia*), and most especially moderation. And the ethical qualities they urge on the king are thoroughly Hellenistic - love of humanity (*philanthrwpia*), generosity (*epieikeia*), and magnanamity (*makrothumia*).[19] Moreover, the literary form and koine Greek of the letter itself reveal Hellenistic influence. The journey to Palestine follows similar patterns in utopian Greek novels, and the king's

---

19 See Tcherikover, *Op. Cit.*, p. 65.

questions addressed to each of the seventy-two translators imitate the pattern of the Greek symposium.[20]

This document reveals that a real metamorphosis was taking place in the Jewish community in Alexandria. Even the representatives of Jerusalem appear as learned men who speak both Hebrew and Greek (121). Jewish dietary rules blend with Hellenistic wisdom. Jewish law and Hellenistic virtue coalesce. A significant number of the community concern themselves primarily with "eat, drink and pleasure" (223), and while the Sabbath law, circumcision and prescriptions against eating pork went unchallenged, other dietary rules, the tefilin and mesusot were neglected or ignored altogether.[21] Thus we see that Hellenistic influence was pervasive and tended to weaken ties with what had historically been the primary symbols of Israel's faith—namely, the land, the temple, and even the covenant faith. So tolerance of the Greek neighbors and acceptance of their ways was at the expense of the ancestral religion.[22] As citizens of the polis became more cosmopolitan, ethnic identity eroded. Yet this erosion sparked off resistance. In a classic essay, Victor Tcherikover argued that the Letter of Aristeas was not written as propaganda to gain support from the gentiles but to confirm the loyalty of Jews to traditions that were being eaten away.[23] But can that dialogue with insiders and propaganda aimed at outsiders be so neatly divorced? The integrity and identity of the community is often secured by rhetoric aimed at outsiders.[24] No internal dialogue can totally ignore one's relationship with outsiders, and no dialogue with the outsider can overlook the role of the insider. Tcherikover, nevertheless, held that in the Letter of Aristeas we find a conservative minority who were unable to free "themselves from the 'lack of education and stubbornness' of their Palestinian brothers...who continued to use the Hebrew Torah in spite of the fact that it was preserved in Alexandria only in bad copies."[25] Tcherikover was correct to point out conflicting tendencies in the letter. Juxtaposed against liberalizing tendencies in the letter, reaffirmations of the power and importance of ancient symbols and rites appear. Contradicting the enthusiastic embrace of the language, literary forms and philosophic views of the Hellenistic world seen in Pseudo-Aristeas' brief summary of the law (128-172) comes

---

20 Ibid. p. 63.

21 V. Tcherikover correctly notes that laws and customs taken for granted and therefore unchallenged needed no defense. Only those in danger of rejection by Jews as irrational prescriptions needed and received a rational defense by Pseudo-Aristeas (128-172). Op. Cit., pp. 60-63.

22 See Schürer, *The History of the Jewish People*, III.l, pp. 140f.

23 "The Ideology of the Letter of Aristeas," *HTR* 51 (1958), 57-85.

24 Festinger's, *When Prophecy Failed*, suggested as much in showing how the attempt to win converts compensated in Lake City, MN for a disconfirmation crisis.

25 Op. cit., p. 83.

a divine mandate for the separation of Jews from gentiles. Verses 139-40 especially insist on the separation of Jews from their "pagan" neighbors: "In his wisdom the legislator [Moses]...being endowed by God for the knowledge of universal truths, surrounded us with unbroken palisades of iron walls to prevent our mixing with any of the other peoples in ANY MATTER, being thus kept pure in body and soul, preserved from false beliefs, and worshiping the only God omnipotent over all creation."

How is one to understand these contradictory tendencies? Tcherikover located this duality in the situation of the Jewish community rather than the contradictions of Aristeas. Turning against conservative Jews stubbornly clinging to a defective Hebrew Torah (30) and its flawed interpretation (144), Pseudo-Aristeas emphasized the advantages of a Greek education.[26] And against those conformist Jews, our author insists on the laws and customs that separate Jews and gentiles. It was this strategy that caused Tcherikover to observe that Pseudo-Aristeas was a citizen of two worlds but belonged to neither. But, Tcherikover's solution is too extreme and leaves the internal contradictions of the opposing contradictions unresolved.

J.J. Collins argues that the contradictions come from the attempt by Pseudo-Aristeas to address two different audiences. He sought to reassure gentiles of Jewish trustworthiness and fidelity to Ptolemaic interests and at the same time he hoped to confirm Jews in their faithfulness to their traditions that distinguished them from gentiles.[27]

Rather than concentrating on the audiences, it might be more useful to concentrate on the high level of ambiguity created by the metamorphosis taking place in the community. That ambiguity is evident in the letter in the emerging conflict between the nostalgia for the coherent religious world of shared meaning represented by the temple and high priest (but without reference to sacrifice!) and powerful pluralistic tendencies of a vibrant, alluring Hellenistic culture. While earnest, pious Jews in Alexandria knew cultural alienation, Jews at home in the discourse of the Hellenistic world experienced religious alienation. But this work is hardly about the divorce of those worlds but about their co-existence within the community itself and the ability of Jews to live with the resulting ambiguity. Consequently, Pseudo-Aristeas' interpretation of the nature and function of law saw the law as an instrument for mediating but not resolving the tension. He found confirmation for the authority of the law in the Hellenistic world itself with the independent recognition by the king of "your law"(32). King Philadelphus is summoned by Pseudo-Aristeas to pay homage to the law as the very *logia theou* (177,179) and even Greek

---

26 Ibid., p. 83.

27 *Between Athens and Jerusalem, Jewish Identity and the Hellenistic Diaspora* (New York: Crossroad, 1983), p. 86.

poets and writers appear in the letter offering testimonials to the sacred character of Torah(3l). Thus, ironically, Pseudo-Aristeas found in the cosmopolitan Hellenistic culture itself support for placing limits on pluralism.

The central significance of the law for the Diaspora community was hardly in question, but a fresh interpretation of the law was required by the sophisticated, urban Hellenistic milieu framing Alexandrian Judaism. The condemnation of idol worship (135-138) as well as the allegorical interpretation of the laws of purity would have offended no member of the Hellenistic intelligensia. Pseudo-Aristeas thus offers a common meeting ground for both serious, inquiring Jews and gentiles. But he did more. He provided a corrective for those tempted to abandon the Law altogether in the pursuit of "eat, drink and pleasure."(223) Thus we see that it was the interpretation not the translation that was of primary importance to Aristeas(15). The combination of his commentary on law observance and his stress on the classic Hellenistic virtues was not without tension.[28] Pseudo-Aristeas strained to be a citizen of both worlds. He sought a way, as did the Septuagint of Isaiah, to remain loyal to the ancestral Jewish traditions while remaining open to the surprises and fruits of the Hellenistic encounter. The tensions in the narrative reflect the tensions of his situation, tensions that were to remain unresolved for some centuries to come. But what is distinctive about Pseudo-Aristeas' vision of *oikoumene* is the high level of ambiguity he allows in the enormously complex interaction between the Jewish community and its pluralistic setting.

Philo

In a rare personal outburst Philo opens book three of the Special Laws with an outpouring of devotion to his two great loves, the Pentateuch and philosophy:

There was a time when I had leisure for philosophy and for contemplation of the universe and its contents, when I made its spirit my own in all its beauty and loveliness and true blessedness, when my constant companions were divine themes and verities wherein I rejoiced with a joy that never cloyed or sated....(3:1)

Kept from his beloved studies by "civil cares," Philo, nevertheless, kept alive in his soul, "the yearning for culture which...lifts me up and relieves my pain." (3:4) Thus Philo was emboldened not only to "read the sacred messages of Moses, but also in my love and knowledge to peer into each of them and unfold and reveal what is not known to the multitudes"(3:6). This philosophi-

---

28 For example, he extolls moderation which brings health (237, 245), restrains anger (253), promotes self discipline (211, 221), and enhances self-esteem (223-4). He stresses piety, love of humanity, generosity, magnanimity, prudence, justice and temperance, all Hellenistic traits of the ideal Hellenistic man or *kalokagathos*.

cal lens through which Philo read "Moses" goes far to explain the tension between his understanding of *oikoumene*, a Hellenistic creation, and his ancestral religion.

Although Philo employed a rich vocabulary to express his universalistic outlook, one of the most important words in that vocabulary was *oikoumene*. Given the Stoic and Cynic influence on Philo, the frequent appearance of *oikoumene* in his writings—57 times—comes as no surprise. Nevertheless, in his use of *oikoumene* as in that of Pseudo-Aristeas ambiguity abounds. Certainly Philo recognized the importance of the polis and its laws for both Jews and Greeks. At one level, as a Jew Philo was at home with the idiom and ways of his Hellenistic habitat. Yet he found in the Stoic view of the world as a cosmopolis a critique of the traditional polis that well suited his marginal status as a Diaspora Jew. Appealing to this Stoic concept, Philo went beyond the biblical text to claim citizenship in a world city ruled by a single law and polity: "For this world is the Megalopolis or 'great city,'and it has a single polity and a single law, and this is the word or reason of nature (*logos physews*)" (Iosepho, 29). Elsewhere, he noted the harmony of the law with the world and the world with the law that makes the observer of the law a "loyal citizen of the world (*kosmopolitou*)" (Opif. 3; also Abr. 61).[29] Everywhere, equally uniform and valid, loyalty to this law transcended one's duty to any particular polis.

In Moses I, 156-7, Philo offers his most cogent summary of this universalism. Referring to Moses, Philo says,

Each element obeyed him as its master, changed its natural properties and submitted to his command, and this perhaps is no wonder. For if, as the proverb says, what belongs to friends is common, and the prophet is called the friend of God, it would follow that he shares also God's possessions, so far as it is serviceable. For God possesses all things, but needs nothing; while the good man, though he possess nothing in the proper sense, not even himself, partakes of the precious things of God so far as he is capable. And that is but natural, for he is a WORLD CITIZEN (*kosmopolites*), and therefore not on the roll of any CITY OF THE HUMAN HABITATIONS OF THE WORLD (*oudemia two kata ten OIKOUMENEN polewn enegraphe*), rightly so because he has received no mere piece of land but THE WHOLE WORLD as his portion (*holon ton kosmon kleron labwn*).

In addition to Moses, Philo spoke of Adam, Abraham, and all the wise as citizens of the world (*kosmopoliten;* On the Creation, 142): "Now the world

---

29 One might argue that kosmopolitou here is hardly a universalistic term but rather a term with a sharp vertical dimension with little direct relevance for this discussion. But its association with the creation of the world would seen to gainsay that position.

of the wise man, the world citizen (*ho kosmopolites sophos*), is filled full of good things many and great, but the remaining mass of men experiences evil things in greater number, but fewer good things" (The Mig. of Abraham 59). And he extended world citizenship (*kosmopolitides*) to all those who consecrate themselves as an offering to God from which no mortal attraction dissuades them (On Dreams, I, 243). While the citizenship in the cosmos had a vertical dimension, Philo extended it horizontally to embrace the whole of the inhabited world (Iosepho, 29). This view of the Hellenistic world was informed by a vital biblical tradition to which he appealed for support, but inevitably tensions arose when that tradition collided with the polities of Hellenistic cities. Drawing on his understanding of Septuagintal Law, he condemned the covetous designs of the fractured and contradictory laws of various cities (Iosepho, 30) that were nothing more than human addenda to the "single polity of nature" (Iosepho, 3l). And, he drew an unfavorable contrast between Jewish solidarity and Greek and barbarian factiousness. That the fate of traitors was shared by children, he called repulsive, and that a poll tax was levied not on property but on bodies he criticized as uncivilized and devoid of "humane culture" (Spec. 3.163, 164). Unlike the laws of Rome, Philo had Moses propose swift justice for poisoners lest the offender multiply the crime (Spec. 3.l02). He detested Solon's practice of permitting marriage with "half sisters" on the fathers side,[30] and the Egyptian permission of marriage with sisters on both sides of the family.[31] He condemned the Spartans as too austere and the Ionians too lax. By contrast, Moses followed the golden mean, relaxing the overly strict laws and tightening the loose, and thus achieving "harmony and concord" (Spec. 4.l02). According to Philo, when Moses forbade the consumption of meat from animals dying naturally or being killed by beasts, he repudiated the practice of skillful, aristocratic Greek hunters who bagged their game and parcelled it out in an act of generosity (Spec. 4.l20). Finally, he applauded the "holy Moses" for condemning child sacrifice and the burning of sons and daughters as an abomination and a dastardly, polluting deed (Abr. l8l). This stark contrast between Jewish and Hellenistic polity he used to emphasize the superiority of Mosaic law, nevertheless, his description of Mosaic law as a perfect copy of the invisible, eternal, divine natural law depends on Hellenistic concepts. Furthermore, his description of the true *cosmopolites* as the observer of the Mosaic law links Jewish tradition and Hellenistic culture. So even in differentiating Jewish and Hellenistic ways, Philo forges links between them.

In this uneasy coupling of the two traditions, the emphasis was not always balanced. Because of the weak position of the Jewish community in a domi-

---

30 For example Themistocles' daughter married her brother (Plutarch, Them. 32).

31 Perhaps following the example of the marriage of Isis and Osiris.

nant culture the greater risk was excessive conformity to the Hellenistic culture. Without defining its nature, Philo repeatedly warned his people of the evils of apostasy,[32] but he sharply criticized rigorist Jewish conservatives as well. He condemned scriptural literalists as "slow witted" (*On Flight and Finding* 179; *On Dreams* I, 39), "obstinate," "rigid," and "resentful" (*On Dreams* II, 301), and accused them of rejecting the truth of the Scriptures and even of apostasy (*On the Confusion of Tongues*, II, 6-8; *On Husbandry* 157). He simultaneously repudiated symbolic and intellectual readings of *nomos* that treated the literal sense of *nomos* with "easy going neglect." He rejected a spirituality that so elevated "what is not seen" that it eclipsed "what is seen" (Ebr.) in the text. He castigated Jews who neglected the letter of the law, arguing that "they ought to have given careful attention to both aims, to a more full and exact investigation of what is not seen and to a blameless stewardship of what is seen." (Mig. 89-94) As he scolded sophisticated, conformist Jews, and chided rigorist Jews obsessed with the literal message of texts, he aimed to steer a middle course between the two. That middle course was inevitably steadfastly held by tension between the extremes. Given Philo's own sophistication and the ease with which he moved in Hellenistic circles, his condemnation of other Jewish sophisticates may sound hollow or even hypocritical unless one realizes that these condemnations reflect the tensions within Philo's own soul.

The need for Philo to defend proselytes from discrimination within the Jewish community itself and his simultaneous endorsement of Hellenistic philosophy may indicate the level of tension within the community itself. Only the fruitful interaction between Judaism and Hellenism would protect the Jewish community from total alienation or complete assimilation. One way Philo escaped alienation was by incorporating the great philosophers into the traditions of Israel. By making Moses the source of their genius. he was able to see Judaism's self in the other, and rejection of that world inevitably would mean self-rejection. Equally important, however, was Philo's concern for the welfare of the proselyte. That proselytes participated in the life of the Jewish community is clear,[33] but their status was ambiguous. By identifying the Israelites

---

32 Unfortunately few deviants are allowed to speak for themselves so we do not know if they intended to abandon Judaism. Certainly the boundary beyond which one became an apos-tate is unmarked. Denial of the God of Israel, or initiation into one of the mysteries (SpL 319) would make one an apostate, but would loyalty to the Roman Imperial administration make one an apostate? What had Philo's nephew, Tiberius Alexander, done to earn the condemnation Philo heaped on him?

33 S.J.D. Cohen, "Crossing the Boundary and Becoming a Jew," *HTR* 82 (1989), 13-33 argues that "in Alexandria in the first century, the tension between the Jews and the gentiles was so great that virtually no gentiles became adherents or proselytes." pp. 32-33. Philo's repeated defenses of the rights of the proselytes does suggest tensions existed but Cohen goes too far with his claim that proselytism essentially ceased.

themselves as proselytes and recipients of God's gift and promise, Philo elevated the status of the proselytes in his own community (On the Cherubim, 108; On Dreams II, 272-3; Special Laws I, 308). By exhorting the community to accept and encourage proselytes Philo was asking the marginalized not to marginalize others in turn. When gentiles married to Jewish men were diminished, Philo cited with approval Moses' decision to allow Hebrew fugitives from Egypt to keep their Egyptian wives. In reconciling Jews and gentiles within the community Philo's *oikoumene* received a very immediate relevance.[34] In his Special Laws I, 51, 52, Philo embraces the proselytes with a special tenderness:

> they have left...their country, their kinsfolk and their friends for the sake of virtue and religion. Let them not be denied another citizenship or other ties of family and friendship, and let them find places of shelter standing ready for refugees to the camp of piety. For the most effectual love-charm, the chain which binds indissolubly the goodwill which makes us one is to honor the one God.

Had the community not felt attenuated by the proselyte presence such an exhortation would have been unnecessary. Although Philo knew that observance of the Jewish religion sometimes brought one into conflict with the gentiles in the polis, he insisted that Jews embrace believing gentiles. Philo's aim was, as Tcherikover noted, to allow the Jew to remain a Jew and, at the same time, to belong to the elect society of the Greeks, the bearers of world culture.[35] Yet this synthesis was always being tested by centrifugal forces from within and centripetal forces from without.

We see, therefore, that in Philo as in Pseudo-Aristeas and the LXX of Isaiah, tension was the norm. The obligations of membership in the polis often clashed with the claims of citizenship in the megalopolis. And definition of a *cosmopolites* as a person made wise by a deep understanding of the scriptures placed Jews at odds with Hellenistic conventions. And Jews easily swayed by the claims of the dominant culture quarreled with members of the Diaspora who were more hostile to Hellenism. The conflict without was matched by a struggle within as the individual debated the wisdom of a cosmopolitanism that undermined Jewish identity. Twin forms of alienation were the Scylla and Charybdis of Alexandrian Jews. According to Philo, only a steady course between these twin perils could save the community from being devoured by

---

34 Schürer, *The History of the Jewish People*, III.1, p. 140 correctly notes the tendency in the Diaspora community to emphasize general religious ideas such as the idea of the supreme God to harmonize Jewish and Greek culture, and the emphasis on the universal elements evoked tolerance from the Greek environment. Proselytism, so Vermes et al, maintain "may itself have brought about a tendency towards an 'attenuated Judaism.'"

35 Tcherikover, "The Ideology of the Letter of Aristeas," *HTR* 51 (1958), 81. See also pp. 59-85.

the dominant culture and a consequent alienation from one's Jewishness or being wrecked by total withdrawal into a cultural ghetto and alienation from the dominant culture. To guard that balance was an important part of the task of Philo, Pseudo-Aristeas, and even the LXX of Isaiah.

Paul

Werblowsky maintains that the portrayal of Paul as a "typical 'Dispersion Jew' is sheer nonsense."[36] Given Paul's upbringing in the Diaspora, his Diaspora Bible (the LXX), his Greek language, and his education in the Diaspora, one must respond that a consideration of Paul that does not take account of the influence of the Diaspora on his theology is also absolute nonsense. Some such connection was suggested by Nils Dahl whose commentary on Romans 3:29-30 suggested that "In drawing the consequence that radical monotheism excludes any distinction [i.e. between Jew and gentile], Paul shows some affinity with Greek philosophical monotheism, which was universalistic and more or less cosmopolitan. Since Xenophanes, it could include polemic against religious particularism."[37] Dahl believes such influences were mediated by a Hellenized Judaism that used them for apologetic purposes "to prove the excellency of the Mosaic legislation and of the Jewish nation."[38] Our presentation focuses on the contradictory impulses within the Diaspora community, and on the unresolved tensions between *oikoumene* and particularism within that circle. If we take Paul's Diaspora experience seriously, the question inevitably rises whether those same tensions characterized Paul's outlook and if so to what extent.

Oikoumene appears only once in Paul's letters and then only in a citation from the LXX of the Psalms.[39] That single appearance, however, comes at a critical juncture in Paul's argument. In a justification of the gospel mission that sounds quite autobiographical Paul uses Psalm 19:4 to frame his rhetorical question: "have they [the gentiles] not heard?" He answers the question with a citation from the Psalms:

36 See R.J.Z. Werblowsky, R.J.Z., "Paulus in jüdischer Sicht" in *Paulus—Apostat oder Apostel* ed. M. Barth et al (Regensburg, 1977), 135-146, esp. 139.

37 "The One God of Jews and Gentiles, (Romans 3:29-30)," in *Studies in Paul* (Minneapolis: Augsburg, 1977), p. 190.

38 Ibid., and p. 190.

39 One might agree with Mussner, however, that *pas* is the key word for understanding Romans. F. Mussner, "Heil für Alle," *Kairos* 23 (1981), 207-214. But, to emphasize inclusion with no sense of its history in the Diaspora is to miss important dimensions of its development and application. I agree with Lloyd Gaston that this inclusion "must not be interpreted in a disinterested, even-handed, universalizing theological manner." See L. Gaston, *Paul and the Torah*, (Vancouver: University of British Columbia Press, 1987), pp. 116-134. But I might be more attentive to the universalizing tendencies of Diaspora Judaism than is Gaston.

Their voice has gone out to all the earth,
and their words to the ends of the *oikoumene*.
(*eis ta perata tes oikoumenes*, 10:18)

Then Paul observes (not questions as in RSV): "Again, I say, Israel did not understand." (10:19) But Paul is soon to insist from different points of view that the inclusion of the gentiles of the *oikoumene* does not mean either (a) that God has rejected his chosen (11:1) or (b) that Israel has stumbled so as to fall (11:11).

Of course, as Mussner has shown, the economical use of the word, *oikoumene*, hardly means that Paul's universal perspective is inconsequential.[40] As Lloyd Gaston has successfully argued, *the pas* or "all" vocabulary in Romans is "inclusive language" that shows how self consciously ecumenical Paul's thinking really was.[41]

We have time to only briefly note the enormous tension between Paul's kerygma for the *oikoumene* and his pledge of loyalty to Israel in chs. 9-11. Paul stands on the boundary between Israel and the gentiles. This stress of living on the boundary resembles the tension between boundlessness and boundedness which Victor Turner believes is characteristic of the liminal stage of myth and ritual. Following the mythic structure developed by Arnold van Gennep of *rites de passage*,[42] Turner shows how in the liminal stage tensions are created by competing tendencies—a straining toward universalization (or boundlessness) and a desire to impose structure (or limit, or boundedness) on the surge toward universalization.[43] Such a model aptly characterizes Paul's position and tendency. Certainly Paul's apocalypticism placed him in a liminal stage or transitional phase which allowed him to go beyond the Alexandrian community in his embrace of "gentile sinners" while defending his loyalty to the ancestral religion of the Jews. His argument thus pulled in contrary directions—affirming first of all God's freedom to include gentiles *qua* gentiles even if that meant rejection for Israel, and second somewhat paradoxically asserting that God's commitment to the salvation of gentiles *does not exclude* Israel. Paul buttresses this difficult position with a cascade of scripture citations (29:16; 10:22; 28:22; 1:9; 28:16). And finally, the tension between Paul's vision

---

40 F. Mussner, "Heil für Alle," *Kairos* 23 (1981), 207-214.

41 Lloyd Gaston, "For *all* the Believers, The Inclusion of Gentiles as the Ultimate Goal of Torah in Romans," in *Paul and the Torah* (Vancouver: University of British Columbia Press, 1987), pp. 116-134.

42 Arnold van Gennep, *The Rites of Passsage* (London: Routledge, 1960. French edition 1909.

43 *The Ritual Process, Structure and Anti-Structure* (Ithaca, New York: Cornell University Press, 1969). This tendency, however, according to Turner, is not limited to ritual. See his "Myth and Symbol," in the *International Encyclopedia of Social Sciences*, 17 vols., ed. David L. Sills (New York: Macmillan & the Free Press, 1968), vol. 10, pp. 576-79.

of *oikoumene* and his loyalty to Israel reaches the breaking point in chapter eleven. In 11:11 he recalls a sports metaphor ("Have they stumbled [in the Torah race] so as to fall?") which he had introduced in 9:30-33. Incredibly both Israel who ran the Torah race, stumbling over a rock which *God* placed on the track, and the gentiles who did not compete in the Torah race, both emerge as winners. Against all conventional sporting rules or traditions, Paul argued that in God's eschatological race winners do not require losers. The gentile victory does not dictate a loss for Israel, and a prize for Israel does not leave the gentiles empty handed. How such a preposterous suggestion is realized is left open. There is no human resolution, Paul realizes, of how this can be accomplished. The answer is hidden in the mystery of the Godhead itself. Paul can only wonder at this mystery as he launches into a soaring benediction (11:33-36): "O the depth of the riches, and wisdom and knowledge of God. How inscrutable are his judgments and untraceable his ways. For who has known the mind of the Lord? Or who has been his counselor? For out of him and through him and in him are all things. To him be the glory forever. Amen."

Paul's logic was thus extended to the breaking point. At one end of the spectrum, but still within the circle of the ancestral faith, Paul argued that God will include gentiles of the *oikoumene* while remaining faithful to Israel. Thus his dialogue with the synagogue was complicated by inclusive tendencies set loose by his gospel. And while the limit of pluralism for Philo was found where *nomos* and *anomia* collided, a similar limit may have been assumed by Paul except that now *nomos* was redefined as being *en nomos Christou* (1 Cor. 9:21) or by the *nomos tou pneumatos* he had already mentioned in Romans 8:2. And the life now lived in *dikaiosune* was seen as the antithesis of the life once lived in *anomia* (Rom. 6:19)[44] Paul still belongs somewhere on the spectrum of Diaspora Judaism, though admittedly at one end of the spectrum. His apocalypticism or Messianism may have pushed him toward a more radical vision of the *oikoumene* and the role of the gentiles in the people of God than we have seen in Alexandrian Judaism. But, Paul's radical monotheism that eliminated any distinction between Jews and gentiles shows "some affinity with Greek philosophical monotheism, which was universalistic and more or less cosmopolitan."[45] Nevertheless, Paul argues that he still belongs within the

---

44 The position of W. Gutbrot that "In Judaism *ho anomos* or *hoi anomoi* is a common term for the Gentiles" (*TDNT* IV, 1087) while generally correct ignores the ambiguities created by gentiles living on the boundary of Judaism, and misses the tension let loose in the Diaspora Jewish community by its interaction with the dominant culture. Once one sees the Hellenistic culture as a lively cohort in active conversation with the Jewish community the neat distinctions become less useful.

45 See Nils Dahl, "The God of Jews and Gentiles," in his *Studies in Paul,* (Minneapolis: Augsburg, 1977), p. 190.

circle of faith drawn by God's covenant with Israel (2 Cor. 11:22-23). Thus we see that tension between universalism and particularism was present in both the Alexandrian and Pauline writings; the difference between them was one of degree not of kind. If our suggestion is correct, the Alexandrian exemplar may offer a useful model for understanding both the nature of those tensions and the way they were mediated in the Pauline letters. Far from being sheer nonsense, the assessment of Paul's place in Diaspora Judaism may be crucial to understanding the dynamic of Paul's theology.

The Jews in Acts
Howard Clark Kee

Studies by A.T. Kraabel of Diaspora Judaism in Late Antiquity have not only provided important insights and information but have also provoked profitable ongoing discussion of related issues[1]. This stimulus to debate is especially evident with respect to his historical judgments about the "God-fearers" in the Book of Acts. The belated publication of the inscription from Aphrodisias in which *theosebes* is used[2] indicates that Kraabel's negative judgment about the origin and significance of this and related terms for those on the borders of Judaism has stimulated and deepened rather than terminated this discussion about the social and ethnic context of Judaism in the first centuries of the Common Era.

A major component in the difficulty that has charcterized this debate has been a lack of clarity about the relationship of Gentiles to Jews within Judaism during the first two centuries of the Common Era, as well as the definition of the respective Jewish and Christian communities. By extension these differences of opinion and group understanding are reflected in the early Christian writings, and especially in the Book of Acts [3].

---

1 Kraabel's publications include basic surveys of the evidence concerning the Diaspora Synagogue: "The Diaspora Synagogue: Archaeological and Epigraphic Evidence since Sukenik (in *Aufstieg und Niedergang der roemischen Welt* (Principat II; 19.1, 477-510. Berlin: De Gruyter, 1979); "Social Systems of Six Diaspora Synagogues", in *Ancient Synagogues: The State of Research*, ed. Joseph Gutman (Brown Judaic Studies 22. Providence: Brown University, 1981, 79-91); "Unity and Diversity among Diaspora Synagogues", in *The Synagogue in Late Antiquity*. ed. Lee I. Levine. (Philadelphia: American Schools of Oriental Research, 1987, 49-60). More problematical is Kraabel's essay, "The Disappearance of the God-Fearers", in *Numen* XXVIII,2, 1981, 113-126.

2 Joyce Reynolds and Robert Tannenbaum, *Jews and God-Fearers at Aphrodisias: Greek Inscription and Commentary*. Cambridge: Cambridge Philological Society, 1987.

3 Among the more important discussions of the picture of Jews in Acts are those of J. Jervell, J.T. Sanders, R. Brawley, and Etienne Trocme. Jervell, in *Luke and the People of God* (Minneapolis: Augsburg, 1972), declares that Luke can think only of Israel; the conversion of Gentiles is a problem for him, since he is "not acquainted with the later solution of this difficulty by means of a conception of the church as the new Israel made up of Jews and Gentiles; and this hardly fits with his view of history." Accordingly, he assumes that Luke knows only one Israel: the Jewish people (68). At the opposite end of the discussion is Jack T. Sanders, in *The Jews in Luke Acts* (Philadelphia: Fortress, 1987), who asserts that Luke understands the Jews to become by the end of Acts what they were from the beginning. This, expressed by what Jesus, Stephen, Peter and Paul say constitutes the Jew's "intransigeant oppostion to the purposes of God, about their hostitlity toward Jesus and the gospel, about their murder of Jesus." What they become in their hostility "was no more nor less than what they always, from the days of their creation as a people were" (81). Robert L. Brawley takes a position well-removed from Jervell or Sanders when he says that "Acts presents Paul as completely Jewish" (83). Paul portrays the development of an essentially Jewish sect that, in fulfillment of God's promises, includes Gentiles. He conforms to the demands of the law, continues to claim to be a Pharisee, and is conciliatory
(continued...)

A major factor in the wide disagreements that characterize much of the discussion of these matters is the historical and exegetical assumption that to be a Jew in this period (first and second centuries C.E.) had a commonly accepted ste of requirements. Ignored is the mounting evidence of widespread debate and basic differences of opinion within Judaism on the matter of qualifications for membership, and that by extension, in this period Christianity was able to develop a clearly definition of itself over against the Jewish alternative. Careful analysis of the evidence discloses, rather, the fluidity of these issues and the diversity of answers offered from both the Jewish and the Christian sides. Indeed, the serious modern investigator of Christian origins or of pre-rabbinic Judaism cannot even responsibly use terms like "Jew" or "Christian" as though they had unambiguous, self-evident meaning.

While it would be an enormous task to examine all the evidence that bears on this issue, a more modest undertaking may be useful: that is to proceed with an analysis of the critical terms by which Jews and Christians are described and their differences defined in a document that has been perhaps the center for debate and disagreement on the larger issue: the Book of Acts. Even this limited line of inquiry points up the complexity of the historical questions, but at the same time it may offer some suggestions as to how one segment of early Christianity—that represented by the two-volume work, Luke-Acts—was undertaking to clarify and resolve the urgent and existential issues of community definition. It may be useful to begin by differentiating the variety of connotations with which the basic terms "Jew" and "Jews" are used in Acts. We begin be noting that these basic terms appear with by no means uniform connotations in Acts, thereby illustrating the complexity and fluidity of a familiar term which one might assume to have self-evident meaning.

1.   Jews/Israel as the Historic People of God.

The importance of the question of continuity in the history of God's covenant people, reaching from the past into the future, is highlighted on the opening page of Acts. There, when the risen Jesus is described as meeting with the reassembled disciples/apostles and promises them the outpouring of the Spirit, their first and basic question is, Lord, will you at this time restore the kingdom to Israel" (Acts 1:6). He had been "speaking to them of the king-

---

3(...continued)
toward Jewish Christians, as the agreement reached at the Jerusalem Council in Acts 15 demonstrates. Luke does not set Christianity free from Judaism; he ties it to Judaism. Trocme in his essay, "The Jews as Seen by Paul and Luke" (in "To See Ourselves as Others See Us": Christians, Jews, 'Others' in Late Antiquity, ed. Jacob Neusner and E. S. Frerichs. Chico: Scholars Press, 1985) notes the mixed response to the gospel on the part of Jews and others in Acts, and observes that "the Jews are not ignored or despised" (160).

dom of God" (1:3), which is apparently a matter of eschatological promise about the final establishment of God's rule in the creation and over humanity. What is problematical for the apostles here is two-fold: Will the restoration of the kingdom take place "at this time"? And will it be achieved through or for "Israel"?

The first of these questions is answered directly, though in a way which precludes an unequivocal solution to the problem. The apostles are told that "it is not for you to know the times or seasons". The unfolding of the ages "the Father has fixed by his own authority" (1:7). But also unaddressed is the second part of the question: How should one identify Israel to whom the kingdom is to be restored?

Fortunately, the issue of the definition of Israel is offered, at least implicitly, in detail in Stephen's speech before the council, which has accused him of speaking against the temple and the law, of announcing that Jesus would destroy the sanctuary, and of changing "the customs that Moses delivered to us" (6:13-14). Stephen's reply to these charges is to recite the history of Israel (7:2-49), beginning with Abraham and the patriarchs, including the origins in Mesopotamia, the migration to "this land" (7:4), the period in Egypt (7:9-16), the emergence of Moses as leader and deliverer of the people (7:17-36). He also was the one through whom God spoke at Sinai, and who promised the people "a prophet from your brethren", whom God would raise up as he had lifted Moses into this role of definer of the covenant people (7:37). In amplification of Moses' role he transmitted to Israel at Sinai "living oracles" (7:38). Stephen's positive identification with this historic people is implicit in the detail that these oracles had been given "*to us.*"

At this point, however, the thrust of Stephen's speech shifts from rehearsal of Israel's history to sharp critique. Yet even here Stephen continues to identify with the historic people: those who "refused to obey" Moses or the God speaking through him were "*our fathers*" (7:39). Their turning to idolatry was matched by God's giving them "over to worship the host of heaven", which Amos had later perceived to be the reason for Israel's subsequent exile in Babylon (7:42-43 = Amos 5:25-27).

Again it was "our fathers" who had erected the "tent of witness in the wilderness", and had brought it into the land when the nations were "thrust out before our fathers" (7:44-45). It was later replaced by the temple which David had asked to build, but which was actually built by Solomon (7:46-47). Stephen, however, goes on to quote 2 Isaiah to the point that not even this house is where God actually dwells, since heaven is God's throne, and it is inappropriate to build a house as his dwelling place (Acts 7:48-50; Isa 66:1). The indictment of the people which brings to a conclusion Stephen's address describes them as "stiff-necked", echoing God's description of them to Moses at Sinai (Ex 33:5) and "uncircumcized in heart and ears", recalling the charges made against Israel in the law (Lev 26:41; Num 27:14) and the prophets (Isa 63:10; Jer 6:10). It is their ancestors' pattern of resistance to God and his purpose for his people that they are emulating, as is apparent from the earlier rejection and persecution of the prophets (I Kgs 19:10; 2 Chron 36:16; Neh 9:26). The culmination of this repudiation of the God of the covenant came. Stephen declares, in the murder of God's ultimate agent, "the Righteous One", and of those who had announced his coming. Though they had received the law from God through angels (Ex 33:2), they did not obey it. The pattern of divine disclosure which is then rejected by the covenant community is not new, but goes back to the days of Moses at Sinai and continued through the subsequent history of Israel. What is stated here is not God's withdrawal or repudiation of the covenant promises, but a historical comment on the ongoing rejection of the covenantal obligation by the intended recipients of its benefits.

The outrage of Stephen's hearers at this indictment contrasts with the divine approbation of his diagnosis through the vision that is granted him of Jesus exalted at God's right hand (Acts 7:54-56; cf. Psa 63:3; Isa 6:1). There is here no Marcion-like repudiation and replacement of God's covenant with Israel, but rather an affirmation of its continuing validity in spite of the widespread rejection it has met and continues to meet.

An important dimension of participation in God's people according to Acts is the representative group of Jews living in Jerusalem, including "devout men from every nation under heaven" (2:5). The geographical, linguistic and ethnic inclusiveness of this group is further specified by the enumeration of their places of origin reaching from Rome and Africa across Mesopotamia and the Middle East (2:9-10). But further, they include both Jews and proselytes, as well as former residents of Rome who are now living in Jerusalem. The appeal of the covenant with Israel extends not only to Jews throughout the disapora but also to non-Israelites who identify with the covenant by a range of relationships, extending from choice of residence in Jerusalem (the sojourners) to formal, ritual participation (the proselytes). The subsequent outpouring of the Spirit and the miraculous ability of all who are present to hear in their own languages (2:6) is declared to be in fulfillment of the prophet (Joel 3:1-5), which culminates in the promise that "whoever calls on the name of the Lord shall be saved" (Acts 2:21). In Peter's address which follows, the identification of Jesus as God's Messiah is to made to "all the house of Israel" (2:36), while the invitation to receive forgivenss of sins and the gift of the Spirit is extended to Israel ("you and your children") as well as "all that are far off" and "every on whom our Lord calls to him" (2:39). There are no humanly imposed preconditions to hearing and responding to the message, and thereby to participation in the community of God's people.

2. Jew as a Mode of Ethnic and Geographic Identity.

The opening phrases of Peter's speech at Pentecost do, however, use the term *Ioudaioi* with an implication of ethnic and geographical identity. A literal rendering of *andres Ioudaioi* would be "Jewish men". To this is added the phrase "and all who have taken up residence (*katoikountes*) in Jerusalem. Similarly, Peter's speech in house of Cornelius (Acts 10:34-43) notes the witness of the apostles to all that Jesus—anointed by God and empowered by the Holy Spirit—did "both in the country of the Jews and in Jerusalem".

Ioudaioi is also used in Acts with reference to Jews who live outside of the "country of the Jews", as in the case of the Jews with whom Paul argues in Damascus and who consequently seek to kill him (9:22-23). Similarly, when Paul and Silas are brought before the authorities in Philippi as disturbers of the peace and as advocates of anti-Roman practices, they are identified to the magistrates as "Jews".

3. Those who Identify Themselves with the Jewish Community.

The close relationship between Jews and Gentile proselytes, which is implied in Acts 2:10, is indicated more explicitly in the story of the conversion of Cornelius. He is described as "a centurion, an upright man who fears God (*phoboumenos ton theon*), who is well spoken of by the whole Jewish nation." In the synagogues of Thessalonica and Beroea, the primary targets of Paul's argument from the scriptures are the Jews (17:1-2, 11). But also involved in the debate about Jesus as the Christ are "a great many of the devout (*sebomenon*) Greeks and not a few of the leading women" (17:4). Among those who become believers in Beroea are "not a few Greek women of high standing as well as men" (17:13). In Corinth, the primary associates of Paul are Prsicilla and Aquila—both of them with Greek names, and from the Gentile province of Pontus—who had been recently expelled from Rome along with other Jews by the order of the emperor Claudius. But Paul's preaching there "in the synagogue on every sabbath" involved both Jews and Greeks (18:1-4), although it is said to be primarily Jews whom he seeks to persuade that "the Christ was Jesus". A similar task is undertaken by Apollos at Ephesus (18:24-28), where Paul later is reported to have shifted his place of debate "about the kingdom of God" from the synagogue of the Jews to the public hall of Tyrannus. The result is "that all the residents of Asia heard the word of the Lord, both Jews and Greeks" (19:8-10). The synagogue is not the exclusive province of Jews, but through it the issues about the messiahship of Jesus and the identity of God's people reaches out to the wider Gentile, Greek-oriented populace.

The terms to describe those who are not birthright Jews but active parti- cipants in the synagogue include (1) *eulabeis* ("devout", or "pious") as in 2:5; 8:2; (2) *sebomenoi* ("worshippers"); (3) *phoboumenoi ton theon* ("those who fear God"), as in 13:26; and (4) *proselytoi*. Among these—in a curoius combination of terms—are the *sebomenoi proselytoi* who, along with "many Jews" join to follow Paul in response to his preaching in the synagogue at Antioch in Pisidia. Likewise Lydia is described as *sebomene ton theon*, prior to her being persuaded by what Paul said at the *proseuche* outside Philippi (16:14). We noted earlier the similar phenomenon of the *sebemenoi* Greeks and leading women who respond in faith to Paul's message about Jesus (17:4). At Athens Paul argued in the synagogue with the Jews and *sebomenoi* (17:17). The picture is consistent that members of the new community are drawn from among those who previously were birth-right Jews and those who had come to worship the God of Israel in the context of the voluntary assembly, the synagogue.

This dramatic convergence is vividly evident in the story in Acts 18:5-8 when Paul is expelled from the synagogue, but when he moves next door to the house of Titius Justus, who is described as *sebomenos ton theon*. Among the converts who go along to the new community are the *archisynagogos*, Crispus, and his entire household. Although in a few texts the proselytes are mentioned separately (2:10; 6:5), elsewhere the term is linked with the *sebomenoi*, as in 13:43. Paul's report to the Ephesian elders of his activity reminds them of his having testified to both Jews and Greeks about "repentance toward God and faith in our Lord Jesus Christ" (20:21). The blending of Gentiles with Jews in the synagogues where Paul preaches the gospel is a pervasive feature of Acts.

4.   Jews as Leaders of the Oppostion to Paul and the Gentile Mission.

One strand of the tradition in Acts represents "the Jews" as taking the initiative to destroy Paul. It is reported in 9:22, following the Acts account of the conversion of Paul, that he "caused consternation among the Jews who lived in Damascus by proving that [Jesus] was the Christ" (9:22). As a result, "they plotted together to kill him" (9:23), although he learned of their plan and escaped. At Pisidian Antioch, the reaction of Jews to the huge numbers ("the whole city") that gathered to hear Paul proclaim "the word of God" was one of fierce jealousy, a determined effort to contradict what he preached, and denouncing him bitterly (*blasphemountes*) (13:45). Ironically, those who join in this Jewish-led attack on Paul through the urging of the Jews are "the devout women (*tas sebomenas gunaikas*) of high standing and the leading men of the city (*tous protous tes poleos*). The result is persecution (*diogmon*) of Paul and Barnabas, and they are driven from the district (13:50). Similarly, at Beroea Jews from Thessalonica came to combat Paul's work by "stirring up and inciting the crowds" (17:13).

More formal is the charge brought against Paul before the Roman proconsul of Achaia, Gallio, that "This man is persuading men to worship God contrary to the law." Gallio responds to their "united attack" by dismissing the charge as an issue involving "words and names and your own law", rather than as "wrongdoing or a vicious crime" by the standards of Roman law (18:12-14). Twice in Acts 20 there is mention of Jewish plots against Paul: once in Greece "as he was about to set sail for Syria " (20:3), and the reference in his speech to the Ephesian elders of the multiple "plots of the Jews" which had brought him such sorrow and times of testing. The effort of one Alexander in Ephesus to discredit Paul before the public assembly in Ephesus and to do so from a Jewish perspective (19:33-34) is significant even though he is outshouted by the devotees of Artemis. The curious story of the Jewish exorcists related to one of the high priests who want to exploit power of "the name of the Lord Jesus" depicts dramatically the ambivalence of some Jews about Jesus and the claims made in his behalf. Their attempt backfires, when they are physically attacked by the one from whom they try to expel the evil spirit through the name of Jesus (19:11-20). The report of this attempt and the result of the use of Jesus' name has a powerful impact on "both Jews and Greeks" in Ephesus, leads to confession of exorcistic practices by believers, and an abandonment of magic by others. Here, too, the initial impetus was provided by Jews.

5.   Ambiguity and Ambivalence about the Jewish Law on the Part of Paul and the Jerusalem Apostles.

Clearly in Acts there is not envisioned a total break between Jewish legal tradition and Christian moral and ritual responsibility. The issue is central when Paul makes his formal visit to the apostolic leaders in Jerusalem according to Acts 15. The declaration of Christians from Judea to the community in Antioch is, "Unless you are circumcized according to the custom of Moses, you cannot be saved " (15:1). After extended discussion of the question as to how much the Mosiac law is binding on members of the new community, and the quotation from Amos which is interpreted as promising a share by the Gentiles in the new people of God (15:16-17 = Amos 9:11-12), the decision is announced that Gentiles who turn to God are not to be troubled by obligation to observe the law (15:19). But James goes on to offer as his judgment that Gentiles are "to abstain from the pollution of idols and from unchastity, and from what is strangled and from blood. This latter phrase of dietary restriction that is to be binding on Gentile Christians echoes Lev 17:10-14. This contrasts sharply with Paul's version of the obligation placed on Gentile Christians by the Jerusalem-based apostles according to Gal 2:10, which was that the Gentile converts were to make a contribution to the church in Jerusalem: that is, "to remember the poor" (Gal 2:10). Clearly for the author of Acts, Paul's version of a non-legal obligation was not enough for Gentile Christians to fulfill. The minimal dietary requirements for Gentile Christians are repeated in Acts 21:25, so it clearly is regarded as a basic obligation.

Acts also reports Paul's having been charged with teaching "all the Jews who are among the Gentiles to forsake Moses, telling them not to circumcize their children or observe the customs" (21:21). In response to this charge, Paul manifests willingness to go beyond these minimal Jewish purity requirements in that he joins four others who have taken the Nazirite vow, have purified themselves ceremonially and have shaved their heads (Acts 21:23-26; cf. Num 6:1-21 [4]. This is to prove to his critics that "there is nothing in what they have been told about you"—that you teach Jews and Gentiles to abandon the law —"but that you yourself live in observance of the law" (21:24).

In his self-defense before Felix (24:10-21) Paul is quoted as saying that he had come to Jerusalem in order to worship, that he had caused no disturbance and raised no issues "either in the temple nor the synagogues", that none of their charges against him as a law-breaker can be upheld by evidence, and that he believes "everything laid down by the law or written in the prophets". His antagonists are invited to make a specific charge against him as one who violates the law of Moses. No such accusations are reported as forthcoming. Similarly, at the Roman tribunal in Caesarea (25:6-7) the Jews from Jerusalem brought "many serious charges" against Paul, "which they could not prove". Paul goes on to deny that he has done anything in defiance of the Jewish law, and declares that he is ready to die if he has deonstrably done so (25:8-10). Later in his testimony before King Agrippa (26:19-23) he asserts that his message about Jesus as the Christ involves "nothing but what the prophets and Moses said would come to pass". In his speech to the Jews in Rome (28:17) he testifies that he "had done nothing against the people or the customs of our fathers". Thus the picture of Paul in Acts makes the repeated point that Paul's convictions and personal behavior are not in conflict with the requirements of the Jewish scriptures. Paul emphatically and frequently in Acts identifies himself with the traditions of the Jews, not merely prior to his conversion, but also down to the end of his career as it is depicted in the Acts account.

The kind of clarity in differentiating membership in the covenant community of Israel from membership in the new covenant people that Paul achieves in his letters to the Galatians and the Romans is not attained in Acts. The author portrays Paul down to the end of his career as maintaining a strong commitment not only to the law and the prophets in a general sense as the sources from which the purpose of God for his people can be inferred and understood, but also as providing certain norms which Paul as a Christian

---

4. Although the details and procedures of Paul's self-purification do not fit the requirements set forth in Num 6:1-21, the basic point is clear: that Paul is portrayed as observing certain forms of ritual purity in order to persuade the Jews that he is not subverting the Mosaic law or encouraging Gentile Christians to do so. Cf. the discussion on E. Haenchen, *The Acts of the Apostles: A Commentary* (Philadelphia: Westminster, 1971, 610-614).

feels obligated to fulfill. Acts seems to represent one stage or stream in the development of early Christianity which is trying to affirm more continuity with Judaism than Paul himself appears to do in his preserved letters.

6.   The New Community Composed of Jews and Gentiles.

In the Acts account of the conversion and commissioning of Paul (9:1-18), Ananias is reluctant to obey the vision that called him to go and restore the sight of Saul/Paul because he has heard "how much evil he has done to the saints in Jerusalem" (9:13). But he is then told by "the Lord" that Paul "is a chosen instrument of mine to carry my name before the Gentiles and kings and the sons of Israel" (9:15). On his initial visit to Jerusalem following his conversion, the "disciples...were all afraid of him, for they did not believe that he was a disciple" (9:26), but regard him as an impostor who seeks access to their group in order to destroy it. The relationship between the traditional and the new community remains unclear.

It is Peter who is credited in Acts with enunciating the basic principle in his sermon at the house of Cornelius, who is pictured in Acts as "a centurion, a *dikaios* man who fears God (*phoboumenos ton theon)"*. Peter's vision of the animals, reptiles and birds in the sheet let down from heaven and the instruction to him to "kill and eat" (10:11-13) is seen as posing for him the basic dietary questions which establish boundaries that preclude observant having Jews social relations with those who do not obey these rules. Eating is the symbol of personal relationships within the covenant community, as indeed it was in the various parties of Judaism in the first century, especially for Pharisees and the Dead Sea community. Not only is he instructed repeatedly to kill and eat, but he is advised, "What God has cleansed, you must not call common (*koinon*) or unclean (10:14)."

Peter's sermon in the house of Cornelius (Acts 10:34-35) opens with the broadest theoretical statement on the issue of whether or not there are preconditions for participation in God's people: "Truly I perceive that God shows no partiality, but in every nation anyone who fears him (*phoboumenos auton*) and who does righteousness (*ergazemonos dikaiosunen*) is acceptable to him." The first and last parts of this sentence are radical, even revolutionary in import: no preferential treatment for any nation (*ethnei*), which would of course include the Jews; anyone who fears him is acceptable to him. But complicating the picture, and left unclarified by Peter in this statement is the qualification: "who does righteousness". The inclusive dimension appears again in 10:43 where Peter declares that "everyone who believes in him receives forgiveness of sins through his name." The confirmation that this is an accurate understanding of how God is working to form his new people comes when the Spirit falls "on *all* who hear the word" (10:44). The Jewish believers—here referred to as "the believers from among the circumcised"—were astounded "because the gift of the Holy Spirit had been poured out even on the Gentiles". Further assurance of Gentile participation in God's people is provided when they began "speaking in tongues and extolling God" (10:46). The rhetorical question about whether these Gentiles who have received the Holy Spirit should now be administered the rite of water baptism receives no challenge, and is followed by the baptism of these Gentile believers. Although the specific question of what "doing righteousness" involves is not addressed, much less answered here, remaining rather in the area of unelaborated peripheral detail.

Similarly, Paul's address in Pisidian Antioch (13:16) is aimed at "Men of Israel and you that fear God (*phoboumenoi ton theon*), and then proceeds to trace the history of Israel. It is from the posterity of Israel's king, David, that "God has brought a savior to Israel, Jesus" (13:23). But Paul goes on to declare that "those who lve in Jerusalem and their rulers, because they did not recognize [Jesus] nor understand the utterances of the prophets which are read every sabbath, fulfilled these by condemning him" (13:27). After showing how the scriptures were fulfilled in the death and resurrection of Jesus, he asserts that "Through this man forgiveness of sins is proclaimed to you [Jews] and by him *everyone that believes* is freed from everything from which you could not be freed by the law of Moses" (13:38-39). Once more there is an unqualifiedly conclusive declaration about the significance and availability of salvation through Jesus to everyone (*pas ho pisteuon*). As we noted earlier, the effect of this open invitation is evident in the result reported: "Many Jews and devout proselytes (*sebomenon proselyton*) followed Paul and Barnabas."

Returning to the policy discussion that takes place in Jerusalem when Paul and Barnabas sought aprroval of the apostles for their mission to the Gentiles (15:12-21), James recalls Peter's report "how God first visited the Gentiles, to take out of them a people for his name". Scriptural justification for this is provided through a quotation from Amos 9:11-12, supplemented by a line from Isa 45:21 which declare that "the rest of humanity will seek the Lord" and that these things have been made known by the Lord "from of old". The potential for humanity-wide participation in God's people is clearly announced in this policy-making apostolic conclave. It is in these terms of continuity with scripture and Jewish tradition that Paul offers his defense before King Agippa. Noting that his proclamation of the gospel had been "first to those at Damascus, then at Jerusalem and throughout all the country of Judea, and also to the Gentiles" (26:20), he declares that he had received "help from God" in his endeavor, and that he had said "nothing but what the prophets and Moses said would come to pass" (26:22). That divinely commissioned task of Paul's was to proclaim through Christ "light both to the people [that is, to Jews] and to the Gentiles" (26:23).

That same conclusion was confirmed following Peter's report to the Jerusalem apostles of his preaching to the household of Cornelius, when the apostles declare, "Then to the Gentiles also God has granted repentance unto life" (11:18). Similarly, following the preaching of Paul and Barnabas in Pisidian Antioch, there is a report that "when the Gentiles heard this [report that God was sending a light to the Gentiles] they wee glad and glorified the word of God, and as many as were ordained to eternal life believed" (13:48). Similar mixture of Jewish and Gentile response to the message of Paul is reported in 14:1 ("a great comapny believed, both of Jews and Greeks). The report to the church in Antioch in 14:27 is that the door of faith has been opened to the Gentiles, as it is to the Christian communities in Phoenicia and Samaria (15:3). This policy is confirmed by Peter (15:7) as well as by Paul and Barnabas (15:12) and James (15:14-17). The report of the apostolic council declaring them free of such Jewish legal obligations as circumcision—though not of minimal dietary requirements, as we have noted—is addressed to "the brethren who are of the Gentiles in Antioch and Syria and Cilicia" (15:23). Similarly, Acts 21:18-19 describes Paul's relating to the apostolic circle in Jerusalem "one by one the things God had done among the Gentiles through his ministry." The author of Acts leaves the reader with no question about the full participation of Gentiles along with Jews in the common life of the new people of God, even though the issue of the degree to which Gentiles are to conform to certain basic ritual requirements deriving from the Jewish law is not neatly resolved in this account.

7.   The Shift of Focus from Jews to the Gentile Mission.

In the latter half of Acts, the author not only reports the believing response to the gospel on the part of Gentiles, but also explicitly declares a shift from Jews to Gentiles as the hearers of the gospel. The bitter Jewish opposition to his preaching "that the Messiah was Jesus", when they "opposed and reviled him", led him to "shake out his garments" as a symbol of his responsibility discharged toward them and to declare, "Your blood be on your own heads! From now on I go to the Gentiles" (18:5-6). Following the subsequent hearing and the "united attack on Paul" by the Jews who had brought the accusations against him before Gallio, the proconsul, only to have him dismiss the charges and drive them "from the tribunal" (18:16), the ambivalence and ambiguity about ritual purity for Christians appears when Paul "cut his hair, for he had a vow" (18:18). And the report continues that at Ephesus Paul "went into the synagogue and argued with the Jews" (18:19).

In his self-defense before the crowd that had attacked him in Jerusalem, Paul identifies himself as a Jew and speaks in the Hebrew language (21:39-40), but declares that the Lord instructed him, "Depart; for I will send you far away to the Gentiles" (22:21). It is this claim that rouses the Jews to demand his execution (22:22). We have already noted that in his defense before Agrippa he claimed that his "heavenly vision" had led him to call Gentiles as well as Jews to repentance (26:20) and to see that the light of God should go out "to the [Jewish] people and to the Gentiles" (26:23).

The final pages of Acts are especially emphatic in documenting the shift by Paul from predominantly Jewish to primarily Gentile audiences for the proclamations of the gospel. The incident that takes place on his arrival in Rome dramatizes this shift in audiences. Initially he "called together the local leaders of the Jews" (28:17), who came to him at his lodging in great numbers (28:23). His attempt to persuade them about Jesus from the Jewish scriptures is partly successful, in that "some of them were convinced by what he said, while others disbelieved" (28:24). The climax of the Jew/Gentile issue in Acts comes at 28:25-28, however, where Paul turns to the prophecy of Isaiah 6:9-10 to show that evangelistic efforts to persuade the traditional people of God will come to nothing: they will "indeed hear but never understand". The text as quoted goes on to describe the historic Israel's lack of perception and response to God's message to his people. Paul concludes with the declaration, "Let it be known to you then that this salvation of God has been sent to the Gentiles: they will listen."

* *

Acts presents the reader with a complex portrait of the place of Jews in the new covenant people. The continuity between what God is now described as doing through Jesus with the history of Israel, and especially with the law and the prophets, is repeatedly affirmed. On the issue of the freedom of Gentile Christians from conformity to Jewish ritual requirements, however, there are both broad affirmations and indications of equivocation or at best synthesis of new freedom and traditional ritual obligations. It is inappropriate, therefore, to picture Acts as anti-Jewish with respect to either membership in the new community or sharp break with modes of community identity and piety that were part of the Jewish tradition. At the same time, Acts pictures Paul as the one who launches the new enterprise of inclusion of Gentiles in the covenant people. Yet Paul is seen as agreeing to minimal ritual requirements for Gentile Christians and for himself, even while affirming the new enterprise which is to include Gentiles in God's people. The earlier Jewish requirement for proselytes to accept circumcision in order to enter the covenant is rejected, as is the pattern of God-fearers who remain on the periphery of the covenant people. Yet the author of Acts is unwilling to go as far as Paul does in his preserved letters in dismissing all ritual obligations as requisite for participation in the new people of God. It is possible that early Christian reading of the Jewish scriptures led some of them unconsciously to adopt certain minimal requirements from ancient Israel's rules for covenantal participation. It is even conceivable that Acts represents a reaction to the radical disjunction between the Old Testament and the New that can be documented in the second century as being promoted by Marcion. Whatever the origin, Acts represents forthright affirmation of the full participation in the covenant. Yet its point of view is at the same time more subtly influenced by the desire to provide visible cultic signs of both continuity with the traditions of Israel and overt, public identity for Christians in a culture permeated by competing religious claims.

Melito the Bishop and the Synagogue at Sardis: Text and Context[1]

A.T. Kraabel

For the historian of ancient religions,[2] the Harvard-Cornell expedition to Sardis became impossible to ignore on 28 July 1962 when Prof. G.M.A. Hanfmann identified the synagogue of Sardis.[3] Subsequent excavation and research have revealed that the Sardis Jewish community was a large one, with a degree of wealth, social status and political power,[4] and that the synagogue, on a choice location in the center of the Roman city, is by far the largest yet discovered anywhere in the ancient world.[5]

---

1 Frequently used works are abbreviated as follows: Bonner, *Homily* = *The Homily on the Passion, by Melito Bishop of Sardis, with Some Fragments of the Apocryphal Ezekiel,* ed. Campbell Bonner (Studies and Documents, ed. K. and S. Lake, no. 12, 1940).. Blank, Meliton = *Meliton von Sardes: Vom Passa,* ubersetzt, eingeleitet und kommentiert von J. Blank (Sofia, ed. J. Tyciak and W. Nyssen, no. 3, 1963). Perler, *Meliton* = *Meliton de Sardes, Sur la Paque et Fragments,* ed. O. Perler (Sources chretiennes, no. 123, 1966). Hanfmann, *Sardis und Lydien* = G.M.A. Hanfmann, "Sardis und Lydien," *Abbandlunger der geistes- und sozialwissenschaftlichen Klasse,* Akademie der Wissenschaften und der Literatur 6 (Mainz 1960) 497-536. Johnson, "Christianity in Sardis" = S.E. Johnson, "Christianity in Sardis," in *Early Christian Origins, Studies in Honor of H. Willoughby,* ed. A. Wikgren (1961) 81-90. Mitten, "A new Look at Ancient Sardis" = D.G. Mitten, "A New Look at Ancient Sardis," *Biblical Archaeologist* 29 (1966) 38-68. Annual reports of the Sardis excavations by Prof. Hanfmann in BASOR are cited by fascicle number, year of publication, and page number. Eusebius, *Ecclesiastical History,* is abbreviated *HE* and cited by book, chapter and paragraph.

    Editor's note: This essay appeared in *Studies Presented to George M.A. Hanfmann,* edited by D.G. Mitten, J.G. Pedley and J.A. Scott, by the Fogg Art Museum, Harvard University, Monograph in Art and Archaeology II (Mainz, Germany: Verlag Philipp von Zabern, 1971) 77-85.

2 One of the first to recognize the building's importance was Prof. E.R. Goodenough. At the time of my first meeting with him, he was already weakened by the disease which was to take his life; we were to discus quite another matter, but almost before I knew it he had plans, photographs and reconstructions of the synagogue spread out before me and was commenting on them with obvious pleasure and excitement. His preliminary observations were inserted in his *Jewish Symbols in the Greco-Roman Period* (New York 1965) XII 191-195.

3 Prof. Hanfmann has described the events leading up to the discover in "The Ancient Synagogue of Sardis," *Fourth World Congress of Jewish Studies, Papers, I* (Jerusalem 1967) 38.

4 Josephus preserves two Roman decrees which demonstrate the extent of the influence of Sardis Jews by the first century B.C.E. The wording of one decree indicates that by this time they had established themselves firmly enough to claim before a Roman official that "from of old they have had their own assembly [in Sardis, governed] by ancestral laws, and their own place where they [handle] their own affairs and decide their own controversies," *AJ* 14.235. In the other decree a Roman proconsul on Caesar's order writes to the magistrats and *boule* of Sardis, forbidding interference in the collection of the tax for the Jerusalem temple, *AJ* 16.171. Further on these decrees, A.T. Kraabel, "Judaism in Western Asia Minor under the Roman Empire," forthcoming in the series *Studia Post-Biblica,* ed. J.C.H. Lebram.

5 Reports of the work on the synagogue appear in the annual excavation reports, beginning

(continued...)

But other religions were represented in Roman Sardis as well,[6] in particular Christianity; Asia Minor was the first area outside Syria-Palestine to be
reached by the Christian mission.

By the end of the first century C.E., when the first literary evidence for
Sardis Christianity appears,[7] a congregation had existed long enough to be
compared (unfavorably) with the church of the past: "You have the reputation
of being alive, but you are dead," (Revelation 3:1, cf. 2-6). As the site of one
of the "Seven Churches of Asia" the city attracted—and continues to attract—
numerous Christian pilgrims and tourists. The remains of four Christian
churches or chapels built between the fourth and the thirteenth centuries are
still to be seen.[8]

Given the close connection between ancient Judaism and ancient Christianity, it now becomes necessary to re-examine the relations between Sardis
Christians and Sardis Jews during the time the synagogue was in use. A decade ago we knew that Jews and Christians lived in this city, but no one could
have predicted the size and influence of the Jewish community; now, thanks
to Prof. Hanfmann and those who worked with him, much more is known about
Sardis Jews. What does this new information indicate about their Christian
contemporaries? Does it only supplement, or does it contradict and revise
what had been said about Sardis Christianity? What results when excavations

---

5(...continued)
with *BASOR* 170 (1963); other publications about the site, including those on the synagogue, are
customarily listed in the first footnote of each annual report. Important inscriptions discovered
in 1962 were published with exhaustive commentary by L. Robert, *Nouvelles inscriptions de
Sardes* (Paris 1964) I 37-58. See also Mitten, "A New Look at Ancient Sardis," 63-66 and the
section on Sardis in Kraabel (*supra*, n.4).

6 J. Keil, "Die Kulte Lydiens," *Anatolian Studies Presented to Sir. W.M. Ramsay*, ed. W.H.
Buckler and W.M. Calder (Manchester 1923) 239-266 is still a useful summary. On evidence from
the present excavations: G.M.A. Hanfmann and M. Balmuth, "The Image of an Anatolian
Goddess at Sardis," *In Memoriam H.T. Bossert*, ed. U.B. Alkim *JKF* 2 (1965) 262-269. L. Robert,
(*supra*, n.5) 23-36. S.E. Johnson, "A Sabazios Inscription from Sardis," *Religions in Antiquity:
Essays in Memory of E.R. Goodenough*, ed. J. Neusner (supplements to *Neumen* 14 [1968]) 542-
550. A.T. Kraabel, "*Hypistos* and the Synagogue at Sardis," *Greek, Roman and Byzantine Studies*
10 (1969) 81-93. A comprehensive treatment of the religious life of Roman Sardis, using all the
new evidence, is yet to be done.

7 On Christianity in Sardis: Johnson, "Christianity in Sardis" and the biblical dictionaries.

8 These may be located on the map of Sardis in *BASOR* 174 (1964) 6, reprinted in Mitten
"A New Look at Ancient Sardis" 39: the small, fourth-century chapel attached to the Artemis
temple (map, no. 12), *BASOR* 166 (1962) 49-54. The "baptistry," perhaps of the sixth century
A.D. (Hanfmann, *Sardis und Lydien*, pl. 15:23), originally one of the shops just west of the synagogue (map, no. 16) and south of the gymnasium (map, no. I), *BASOR* 157 (1960) 32f. The
Byzantine church "E" (map, no. 17) of ca. the twelfth century, *BASOR* 174 (1964)14-20. An unex-
cavated Byzantine church (map, no. 4) of the twelfth or thirteenth century: Mitten, "A New Look
at Ancient Sardis" 67.

suddenly supply a context, a "social location" for ancient religious texts, and the discipline of archaeology provides important new data for the discipline of patristics? The obvious place to begin is with Melito,[9] for several reasons. He was bishop of the Sardis Christians in the latter part of the second century C.E., when the Jews were first putting their fine building into use. He was known previously only through literary evidence: fragments[10] scattered in later patristic texts and (since its discovery in 1937) one nearly complete work, the *Peri Pascha*. Finally, he held to a theology which had its roots deep in earliest Christianity, which was nevertheless condemned by the later Church, and which has intriguing and complex relationships with ancient Judaism: he was a Quartodeciman (of which, more later).

The major source for understanding Melito is, of course, the *Peri Pascha*; what was known about him before its publication may be quickly summarized:

1. He is numbered with the disciples Philip and John and the martyr bishop Polycarp of Smyrna as one of the "great luminaries" of the Church in Asia Minor; he is "melito the eunuch,"[11] who lived entirely in the Holy Spirit (and) who lies (buried) in Sardis"—so Polycrates of Ephesus (ca. 195 C.E.) as quoted by Eusebius (*HE* 5.24.2 and 5).

2. As bishop, Melito addressed an Apology to the emperor Marcus Aurelius (fragments in *HE* 4.26.5-11) in which for the first time it is argued that the Empire should support the Church because they began together in the time of Augustus, prospered when together, and thus belong together: "Our philosophy first grew among the barbarians, but its full flower came among your nations during the glorious reign of your ancestor Augustus; it became a good omen for your empire, since from that time the power of the Romans has grown mighty and magnificent" (*HE* 4.26.7).[12] It has

---

9 Generally on Melito, see the introductions to the *Peri Pascha:* Bonner, *Homily;* Blank, *Meliton*; and Perler, *Meliton*; also A. von Harnack, *Die Uberlieferung der griechischen Apologeten des zweiten Jahrhunderts in der alten Kirche und im Mittelalter* (Texte und Untersuchungen zur Geschichte der altgriechischen Literatur I, 1-2 [Leipzig 1882]) 240-278; Johnson, "Christianity in Sardis" 83-85; J. Quasten, *Patrology* (Westminster, Md. 1962) I 142-248. I use here the Perler text, citing both section (as divided by Bonner and continued by subsequent editors) and line. A useful though incomplete bibliography of Melito has been published by R.M. Mainka, "Meliton von Sardes," *Claretianum* 5 (1965) 225-255.

10 These fragments were most recently reprinted by Perler, *Meliton* 218-244; he also gives on 128 the text of a hymn-fragment (*Papyrus Bodmer* XII, publ. 1959) which he attributes to Melito.

11 On this adjective, Perler, *Meliton* 7f.

12 On this argument, E. Peterson, "Der Monotheismus als politisches Problem," (first published in 1935) in *Theologische Traktate* (Munich 1951) 85f. and H. Fuchs, *Der geistige Widerstand*

(continued...)

been suggested that this Apology may have been presented by Melito to the emperor's colleague, Lucius Verus, who passed through Asia in 166 C.E. and is known to have visited Ephesus; a statue of Verus was erected in the Sardis gymnasium about that time, and a Hebrew inscription may have been put up in his honor in the synagogue as well, increasing the likelihood that Verus' trip included a stop at Sardis.[13]

3. Melito was an accomplished orator, a man of *elegans et declamatorium ingenium*—so Tertullian (as quoted by Jerome in *De Viris Inlustribus* 24). His rhetoric closely resembles the "Asian" style of the Second Sophistic,[14] and his use of allegory follows earlier Stoic models.[15]

The *Peri Pascha* was to furnish additional evidence of Melito's oratorical skill; its opening lines indicate his procedure: "The text from the Hebrews' Exodus has been read, the words of the (saving) mystery have been plainly stated..." The biblical text upon which Melito is to speak is Exodus 12, the account of the *pascha*, the Passover; it is read and the *Peri Pascha* then follows, an intricate,[16] ornamented, often florid Christian interpretation and application of that text. Both scripture and sermon were doubtless in Greek; earlier suggestions that the biblical text was first read in Hebrew and then freely translated into Greek seem unlikely in view of the fact that even within

---

12(...continued)
gegen Rom (Berlin 1964) 76f. Generally K. Aland, "The Relation between Church and State in Early Times: A Reinterpretation," *JThS* 19 (1968) 115-127.

13 Mitten, "A New Look at Ancient Sardis" 62; Johnson "Christianity in Sardis" 87. The inscription for the statue (IN 58.4) was published by Johnson, *BASOR* 158 (1960) 7-10, no. 4, cf. L. Robert, "Bulletin epigraphique," *REG* 75 (1962) 200f. no. 290. The Hebrew inscription, a fragment (IN 62.79) has been read by Prof. I. Rabinowitz as *beros*, a transliteration of "Verus," *BASOR* 187 (1967) 25. Earlier, Sordi had suggested that the Apology was composed a decade later, when Marcus Aurelius was in the East, M. Sordi, "I nuovi decreti di Marco Aurelio control i Cristiani," *Studi Romani* 9 (1961) 365ff., especially 368ff.

14 Bonner, *Homily* 27, originally claimed that, in style, the *Peri Pascha* followed chiefly Jewish texts (the Septuagint above all), but A. Wifstrand produced sufficient parallels from the Second Sophistic (e.g. Maximus of Tyre) to prove it the dominant influence, A. Wifstrand, "The Homily of Melito on the Passion" *VigChr* 2 (1948) 201-223. Melito probably had ample opportunity to experience and appreciate this kind of rhetoric, since "the homeland [of the Second sophistic] is above all the cities of Asia Minor: Ephesus, Miletus, Mytilene and Smyrna," K. Gerth, "Die zweite oder neue Sophistik, " *RE* Supp. 8 (1956) 719f. cf. A. Lesky, *A History of Greek Literature* (London 1966) 829ff. and Perler, *Meliton* 26-28.

15 R.M. Grant, "Melito of Sardis on Baptism," *VigChr* 4 (1950) 33-36, discusses a fragment of Melito's *De Baptismo* and concludes: "Melito is the first Christian writer in whom we find Stoic exegetical theology newly baptized for Christian use," 36. Perler prints the fragment (*Meliton*, 228-232), appears to agree with this analysis, but does not cite Grant's article.

16 On the involved structure of the *Peri Pascha*, J. Smit Sibinga, "Melito of Sardis. The Artist and His Text," *VigChr* 24 (1970) 81-104.

the Sardis synagogue the language of the inscriptions is not Hebrew but Greek. Of the more than eighty Jewish inscriptions now known from Sardis, only three are obviously in Hebrew: two one-word fragments, IN 62.66f ("Shalom!") and IN 62.79 ("Verus"?) and a medieval graffito, IN 64.53.[17] Even before the Sardis excavations it was becoming clear that the Jews of western Asia Minor used Greek, not Hebrew; before 1962 the only published Anatolian Jewish text in Hebrew was the fragmentary Greek-Hebrew bilingual (*MAMA* VI 334), a biblical blessing from the Jewish community in Acmonia, Phrygia. If the Jews of Asia Minor wrote in Hebrew so infrequently, it appears doubtful that their Christian neighbors would have made use of it in their worship.[18]

4.   Melito is also the first Christian known to have made a pilgrimage to "the Holy Land."[19] The purpose of the journey was to secure an accurate canon of the books of the Jewish scriptures. The list he gives (quoted in *HE* 4.26.14) is "the earliest Christian Old Testament list of certain date" and closely resembles that ratified by the Jews in Palestine at the "Synod of Jamnia" in the last part of the first century C.E.[20] On the basis of this list Melito then compiled the *Eklogai*, a six-volume anthology of scripture selections.[21]

5.   Finally, Melito was a Quartodeciman: like many other Anatolian Christians of his time, he celebrated Easter (the Christian "Passover") on the

---

17 On IN 62.66 and 79, see *BASOR* 170 (1963) 44 and the discussion *supra*, n. 13. The following fragments have sometimes been considered Hebrew, but are too incomplete (a single letter? one or two half-letters?) for identification: IN 62.63, 67, 68, 78, 83, 88, 123, and 182.

18 The opening lines of the *Peri Pascha* allow a translation which suggests that the biblical text was first read in Hebrew and then translated or paraphrased; such a procedure is known to have been used in the synagogues and the Jewish-Christian churches of Palestine (where the translation was usually Aramaic, a *targum*). Those who argued that Melito's congregation acted similarly cited this Palestinian custom and all but ignored the evidence from Asia Minor, whether archaeological, epigraphic or literary. The discussion is summarized in Perler, *Meliton* 131-133, but the archaeological evidence available to Perler in 1966 is not mentioned; indeed, Perler's edition makes no reference to Sardis *as a city* at all, or to any of the excavations done there.

19 *HE* 4.26.13 reproduces Melito's description of the journey, cf. J. Finegan, *The Archeology of the New Testament* (Princeton 1969) v, xii.

20 A. Sundberg, *The Old Testament of the Early Church (Harvard Theological Studies*, no. 20, 1964) 56, cf. 133f. Not all Church leaders agreed the Christian Old Testament should conform to the Jewish canon; soon after Melito, Origen would make a clear distinction between Jewish and Christian canons and consider "some books as authoritative in the church even though they were not included in his list of the Hebrew canon," Sundberg 138, cf. 134-138.

21 In addition to the *Peri Pascha*, the *Eklogai* and the Apology already mentioned, Melito wrote sixteen other works whose titles are known, see the list in *HE* 4.26.14 and the discussions in Harnack (*supra*, n. 9) 240-270 and in Perler, *Meliton* 11-15. Except for the *Peri Pascha* and a few fragments, these writings are lost, either because they seemed no longer relevant to later Christians (so Harnack 248) or, more probably, because their theology was no longer acceptable, so W. Bauer, *Rechtglaubigkeit und Ketzerei im altestern Christentum* (Tubingen 1964[2]) 155-157.

day of the Jews' Passover (14 Nisan in their calendar) no matter what day of the week it might be; other Christians, those in the West in particular, celebrated Easter on the Sunday following Passover. The Quartodeciman practice was condemned by the Roman church as "Judaizing," a judgment which was repeated at the Council of Nicea, 325 C.E.[22]

The above summarizes what was known about Melito before the discovery of the *Peri Pascha*; there is thus far no obvious hostility toward Jews in his character or theology.[23]

Upon publication, the *Peri Pascha* proved to be a Quartodeciman sermon, prepared to be preached at the celebration of the Christian *pascha* immediately after the reading of the Jews' traditional Passover text, Exodus 12. Perler, the most recent editor, has outline the sermon as follows:[24]

Prologue, 1.1-11.72: An introduction to the typological import of the Passover.

I.   The typology of the Jewish Passover, 11.73-71,522.
II. Israel's denial—denunciations directed at her, 72.523-100.766.

Epilogue, 100.767-105.823.

While none of what was previously known about Melito was contradicted by the new text, nothing in that earlier evidence is sufficient explanation for the

---

22 The literature on Quartodecimanism is vast, all but a fraction of it on the dogmatic question of the proper understanding of Easter; see B. Lohse, *Das Passafest der Quartadecimaner* (Beitrage zur Forderung christlicher Theologie, 2. Reihe, no. 54, 1953) *passim*. H. Leclercq, "Paques," *DACL* 13:2 (1938) 1521 ff. (on Nicea, 1541ff.). Important articles: N. Zernov, "Eusebius and the Paschal Controversy at the End of the Second Century," *Church Quarterly Review* 116 (1933) 24-41, esp. n. 3, p. 38, on the church-political effectiveness of charging one's enemies with "Judaizing." O. Casel, "Art und Sinn der altesten christlichen Osterfeier," *Jabrbuch fur Liturgiewissenschaft* 14 (Munster 1938) 1-78. C. Richardson, "The Quartodecimans and Synoptic Chronology," *HThR* 33 (1940) 177-190, cf. bibliography, 177, n. 2. C. Dugmore "A Note on the Quartodecimans," *Studia Patristica IV (Texte und Untersuchungen zur Geschichte der altchristlichen Literatur* 79, Berlin 1961) 411-421. M. Richard, "La question pascale au IIe siecle," *Orient Syrien* 6 (1961) 179-199. Whatever the degree of "Judaizing" in this practice (and that depends greatly on one's definition of the term), a large problem which it raised stemmed from the fact that the Church was less and less comfortable with the idea that the date of a major Christian festival should depend on the Jews' calendar and calculations, cf. pseudo-Cyprian, *De Pascha Computus,* tr. G. Ogg (London 1955), paragraph 1: "we desire to show...that Christians need at no time...walk in blindness and stupidity behind the Jews as though they did not know what was the day of Passover..." (written 243 C.E.; probably in Africa).

23 It might be argued that Melito seems rather favorably inclined toward the Jews. This impression would be further strengthened if Lohse were correct in his assumption that a "fast on the Jews' behalf" was a major part of the Quartodeciman celebration (*supra*, n. 22) 62-75; but strong arguments against Lohse on this point have been raised by N. Hyldahl, "Zum Titel *Per Pascha* bei Meliton" *Studia Theological* 19 (1965) 55-67, esp. 65f.

24 Perler, *Meliton* 43f.

fact that a fourth of the *Peri Pascha* is a prolonged, bitter, personal attack on "Israel."[25] It occupies Perler's entire second section, but the language of 73.534-80.595 and 93.695-94.726 is perhaps the strongest:

Israel! Why have you committed this new injustice? you dishonored the one who honored you. You scorned the one who glorified you. You denied the one who acknowledged you. You repudiated the one who preached to you. You killed the one who gave you life. Israel! Why did you do this? Was it not written on your behalf: 'Do not spill innocent blood lest you die an evil death?' Israel answers, 'It was I who killed the Lord.' 'But why?' 'Because he had to suffer.' Israel, you deceive yourself when you spin such sophistries about the slaughter of the Lord. He had to suffer, but not at *your* hands. He had to be abused, but not at *your* hands. He had to be condemned, but not at *your* hands. He had to be nailed [to the cross], but not by *your* right hand...(73:534-75:549).

At night you made everything ready for the murder of the Lord; you prepared for him sharp nails and false witnesses and snares and scourges and vinegar and bile and a sword and oppression, as though for a murderous thief. You laid whips to his body and the crown of thorns to his head; you bound his fine hands which formed you of earth, and that fine mouth of his which gave you life to eat—you fed it bile and you killed your lord on the great festival...(78:571-79:579).

The "great festival" mentioned also in 93.694 is further described in 93.695 as "the festival of unleavened bread."

Paragraph 80 which follows the above quotation is an elaborate contrasting of the holiday celebration of the Jews and the suffering of Jesus, occurring simultaneously. Paragraph 93, playing on the bitter herbs associated with Passover, lists the "bitter things" done to Jesus at the Crucifixion, while paragraph 94 draws the attention of the gentiles to these horrors of the Jews:

Listen all you gentile nations! Look! A new murder has taken place in the midst of Jerusalem, a city founded on law, a Hebrew city, a prophet's city, a city thought just...in the middle of the street and city, in the midst of the city with everyone looking on, occurred the just man's unjust death (94.711-16, 724-26).

---

25 I am unable to explain how a generation could read the *Peri Pascha* without calling attention to the implications of this polemic. L. Goppelt, in a book titled (!)*Christentum und Judentum im ersten und zweiten Jahrhundert* (Beitrage zur Forderung christlicher Theologie, 2. Reihe, no. 55, 1954) devotes one sentence to Melito, p. 267. Neither the Bonner nor the Perler edition comments on the polemic. J. Quastern (*supra*, n. 9) 243 and Johnson, "Christianity in Sardis" 83 each devote one sentence to Melito's attack on the Jews.

Quartodeciman practice furnishes no theological motive for such vituperation; few extended texts from this movement still exist outside the *Peri Pascha,* but the basic ones studied by Lohse show no such hostility.[26] Bonner has
compared to the *Peri Pascha* and even quotes Exodus 12:1-15, 43-49 verbatim
in paragraph 5.[27] References to the Jews are bitter, but quite brief, e.g. 24
and 55.2. Although it is an Easter sermon, Easter is dated to 14 Nisan. Since
Melito and pseudo-Chrysostom use Exodus 12 as a text, we might expect more
correlation than appears between them.

Comparisons of the *Peri Pascha* with contemporary examples of *Adversus
Judaeos* literature yields little, since few second-century texts are available;
such writings become important and extensive in the third and fourth centuries
and later.[28] Of the two major texts extant, Justin's *Dialogue with Trypho* contains nothing approaching Melito's frontal attack on the Jews, but this could
be attributed to Justin's dialogue form, which might make verbal barrages less
desirable.[29] In Tertullian's *Adversus Judaeos,* however, something comparable
to Melito might be expected; the author is usually most combative, cf. his
writing against gentile pagans, e.g. the second book of *Ad Nationes,* 197 C.E.
His *Adversus Judaeos,* however, is less a personal attack than a battle over the

---

26 Lohse (*supra,* n. 22) 10-20. It might be argued that Melito's attitude is only a continuation
of the hostility toward "the Jews" which appears in the Gospel of John, since Quartodecimanism
is usually considered an example of Johannine influence upon Anatolian Christianity; but then
the polemic should appear generally throughout the Quartodeciman texts, and it does not. On
the "anti-Semitism" of the Gospel of John: E. Grasser, "Die Antijudische Polemik im Johannes-
evangelium," *New Testament Studies* II (1964) 74-90.

27 Bonner, *Homily* 57-62, cf. J. Quasten, *Patrology* (Westminster, Md. 1962) II 178f. and the
edition of P. Nautin, *Homilies Pascales* I (Sources chretiennes, no. 27, 1950). Hippolytus and less
frequently his opponent Callistus (both of Rome, first half of the third century A.D.) have each
been credited with this text, but recently a strong case has been made that the actual author is
an unknown contemporary of Melito from western Asia Minor, R. Cantalamess, *L'omilia "In S.
Pascha" dello Pseudo-Ippolito di Roma* (Milan 1967), known to me through the review by J.
Danielou, *RecSciRel* 57 (1969) 79-84.

28 See the traditionalist in J. Juster, *Les juifs dans l'empire romain* (Paris 1914) I 54ff. Lost
works of this type include the *Discussion between Jason and Papiscus,* by Aristo of Pella (J. Quasten *supra,* n. 9 195f.) and two Anatolian writings titled *Against the Jews,* one by Miltiades, the
other by Apollinaris of Hierapolis, Phrygia (Quasten 228f.). The anti-Jewish addition to *Fourth
Ezra,* so-called *"Fifth Ezra,"* perhaps also belongs here, but since it is attributed to the biblical
Ezra, direct references to Jewish-Christian controversies are not to be expected; see the translation in E. Henneck, *New Testament Apocrypha,* ed. W. Schneemelcher (Philadelphia 1965) II
691-695 with an introduction by H. Duensng, who dates the test ca. A.D. 200 (p. 689).

29 As Justin sets up the discussion, extended acrimony is out of place, cf. A. von Harnack,
*Judentum und Judenchristentum in Justins Dialog mit Trypho (Texte und Untersuchungen zur Ges-
chichte der altchristlichen Literatur,* 39.1, Leipzig 1913) 92: "In reality the Dialogue with Trypho
is a monologue by the victor, with the opponent speaking not for himself, but as Justin wishes
him to speak." But see also M. Simon, *Verus Israel* (Paris 1964²) 167ff.

Old Testament in which Tertullian sees Jesus everywhere prefigured. On comparison, Melito appears to be thinking of flesh-and-blood Jews, Tertullian of shadow-figures, theological abstractions.[30]

If neither Quartodeciman theology nor the conventions of *Adversus Judaeos* literature fully account for the bitterness of Melito's attack, new evidence might profitably be consulted; the results of the Sardis excavations to date suggest two hypotheses: that Melito was driven to take the offensive in the *Peri Pascha* by the size and power of the Jewish community, and that the new arguments which Melito used in his *Apology* put him on collision course with Sardis Jews. To take this in order:

The size, the grandeur and the choice location of the synagogue suggest that is was owned by a powerful group.[31] The titles used by Jews in the synagogue inscriptions are also impressive.[32] Three members of the Roman provincial administration are mentioned, among them a former procurator; as an imperial agent, he may well have been a powerful man, able to reach the ear of higher provincial officials. Nine men use the title *bouleutes*, indicating that they were members of the city council, thus men of substance, economic and social power, as well as political leaders. Under the Empire the city *boule* had grown to resemble the Roman senate: members were from the wealthier and better educated class; membership tended to be for life.[33] The impression is that certain Jewish families had been in Sardis a long time and had accumulated power and status. It is likely that some of the Sardis Christians

---

30 On Tertullian *Adversus Judaeos*: J. Quasten (*supra*, n. 27) 268f. The difference between the two writers is made even more striking in view of the fact that Harnack (*supra*, n.9) once called Melito "the Tertullian of Asia Minor" and drew up a detailed list of the similarities between the two writers, 249, with n. 355.

31 The extent of this power, both political and economic, would be even greater if a theory of the late A.H. Detweiler proves correct (cf. *BASOR* 187 [1967] 23, 25); he argued that the building began as a civil basilica and was later turned over to the Jews, who remodeled it into a synagogue. He suggested that the wealthy Jewish community received the building in return for financial assistance in the rebuilding of the city after the disastrous earthquake of A.D. 17, a reconstruction which is known to have extended over at least a century and a half. The synagogue *is* architecturally an integral part of a complex of *public* buildings, the Marble Court, the gymnasium, etc.; this is a location of prominence unparalleled in the Diaspora and Detweiler's explanation for it is the most plausible yet advanced.

32 Information on these titles from p. 6f. of the 1966 Final Report of epigrapher J.H. Kroll (Sardis Expedition files, unpublished typescript, by courtesy of the author and the Sardis Expedition).

33 So G. Bowersock, *Augustus and the Greek World* (Oxford 1965) 85f.; D. Magie, *Roman Rule in Asia Minor* (Princeton 1950) 639ff. The example of these Sardis Jews calls into question the extreme statement of A. Sherwin-White, *The Roman Citizenship* (Oxford 1939) 255 about the "intransigence" of the Empire's Jews who "could not come within the (Roman) *civitas* because they would not."

in Melito's time were converted Jews or descendants of converted Jews, and that the relationship of Christianity to Judaism was a perennial issue. The Jews' attitude might have been one of hostility toward "apostates" or one of openness; either way, in the face of such a large and powerful Jewish community Melito felt forced to adopt the stance demonstrated in the *Peri Pascha*. Additional pressure to take such a position would come from the fact that (as a Quartodeciman) he as liable to the charge that his Christianity was little different from Judaism. The *Peri Pascha* is then a strong attempt on Milito's part to establish and preserve the identity of his religion over against the Jews, while retaining the Quartodeciman practice almost universal in the Christianity of his area.

The line of argument taken by Melito in the *Apology* might also have brought him into conflict with the city's Jews; as was mentioned above this text uses a line of reasoning new to second-century apologetic: The Empire should support and protect the Church because they were begun at the same time, and the state has prospered since. But in Sardis this approach means a direct conflict with the Jews, who had long sought a privileged position with the state. Melito may be taking the offensive against the Jews when he writes to the emperor, "Our philosophy first grew up among the barbarians" (*HE* 4.26.7); are "the barbarians" the Jews?

If Verus did in fact visit Sardis ca. 166 C.E., and if Melito did present him with a copy of the *Apology* at that time, and if the Jews also honored Verus with an inscription in Hebrew, then the elements of a vigorous Jewish-Christian conflict are all present at the time of that visit, something which could have prompted the *Peri Pascha* as well. Such a precise and elaborate hypothesis is not required for the main point however, since the size of the Jewish community and its political power are well enough attested; it seems likely that there is a socio-political motivation, more than a theological one, in Melito's attack.[34]

Using archaeological evidence to solve literary and theological problems is never easy, and frequently the "answers" are not easily accepted. Nevertheless Melito's vehemence *is* there in the *Peri Pascha* and attempts to under-

---

34 The existence of Christians throughout the Empire and perhaps particularly at Sardis may have become increasingly precarious in the next few years as the indirect result of an act of the Roman senate, partially preserved in an inscription discovered by the H.C. Butler expedition to Sardis, *Sardis* VII:I: *The Greek and Latin Inscriptions,* ed. W.H. Buckler and D.M. Robinson (Leyden 1932) no. 16; see J.H. Oliver and R.E.A. Palmer, "Minutes of an Act of the Roman Senate," *Hesperia* 24 (1955) 320-349. The act is dated to A.D. 177; Melito's death is usually placed within the ninth decade of the second century. The Oliver-Palmer interpretation of this inscription was first brought to my attention by J.D.B. Hamilton, S.J., of the University of Minnesota; it is accepted, and the act is placed within the context of Marcus Aurelius' career, by Anthony Birley, *Marcus Aurelius* (London 1966) 275-279,cf. 328-331.

stand it by fitting it into his theology have not been satisfactory.[35] If new explanations are to be attempted, the evidence provided by Prof. Hanfmann and his colleagues may no longer be ignored.

---

35 They have produced more than dissatisfaction; note the anguish of the Christian commentator, Blank (*Meliton* 81ff.) and the rage of E. Werner, a Jew, in his "Melito of Sardis, the First Poet of Deicide," *Hebrew Union College Annual* 37 (1966) 191-210.

Christian Self-definition in the *Adversus Judaeos* Preachers in the Second Century[1]

Robert S. MacLennan

A.T. Kraabel in referring to the *pascha* controversy in the fourth century[2] makes the following comment:

References to Jews occur in many places in the Christian literature of this period: in the sermons and theological treatises of course, but also in the martyr-acts and in the genre called adversus Judaeos literature. Yet there was little interest on the part of non-Jews in studying these Jews dispassionately or in portraying them objectively. This leads to two further conclusions: [1] the "information" which we thought we had about these Jews and their Judaism must now be viewed with great skepticism, for from the Christian sources at least, we really know less than we think we know; [2] but that also requires taking a second look at what is sometimes called the "anti-Semitism" of this period. The tensions between Jews and gentiles may have been greater or less than they appear. There was no uniformity of treatment, and it would be misleading to assume that what held for one period or location was true necessarily for another. There is no way to tell until each source has been tested first for its inner biases.

The same observations and advise could be given for the references to Jews and their Judaism in the Christian literature of the second century. The Christian writings known as *adversus Judaeos* interestingly have never been studied with an eye to discover the "Jews" or the "Judaism" to which they refer. Few scholars have viewed these writings which speak about Jews and Judaism with enough "skepticism." It is still assumed that there was tension between Jews and gentiles in the early centuries of emerging Judaism and Christianity.

Kraabel's suggestion that we "test" each of these writings for their "inner biases" leads us in a very different direction. The purpose of this essay is to present one example of an early *adversus Judaeos* preacher which demonstrates how a more careful look at the environment out of which these early Christian writers worked gives a more adequate picture of the relationships between gentiles and Jews in the second century.

---

1 Editor's note: Sections of this chapter have been borrowed from my chapter on Melito in *Early Christian Texts on Jews and Judaism, BJS* 194, (Atlanta, GA: Scholars Press, 1990).

2 *"Synagoga caeca.* Systematic Distortion in Gentile Interpretations of Evidence for Judaism in the Early Christian Period." In *"To See Ourselves as Others See Us": Christians Among Jews and Gentiles,* edited by Jacob Neusner and Ernest S. Frerichs, (Chico, CA: Scholars Press, 1985) 241.

As a result of reading the *adversus Judaeos* writings with more "skepticism" the following conclusions can be made:

(1) Each *adversus Judaeos* writing is unique and the result of one writer's concern about the relationship between Christians and Jews. The writer was not stating a universally accepted view of Jews and their Judaism.

(2) Each city had its own particular relationship with Jews. In many cities Jews were "at home" and contributed to the general welfare of their towns.

(3) Each author of the *adversus Judaeos* writings was more concerned with Christian self-definition then with attacking Jews or their Judaism.

(4) When the *adversus Judaeos* writer does talk about Jews or Judaism, he is speaking about them either as he is experiencing them in his particular time and place or as "Bible-people."[3] Curiously, the writers never seem to talk directly to or about Jews, unless the Jews are invented for a dialogue. But generally there is no dialogue taking place between these two groups.

These conclusions hold true for four second century *adversus Judaeos* preachers: Justin's *Dialogue with Trypho the Jew*, Barnabas' *Epistle*, Tertullian's *Answer to the Jews*, and Melito's *Paschal Homily*.

To illustrate the reason for these conclusions, I have chosen Melito's *Paschal Homily* which is known as one of the earliest and most influential Christian *adversus Judaeos* sermons. E. Werner has called Melito the first poet of deicide.[4] The sermon speaks directly about Jews and Judaism, and would seem to offer a clear view of the relationship between Jews and Christians in Sardis. The *Homily* was written in or near Sardis sometime late in the second century (c.180). Eusebius of Caesarea, (c. 263-340), tells his readers that Melito was the "Bishop of the parish of Sardis," and wrote some very important essays for his Church during the late second century.[5]

Yet in spite of the direct comments about Jews and Judaism in the *Homily* it is not possible to present a clear picture of Jews and Christians in Sardis using only Melito's *Homily*. There is another *text* which we must read along side the written text; the *text* I am referring to is the city of Sardis itself.

---

3 The phrase, "Bible-people," is used here to refer to how most second century Christian writers of the *adversus Judaeos* view Jews. For the most part they are the people of the Bible and not their contemporaries.

4 E. Werner, "Melito of Sardes, The First Poet of Deicide," *Hebrew Union College Annual* 37 (1966): 191-210.

5 Eusebius, *Ecclesiastical History*, translated by K. Lake and J.E.L. Oulton, in the Loeb Classical Library, (Cambridge: Harvard, 1926): 4.26.1-3.

To demonstrate what I mean let us look briefly at the contents of the *Homily* and then review the non-literary evidence for Jews and Christians in Sardis. A Greek text of the *Homily*, discovered fifty years ago, has made it possible to have a clean text of the Homily and more direct access to the thoughts of some Christians in Sardis.[6]

The *Homily* was a sermon in poetic form, used as a commentary on the meaning of the Exodus 12, the Passover, for Christians. Melito argued that everyone who read the Exodus story knew both the "old" way of looking at the event of the Exodus, and a "new" way of looking at it.

"Understand, therefore, beloved,
  how it is new and old,
    eternal and temporary,
    perishable and imperishable,
    mortal and immortal, this mystery of Pascha:
  old as regards the law,
    but new as regards the word;
  temporary as regards the model,
    eternal because of grace;
  perishable because of the slaughter of sheep,
    imperishable because of the life of the Lord;
  mortal because of the burial in earth;
    immortal because of the rising of the dead.
                (1.5-18)[7]

The second half of the *Homily*, beginning with section 72[8], is anti-Israel.[9] There are many phrases in this section which would lead one to assume that

---

6 C. Bonner, *The Homily on the Passion by Melito Bishop of Sardis and some Fragments of the apocrypha Ezekiel* (Studies and documents 12, London and Philadelphia, 1940); M. Testuz, *Papyrus Bodmer XIII, Meliton de Sardes, Homilie sur la Paque,* Geneve, 1960. An up-to-date and critical edition of the Homily is from S.G. Hall, ed. and trans., *Melito of Sardis, ON PASCHA and Fragments,* (Oxford: Clarendon Press, 1979): see page xvii in that volume for a description of the discovery of the text.

7 All of the references to the *Homily* in this chapter are from S.G. Hall, *ON PASCHA* (Oxford: Clarendon Press, 1979).

8 The argument at this point in the *Homily* changes from a description of the meaning of Christ and his work to a condemnation of Israel. Hall, *ON PASCHA*, suggests in a note (39, n.40): "[t]hroughout [paragraphs] 72-99 Melito shares with *Evangelium Petri* the tendency to attribute the crucifixion directly and exclusively to Israel."

9 "Israel" is used here in order to stay consistent with Melito's language in describing Jews. He was not condemning Jews, as such, but asking them to reconsider their understanding of the biblical texts. This seems like a worthwhile distinction when one is considering the meaning of the anti-Israel discussion in the *Homily*.

Melito was trying to stir up hostile feelings among Christians toward Jews in Sardis. The text seems to support this notion. For example, Melito wrote:

It is he that has been murdered.
And where has he been murdered? In the middle of
Jerusalem.
By whom? By Israel.
Why? Because he healed their lame
and cleansed their lepers
and brought light to their blind
and raised their dead,
that is why he died.[10]

This is not the only argument against Jews. He continues to press two further issues: 1) the parochialism of Judaism and 2) the allegation that Christianity has superseded Judaism which add to the perception that Melito tried to inflame Christian passions against Jews in Sardis.

In the section on Jerusalem and the Temple Melito wrote:

The Jerusalem below was precious,
but it is worthless now because of the
Jerusalem above;
the narrow inheritance was precious,
but it is worthless now because of the
widespread bounty.
For it is not in one place nor in a little plot
that the Glory of God is established,
but on all the ends of the inhabited earth
his bounty overflows,
and there the almighty God has made his dwelling
through Christ Jesus;
to whom be glory for ever. Amen.[11]

Notice that the "inheritance was precious" but is now worthless because the bounty is now widespread and not limited to the "little plot." This sounds similar to the ideas in Justin and Tertullian, which accuse Jews of being too narrowly focused on their own land and race.

---

10 Translation by Hall, *ON PASCHA*, see 72.505-512. There are many other equally harsh words used by Melito against Israel. See 79.505; 81.631; 92.677; 94.693-96.716; 97.717; 96.715 (This text was used by Werner, "Deicide," to prove that Melito was the first poet of deicide; the one who articulated the idea that Jews killed Jesus who is God); 93.692.

11 Hall, *ON PASCHA*, 45.290-300.

The other claim was that Judaism had been superseded by Christianity. This view of Judaism is still held by many Christians to this day.[12] Part of Melito's argument on this issue was the fact that everything in Israel's history was a "prefiguration"[13] of the reality to come. The reality, of course, was the Church. "[T]he Temple below precious, but it is worthless now because of the Christ above" (44.288-289).

When we read the *Homily* without any reference to the city of Sardis as a "text" we may concluded that there was a thriving Christian presence that was a forceful part of the community and a major threat to Jews living there.

The non-literary "text" we read is the archaeological evidence from Sardis.[14] This evidence suggests that Jews and Judaism in Sardis of mid-second century were "proud, prosperous and highly respected . . . active in civic and commercial affairs, . . . influential enough to build and maintain a huge house of worship in a location unparalleled elsewhere."[15] The most impressive evidence for a Jewish community in Sardis is the large synagogue which "formed the focus of a thriving bazaar area, [s]tretching along the north side of the colonnaded street for 200 meters . . . The existence of a large Jewish community at Sardis is known as early as the 1st century B.C. . . . It was from this community that the first Christians, to whom the letter of St. John was addressed, must have come."[16]

This last statement by Mitten seems to shift from the importance of the Jewish community to the Christianity community without making a proper transition. The evidence is more descriptive of a venerable Jewish community in Sardis than a Christian one.

The only archaeological evidence from the first through the third centuries of a religious community in Sardis is the Synagogue and the pagan temples. Christian evidence[17] and some minor relics have been discovered in Sardis, but none is earlier than the fourth century C.E. G. Snyder has concluded that

---

12 Recently the 199th General Assembly of the Presbyterian Church (USA), meeting in Biloxi, Mississippi, from June 8-16, 1987, began to modify the position of supersessionism in its paper "A Theological View of the Relationship Between Christians and Jews."

13 *Homily*, 34-45, 36.226-234; 39.360; 40-43; 43.275-279; 44.28-45.300.

14 See G.M.A. Hanfmann, *Sardis from Prehistoric to Roman Times: Results of the Archaeological Exploration of Sardis 1958-1975*, (Cambridge MA: Harvard University Press, 1983) the definitive work on Sardis to 1975.

15 D.G. Mitten, "A New Look at Ancient Sardis," *Biblical Archaeologist* 29.2 (1966): 65.

16 Ibid. 65. Mitten's confidence about the origin of the Christian community demonstrates his acceptance of the conventional wisdom about the beginnings of the Church in Sardis.

17 G.M.A. Hanfmann and Hans Buchwald, "Christianity: Churches and Cemeteries," in Hanfmann, *Sardis*, 191-210. For a complete discussion of the reason for little archaeological evidence of Christianity in the Roman Empire before Constantine see G.F. Snyder, *Ante Pacem: Archaeological Evidence of Church Life before Constantine*. (Macon, GA: Mercer University Press, 1985).

there was a reason for this lack of architectural evidence. They were probably meeting in houses or other public places. Constantine would change that in his building programs in the early fourth century.[18] Even without literary sources for Jews in Sardis, it is easier to reconstruct the prominence of Jews in the city because of the location of the large synagogue there.

Further, after the earthquake in Asia Minor in 17 C.E., Sardis was rebuilt with the aid of funds from emperors Tiberius and Claudius. Following the initial planning, the reconstruction took several centuries to complete. Buildings were rebuilt with much stronger foundations in the hope, apparently, that a disaster similar to the one in 17 C.E. would never again destroy the city.

The rebuilt central area was dominated by two impressive buildings: the Roman Gymnasium and, later, the large, impressive synagogue within it. The original purpose of this basilica-like structure is unclear, but the fact that it eventually became a synagogue cannot be disputed. These structures remained in place until Sardis fell to the Persian invasion in 616 C.E. The full archaeological description of the synagogue[19] provides ample evidence for a lively and prosperous Jewish community in Sardis for many centuries.

Some scholars estimate that between 5,000 and 10,000 Jews lived in Sardis during the middle of the second century C.E., approximately 10% of the total population. There is no evidence prior to the Byzantine period to determine the number of Christians in the city.

The Jewish population was apparently well established and intimately involved on every level of Sardis life. The large synagogue was one of the dominant buildings in the center of a complex of buildings including a large Roman Bath. Nothing indicates that the synagogue stood out as an unusual structure in the city. It was of a piece with the other buildings. This fact indicates that Jews of Sardis were "at home" there.[20]

The inscriptions and the design of the synagogue suggest that it was a center for the Jewish community and not used as some kind of a "paganized" meeting place. The inscriptions found in the synagogue itself indicate that the Jews maintained a connection with their tradition even though they borrowed art and other cultural forms in which to express their rituals. Greek language itself is a cultural form which Jews in Diaspora freely employed to express their most treasured thoughts and ideas. It was often assumed[21] that "the

---

18 See G. Snyder, *Ante Pacem: Archaeological Evidence of Church Life before Constantine*, (Macon GA: Mercer University Press, 1985): 67-119.

19 See the extensive bibliography in Hanfmann, *Sardis*, xvii-xxxv.

20 See specifically, Kraabel, "Impact of the Discovery of the Sardis Synagogue," in *Sardis* edited by Hanfmann, 178-190.

21 See Kraabel, "The Roman Diaspora: Six Questionable Assumptions." (Yadin Festschrift) *Journal of Jewish Studies* 33.1-2 (1982): 450.

Jewish Diaspora was syncretistic, and that substantial elements of pagan piety were mixed in with the ancestral religion." This assumption,[22] which has been challenged recently by Kraabel, is simply not the case in Sardis.

The setting of the synagogue next to a significant pagan structure indicates that the Jews were not hiding somewhere in Sardis. They had an identity which had never been completely assimilated into the surrounding pagan culture.[23]

What the evidence does not indicate is what kind of Judaism is represented by the synagogue in Sardis. Discoveries at Dura-Europos, at Bet She'-arim in Israel, and at Qumran have indicated a diverse and multifaceted Judaism both in Palestine and in the Diaspora. There is no reason to believe that Jews in Sardis were any different in their independence of religious expression.

The fact that there is no evidence in Sardis of the presence of the "God-fearers" in the numbers assumed by some scholars is another indication that it is inappropriate to suggest that Christianity somehow emerged out of such a group in the synagogue there.

What is more likely is that citizens of Sardis lived and worked well with most Jews in the city during the middle of the second century C.E. A commonality existed on all levels, which made the synagogue an integrated part of Sardian society.[24]

This new look at some of the evidence of Jews in old Sardis provides a "text" we can read in several significant ways:

First, the Jews were longtime residents of Sardis.[25] If one accepts the arguments that 'Sepharad'[26] in Obadiah 20 (postexilic), is a reference to Sardis, it is likely that the Jews survived in the Lydian capital for many centuries as an independent and identifiable ethnic group. Their community life and religious practices certainly developed and changed from the way they had

---

22 Ibid. 450 n.20-24.

23 See Kraabel, "Impact," 178-190, for a more complete description of the Jews and Christians in Sardis.

24 See G.M.A. Hanfmann's detailed description of the city, in which he suggests such a situation, *Sardis*, 1-16. See especially pages 5 and 14, in which the makeup of the population and the importance of the city is mentioned. For a recent study of the evidence about Jewish communities in Asia Minor see Paul R. Trebilco, *Jewish Communities in Asia Minor*. SNTSMS, 69. Cambridge UK: Cambridge University Press, 1991.

25 Kraabel, "Impact," 178-180.

26 Called "Saparda" in Persian cuneiform inscriptions. See note j, Obadiah 20, in *The Prophets, Nevi'im*, (Philadelphia: The Jewish Publication Society of America, 1978).

lived in Jerusalem[27] in 597 B.C.E. But it is clear that a Jewish presence of some form survived nearly without a break, and possibly flourished, in Sardis until 616 C.E. There is no extensive evidence for Christians in Sardis until after 350.

Second, all of the evidence indicates that Jews in Sardis used Greek in every area of their social, cultural, economic, and religious life. Inscriptions indicate that there was some use of Hebrew in Sardis.[28] But the extent of the use is not certain. The single inscription in Hebrew found in Sardis to date is fragmentary. Although it is not clear to whom the inscription was actually referring, it may be a dedication to the Emperor. It is clear from the synagogue evidence that Greek was the language used to communicate important information, such as the names of the benefactors for the synagogue.

Kraabel states that "there is more Hebrew in the decoration of a synagogue in the American Diaspora than in the ones which have been excavated from the Mediterranean Diaspora; does that say something about the popularity of the language in each case?"[29] Certainly, to survive economically and socially, a group must be able to do business in the *lingua franca* of the place in which it lives.

Third, Jews in Sardis maintained contact with Jewish communities around the Roman world, including Palestine. But this does not mean that they were supervised by a patriarch in Palestine.[30] The evidence from Sardis presents a portrait of a Jewish community that is international and intercultural, with some contact with Jerusalem when the temple tax was collected.[31]

Jewish communities in the Diaspora often developed in their own ways. When one investigates the unique expressions found in various synagogues around the world, this conclusion seems obvious.

The sculpture pieces of animals within the synagogue in Sardis, for example, the paintings on the walls of the Dura-Europos synagogue[32] far to the East, and the zodiac on the floor of several Palestinian synagogues[33] are examples of this variety, and present more questions than answers to the discussions about the nature of Jews and Judaism in the Diaspora.

---

27 According to Obadiah 20 the Jews who were living in Sepharad were part of the "Jerusalem exile community," (*galut yrushla'im*).

28 Hanfmann, *Sardis*, 179. The Hebrew inscription honors Lucius Verus during his visit to the city about 166 C.E.

29 Hanfmann, *Sardis*, 189.

30 See Kraabel, "Impact," 182-183.

31 Ibid., 179.

32 See M.I. Rostovtzeff, *Dura-Europos and its Art*, (Oxford, 1938).

33 See S.J. Saller, *Second Revised Catalogue of the Ancient Synagogues of the Holy Land*, (Jerusalem, 1972), 25, fig. 4, who summarizes the scholarship of the early synagogues.

As has been pointed out by Kraabel,[34] besides the variety demonstrated in the various synagogues in the Diaspora, it is also clear that the rabbis in Palestine did not control the Jewish communities. The communities appear to have been totally independent and free to work within their own city to establish their identity there.

Fourth, Jews in the Greco-Roman world, as the Greek translations of the Old Testament and the works of Josephus and Philo amply attest, were able to maintain their identity because of their flexibility and their willingness to integrate into their host culture without assimilating into it. This intellectual and religious agility seems to have been present in the Jewish community in Sardis.

What emerges as one examines the old data in light of the new is a Jewish culture and a form of Judaism capable of being a critical partner in its host culture. Symbols used in the synagogue, which reveal that the Jews were at home with the surrounding culture, need not suggest assimilation. Kraabel[35] suggests that early in the third century a coalition of Jews and pagans may have existed in Sardis. This "coalition" was perhaps a social necessity based on the need to oppose an aggressive (and ultimately successful) Christian mission. Kraabel further suggests that because of this coalition the synagogue did not pass into the Christians' hands during the time of Justinian, (527-565 C.E.), when there was surely a large Christian community in Sardis.

If there was a "coalition" of some kind between the Jews and the pagans in Sardis, as Kraabel has suggested, then we can begin to understand why Melito would have written a rather negative, even hostile, homily against Jews.

Fifth, the Jews were protected by Roman Law and apparently flourished under that arrangement. In Josephus's *Jewish Antiquities*,[36] in a text dated to the first century B.C.E., reference was made to long-standing laws protecting the Jews in Sardis:

> Lucius Antonius, son of Marcus, proquaestor and propraetor, to the magistrates, council and people of Sardis, greeting. Jewish citizens of ours [variant reads "yours"] have come to me and pointed out that from the earliest times they have had an association of their own in accordance with their native laws and a place of their own, in which they decide their affairs and controversies with one another; and up-

---

34 Kraabel, "Impact," 183.

35 Kraabel, "Impact," 186.

36 Flavius Josephus, *Jewish Antiquities,* translated by Ralph Marcus, in the *Loeb Classical Library*, vol. VII (Cambridge:Harvard, 1926): 14.235. As to the reliability of Josephus as a historian, see S.J.D. Cohen, *Josephus in Galilee and Rome: His Vita and Development as a Historian* (Leiden: Brill, 1979).

on their request that it be permitted them to do these things, I decided that they might be maintained, and permitted them so to do.[37]

A decree of the people of Sardis preserved in the *Antiquities* allows one to gain some insight into the interaction between Jews and pagans in Sardis:

> Decree of the people of Sardis. The following decree was passed by the council and people on the motion of the magistrates. Whereas the Jewish citizens [?] living in our city have continually received many great privileges from the people and have now pleaded that as their laws and freedom have been restored by the Roman Senate and people, they may, in accordance with their accepted customs, come together and have a communal life and adjudicate suits among themselves, and that a place be given them in which they may gather together with their wives and children and offer their ancestral prayers and sacrifices to God, it has therefore been decreed by the council and people that permission shall be given them to come together on stated days to do those things which are in accordance with their laws, and also that a place shall be set apart by the magistrate for them to build and inhabit, such as they may consider suitable for this purpose, and that market-officials of the city shall be charged with the duty of having suitable food for them brought in.[38]

Jews in Sardis were permitted to have their own courts and a meeting place in the center of the city. The recent archaeological discoveries in Sardis generally affirm the accuracy of Josephus's record. A letter (first century B.C.E.) from the proconsul Flaccus to the council of Sardis was confirmation of a tradition of legal rights of Jews in Sardis.[39]

It is no longer possible to suggest that a Jewish community in Sardis had been absorbed by the local culture. The data suggests that there was a two way conversation between Jews and the non-Jewish culture there.

In contrast to the evidence of a venerable Jewish community in Sardis is the meager and mainly literary (*The Revelation of John* and Melito's *Paschal Homily*) evidence of Christianity in this city. The text of *Revelation* obviously

---

37 *AJ* 14.235.

38 *AJ* 14.259-260.

39 "Gaius Norbanus Flaccus, proconsul (56 B.C.E.), to the magistrate and council of Sardis, greeting. Caesar has written to me, ordering that the Jews shall not be prevented from collecting sums of money, however great they may be, in accordance with their ancestral custom, and sending them up to Jerusalem. I have therefore written to you in order that you may know that Caesar and I wish this to be done." from Josephus, *AJ*, 16.171.

had a rhetorical purpose[40] and must be interpreted with this in mind. Yet, in spite of the very sketchy information about the development of the church in Sardis, scholars lead us to believe that the Christian community had a long and vital history there. "When the apocalyptic prophet John wrote,[41] the church in the ancient Lydian city may have existed for some time, for it has the name of being alive but is dead. John recognizes that in Sardis there are still a few who have not soiled their garments and are worthy, but the church must awake and strengthen what little remains. Its decadence may have been a relapse into paganism or into the error of the *Incognitas* mentioned in the letters to Pergamum and Thyatira."[42]

There is no significant archaeological evidence, for instance, for a church building in Sardis until c. 350, leaving the scholar with little architectural evidence about the Christians in one of the leading cities of Asia Minor.

The literary evidence, as we have suggested, for a Christian presence in Sardis available for the late first and middle second centuries is inadequate.[43] Most commentaries avoid mentioning anything about the Church, even though *Revelation*, a first-century apocalyptic[44] writing, is meant for the Church in Sardis, as well as the other churches mentioned at the beginning of the book.

Eusebius mentioned the Christian community during Melito's time in Sardis, but said nothing about its organization, community life, and relation to the other cultures in the city. Eusebius is understandably more concerned with the Quartodeciman debate than with the social context. The reference in Eusebius's *Ecclesiastical History*[45] simply mentions Melito's work and calls him the

---

40 See R.H. Charles, *The Revelation of St. John, A Critical and Exegetical Commentary*, 2 vols. *ICC*, (Edinburgh: T & T Clark, 1920), 78. and the more recent work of J.M. Ford, *Revelation. The Anchor Bible* 38 (New York: Doubleday, 1975) 410-413.

41 See Revelation 3:1-7

42 S.E. Johnson, "Christianity in Sardis," in *Early Christian Origins: Studies in hone of Harold R. Willoughby* edited by Allen Wikgren (Chicago: Quadrangle Books, 1961) 81. The text Johnson is referring to is Revelation 2:15, 20ff.

43 Ford, *Revelation*, deals almost exclusively with the evidence for the synagogue and follows Charles, *Revelation*, commentary in describing the cultural and social background of the letter to the Church in Sardis. The evidence points to a very weak Christian presence in Sardis until the late third-early fourth centuries. For some reason the Christians could not gain a foothold in Sardis. None of the archaeological evidence to date (summer 1990) indicates a strong Christian presence.

44 96 C.E. Most commentaries simply follow the work of R.H. Charles, who sketches the social and cultural images reflected in Revelation 3:1-6, or they simply talk about the Jews in Sardis. There is no substantive description of the Christians in Sardis in R.H. Charles's commentary. See the list of commentaries provided by Ford, *Revelation*, 59-64.

45 Eus., *HE*. 4.26.1, 4.13.8 where Eusebius referred to *"tes en Sardes in ekklesias episcopos."*

"bishop of the diocese of Sardis." The other reference in Eusebius to Sardis is a brief comment about the burial place of Melito.[46]

Melito's *Paschal Homily* is the other literary reference used as evidence for the Christian presence in Sardis. But we have already suggested that we need more than the *Homily* itself to understand its anti-Jewish or anti-Israel bias. It is not possible to agree with most scholars that this work was the product of an extremely antagonistic anti-Jewish writer. Nor can we agree with W.H.C. Frend who finds this document as expressing "his attitude toward his orthodox [*sic*] Jewish neighbors,"[47] and insists that the "incitement of the Jews in Smyrna against Polycarp (c.166 C.E.) was being answered in kind by Christian leaders in other towns in Asia Minor." Frend continues his argument by suggesting that "In these years the seeds of Christian anti-Semitism were sown, and it would seem that the closer the two communities resembled each other the more deadly the enmity became."[48] Contrary to this view there is no evidence that the Christian community "resembled" the Jewish community in any way.

Now what can be said about the relationship between Christians and Jews in Sardis in the later part of the second century?

First, the *Homily* is a sermon in poetic form, written by a person who led a group of Christians who apparently did not occupy a prominent place in Sardis during the later part of the second century but who struggled for self-understanding. The evidence presented above indicates that the Church in Sardis might have lived under the shadow or even the threat of a venerable and well-established attractive Jewish community.

It is possible that some Christians in Sardis were part of the synagogue as full members of the religious life of the Jewish community because of the vitality these Christians felt in the form of Judaism they experienced there. Melito may have used an effective rhetorical and kerygmatic poem to call Christians back to the Church and away from the synagogue. This might be one was to explain Melito's anti-Jewish themes in the homily. He needed to define the uniqueness of Christianity *against* Judaism.

Along with the threat of Christians converting to Judaism, Judaism threatened the fundamental presuppositions of Christianity. The messianic era

46 Ibid., 5.24.5 "and Melito the eunuch, who lived entirely in the Holy Spirit who lies in Sardis, waiting for the visitation from heaven when he will rise from the dead?"

47 Frend, *Rise*, 240. The Jews are often referred to by Frend as a religious group; never as an ethnic community which may or may not be actively involved in some kind of religious activities. See most of Kraabel's works for a critical evaluation of this position.

48 Frend, *Rise*, 241. This assumes, of course, that the Christian and Jewish communities resembled each other and that the Jewish community, like the Church, was viewed as a "religious" community.

had not come with universal peace, and the Jews had not all converted to Christianity, so the Christian poet had to come up with reasons for its delay. As the evidence now shows, Jews were NOT converting to Christianity in great numbers, which was a constant thorn in the side of Christian missionaries from the beginning (see Romans 9-11).

Second, political positioning was another threat to Christianity from Jews and Judaism. The laws protecting the rights of Jews[49] suggest strong Jewish influence in the Empire long after the Empire became Christian under Constantine in the early fourth century.

Jon D. Levenson[50] concluded the first section of his essay with this comment:

> There is a tragicomical irony here, that a tradition which sets such a great store on love and reconciliation should have canonized literature deriving, in part, from a situation of hatred and strife. However, read against their historical context, the New Testament documents exemplify a truism of human nature: We are rarely generous with our competitors, especially when the competitors have *prima facie* first claim upon the status to which we aspire. If we are to replace them, we had better show that they deserve to be replaced, and, if we dare not boast that we are better than they, then let us at least portray them as worse than we.

If Melito presented his ideas out of his own feelings of insecurity and inadequacy against an established, venerable, and appealing Judaism then one may understand why he focused on "the superiority of Christianity to Judaism." He tried to prove to his fellow Christians the superiority of his form of Christianity over the type of Judaism that he and they experienced in Sardis.

Third, to convey his message in a dramatic way, Melito used rhetoric and liturgical forms in his poem. An example of the rhetorical style may be found in the section of the *Homily* that introduces the discussion about the murder of Christ (72.505-513):

> It is he that has been murdered.
> And where has he been murdered? In the middle of
>   Jerusalem.
> By whom? By Israel.
> Why? Because he healed their lame
>   and cleansed their lepers

---

49 See *The Theodosian Code and Novels and the Sirmondian Constitutions,* a translation by Clyde Pharr (Princeton: Princeton University Press, 1952).

50 J.D. Levenson, "Is there a Counterpart in the Hebrew Bible to the New Testament Antisemitism?" *Journal of Ecumenical Studies* 22.2 (Spring 1985): 245.

and brought light to their blind
and raised their dead,
that is why he died.[51]

In 14.3-15.91 Melito regards the "Pascha as an initiatory rite with apotro-paie effect, and insinuates into sections 14-16 the language of Christian Baptism and unction, especially 'marked,' 'smear,' 'spirit.' Justin draws a close parallel between the paschal blood and the saving faith of Christians in *Dialogue* 40.1 and 111.3."[52] Rhetoric and liturgy were a part of the way Melito conveyed, throughout his poem, his message to his audience, Christians who for some reason needed reassurance.

Fourth, the *Homily* was not directed against the Jews of Sardis, or any other Jewish group in particular, but was written to Christians who defined themselves against the Israel of the Bible (including the Israel of the New Testament). This "over-againstness" created the impression that all Jews were to be condemned by Christians, which was not necessarily the case.

One of Melito's concerns was to prove that Christians possessed something that was more precious than Judaism. This is the reason for the super-sessionistic teachings found throughout the *Homily*:

> [J]ust so also the law was fulfilled when the
>   gospel was elucidated,
> and the people was made void when the church
>   arose;
> and the model was abolished when the Lord was
>   revealed,
> and today, things once precious have become
>   worthless.
> since the really precious things have been
>   revealed. (43.275-279)

The church superseded Israel. But instead of interpreting these words as polemic directed at Jews in general, we must (in light of the new evidence) consider them as words which provided encouragement for the struggling church of the Sardis area. The *Homily* was written for that church.

Fifth, the *Homily* made a statement to a secondary and more universal audience. The Jews mentioned in the *Homily* were a type of "men" who rejected God. There is an interesting shift in the argument of the *Homily*. It occurs in sections 87, 94, 103, and 104.

---

51 Hall, *ON PASCHA*, 39.

52 Ibid. 9, n. 5.

> Ungrateful Israel, come and take issue with me
>   about your ingratitude. (87.634-635)
> Listen, all you families of the nations, [53]
>   and see! (94.693).
> Come then, all you families of mankind who
>   compounded with sins,
>   and get forgiveness of sins. (103.766-768).
> [W]ho has power to save everyone,
> through whom the Father did his works from
>   beginning
>   to eternity. (104.790-791).

The words in these sections are harsh and do condemn Israel for the murder of "your Lord" (92.677, 93.692, 695) but there is a call in these words to "all the families of mankind," and "all you families of the nations." This is the universal appeal of the poem and becomes the "other" audience.

Sixth, in Melito's view *Christianity replaced* the Judaism that he knew.

> [A] speechless lamb was precious,
>   but it is worthless now because of the spotless
>   Son;
>   the temple below was precious,
>   but it is worthless now because of the Christ
>   above. (44.286-289)

Everything in Israel's history was merely a prefiguration of the reality which was to come (34-35; cf. 42.270-271). The model, Judaism, was made void when the real (that is, the Church) came, (40-43; 43.275-279).

A Christian community which did not seem very substantial next to the venerable and substantial Jewish community would feel affirmed if it superseded Israel in its God-given task. This theme also appears in some other *adversus Judaeos* writings.[54]

Reading the city as "text" leads to the conclusion that Melito's *Homily* as an *adversus Judaeos* writing was the product of a fledgling Christian church struggling for its existence in or around Sardis in the latter part of the second century. The Christians were overshadowed by the venerable Jewish community in the same area. Christians were insecure and defensive in relation to the

---

53 Hall, *ON PASCHA*, 53, provides a textual variant here for nations: *"ethnon"* or *"anthropon"* (both genitive plural. Either way it is clear that Melito had a universal audience in mind.

54 See *Barn.* 4.6-7; 6.16-19; 5.7; 7.5, among many other texts. Justin Martyr, *Dial.* 82.1; 29.2; 116; 119; 123.6; 124. Tertullian, *Ad.Jud.* 3.10; 6.1-4; 13.13; 13.19. These are only a few references in the other *adversus Judaeos* writings.

Jews and the form of Judaism present there. Their pastor, Melito, preached his *Homily* within relative isolation; from within a closed community, and was not meant to directly criticize a Jewish community in Sardis.

The Jews in Sardis during this same period were prosperous, integrated into the society, and secure without being assimilated. Judaism threatened Christianity and its leaders' social status. But there is no evidence that Christianity disturbed the Jewish community in the same way. Jews were cosmopolitan in their outlook and international in their experience.

When one reads Melito's *Homily* in the context of the "city as text" it becomes clearer that this *adversus Judaeos* preacher was more concerned with Christian self-definition that with an attack on Jews and their Judaism. The same applies to the other second century *adversus Judaeos* preachers.

The Synagogue at Sardis: Jews and Christians[1]

A.T. Kraabel

I

Let us begin with a certain hundred years, those from the middle of the second century of the Common Era to the middle of the third. In the year 150 the Jews of the Holy Land were still trying to recover after the second of two disastrous wars with Rome. Jewish militancy was over. Jews as a nation would conduct no such battles again until the establishment of the State of Israel in our own time. The center of nation and cult, the Temple in Jerusalem, was in ruins and under gentile control; it would not be rebuilt. Within a century, however, the *Mishnah*, the text at the heart of post-Biblical Jewish teachings, would receive its final form in the Galilee at the hands of the great Rabbi Judah "the Prince."

Just beyond the boundaries of the Holy Land, in the Roman garrison town of Dura Europos, another Judaism was preparing to express itself in much different fashion, in wonderful folk art; the congregants of the little Dura synagogue would cause its walls to be covered with glorious frescoes of Biblical symbolism. Varieties of Judaism flourished also west of Dura and of the Holy Land, all around the Mediterranean rim, where Jews lived as one of many minorities in the cities of the Roman world.

Among Christians the various documents which would make up the present New Testament had only just been completed by the year 150, along with other Christian texts of many kinds. However, the decisions which would place certain texts into the Christian Bible were only just beginning to be made; the debates would continue for a century and a half. In Asia Minor and then in Rome Marcion, a bright disciple of Saint Paul, was arguing that the scripture of the Jews, the "Old Testament," had no place in Christianity; the God it described, Yahweh, was in fact sub-Christian, and His followers were to be repudiated by proper members of the Church. It was Marcion himself who was finally repudiated, after some debate. Meanwhile, many Christians in Asia Minor were setting the date of Easter with the help of the old Jewish calendar, for they believed that to be proper according to the earliest Christian tradition; this "Jewish" practice was frequently the cause for dispute with Christians to the west. For Christianity, which had begun as a Jewish sect in the Holy Land, was now almost exclusively gentile, its centers of power and growth farther west in the gentile world.

Christians were increasingly in conflict with the Roman State and with local authorities. Polycarp, Bishop of Smyrna, not far to the west of Sardis, on the coast of Asia Minor, died a martyr in his city in the middle of the second

---

1 Editor's note: This article appeared in *Sardis: Twenty-Seven Years of Discovery.* Papers presented at the Oriental Institute March 21, 1987, edited by Eleanor Guralnick, (Chicago, 1987) 62-73.

century. But for the Roman Empire in general, the year 150 was a time of prosperity, growth and peace. The Emperor was the conscientious Antoninus, nicknamed *Pius*. His successor would be his adopted son, the introspective stoic philosopher Marcus Aurelius.

The historian Edward Gibbon called this period the most prosperous age the world had ever known. But there was a whiff of smoke in the air, and flames apparent at the edges of things. Marcus Aurelius wrote much of his immortal *Meditations* in his field tent, on campaign against the enemies of the Empire and often on its farthest borders. His successor Commodus (ruled 180-192) was the beginning of decline, and things grew significantly worse in the early third century. In the half-century before Diocletian, who ruled from 284 to 305, every Emperor died by violence, and the average length of reign was two or three years. (It was Diocletian who would conduct the last systematic persecution of Christians.)

There was more order, but not much less violence when Constantine took over less than a decade after Diocletion, and began to make Christianity the new state religion.

Somewhere in the hundred years between 150 and 250 the Jewish community at Sardis created its magnificent synagogue. By the year 200 Jews had lived in Sardis for half a millennium or more. They enjoyed a striking amount of acceptance, respect and indeed power within the city and within the Roman province. Their central artifact is of course the synagogue itself, crammed with gorgeous decoration and many more Jewish inscriptions than are known from all the rest of Asia Minor put together. On the basis of this new evidence and what was previously known about the context of Sardis, it is possible to offer a hypothetical but very detailed, reconstruction of the Jewish community, its piety, its economics and its life among gentile neighbors. The purpose of this essay is to summarize that fascinating story.

II

As any present-day visitor to the site can attest, the reconstruction of the synagogue gives a vivid picture of what it must have been originally. No one riding the inter city buses from Ankara to Izmir today can fail to be impressed as a massive structure looms up on the right a few kilometers west of Salihli. The basilica which would become the synagogue was not a free-standing building, but rather the southeast unit of the huge bath-gymnasium complex at Sardis. The original intent was that the southeast corner would be devoted to a row of three large rooms opening north into the gymnasium *palaestra*. But at some point during the construction the plans were changed. The space became instead a civil basilica accessible only from the street to the east, from outside the bath-gymnasium. There was a small forecourt in the east end, and in the west end an apse provided with a platform or stage looking out over a long, narrow hall. Niches in the wall of the apse contain statues of deities or emperors.

This is the first phase actually put to use by the people of Sardis, beginning somewhere in the second century. From the beginning, that is, Sardis knew this space as a basilica accessible to all. From the beginning it differed from the parallel hall to the north, the three rooms of which always opened into the palaestra itself.

In the second phase of use, a three-tiered bank of semi-circular benches was added to the apse, and the crosswall separating main hall from forecourt was removed, creating a single hall over eighty meters long from east to west. It was at some point during this phase that the space came under the control of the Jewish community. After it became their synagogue, however, it was still not out-of-bounds to Sardis gentiles; the basilica had been city property for too long to imagine that once in Jewish hands it would be closed to the rest of the city forever. The "fountain of the synagogue" was surely public, and it seems unlikely that Jews whose community had been a part of the city for half a millennium would totally exclude their gentile neighbors from what would now be the center for Jewish life in Sardis.

The third phase of use is the synagogue which has been reconstructed; it dates from the fourth century. Congregants and visitors entered from the east, from the same colonnaded street which served the palaestra; their entrances were less than fifty meters apart. Three doorways led into the synagogue forecourt, an attractive space, roofed on four sides but open to the sky over the fountain in the center. The west wall of the forecourt was pierced by another three doorways leading into the main hall.

Just inside the main hall were two marble Torah shrines, one on each side of the central entrance. The south shrine was evidently the more important; the construction was of better quality, and the few fragments of Hebrew inscription from the building were found here. When the Scripture was to be read aloud from the apse at the west end of the building, the proper scroll must have been brought, perhaps in a formal procession, from one of these shrines; afterwards it would be returned in the same fashion.

Many synagogues today have only one shrine or Ark or *Aron ha-Kodesh*, but the Sardis Jews erected two, probably for reasons of symmetry. The shrines and the crosswall between the forecourt and the main hall are new in this stage of the building; they indicate architecturally the increasing importance of the Scripture, and permit the scrolls to be stored on the wall closest to Jerusalem, a synagogue feature as common in the Diaspora as in the Holy Land. The Sardis Jews had a significant name for such a structure; in one of the inscriptions it is called a *nomophylakion*, "that which protects the Law."

West of the shrines, precisely in the center of the main hall, is the synagogue's most important inscription, introducing "Samoe, priest and *sophodida-*

skalos." Sacrificial ritual had ended among Jews centuries before Samoe, when the Temple in Jerusalem was destroyed by Roman armies. A priest is never essential to the function of a synagogue, but Samoe was a descendent of the Biblical high priest Aaron and bore the title proudly. *Sophodidaskalos* means "wise teacher" or "teacher of wisdom"; it is likely that Samoe was the closest thing Sardis had to a rabbi.

The west end of the synagogue was the architectural focus of the building. For the services, important members of the community and honored guests were seated on the benches of the apse; they looked out across the semi-circular apse mosaic, over the apse railing and the massive lecturn and out to the rest of the congregation. The lecturn was actually a colossal stone table; it has been dubbed the "Eagle Table" after the massive Roman eagle depicted on the supports at each end, architectural fragments from earlier Roman times, in reuse. The table was flanked by pairs of marble lions, also in reuse, but still earlier, from the Lydian period. A large stone menorah discovered in the excavations may have stood on a small, carefully carved monument discovered nearby. The menorah bears its donor's name: Sokrates.

Eagles, lions and menorah were all rich in symbolism for the assembled community. At the proper time in the service the scroll of the Scriptures was unrolled on the Eagle Table; a member of the community stood on a small pedestal at the table, his back to the apse, and read aloud the test designated for the day.

III

It would be a mistake however to see this building as primarily cultic in purpose, like the Jerusalem Temple or an early Christian church. In the Greco-Roman world outside the Holy Land, Jews like those responsible for the Sardis synagogue are best understood not as a *religious* movement but as an *ethnic* minority, albeit one with some unusual religious practices. It is important to realize that this building was the only one controlled by the Sardis Jewish community in this period; most if not all of the activities of the community would have taken place within it.

A similar situation obtained even before this building existed: according to a Roman decree from the first century B.C.E., the Sardis Jews had been given their own "place" or "location" where decisions were made on community matters, religious and non-religious. This earlier meeting place could have been an entire building, an assembly hall, the forerunner of the mammoth synagogue described above; or it may have been nothing more than a designated space in some public building.

Several features of the present Sardis synagogue recalled the famous Diplostoon or "double-colonnaded" synagogue at Alexandria destroyed by Trajan. The Talmud indicates that people seated themselves in the Diplostoon by trades—all the goldsmiths together, all the weavers together, all the carpet makers together—so that a new person in the community associated himself with others in his profession in order to gain employment; the Sardis synagogue too may have functioned as a kind of hiring hall. It was also a school. It may have been used on occasion as a dining hall. And since a main highway from the Aegean to the Holy Land and the east was just outside, Jewish travellers may often have spent the night in the building as guests of the Jewish community.

The occupations of Jews in this part of the ancient world are not much different from those of gentiles. There is no indication at Sardis that particular crafts were associated with Jews. Goldsmiths must have been in demand; three of the synagogue donors were Jews of that occupation. Others were merchants; some sold glass, some paints and dyes. One may have been a sculptor, others held government positions.

It is their status in the city and the government which Sardis Jews stress in the synagogue inscriptions. Many donors proudly identify themselves as a "citizen of Sardis," and no less than nine use the privileged title "city council member"; perhaps because of their wealth, these must have possessed considerable social status. In addition, three donors were part of the Roman provincial administration: one was a "Count," another a procurator, a third an assistant in the state archives.

IV

The Sardis Jewish community must have been a strong and influential one to gain control of such a large and impressive buildling. One reason for this strength in the city was the Jewish community's long history, which may have begun as early as the sixth century B.C.E. The book of Obadiah in the Hebrew Bible mentions (verse 20) exiles from Jerusalem who lived in *Sepharad* after the Babylonian destruction of Jerusalem in 587. Sepharad is the Semitic name for Sardis.

Another group of Jews settled in the area three centuries later. In an effort to pacify Lydia and Phrygia to the east by increasing the number of his own supporters there, the Seleucid king Antiochus III brought in two thousand loyal Jewish families from his forces in Babylonia and Mesopotamia, provided them with houses, and gave them a decade's relief from taxation. Since Sardis was the headquarters of the Seleucid governor responsible for these immigrants, it is likely that some of them came to settle in the city.

In all probability it was descendants of this group who established the meeting "place" or "location" whose existence was later guaranteed by the Roman decree mentioned above; this would have been the *first* Sardis "synagogue." There must have been another as well, whatever building or meeting place was utilized by the community after most of Sardis had been heavily damaged by the earthquake of 17 C.E. This would have been the *second* Sardis "synagogue." The *third* would be the presently reconstructed third-fourth

230 A.T. Kraabel

century building. Sardis thus had a series of at least three synagogues or
Jewish community assembly sites, even more if the history of the community
was more complex than what has been sketched here.

V

The present building and its inscriptions are the central artifact of Sardis
Judaism. When these data are taken together with the literary evidence,
Jewish, Christian and pagan, the story of this community's life is expanded
considerably.

These Jews were apparently on good terms with their gentile neighbors
in Sardis. For one thing, this community—like others in the Diaspora—had the
support of the Roman government. Jews were a powerful enough minority
within the Empire that the Romans usually preferred to placate them rather
than risk their destabilizing the status quo. On the Empire's eastern border
the Jewish homeland provided an essential buffer to such enemies of Rome
as the Parthians farther to the east. It was when this bulwark seemed at risk,
and the eastern frontier less secure, that the situation between Roman troops
and Palestinian Jews moved from uneasy truce to pitched battle in the two
"Jewish wars" of the first and second centuries C.E. It is significant that the
Jews of the western Diaspora did not take part in either case; nor did peaceful
Jewish communities like the one at Sardis suffer at Roman hands thereafter.
(Alexandria in Egypt was always a more volatile city; in that explosive atmo-
sphere, Jews *and gentiles* suffered more from civic strife.)

In addition to Roman support, the Sardis Jews had their own sources of
power, both economic and political. That is clear from the evidence of the
inscriptions, already mentioned, and from the grandeur of the synagogue itself.
Had this not been a strong community in the second and third centuries, the
building would likely not have become theirs.

Some of that stature was due to the community's long history *in Sardis*.
They were not aliens; by this time they belonged in the Lydian city. Their long
history there was one of the things being recognized by the transfer of the
building to their possession. Relative newcomers are unlikely to have been
given such an opportunity. To an extent unparalleled elsewhere among the
Jews of the Roman Empire, this Jewish community was fully a part of the
gentile city which was its home.

VI

If the Jews fit into the larger life of Sardis so well, does that mean that
they had cut their ties with the Homeland? Did Sardis Jews abandon the Holy
Land in which their religion centered in order to take up membership in Anatolian gentile society? That might seem likely, particularly when it is recalled
that this community may not have begun out of Palestine, but rather from
Babylonia and Mesopotamia, the result of the action of Antiochus III already

described. But the break with the Holy Land never occurred; the Jews of this community never lost their roots. (I have argued elsewhere that this may have been just because the community grew out of another Exile, that is, from Jews who had learned the importance of their heritage *in exile* when they were taken as hostages to Babylon after the capture of Jerusalem and the destruction of the first Temple there in the late sixth century B.C.E. I suspect too that by the third and fourth centuries C.E., a millennium later, the real tie was not so much to the Palestine of their own times as it was to biblical Israel raised to mythic status.[2]

Another piece of evidence for the importance of this link is financial: Sardis Jews faithfully donated the annual half-shekel offering for the support of a Temple in Jerusalem, a privilege guaranteed them by the Roman government according to a decree preserved from the first century B.C.E. Other communities did as well, according to evidence provided unwittingly by the great Roman lawyer and politician Cicero. One of the best known incidents in the life of Anatolian Jews occurred in the first century B.C.E.: it is the attempt by the Roman governor Lucius Valerius Flaccus to divert to his own use the gold these Jews were sending to Jerusalem to support the Temple. When prosecuted, Flaccus engaged Rome's most famous lawyer to defend him; Cicero's successful speech in Flaccus' defense, the *Pro Flacco*, may still be read. Jewish funds deposited in four cities are mentioned there, two in the interior, in Phrygia east of Sardis, and two in Mysia on the northwest coast.[3] The speech reveals two things relevant to our story. These Jews took their traditional obligations seriously; far from ancient Palestine they had not cut their ties to Jerusalem. And collectively they had substantial disposable income; over two hundred pounds of gold are involved in the suit. It was not only the Jews in Sardis who controlled funds in quite respectable amounts.

Pilgrimage was another important link to the Homeland from the Diaspora, particularly at the annual observances of the three major pilgrim festivals, *Pesah* (Passover), *Shavuot* (Pentecost) and *Sukkot* (Tabernacles). Sardis was located on the main land route for pilgrims coming from the west, and members of the Sardis Jewish community must have been among these pil-

---

2 Kraabel, "Unity and Diversity Among Diaspora Synagogues," in *The Synagogue in Late Antiquity*, A Centennial Publication of the Jewish Theological Seminary of America, edited by L.I. Levine, (Philadelphia: ASOR, 1987) 49-60, see also G. Nickelsburg, *Jewish Literature Between the Bible and the Mishnah*, (Philadelphia, 1981), and J.J. Collins, *Between Athens and Jerusalem* (New York, 1983).

3 H.J. Leon, *The Jews of Ancient Rome* (Philadelphia, 1960).

grims on occasion; the only Sardian who claims to have travelled to the Holy Land, however, is the second-century Christian bishop Melito.[4]

We know a little about traffic from the other direction, even though Asia Minor and Sardis were on the edge of the rabbinic world; little attention is paid to this area in rabbinic literature. (Even the meaning of the term "Asia" in the literary evidence is unclear; sometimes it designates what we have been calling Asia Minor, sometimes a single city, sometimes a non-Anatolian location.) Rabbinic texts tell of rabbis sent into the Diaspora to collect funds and to keep the official ritual calendar synchronized with that of the Holy Land. The famous second-century rabbi Meir once went to "Asia" for the second purpose. The story goes that when he found the community there without a copy of the Book of Esther (for the Purim Festival) he wrote one out from memory. Meir is also reported to have died in "Asia." Did these two events take place in the same area or the same city? If an Anatolian community lacked Esther, was it because the community was so far out of touch with the majority of Jews as even to lack a complete text of the Scriptures? Or was it because the people of "Asia" refused to accept the Festival of Purim because of its political and anti-gentile emphases, that is, not because they were marginal Jews but because their kind of Judaism was self-consciously independent of the nationalism of the Palestinian homeland?

The most convincing evidence for the allegiance of Sardis Jews to their traditions and their origins remains however the synagogue itself, a building where the community assembled at the appointed times, where the Torah was central, where Samoe (and others) taught and where in the architecture itself, in the Torah Shrines, the connection with Jerusalem was maintained.

And yet Sardis Jews remained open to, indeed at home in, a world where gentiles were the vast majority. This rhythm of allegiance to one's origins and openness to one's neighbors may seem contradictory, and surely was not always easy to maintain. But it was the key to the continued existence of the Jewish community. To relinquish either, and thus to relax the tension, would have meant the disappearance of the Jews of Sardis.

A final reason for the tie to the Holy Land is one not often recognized: in the Mediterranean world *antiquity* was important. In Greco-Roman culture it helped to have a long history. This is what Homer represented for the Greeks. The parallel story for Rome was given classic form by Virgil in the *Aeneid*. Egypt's great age was respected, and so was Israel's. When the Jews of Sardis claimed Israel's history as their own, they were signalling that they too had their proper place in the vast Greco-Roman civilization.

---

4 Kraabel, "Melito the Bishop and the Synagogue at Sardis: Text and Context," *Studies Presented to George M.A. Hanfmann* edited by D.G. Mitten, J.G. Pedley and J.A. Scott (Cambridge, MA, 1971).

VII

There were also Christians at Sardis, from the earliest times of the history of the Church. Christian missionaries could reach the city easily *via* the Roman road system; the first ones had arrived by the middle of the first century, that is, they were contemporaries of the Apostle Paul. By the last decade of the first century, when the community receives the letter to it preserved in the New Testament (*Revelation* 3:1-6), it had been in existence long enough to have a good reputation which it no longer deserved; there had been a decline from earlier accomplishments. Sardis was thus a very early Christian center of some importance. One of its bishops, Melito, was highly influential in the late second century and thereafter, not always in happy ways. The strength of Sardis Christianity increased greatly after Constantine; sometime late in his reign, or perhaps under his sons, the decision was made to build an entire "Christian quarter" just outside the city gate.

While the Jews might have wanted to ignore this new movement and maintain their life in Sardis as it had continued for centuries, Christians could not really afford to leave Jews undisturbed. Once Christianity moved out of its Jewish context in the Holy Land west to areas where gentiles were greatly in the majority, its ties with Judaism became a problem, and soon an embarrassment *for Christians*. The Christian claim was that Jesus was the Christ, the Messiah whom the Hebrew scriptures had promised; but nearly all Jews rejected that claim. In the Holy Land, where the first followers of Jesus constituted a sect among other Jewish sects, this was in one sense an internal disagreement, a "family argument"—and there had been plenty of those in the Jewish Homeland! But in the gentile world the problem of credibility arose very quickly. Christians, whether of Jewish or of gentile descent, made the same assertions: Jesus was the Jews' Messiah, and he matches the promises—or fits the pattern—of the Hebrew scriptures. Diaspora Jews rejected both claims and in the process forthrightly distinguished themselves from the followers of Jesus. One result was that the protection and patronage the Roman government had provided to Jews would not be available to Christians even if they were of Jewish descent. Further, the assertion of antiquity, of having a long and illustrious past—which, as noted, was very significant for the Greco-Roman world—was blocked for Christians if they could not claim somehow to be "Jewish." The only "past" the Christians had was that of the Old Testament Israelites; if that was not available to them, their standing in the ancient world became even more precarious.[5]

---

5 *Anti-Judaism in Early Christianity,* Studies in Christianity and Judaism 2-3, Vol. 1: *Paul and the Gospels,* edited by P. Richardson and D. Granskou, Vol. 2: *Separation and Polemic,* edited by S.G. Wilson, (Waterloo, Canada: Wilfrid Laurier University, 1986).

Eventually Christianity would sort these things out, but in the early centuries they were acute concerns. And of course they were *Christian* problems; they came from the Christian side, from Christians' understanding of who they were and whence they had come. There were no parallel concerns from the side of the Diaspora Jews.

They became problems very early too, as soon as the Christian mission was catapulted into the Diaspora. And Asia Minor was one of the very first places these missionaries reached after they left the Holy Land.

One of Bishop Melito's sermons from the later second century is still in existence, and it is such a violent attack on Jews and on "Israel" that it earned him the title "the first poet of deicide," that monstrous charge that because of the Crucifixion *all* Jews were guilty of "murdering God."[6] The impression Melito creates is one of great hostility between Christianity and Judaism at Sardis. That image is suspect, as are suggestions of similar conflict elsewhere. I say this first because Christianity was not often an issue for Diaspora Jews in this period. In the beginning Christians were not very numerous in the world of Diaspora Judaism. Later most Christians there were gentiles, as Christianity became pretty quickly a gentile religion. For Christian leaders Judaism *did* matter, for the reasons given earlier. Most responded with hostility; while Melito's attack is one of the earliest and most bitter, it is not at all isolated.[7]

The gentile Christian *laity* however may have been of a different mind, at least at Sardis. Theological issues may have been less important for them. And Jews had been a part of the city's life centuries longer than Christianity had. Jews and Christians (and pagans) had shops side-by-side just outside the bath-gymnasium complex and the synagogue. The central location of the synagogue makes it unlikely that there was anything like a "Jewish quarter" or ghetto there.

And there is one last piece of evidence that Jews and Christians may have lived in relative harmony in this city: the synagogue itself, though it would have made a wonderful church, was *never* taken over for that purpose. To the end of Sardis' history, when the city was destroyed by Persian forces in 616, three centuries *after* Constantine, the building remained in Jewish hands.

The Sardis Jews are not the typical example of life in the Greco-Roman Diaspora: there is no such typical community known to me. But with their centuries-long history there, their economic and political substance, their com-

6 E. Werner, "Melito of Sardis, the First Poet of Deicide, *Hebrew Union College Annual* 37 (1966): 191-210.

7 Kraabel "Melito the Bishop" 1971, and "*Synagoga Caeca*. Ssytematic Distortion in Gentile Interpretations of Evidence for Judaism in the Early Christian Period," in "*To See Ourselves As Others See Us*" *Christians, Jews, "Others" in Late Antiquity,* edited by J. Neusner and E.S. Frerichs, (Chico, CA: Scholars Press, 1985) 219-246.

bination of an integration into gentile life with a concern for their "roots," their own history and traditions, they do not fit the traditional stereotype of the frightened and powerless minority lost in a sea of non-Jews and yearning to return to their Homeland. The silent evidence from Sardis deserves to be heard in more places in our own world. I hope you are grasped by their story, and never quite forget them.

Bibliography

Anti-Judaism
1986   *Anti-Judaism in Early Christianity*. Studies in Christianity and Judaism 2-3. Vol. 1: Paul and the Gospels, edited by P. Richardson and D. Granskou. Vol. 2: Separation and Polemic, edited by S.G. Wilson. Waterloo, Ontario.

Collins, J.J.
1983   *Between Athens and Jerusalem*. New York.

Foss, C.
1976   *Byzantine and Turkish Sardis*. Archaeological Exploration of Sardis Monograph 4. Cambridge MA.

Green, W.S. (ed)
1985   *Approaches to Ancient Judaism. Volume V. Studies in Judaism and Its Greco-Roman Context*. Atlanta.

Hanfmann, G.M.A.
1983   *Sardis from Prehistoric to Roman Times*. Cambridge MA.

Kraabel, A.T.
1971   "Melito the Bishop and the Synagogue at Sardis: Text and Context." *Studies Presented to George M.A. Hanfmann*. Edited by D.G. Mitten, J.G. Pedley and J.A. Scott. Cambridge MA. Pages 77-85.
1979   "The Diaspora Synagogue." In *Aufstieg und Niedergang der römischen Welt: Geschichte und Kultur Roms im Spiegel der neueren Forschung*, II.19.1: 477-510.
1982   "The Roman Diaspora: Six Questionable Assumptions." *Journal of Jewish Studies* 33:445-64 (Yadin *Festschrift*).
1983   "Impact of the Discovery of the Sardis Synagogue." In Hanfmann 1983. Pages 178-190.
1985   "*Synagoga caeca*. Systematic Distortion in Gentile Interpretations of Evidence for Judaism in the Early Christian Period." In Neusner and Frerichs, 1985. Pages 219-246.
1987   "Unity and Diversity Among Diaspora Synagogues." In *The Synagogue in Late Antiquity*, edited by L.I. Levine. Philadelphia.

Leon, H.J.
1960   *The Jews of Ancient Rome*. Philadelphia.
Millar, F.
1967   *The Roman Empire and Its Neighbours*. New York.
Neusner, J.
1985   "The Experience of the City in Late Antique Judaism." In Green, 1985, 37-52.
Nickelsburg, G.
1981   *Jewish Literature Between the Bible and the Mishnah*. Philadelphia.
Werner, E.
1966   "Melito of Sardis, the First Poet of Deicide." *Hebrew Union College Annual* 37: 191-210.
Yegül, F.K.
1986   *The Bath-Gymnasium Complex at Sardis*. Archaeological Exploration of Sardis Report 3. Cambridge MA.

Paganism and Judaism: The Sardis Evidence[1]

A.T. Kraabel

Introduction[2]

The title of this *Festschrift* and its three-part organization directly reflect that element in the work of Marcel Simon which is most important for many of us in the Western Hemisphere: his research on the *boundaries* between and among the religions of the Greco-Roman world. Examples from his bibliography may be selected almost at random: Θαρσει οὐδεὶς ἀθάνατος (1936), on a grave-formula used by paganism, Judaism and Christianity; "Alexandre le Grand, juif et chretien" (1941); *St. Stephen and the Hellenists in the Primitive Church* (1958);[3] "Bellerophon chretien" (1966); "Early Christianity and Pagan Thought; Confluences and Conflicts" (1973). Simon has often surveyed these boundary-areas in the broadest terms, witness the volume which first brought his name to the attention of many Americans of my generation, *Verus Israel, subtitled Etude sur les relations entre chretiens et juifs dans l'empire romain (135-425)*. When guides are needed for these large areas, we are not surprised to see his name on them: *Le judaïsme et le christianisme antique* (1968, with A. Benoit) and *La civilisation de l'antiquite et le christianisme* (1972).

The present essay is also about boundaries and relationships among ancient religions, but on a much smaller scale; it is restricted essentially to one ancient city. Archaeological excavation frequently provides opportunity for testing hypotheses about ancient religions by offering particular and controlled examples as "case-studies": individual Jews, particular pagans, specific Christians in a single time and place. For the subject of *Jews and Pagans*, Dura,

---

1 Editor's note: This essay first appeared in *Paganisme, Judaïsme, Christianisme: Influences et affrontements dans le monde antique*, (Mélanges offerts à Marcel Simon) (Paris: Édition E. de Boccard, 1978) 13-33.

2 Abbreviations: BASOR=*Bulletin of the American Schools of Oriental Research*. Annual preliminary reports on the Sardis excavations have been published in BASOR since 1959 and are referred to by issue number, year of publication and page number. Robert, "Bull. épigr." = the Roberts' annual review of the year's work in Greek epigraphy; the entry is followed by the year and number (#), indicating that the reference is to that year's volume of REG, in the section "Bulletin epigraphique" and at the number cited.

3 When a famous American Episcopal bishop, James A. Pike, began to study in earnest the boundaries between Christianity and Judaism in antiquity (as he was himself in the process of moving from "just inside" the Church to "just outside" it), he became an avid reader of this book; it is the only such volume quoted (from pages 46f.) in his biography, *The Death and Life of Bishop Pike* by W. Stringfellow and A. Towne (Garden City, New York, 1976), page 404. Pike's intense interest in the topic led to his death from exposure in the Judean desert near Qumran in September, 1969, four months after the announcement of his decision to leave the institutional church.

238 A.T. Kraabel

Delos, Ostia are ready-to-hand.[4] The evidence from Sardis,[5] on the other hand, is only beginning to appear in print, but this site will eventually offer one of the most widely and carefully documented of these "case-studies" for the historian of ancient religions. Even now it is possible to review the question of *Paganisme et Judaïsme*[6] in a preliminary fashion for Sardis, taking the measure of particular topics within it in an attempt to gain some impression of the complete picture which will be available when all the evidence for this site is before us.

The Evidence from Josephus

Sardis is mentioned by name in four passages of the *Jewish Antiquities* (see below); now, however, the new epigraphic evidence from Sardis has brought a fifth to consideration, the earliest of all.[7] The text is the famous letter of Antiochus III (ruled 223-187) to his viceroy Zeuxis (*Ant* 12:117-153), ordering that two thousand Jewish families be brought from Mesopotamia and Babylonia, settled in Lydia and Phrygia, provided with houses and land and exempted from taxes on produce for ten years. The inscription (Robert, *Nouvelles Inscriptions #1*), discovered in 1960, is a decree of Antiochus, set up in Sardis sometime after he had besieged, captured and destroyed the city in 215-213. It is clear that Zeuxis (who is mentioned by name in line 9) is the Seleucid governor and that Sardis is his capital;[8] but if the discovery of the inscrip-

---

4 On the synagogues at these sites, see most recently A.T. Kraabel, "The Diaspora Synagogue: Archaeological and Epigraphic Evidence since Sukenik," in W. Hasse (ed.), *Aufstieg und Niedergang der römischen Welt* (Berlin, in press), hereafter "Diaspora Synagogue."

5 Further on the synagogue, Kraabel "Diaspora Synagogue," section III. The final publication of the building is A.R. Seager, et al., *The Synagogue and its Setting* (Archaeological Exploration of Sardis Report 5; Cambridge, forthcoming): until it becomes available, the best source of plans, photographs and reconstruction drawings is G.M.A. Hanfmann, *Letters from Sardis* (Cambridge, 1972), hereafter *Letters*. On the history of the city, G.M.A. Hanfmann, *Sardis and Lydien* (AbhMainz 6; Mainz, 1960) 499-536; D.G. Mitten, "A New Look at Ancient Sardis," *BA* 29 (1966) 38-68; G.M.A. Hanfmann and Jane C. Waldbaum, "New Excavations at Sardis and Some Problems of Western Anatolian Archaelogy," in *Near Eastern Archaeology in the Twentieth Century: Essays in Honor of Nelson Glueck*, ed. J.A. Sanders (Garden City, N.Y., 1970) 307-326, hereafter, "New Excavations."

6 On the topic generally: John G. Gager, "The Dialogue of Paganism with Judaism: Bar Cochba to Julian, " *HUCA* 44 (1973) 89-118, with an emphasis on the literary evidence; G. Kittle, "Das kleinasiatische Judentum in der hellenistischrömischen Zeit," *TLZ* 69 (1944) 9-20.

7 The earliest reference to Jews at Sardis (as exiles and therefore temporary residents) is Obad. 20 in the Hebrew Bible, where the city is called Sepharad; on which, see the biblical dictionaries and lexica, and especially I. Rabinowitz, "Sefarad," *Encyclopaedia Biblica* 5 (1968) 1100-03 (Hebrew).

8 On the inscription, see L. Robert, *Nouvelles inscriptions de Sardes I* (Paris, 1964), 9-21, (continued...)

tion substantiates these conclusions, it has left the Josephus text even more in dispute than was the case before 1960.

The authenticity of decrees preserved only in Jewish authors but purported to be from gentile authorities has long been questioned, since the texts award or continue special privileges to Jews; the debate is summarized by Bickerman and Marcus.[9] I follow Teherikover and Robert[10] in accepting the text in question, *Ant* 12: 147-153, as genuine: these Jews were settled in *Lydia and Phrygia* as a means of pacifying the land, i.e., making its inhabitants more succeptible to Selencid rule. Schalit has gone further, arguing that these Jews had proved their loyalty to the Seleucids as soldiers, and *further* that Antiochus provided the settlers with "sacred ministrants," priests and Levites, at state expense, with the result that "synagogues...were no doubt founded almost immediately after their arrival there."[11] The latter point goes beyond the present evidence. Robert argues that a direct connection between the new inscription and the Josephus text on the resettlement of the Jewish veterans has not been proved; the inscription does not mean that the Jews were installed *at Sardis*.[12] Nevertheless, it seems quite probable that at least some of these pro-Seleucid Jews made their homes in Zeuxis' Seleucid capital, enjoying the protection of this government as they would the protection of the Romans in the next century.[13] But if at this early date the Jewish community of Sardis and the Jews of Lydia are supplemented in this fashion, the "Judaism" which is inserted into

---

8(...continued)
hereafter *Nouvelles Inscriptions*; Hanfmann and Waldbaum, "New Excavations" 318f.; S. Applebaum, "The Legal Status of the Jewish Communities in the Diaspora," (hereafter "Legal Status"), 431f. and "The Organization of the Jewish Communities in the Diaspora" (hereafter "Organization"), 468-73, in S. Safrai and M. Stern, edd: *Compendia Berum Indaicarum ad Novum Testament I.I* (Assen, 1974), hereaft~r *Compendia,* published in the United States under the title *The Jewish People in the First Century* (Philadelphia), 1974). On the events of 215-213, G.M.A. Hanfmann and Jane C. Waldbaum, *A survey of Sardis and the Major Monuments outside the City Walls* (Archaeological Exploration of Sardis Report I; Cambridge, 1975), 29f., hereafter *Survey*.

9 E. Bickerman, "Une question d'authenticité: les privilèges juifs," *AnnPhil-Hist 13* (1953) 11-34; R. Marcus, "Appendix D. Antiochus III and the Jews," in the Loeb edition of Josephus, vol. 7 (Cambridge, 1943), 743-766.

10 V. Teherikover, *Hellenistic Civilization and the Jews* (Philadelphia, 1966) 287f., with notes, hereafter *Hellenistic Civilization*. Robert, *Nouvelles Inscriptions, 12.*

11 A. Schalit, "The Letter of Antiochus III to Zeuxis regarding the Establishment of Jewish Military Colonies in Phrygia and Lydia," *JQR* 50 (1960) 289-318, quotation from 315. Applebaum agrees, "Organization," 468-470.

12 Robert, as cited in Hanfmann and Waldbaum, *Survey* 30 note 101.

13 Sardis comes under Pergamene control with the defeat of Antiochus III by the Romans in 188. It passes to direct Roman control with the "Bequest of Attalus" in 133, Hanfmann and Waldbaum, *Survey* 6; D. Magie, *Roman Rule in Asia Minor* (Princeton, 1950), chapter one, hereafter *Roman Rule.*

western Anatolia is not from "the Holy Land," at least not directly; it is rather the religion and culture of Jews who have already learned to live as a minority in a gentile world: Babylonian and Mesopotamian, Seleucid.And if these immigrants are the *first* Jewish *residents* of Sardis, then the community with which this paper is concerned is from the beginning sensitive to the issues—problems *and* opportunities—raised by life in the Diaspora, among "pagans."

Not that this means the Sardis Jews would forget their responsibilities to Jerusalem and the Temple; a proconsular decree from the second half of the first century B.C. to "the magistrates and council of Sardis" (*Ant.* 16.171) indicates that they were willing to seek Roman aid to ensure that their "temple-tax" would continue to be collected and sent to Jerusalem,[14] without gentile interference.[15]

The remaining passages from the *Jewish Antiquities* are all from book 14; 14.232 is only a "cross-reference," but the others are more substantial. They are also from the second half of the first century: 235 is another Roman decree, 259-261 a *psephisma* of the people of Sardis.[16] Both refer to the Jewish community or association in the city, and to the *topos*, "place" or "location" ("property"?), which has been theirs "since the beginning" ἀπ' ἀρχῆς (235). In the Roman decree it is a *topos* where the Jews of Sardis "make decisions on their own affairs and controversies." In the Sardis *psephisma* it is also a place for religious activities (260); in this text, which may be a bit later than 235, it is assumed that the Jews have had a *topos*, but also that they are to be given a suitable τόπον...εἰς οἰκκοδομίν καὶ οἴκησιν αὐτῶν, "a place...for them to construct and occupy" (261). Perhaps two *topoi* are implied in the *psephisma*: the earlier one (also referred to in 235?) less formal, an "area" or "space," the second the "location" of a building which the Jews will erect.[17]

Topos is a term used in later texts to mean "synagogue,"[18] and it is often assumed that that is the meaning here.[19] However, Yegul has speculated that the *topos* (one of the *topoi*?) in the Josephus texts might have been a location

---

14 J.G. Pedley, *Ancient Literary Sources on Sardis* (Archaeological Exploration of Sardis Monograph 2; Cambridge, 1972), #212, hereafter *Ancient Literary Sources*. On the date, *Philonis Alexandrini Legatio ad Gaium*, ed., trans. E.M. Smallwood, 2nd. ed. (Leiden, 1970) 309f.

15 Such interference was not always local, cf. the famous case of Lucius Valerius Flaccus, Roman governor of Asia in 62, on which, Cicero, *Pro Flacco* and H.J. Leon, *The Jews of Ancient Rome* (Philadelphia, 1960), 5-8.

16 Generally on the texts, Applebaum, "Organization," 477-479.

17 Assuming the interpretation by Marcus in his note "c" in the Loeb edition. *ad loc.*

18 On *topos*=synagogue, M. Hengel, "Die Synagogeninschrift von Stobi," *ZNW* 57 (1966), 173; S. Krauss, *Synagogale Attertumer* (Berlin/Vienna, 1922), 24f.

19 Cf. the references in the Loeb edition, *ad loc.*, and M. Stern, "The Jewish Diaspora" (hereafter, "Jewish Diaspora") in Safrai and Stern, *Compendia*, 144.

in one of the *public* buildings of Sardis; perhaps the acquisition of the mammoth synagogue over two centuries later (see next section) is only "the culminating step in a long-term progression of establishing simple community and club rooms under the socially permissive roof of a pagan institution."[20] Ordinarily, we would expect that before the small Jewish minority of a given Diaspora city had its own building, the place of assembly would be a private home; this is the case at Dura and Elos, and perhaps at Prience and Stobi.[21] There will perhaps never be direct archaeological evidence to support Yegul's hypothesis, since public space used in this fashion would be unlikely to manifest permanent marks of its temporary status as a "synagogue"; nevertheless, the suggestion is worthy of note, particularly for the precedent thereby offered for later placing a sizable public building under Jewish control.[22]

The Sardis *psephisma* also indicates that the Sardis Jews requested the *topos* as a place for "ancestral prayers and sacrifices (*thysiai*)"(260). A few years before the new discoveries relating to Sardis Judaism, Bickerman had suggested that this request was in fact for "a place for sacrifices to be offered to God by the God-fearing pagans of Sardis," i.e., by "sympathizers" and proselytes.[23] This would allow a Gentile adherent to worship the God of the Jews in the familiar way, with sacrifices like those which had formerly been a part of his everyday life. Bickerman is not talking about apostasy on the part of the Jews; they are not giving up the essentials of their faith by allowing such rites (they would say), but simply making it possible for a prospective convert to incorporate and comprehend it.[24]

This text lastly directs the *agoranomoi* of the city to provide "suitable" food for the Jewish community (261); the assumption must be that this is *kosher* food, suitable for ritual use. Similar concerns are reflected in two other

---

20 F. Yegül, *The Bath-Gymnasium Complex in Asia Minor during the Imperial Roman Age* (Diss., Harvard University 1975), 181f. and note 277. Yegül's value for the present purpose is increased by the fact that his hypothesis is based on architectural comparisons rather than the history of religions.

21 See Kraabel, "Diaspora Synagogue," especially section VI. "Delos."

22 The Jews of Berenice, Cyrenaica were apparently using an amphitheater (public?) as a meeting place (synagogue?) in this period, Applebaum, "Organization," 486-488; on the inscriptions involved, Robert, "Bull, épirgr." 1951, #246; 1955, #278; 1959, #514.

23 "The Altars of Gentiles, A note on the Jewish 'ius sacrum'," *Revue internationale des Droits de l'Antiquite* 5 (1958), 151, hereafter, "Altars."

24 "For a gentile the sacrifice was a part of his everyday life...Gentiles ready to worship the Most High God...would be bewildered, snubbed, lost to the true faith forever, were they forbidden to offer their sacrifices to God," Bickerman, "Altars" 161. But *thysiai* may mean simply "offerings," so R. Marcus in the Loeb edition, *ad loc.*

passages in Josephus, both set in western Asia Minor: 14:225-7 (Ephesus, 43 B.C.), 14:211-216 (Miletus).[25]

A final question is, of course, what do these decrees mean? Why were they necessary? It is usually assumed that, if genuine, the protective acts were promulgated because the Jews of this area required protection from their neighbors, and that for some reason the Romans in particular were willing to provide it.[26] But the new evidence suggests that for Sardis at least these rules were made also because of the power and wealth of the Jewish community. Are they a sign, not of the community's need for protection, but of its prestige?[27]

Evidence from Imagery: Architecture, Art, Mythology

The Sardis synagogue is not a building, but only one segment of a mammoth structure, a monument of Roman Imperial urbanism, the Sardis gymnasium complex. Sardis was devastated by an earthquake in C.E. 17; the gymnasium is a major part of the rebuilding afterward. The center of the excavated area is an open *palaestra*, square, its colonnaded sides roughly east-west and north-south; in the original design, the entrance to the complex was a gate in the middle of the east side of the *palaestra*, with the Roman baths proper on the west. On the north and south sides of the *palaestra* were parallel halls, each with three large rooms opening into the *palaestra* and serving perhaps as its dressing rooms or *apodyteria*. Apparently the north hall remained in this form, but the south hall was extensively remodelled, in about the second century; the openings into the *palaestra* were sealed, the interior north-south walls removed, and an *exedra* was added at the west end of the long room thus formed—the result is a structure which closely resembles the usual Roman civil basilica.[28]

These alterations may have been carried out in order to produce a synagogue; it is more likely, however, that this space too was originally public, and was turned over to the Jewish community only later—thus it was probably not designed to serve as a religious structure. In the second half of the third century, however, already decorated with mosaics and revetments some of which are still in place, it is in the possession of the Jewish community and function-

---

25 On the date of the first text, Magie, *Roman Rule*, 1273. On the possibility of a different explanation for the second, J. Juster, *Les juifs dans l'empire romain* (Paris, 1914) I. 361.

26 This is the conclusion drawn by such widely different scholars as V. Schultze, *Attchristiche Städle und Landschaften II. Kleinasien* (Gutersloh, 1922-26), 40f., and Applebaum, "Legal Status," 443.

27 After all, one might assume that an American mayor bestows upon a visitor a "key to the city" because otherwise the city would be barred to him! But such is not the case.

28 A.R. Seager, The Building History of the Sardis Synagogue," *AJA* 76(1972) 425-435, hereafter "Building History."

ing as their synagogue; remodelled once or twice more, it became the building excavated and reconstructed by the Sardis expedition.[29]

What are the implications of the plan of this baths-gymnasium-*synagogue* complex[30] for the understanding of the relation of "Paganisme et Judaisme" in the Roman world? In the Hellenistic period the introduction of a gymnasium and its customs into Jerusalem by the high-priest Jason (formerly Joshua) as an indication of the presence of an alien, pagan culture, in direct confrontation with Judaism (I Macc 1:11-15; 2 Macc 4:7-17); Teherikover and Hengel use the term "the hellenistic reform," Moore "the religious crisis,"[31] to characterize these events, which will eventuate in the Maccabean revolt. Hengel describes the synagogue-school of "the Holy Land" as the central institution for the preservation of a pure Judaism, unadulterated by the pagan culture *epitomized in the gymnasium.*[32]

At exactly the same time, the gymnasium at Sardis is the central location in the city for the promulgation of "pagan" culture and piety; an inscription of ca. 150 B.C.E. honors

"...Dionysios also called Xanthios son of Menas, (director) of the Boys' (gymnasium), because in honor of Hermes (and Herakles), the gods of the palaestra, (he performed) the mysteries with lavish expense, and four times gave (prizes) for the running competition (in the gymnasium), and is now contributing (a statue of Athena). Neikephoros and, for the (festivals of the goddess),—gilded images; a tribute to his excellence."[33]

This was, of course, a predecessor of the gymnasium complex here under discussion; the events taking place within it are those which are traditional and customary for any gymnasium of the hellenistic world.

When Frend discussed the Diaspora Jews as "a people apart, with their own customs and religion which admitted little intermingling with their Greek

---

29 Generally, Kraabel, "Diaspora Synagogue," section III, "Sardis."

30 Plan in Seager, "Building History," 426, fig. I = Hanfmann, *Letters*, 295, fig. 223. Striking reconstruction drawing in *Letters*, 294, fig. 222.

31 Tcherikover, *Hellenistic Civilization*, part 1, chap. 3. M. Hengel, *Judaism and Hellenism: Studies in their Encounter in Palestine during the Early Hellenistic Period* (Philadelphia, 1974), chap. 4, parts 3-4, hereafter *Judaism and Hellenism*. G.F. Moore, *Judaism in the First Centuries of the Christian Era. The Age of the Tannaim,* I (Cambridge, 1927), 48-55.

32 Hengel, *Judaism and Hellenism,* 65-83.

33 *Sardis: Publications of the American Society for the Excavation of Sardis, 7.1 The Greek and Latin Inscriptions,* ed. W.H. Buckley and D.H. Robinson (Leiden, 1932), #21, hereafter *Sardis 7*; restored words in parentheses. Used as an example of "the intimate connection between the gymnasia and religious rites" by Applebaum, "Legal Status," 447, incorrectly referring to a "Sardis III."

neighbors,"[34] he took Sardis as an example, using as evidence Josephus, *Ant.* 14.259, discussed in the previous section.[35] On the basis of the new discoveries of which Frend was not aware, Applebaum is able to render a more realistic judgment: "no evidence could demonstrate better (than the new archaeological data from Sardis) the intimate and excellent relations which prevailed between the Jews of Asia and the Greeks in the early third century C.E."[36] The architectural evidence provided still more recently by Seager[37] allows even more precision: there may be "intimate and excellent relations" between Jews and gentiles here, but there is no evidence of indiscriminate mixing or "syncretism." The synagogue does not communicate with the remainder of the complex; it may be entered only from outside, from the street. The openings which once existed between the *palaestra* and what is now the synagogue are sealed. However, the "fountain of the synagogue"[38] was public, available to gentiles as well as Jews, and the rest of the building may well have been open to non-Jews, at least on a limited basis.

As the plan indicates, the *palaestra*, the baths, the gymnasium and the synagogue are massive architectural units, related integrally to one another in plan, and yet discrete; there is no question where one ends and another begins. This may be taken as symbolic of the situation between Jews and gentiles as well: the Jewish community is so large, obvious, self-conscious as to disallow the possibility of its becoming submerged unwittingly within Sardis "paganism," or so diluted by it as to lose its distinctiveness.

One may go one step farther: the Sardis synagogue reflects a *self-confident* Judaism,[39] bold enough to appropriate pagan shapes and symbols for itself. This impression is reinforced by the finds within the building. The *exedra* has become an apse; its mosaic is a representation of "a great vine growing out from a gadrooned vase," closely resembling the great *kraler* in the synagogue

---

34 W.H.C. Frend, *Martyrdom and Persecution in the Early Church* (Oxford, 1965), 130, hereafter, *Martyrdom*.

35 Frend, *Martyrdom,* 130 note 18, incorrectly referring to book *10* of the *Antiquities*.

36 "Legal Status," 449 cf. 447-450.

37 "Building History."

38 *Sardis 7*, #17, line 7. Other locations for the fountains: near "the two confraternity halls" *(mysteria)*, line 3; near "the confraternity hall of Attis," line 6; near "the precinct of Men," the Anatolian moon-god, line 17.

39 Further evidence for the attitude here suggested: the several city and provincial officials mentioned in the synagogue inscriptions: nine members of the city council, a procurator, two *adiulores tabularii* and a count; cf. BASOR 187 (1967) 27-32 and, for the count (fifth-sixth century C.E.?), BASOR 206 (1972), 20 cf. the same title in Hebrew transliteration in CII 856, from Hammath Gadera.

forecourt.[40] The donors of the apse-mosaic incorporate their names within it. There is nothing in the design or in the names which suggests anything Jewish; had the mosaic been discovered in an otherwise unidentified building there would be no way to prove it Jewish. Yet this is the mosaic immediately before the eyes of the "elders of the synagogue" who presumably were seated on the benches of the apse.

At the opposite end of the main hall were two *aediculae*,[41] one on either side of the central entrance to the room; one likely served as the Torah shrine[42] of the synagogue in its latest phase. Both *aediculae* are in reuse, and clearly reflect their origin in hellenistic, "pagan" public architecture.

But the most startling example of the inclusion of pagan imagery whole-sale in this building is in the "Eagle Table" flanked by two pairs of addorsed stone lions. The table is more likely the lectern of the building, not (*pace* Goodenough) the place for cultic meals.[43] The top of the table is a two-ton slab of stone, an architectural fragment from an earlier building, but the table gets its modern name from the supports, each decorated with a powerful Roman eagle clutching thunderbolts. The lions are originally Lydian, sixth-fifth century B.C.E. The eagle as a symbol of Rome was perhaps too obvious, hence these eagles were deliberately defaced: the head of each was knocked off.[44] Lions figure in Sardis mythology, but from a much earlier and more remote period; for this reason, perhaps, these lions were left complete.[45]

An inscription may give a clue to the Jews' understanding of one of these symbols; it identifies one of the synagogue donors as being of the φυλὴ Λεοντίων. "the tribe of the *Leontioi*." Robert has suggested that this is a "tribe" or group within the synagogue community, and that Leontioi (from lean,

---

40 Quotation, E.R. Goodenough, *Jewish Symbols in the Greco-Roman Period* (13 vols., New York, 1953-1968), 12:193; the mosaic is shown as fig. 5 on 195; hereafter, *Jewish Symbols*. The mosaic is also shown in Hanfmann, *Letters*, 131, fig. 95, and BASOR 174 (1964) 33, fig. 17. The *kraler* (a copy) in place, *Letters*, plate V, opposite p. 322; this is perhaps the "fountain of the synagogue" mentioned above, cf. Hanfmann and Waldbaum, *Survey*, 27 note 74.

41 Hanfmann, *Letters* 216, fig. 167; 289, fig. 217.

42 On the Torah shrine and its forms, Goodenough, *Jewish Symbols*, vol. 13, index; R. Wischnitzer, *The Architecture of the European Synagogue* (Philadelphia 1964), 13-17.

43 Goodenough, *Jewish Symbols* 12: 195, cf. E. Bickerman, "Sur la théologie de Part figuratif, a propos de l'ouvrage de E.R. Goodenough," *Syria* 44 (1967) 143 note 2.

44 Photograph: BASOR 174 (1964) 36, fig. 19; Hanfmann, *Letters*, 134, fig. 97; restored: *Letters*, 288f., figs. 216f. On the eagle as a Jewish symbol, see Goodenough, *Jewish Symbols,* vol. 13, index; in Anatolian piety (including Judaism), Kraabel, "*hypsistos* and the Synagogue at Sardis," *GRBS* 10 (1969) 89f., hereafter "*hypsistos.*"

45 Photograph: Hanfmann, *Letters,* 135, fig. 98. For a restoration drawing which includes the lions, Goodenough, *Jewish Symbols* 12: 194, fig. 4.

"lion") recalls the biblical "lion of Judah."[46] But the lion is associated with Sardis in Greek Literature since the days of Herodotus, who tells of how Meles, king of Sardis, had been told to carry a lion-cub (borne him by his mistress) around the walls of the city in order to make them impregnable; he overlooked a particularly rugged area of the acropolis, and it was just at that spot that the army of Cyrus was later able to penetrate Croesus' defenses and capture the city (Herodotus, 1.84ff.). The story became so well known that, according to Cicero, when a woman dreams of giving birth to a lion, it is an indication that the state in which the dream occurred will be captured by a foreign power (De divinatione 1.53). It may be with this story in mind that Apollonius of Tyana rebukes the people of Sardis for civil strife by asking, "...trusting in what lion have you all...become infatuated with truceless war?" (Letter 75).[47]

The lions in the synagogue are only a small part of the lion images recovered in the current excavations; most notable are the three which were part of an altar to Cybele in the time of Croesus.[48] It seems likely that the Sardis Jews are not simply "reusing" the lion-statues in their synagogue, but actually associating themselves in some way with this traditional Sardis image, just as in Phrygia there occurs a deliberate conflation of indigenouos and biblical flood myths—or so the coins of the mid-third century Apameia Kibotos suggest.[49] The eagle is of course also a biblical image (Ex 19:4; Deut 32:IIf.; Ps. 103:5, etc.) and common in Jewish art; is the Roman eagle in the synagogue being "reused" as a symbol in this same fashion? This seems to me quite likely.

Goodenough titled volumes 7-8 of Jewish Symbols "Pagan Symbols in Judaism;" most later interpreters are disinclined to go to the lengths he did,[50] yet they would agree that symbols with pagan meaning (and Jewish meaning at the same time) appear in ancient Jewish art. Sometimes, possibly, this is accidental: the Jews do not realize that they are utilizing something pagan. Often, however, it appears deliberate. One obvious example is the Dura synagogue painting showing the Philistine god Dagon at Ashdod collapsed before

---

46 Robert, Nouvelles Inscriptions, 46f.

47 Texts in Pedley, Ancient Literary Sources, ##116, 89, 217.

48 BASOR 215 (1974), 48, fig. 17, cf. Hanfmann, Letters, index s.v. and especially 221f.

49 These coins are most conveniently seen in H. Leclereq, DACL I.2 (1907), 2515f., fig. 825-827, s.v. "Apamee," good photograph of an inferior speciment (238-244 C.E.) in M.B. Comstock, "Greek Imperial Coins," BMFA 65:342 (1967) 163f., fig. 5. See also Goodenough, Jewish Symbols, 2:119f., 3 #700. On the lion as associated with Cybele in this geographical area, G.M.A. Hanfmann and Jane C. Waldbaum, "Kybebe (sic) and Artemis: Two Anatolian Goddesses at Sardis," Archaeology 22 (1969) 264-269, hereafter "Kybebe."

50 See M. Smith, "Goodenough's Jewish Symbols in Retrospect," JBL 86 (1967) 53-68.

the Ark of the Covenant; the images and ritual objects associated with "dagon" in the picture are those of pagan religions *at Dura* contemporary with the synagogue. Goodenough is correct: in showing "dagon" collapsed in ruins before the Ark, the artist is "using the incident from I Samuel to show the collapse of paganism before the reality of Judaism, the collapse of paganism presumably as he knew it directly in Dura itself."[51]

At Sardis and perhaps at Apameia Kibotos the situation between Jews and pagans is not always one of hostility; perhaps when relations are "intimate and excellent" (Applebaum),[52] that too can be stated in "symbolic" fashion. Do the Apameia Kibotos coins (which show Noah and his ark, *kibotos* in Greek) and the Sardis synagogue lions and eagles mean that these Jews see their religion as the equivalent of the paganism, so that one collapses into the other in a syncretistic fashion? At least for Sardis, that is impossible. Jewish self-consciousness there is amply demonstrated in the archaeological data. This is no capitulation by Anatolian Jews to a gentile culture! But these Jews are also *Sardianoi*, as they title themselves in the synagogue inscriptions. They have a building which is their synagogue *at the same time* as it is a part of the gymnasium-baths complex. The Jewish mint-masters of Apameia Kibotos have the biblical flood-story *and* an indigenous "pagan" flood-story and manage to represent a bit of both on their coins. I submit that these are the expressions of self-confident Jewish communities, existing in Asia Minor (in the case of Sardis) for over a half a millennium by now. These Jews believe that they belong there. One wonders whether they are associating themselves with paganism, or paganism with them! These are bold acts, not timid ones, and should not be misrepresented as "syncretism" or "apostasy" simply because they appear strange in the twentieth century.

Nor should it be assumed that such "*rapprochement*" knew no limits. Spoils from destroyed pagan temples were used during the reign of fourth-century Christian emperors as building materials in the synagogue,[53] and in one case images of Cybele and Artemis were deliberately defaced before the steel on which they appeared was used as a part of the forecourt stylobate.[54] Two peacocks in the apse mosaic were later gouged out of the design, presumably by conservative members of the synagogue community; they left the remainder

---

51 Goodenough, *Jewish Symbols,* 10:76, cf. vol. II, plate 13. Most recently on Dura, Kraabel, "Diaspora Synagogue," section II.

52 Cf. page 20 note 36 *supra*.

53 *Paganisme, judaïsme, christianisme!*

54 Hanfmann, *Letters,* 243, *From Croesus to Constantine* (Ann Arbor, 1975), 89; the stele was published by Hanfmann and Waldbaum, "Kybebe."

of the mosaic quite undamaged.[55] Cybele and Artemis would be difficult to use as Jewish symbols at any time, and the defaced mosaic may be the result of a period of iconoclasm[56] or, more probably, the action of a minority.The more common attitude toward "paganism" among Sardis Jews is typified rather by the synagogue and its central location, and by its lions and the Eagle Table.

Evidence from Religious Vocabulary: Sarazios

The new evidence from the Sardis excavations is also going to make significant contributions toward the clarification of ancient religious vocabulary and language, pagan, Jewish and Christian. It has long been recognized that there are striking similarities between the language of Anatolian piety and what might be called "Biblical Greek," i.e., the New Testament, the Greek translations of the Hebrew Bible, and the religious texts influenced by these scriptures.[57] The following examples ought now be reexamined together in the Sardis context:

The so-called "Penitential Inscriptions": one Sardis example has been published by Robert in *Nouvelles Inscriptions;*[58] the texts generally are public confessions, in the form: "I did...and the goddess punished me with...I erect this stele in commemoration of the manifestation of her power."[59] The Sardis example uses specific words common in "Biblical Greek," e.g., *eulogein*, though the deities commonly cited in these texts are Sabazios, Men, Anaitis, or one of the indigenous deities often called "Mother" (*Meler*) or "Zeus" or "Apollo."

The term *pantokrater theos*, found in a synagogue inscription (Robert,*Nouvelles Inscriptions, #7*) and in the *Peri Pascha* of the late second century bishop of Sardis, Melito (line 3:22, ed. Perler).[60] But the epithet is also used on occasion of pagan deities, e.g., Hermes and Isis.

References to *angeloi* and *angelikoi*: the church at Sardis had an *angelos* (Rev 3:1) and the "heresy" in the New Testament letter to the Colossians involved *angeloi*. Colossae is a short distance east-southeast of Sardis, on the main Roman highway: its heresy has been attributed to Jews, to pagans and

---

55 Such defacing is known from other sites; at Dura it was done apparently by a (timid?) minority who perforated the eyes of a number of figures in the paintings, Goodenough, *Jewish Symbols*, 9:23f.

56 But then why leave the lions intact?

57 A complete discussion of this vocabulary will be presented in my *Judaism in Western Asia Minor under the Roman Empire* (hereafter *Judaism*), forthcoming in the series *Studia Post-Biblica* (Leiden).

58 Pages 23-33, #2, cf. *Sardis 7*, ##95f.

59 Summary by A.D. Nock, "Early Gentile Christianity," (1928), as republished in his *Essays on Religion and the Ancient World*, ed. Z. Stewart (Cambridge, 1972), 66, hereafter *Essays*.

60 *Sources Chrétiennes* #123 (1966).

to "apostate" or "syncretistic" Jews by earlier scholars. There are both pagan and Jewish texts which use these terms.[61]

Hypsistos as a divine epithet, used in Asia Minor by pagans, Jews and Christians.[62]

The deity called ὅσιον καὶ δίκαιον, "the holy and righteous (divinity)" (neuter). The adjectives recall themes central to Biblical thought, but they are not foreign to Lydian-Phrygian pagan piety.[63]

Martin Nilsson included most or all of the above in what he called "the Lydian-Phrygian mentality," involving remote and demanding deities, ethical codes, penitent adherents, and often an internalizing and spiritualizing piety.[64] One location with many of the elements under consideration here is Philadelphia, Lydia, the first city on the Roman road continuing east from Sardis. It contained Jewish (e.g., CII 754) and Christian communities, the latter entangled with a "synagogue of Satan" (Rev 3:9) and later with Montanism. In addition, there is epigraphic evidence for a great variety of pagan cults, including those of Sabazios, Men and Hypsistos. The richest example of Philadelphia piety is SIG[3] 985, a first-century B.C.E. text containing the elaborate rules of a religious association under the protection and domination of a host of "Savior Gods." Those who come into the shrine are enjoined to observe ritual purity, and forbidden to use love potions and abortive or contraceptive devices; there are also rules against robbery, murder and sexual assault. The mighty gods who dwell there and oversee these matters will become angry and punish terribly all who disobey, but will love and bless those who observe their commands.[65]

In all, this area of Lydia (and Phrygia) manifests a great religious variety and, frequently, strong religious concerns;[66] given the presence of Judaism

---

61 M. Simon, "Remarques sur l'angélolâtrie juive au début de l'ère chrétienne," CRAI 1971, 120-132; Kraabel, "*hypsistos*," 83f.

62 M. Simon, "Theos Hypsistos," in *Ex Orbe Religionum: Studia Geo Widengren Obala* (Supplements to *Numen 21*; Leiden, 1972) 1:372-385; Kraabel, "*hypsistos*."

63 L. Robert, *Sainte et Juste*, Hosion Dikaion. *Un culte indigène en Asie Mineure*, forthcoming in the series *Études préliminaires aux religions orientales dans l'empire romain*.

64 M.P. Nilsson, *Geschichte der griechischen Religion* 2, 2nd ed. (Munich, 1961) 291, hereafter *Geschichte,* cf. Nock, *Essays* 64-68.

65 On the inscription, O. Weinreich, *Stiftungen und Kultsalzungen eines Privatheiligtums in Philadelphia in Lydein* (SBHeidel; Heidelberg, 1919); Nilsson, *Geschichte,* 290-292; Nock, *Essays,* 65-67.

66 The secondary sources cited above are illustrative, not complete; see also J. Keil, "Die Kulte Lydiens," in *Anatolian Studies Presented to Sir William Mitchell Ramsay,* edd. W.H. Buckler and W.M. Calder (Manchester, 1923), 239-266, hereafter "Kulte Lydiens;" Nilsson, *Geschichte,* index, and G. Kittel, *Theological Dictionary of the New Testament,* 9 vols. (Grand Rapids, Mich., 1964-1974), *s.v.v.*

and Christianity, the question of the *relations among* these pieties is often a major consideration in any examination of the evidence. Thus we are not surprised to hear the suggestion that the Philadelphia association's rules are influenced by Anatolian Judaism (e.g. in the prohibition of contraception) and that this cult was itself instrumental in shaping local Christian piety. When dealing chiefly or solely with such written evidence, inscriptions and literary texts, apart from their social context, it is usually difficult to tell where the important words come from and just what has influenced the meanings they carry. For some students of ancient religions, such overlap of vocabulary as was sketched above is sufficient evidence for religious mixing, "syncretism." When such evidence is used to show that ancient Judaism had picked up elements from pagan cults, such terms as "heterodoxy" and "apostasy" are often used; Judaism is not supposed to be that sort of religion, and is distorted and debased when such things occur, whether deliberately or unwittingly.[67]

But where did they occur? Does similarity in vocabulary (or in iconography or in architecture, for that matter) mean that the Judaism under consideration has become dangerously assimilated? With texts alone, it is difficult to tell, but with the larger context provided by extensive archaeological investigation we are on much firmer ground, at least for that particular location.

The deity Sabazios offers a suitable test case for Sardis: there is new evidence from the excavations, the chief cult centers are in Lydia[68] and Phrygia, the deity is often used as a preeminent example of hellenistic syncretism and theocrasia,[69] and it has frequently been alleged *particularly for Asia Minor* that certain Diaspora Jews were influenced by the Sabazios cult, even to the extent of creating new religious groups, half-Judaism, half-paganism. A complete study is in preparation,[70] but the following may serve as an indication of the way connections between the two religions have been made.

The similarity of names and titles: compare *kurios Sabazios,* "Lord Sabazios," with κύριος σαββάτων, "Lord of the Sabbath," or κύριος σαβαώθ, "Lord of Hosts," in "Biblical Greek."

---

67 In arguments that often appear arrogant, it is sometimes held that the Jews under examination had allowed themselves to become "hellenized" or "paganized" *without realizing* what had been lost.

68 Keil, "Kulte Lydiens," 258f. lists ten sites, to which must now be added Sardis and Ayazviran, ef. P. Herrmann, *Ergebnisse einer Reise in Nordosttydien* (DenkschrWien 80, 1; Vienna, 1962), 50f., #45. On Lydia and Phrygia, F.R. Walton, "Sabazios," OCD²941.

69 Nilsson, *Geschichte,* 291; W.O.F. Oesterley, "The Cult of Sabazios, a Study in Religious Syncretism," in *The Labyrinth,* ed. S.H. Hooke, (London, 1935), 115f., hereafter "Cult of Sabazios."

70 Kraabel, *Judaism.*

There is literary evidence, in Latin and in Greek, to show that Sabazios was identified with the God of the Jews, at least in the minds of some gentiles. Valerius Maximus states that "the Jews" were expelled (?) from Rome in 139 B.C.E. because they had "attempted to infect Roman customs with the cult of Jupiter Sabazios."[71] Plutarch takes up the question "Who is the god of the Jews?" in *Quaest. Conv.* 4.6.1f. and makes some far-reaching combinations: the Jewish god is associated with wine (because of the cultic use of wine by Jews) and hence with Dionysos. The Jewish Sabbath is a holiday (because no one may work), a day for partying, orgiastic perhaps—Dionysos again, and perhaps Sabazios as well, due to the name "Sabbath" and an already established link between Sabazios and Dionysos. In one festival the Jews carry *thyrsoi* (palm branches? as in the Feast of Tabernacles). Their festival musicians are called "Levites," derived from "Lysios" or "Evios," both epithets of Dionysos. Behind this discussion of the *Sabbath* and of *Dionysons* there may well be the equation: Dionysos = Sabazios = the god of the Jews.[72]

The personal names Sabbatios, Sambathios and Sambathion are well attested for Jews in the ancient world, and also for some gentiles.[73]

Finally there are the curious Anatolian deities *Sabathikos* (in Lydia) and *Sabbatistes* or *Sambatistes* (in Cilicia).[74]

It is on the basis of evidence such as this that Cumont,[75] Oesterley,[76] Goodenough,[77] Widengren[78] and to a lesser extent Nilsson[79] write confidently of Jews in Asia Minor heavily influenced, even captivated, by this Anatolian deity. My own suspicion presently is that this reflects the ancient understanding of Diaspora Judaism on the part of some gentile observ-

---

71 Text with full discussion and bibliography in M. Stern, *Greek and Latin Authors on Jews and Judaism, I: From Herodotus to Plutarch.* (Jerusalem, 1974), #147, hereafter, *Authors.*

72 Stern, *Authors* #259. Plutarch also refers to Sabbath practices twice in *De Superstione,* 3 and 8 = Stern, *Authors,* ##255f.

73 V. Tcherikover, "The Sambathions," CPJ 3:43-87, hereafter "Sambathions."

74 Tcherikover, "Sambathions," 46f.; full discussion forthcoming in Kraabel, *Judaism.*

75 Frequently, e.g. "Sabazius," *DarSag, s.v.*; "Les mystères de Sabazius et le judaïsme," CRAI 1906, 63-79; "A propos de Sabazius et du judaïsme," MusB 14 (1910) 55-60; *Les religions orientales dans le paganisme romain,* 4th ed. (Paris, 1929) 60-62.

76 "Cult of Sabazios," Bickerman, "Altars," writes sarcastically of those who, "fascinated by Sabazios...outdo syncretism of the ancient mythologists" (148 note 32); Oesterley's essay is his prize example.

77 *Jewish Symbols* 1:22, 168; 2:49; 6:133.

78 "Die Sabaziosmysterien," in *Religionsgeschichte des Orients in der Zeit der Weltreligionen,* ed. B. Spuler (*Handbuch der Orientalistik* 1.8.2; Leiden, 1961), 62-64, hereafter, "Sabazios-mysterien."

79 *Geschichte,* 662-667.

ers—"historians of religion" perhaps, e.g. Plutarch—rather than what the Diaspora Jews themselves practiced and believed. In any case, the view of Cumont et al. pushed the evidence available to them far beyond what was justified.

To dismantle the older view will be a major undertaking in this paper I will only review the new evidence *for Sardis* (after a glance at Melito) in an effort to determine the possibility of interaction between Judaism and the Sabazios cult when they share a limited geographical context.

There is no indication in the writings of the late-second century bishop of Sardis, Melito, that the Jews there are syncretized or apostate to any degree. Since his sermon is an attack upon the Jews, we might expect him to mention such aberrations if they were obvious. In addition, he would be more concerned with Jewish festivals and holidays than were bishops in other parts of the world, since Melito was a Quartadeeiman, and the Jewish holydays—surely Passover but perhaps also the Sabbath—were of particular interest to him. Had there been "Sabbath/Sabazios" speculation among Sardis Jews, Melito would likely have noticed it.[80]

There is no evidence in the more than eighty Jewish inscriptions of any interest in Sabazios or knowledge of him. The name *Sabbatios* appears on a sherd from one of the shops just outside the synagogue to the south; another sherd from these shops mentions a *Iakob pr(esbyter)os*, "Jacob the elder," a distinctive name and title (Robert, *Nouvelles Inscriptions*, ##20, 22). Shops and men are Jewish, and Sabbatios' name is probably a reference to "Sabbath" rather than to Sabazios; to argue otherwise, in the face of the mass of Jewish evidence from just this area of Sardis, would be absurd.

The furnishings of the synagogue have been discussed in the previous section, but in regard to Sabazios two further points should be made. The first has to do with the Eagle Table, which in shape and positioning resembles nothing so much as an altar in a church. In discussions of Sabazios, the religious meals of the cult are mentioned frequently,[81] often with a reference to the Tomb of Vincentius in the catacombs of Praetextatus in Rome. Goodenough and others before him had drawn a connection between the "table of Sabazios" and Jewish cultic meals; yet while he knew of the Sardis table and in fact discussed it in various sections of the last volume of his *Jewish Symbols*—and though he knew well enough that Sardis was in an area where Saba-

---

80 Kraabel, "Melito the Bishop and the Synagogue at Sardis; Text and Context," in *Studies Presented to George M.A. Hanfmann*, ed. D.G. Mitten et al. (Cambridge 1971) 77-85; R.L. Wilken, "Melito, the Jewish Community at Sardis, and the Sacrific of Isaac," *Theological Studies 37* (1976) 53-69.

81 For example, Nilsson, *Geschichte*, 662; Widengren, "Sabaziousmysterien," 64; Goodenough, *Jewish Symbols* 2:48.

zios had long been popular—Goodenough never claimed (or even hinted) that the Eagle Table evidenced the influence of Sabazios. The reasons for this are clear enough; one glance at a plan of the excavated synagogue shows how inappropriately small the Eagle Table would be for such a use. The main hall of the synagogue would easily hold a thousand people, the table top measures 2.4m x 1.2m, i.e., it has about as much surface as one which might have been found in a middle-class dining room of the last century.[82]

The last piece of evidence from within the synagogue is one of the latest inscriptions to be set into the mosaic of the main hall: it was inserted precisely in the center of the floor, equidistant from the four corners of the room, surely a location of some significance. It commemorates one member of the community who is titled priest (*hiereus*) and *sophodidaskalos* ("wise teacher"? "teacher of wisdom"? rabbi?).[83] This revered person, still holding the title "priest" centuries after the destruction of the Jerusalem temple, was very likely the "rabbi" of this community in one of the last phases of its existence. Such a person in Sardis might be quite different from his contemporaries in the great rabbinic schools farther to the east, e.g., those completing the Babylonian Talmud at about the same time; nevertheless, his function is clear enough from his titles—he is a teacher and mediator of the Jewish tradition, surely an unlikely role if the Sardis Jews had been heavily influenced by paganism.

The new Sabazios evidence from Sardis comes from two inscriptions, one discovered in the first season of excavation, 1958, the other in one of the last, 1974. The first is an altar-dedication by a priest of (Zeus) Savazios (sic) from the second century B.C.E. For our purposes it is important chiefly as positive evidence of the presence of this cult in Sardis contemporary with the Jewish community there known from Josephus.[84]

The other text is much later and much more unusual. According to Robert, it is a copy from the mid-second century C.E. of a cultic regulation of the fourth century B.C.E. Its purpose is not to honor Sabazios or order his cult; it is a command to the religious functionaries of "Zeus" (here the Persian Ahura Mazda), forbidding them to participate in the mysteries of Sabazios, of Agdistis or of Ma.[85]

---

82 Using the standards of *modern* church and synagogue architecture (assuming benches or pews), a room the size of the Sardis main hall would provide space for just under 1000 persons. On the table, Goodenough, *Jewish Symbols,* 12:195f.

83 BASOR 187 (1967) 29 and fig. 48.

84 This inscription was published by S.E. Johnson, "A Sabazios Inscription from Sardis," In *Religions in Antiquity: Essays in Memory of Erwin Ramsdell Goodenough*, ed. J. Neusner (Supplements to Numen 14; Leiden, 1968), 542-550.

85 "Une nouvelle inscription grecque de Sardes: Règlement de l'autorité perse relatif à un culte de Zeus," CRAI 1975, 306-330, hereafter, "Réglemént."

Robert has fully discussed the importance of the text for the religious history of Sardis; his account should be consulted by all who are interested in that subject. For our present purposes, the information it presents is as follows: the second century C.E., a time of increasing interest in matters religious throughout the Roman Empire, was for at least one cult at Sardis not a period of syncretism of "religious creativity" but of conservatism, reinforcing the piety of the past. (A parallel example, also from the second century, is the Sardis column capital published by Hanfmann and Balmuth; it recreates the image of a goddess, the essential features of which are from the seventh century B.C.E. The same deity is represented on coins of Sardis and other Lydian cities from the time of Hadrian on.)[86] Since the text simply repeats a much older regulation, it is likely that this kind of exclusiveness for this cult is nothing new; it is the continuation of a religious attitude half a millennium old!

Surely not all pagan cults in Sardis were this strict; as Robert remarks, it is something unusual for paganism, and much more characteristic of Judaism or Christianity.[87] If it says that the cult of Sabazios invites "syncretism," then it has apparently had that quality for a very long time at Sardis, and some pagan religious officials are aware of it and wish to resist it; their rites would be dishonored if the participants had had anything to do with the mysteries of Sabazios. The Jewish evidence from Sardis suggests that the rules governing the members of the synagogue community were at least this strict![88]

Conclusions

The above is no more than a preliminary sketch of the problem suggested in the title,and of the evidence which bears upon it. A full study would require the construction of a complete chronology of the Sardis Jews and of the relevant archaeological evidence; the examples presented here are discrete and isolated instead.

The Judaism of Sardis is of course more cohesive then its "paganism," and thus easier to discuss; we have said nothing of possible influences of Sardis Judaism on Sardis *gentile* piety, and yet—given the number and strength of the Jews that cannot be excluded.

Given the provisional nature of this essay, firm conclusions would be premature, but the evidence presented here does suggest the following for consideration:

---

86 G.M.A. Hanfmann and M. Balmuth. "The Image of an Anatolian Goddess at Sardis," in *In Memoriam Helmut Theodor Bossert*, ed. U.B. Alkim (JKF 2:Istanbul, 1965) 262-269.

87 Robert, "Règlement," 326.

88 There are also great differences between the liturgical practices and community organization of Anatolian Jews and those known to characterize the Sabazios cult; a full treatment will appear in my *Judaism*.

The old hypotheses as to the nature of Judaism in Asia Minor should be scrapped; in the past they were all too often examples of *ad ignolum per ignolius*. They should now be replaced with new reconstructions based on the abundant new evidence.

Further, while Robert may be correct to remark on how hellenique the Sardis Jews are,[89] Nilsson goes too far in emphasizing the *Vermischung* of Jewish and pagan piety in this area.[90] At Sardis at least, proximity appears to have produced clarity, and the enjoyment of a gentile culture did not automatically produce capitulation to "paganism;" the Jews are strong and self-confident, they have a firm grasp on their Judaism and they express it in their building, their inscriptions and even in their iconography. And that may have happened *because* there were so many pagans so very close nearby.

Ancient religions may coalesce in art and literature, but that is a very different thing from what might happen between self-conscious and specific religious communities. Perhaps we have taken ancient gentile statements about Judaism and its relation to paganism too much at face value, relying too quickly on the garbled descriptions of a Plutarch or the crabbed iconography of an anonymous maker of magical amulets.[91]

With these new discoveries and new hypotheses, there is surely a great deal to be done, for those of us who follow in the footsteps of Marcel Simon. May he enjoy yet many more years to assist and guide us in these labors![92]

---

89 Nouvelles Inscriptions, 57.

90 *Geschichte*, 667.

91 On amulets as evidence of the interaction of Judaism and paganism (and Christianity), see M. Simon, *Verus Israel*, 2nd ed. (Paris, 1964), 394-431; and Goodenough, *Jewish Symbols*, vol. 13, index.

92 The most recent interpretation of several of the matters discussed here is after all that of Marcel Simon himself, in a substantial article which came to my attention only after the present essay was completed: "Jupiter-Yahvé; sur un essai de théologie pagano-juive", Numen 23 (1976) 40-66, see especially 52-56 on Sabazios.

Social Systems of Six Diaspora Synagogues[1]

A.T. Kraabel

I

In a recent survey-article[2] I reviewed the evidence from six Diaspora synagogues, each of them discovered during a larger project to excavate an entire city or town of the Roman Empire. Each is available *with its context*: the Jews and their buildings, but also the larger gentile society within which they were located. These archaeological and epigraphic case-studies (the details of which are not repeated here) now contribute to a definition of what constituted Diaspora Judaism in the larger sense, something for which there is otherwise very little evidence.

The term "social systems" is not used in the sense of modern high-technology social science, but in a more limited fashion; this essay is about the life of each synagogue community and its place in the social system of a gentile town or city.[3]

After a table of dates (II) and a brief sketch of each site (III), the article which follows summarizes what might be gathered from the building plans[4] and the other archaeological data about the origin and functions of the six buildings (IV), the ideology or theology of each community (V) its organization (VI) and its relation with the gentile world (VII). In the concluding section (VIII) the hypothesis is advanced that just as the form of each building is due to local influence chiefly, so the kind of Judaism represented at each site also is heavily influenced by the local situation; such an hypothesis may

---

1 Editor's note: This article first appeared in Joseph Gutmann editor, *Ancient Synagogues: The State of Research* (Chico, CA: Scholars Press, 1981) 79-91. Refer to Gutmann's book for further references and illustrations of ancient synagogues, 103-121.

2 A.T. Kraabel, "The Diaspora Synagogue: Archaeological and Epigraphic Evidence since Sukenik," in *Aufstieg und Niedergang der römischen Welt*, II.19, eds. H. Temporini and W. Haase (Berlin, 1979), 477-510. These are the basic sites, and the best known; in the present article there is no intent to be exhaustive, nor to give a complete secondary bibliography. The next major step in the analysis of the Diaspora Synagogue involves moving beyond the simple description of the archaeological evidence to the understanding of the place of the building and its community within the history of Judaism and—even more—the history of religion in late antiquity. In this regard Dura is the place to begin; here I have found the work of Jacob Neusner particularly stimulating, see especially the articles collected in Part Three (titled "Art: Glosses on Goodenough's *Jewish Symbols*") of his *Early Rabbinic Judaism* (Studies in Judaism in Late Antiquity 13: Leiden, 1975). See also "the Symbolism of Ancient Judaism: The Evidence of the Synagogues," in J. Gutmann, Ancient Synagogues: The State of Research, (Chico, CA: Scholars Press, 1981), 7-17.

3 This article is the better for suggestions by Prof. Arthur L. Johnson, Department of Sociology, University of Minnesota.

4 The synoptic plan was prepared by Sylvia Ruud (Ancient Studies, University of Minnesota) with funds provided by the College of Liberal Arts and the Department of Classics of the University of Minnesota.

be overturned, of course, only by another which better accounts for these new data.

The references cited in the footnotes are items actually used in this essay; a full bibliography is available in my "Diaspora Synagogue."

II

Here are probable dates for the buildings, numbered as on the plan (fig. 19):
1. Sardis (Asia Minor) Second or Third Century C.E. to 616
2. Priene (Asia Minor) Third or Fourth Century? C.E.
3. Dura (Syria) Second Century C.E. to 256
4. Delos (Aegean island) First Century B.C.E. to Second Century C.E.
5. Ostia (Italy) Earlier Synagogue: First century C.E.? Later Synagogue (shown on plan): Fourth Century C.E.
6. Stobi (Macedonia) Polycharmos-synagogue: Third Century C.E. Later Synagogue (shown on plan): Fourth Century C.E.

III

The buildings differ greatly, their locations do as well; here is a summary description of the six sites:
1. *Sardis* was a metropolis before the Trojan War, an economic power and a political and cultural center. It was ruled by Croesus in the mid-sixth century, then captured by Cyrus of Persia; it surrendered to Alexander the Great in 334 and was controlled by his successors. It came under Roman control in 133 B.C.E. Sardis is a powerful representative of the Lydian, of the Eastern Greek, and later of the Roman world, and open to the rest of Anatolia and the east.[5]
2. *Priene* was always relatively small, a Hellenistic "planned city" laid out on a regular grid-pattern; its economic growth was hampered by the existence of powerful Miletus just to the south, and by the gradual silting-up of its own harbor. Its major deities are Hellenism's most familiar: Zeus, Athena, Demeter, Isis and the anatolian Cybele; its culture too was strongly Ionian and Greek.[6]
3. *Dora* was a small caravan- and garrison-city, walled and fortified, on the remote eastern rim of the Empire. Its society was a racial and religious

---

5 On Sardis: Kraabel, "Diaspora Synagogue" (note 1 *supra*) 483–488; A.R. Seager, *et. al.*, *The Sardis Synagogue and its Setting* (Archaeological Exploration of Sardis, Report 5; Cambridge, forthcoming); one-volume Synthesis of Sardis discoveries, ed. G.M.A. Hanfmann, *Sardis from Prehistoric to Roman Times: Results of the Archaeological Exploration of Sardis 1958-1975*, (Cambridge, MA: Harvard, 1983). See "The Building" by A.R. Seager, 168-178; "The Impact of the Discovery of the Sardis Synagogue" by A.T. Kraabel, 178-190 in Hanfmann, 1983.

6 On Priene: Kraabel, "Diaspora Synagogue" (note 1 *supra*), 489-491.

mixture so complex that no one tradition may be said to dominate. Its existence was often precarious; it was only intermittently under Roman authority, and then as a non-Roman community under the control of the Roman army. It was open to non-Roman influence from all directions.[7]

4. *Delos,* the birthplace of Apollo, was a crossroads in the Aegean from prehistoric times. Well known in the literature of classical antiquity, it also attracted merchants, travelers and immigrants from all around the eastern Mediterranean, particularly after it became a free port in the second century B.C.E. In addition to the synagogue, several important sanctuaries of a non-Greek type were established for foreign deities in the Hellenistic period.[8]

5. *Ostia* came to life as the port of Rome during the great expansion of trade in the early Empire; in the first half of the second century its population more than doubled. Excavations reveal a well-planned city, with harbors, large warehouses, traders' offices, guild halls and blocks of private apartments. The people of Ostia include old families of Roman stock and others from elsewhere in Italy, along with traders, slaves and exslaves from all over the Mediterranean. Non-Roman religions are well attested: Cybele, Bellona, Isis and especially Mithras, along with Judaism and Christianity.[9]

6. *Stobi* was a Roman administrative center, a municipium from the first century C.E. on; it grew and prospered in the second and third century but even more in the fourth and fifth, when three Christian basilicas were built within the city and at least two more just outside. The city's most famous resident, Joannes Stobaeus, John of Stobi, had his home and library here in the fifth century.[10]

IV

The main Jewish evidence at each location is the excavated building. Sardis is by far the largest of the six in the plan, but that is in part because there all the community's activities took place apparently in the synagogue itself; Dura, Priene, Ostia and probably Delos had several common rooms in addi-

---

7 On Dura: Kraabel, "Diaspora Synagogue" (note 1 *supra*) 481-483; C. Hopkins, *The Discovery of Dura-Europos,* ed. by B. Goldman (New Haven, 1979). Dura was pulled as strongly to the east by Babylonia as it was to the west by Rome. Neusner's work (cf. note 1 *supra*) has convinced me that my "Diaspora Synagogue" under-emphasizes the importance of Babylonian Judaism for the synagogue community of Dura.

8 On Delos: Kraabel, "Diaspora Synagogue" (note 1 *supra*), 491-494.

9 On Ostia: Kraabel, "Diaspora Synagogue" (note 1 *supra*) 497-500.

10 On Stobi: Dean Moe, "The Cross and the Menorah," *Archaeology,* 30 (1977) 148-157; Kraabel, "Diaspora Synagogue" (note 1 *supra*), 494-497.

tion. The earlier synagogue at Stobi has a *tetrastoon and a triklinion* and also "upper rooms" where the donor Polycharmos and his family lived; the later building too (shown on the plan) may well have been the center of a complex of common rooms.[11]

While the Ostia and Sardis buildings were constructed for public use, the other four are converted residences. (This is not proved for Stobi, but probable.) In all likelihood the faithful first met in homes, then raised the funds to convert one home to community use; such a process is known for other eastern religions in the Roman Empire, and is the rule for early Christianity. It does not follow necessarily then that these "house-Synagogues" were located thus in order to conceal them from persecuting gentiles. The evidence from Dura and Priene is particularly complete at this point: the synagogues there are positioned about as several other religious buildings are in the town, no more or less hidden than were various gentile cults. The handsome Ostia synagogue is built in the local style, with a fine four-columned inter gateway; located just off a busy street, it is private, but not obviously "hidden." And the Sardis building takes advantage of its prime location to put Judaism here "on display"; this is the most probable explanation for its colorfully decorated forecourt, complete with fountain and open to the main street of the city. Here the Jews control a building which looms over the primary east-west thoroughfare, at a main intersection in the city; they take advantage of the location for maximum impact.

Four of the six buildings have permanent Torah shrines. As the plan indicates, Dura has a niche in its west wall, Priene has one in the east wall. At Sardis scriptures were kept in one, perhaps both, of the shrines flanking the central entrance at the east end of the main hall. The Ostia shrine is C-shaped in plan, attached to the south wall just west of the side door. The Stobi excavations nay well produce something similar; they are not complete. Only Delos, the only one of the six from the Second Temple period, clearly lacked this feature.

Some of the functions of the Diaspora synagogues are also evident from the plan. They are community centers of course; they were perhaps the only location where the Jews in each city might assemble "in accordance with their ancestral laws and . . . decide their own business and resolve their differences," in the words of a Roman decree about the Sardis Jews, *apud* Josephus, *Ant.* 14:235. Each is the major Jewish building in a gentile town; it is thus more

11 J.B. Frey, *Corpus Inscriptionum Iudaicarum* (Sussidi allo Studio delle Antichita Cristiane I; Rome, 1936), no. 694 = B. Lifshitz, *Donateurs et fondateure dane les synagogues juives (Cahiers de la revue biblique* 7; Paris, 1967), no. 10, Volume 1 of the *Frey Corpus* was reissued in 1975 by Ktav; Lifshitz supplied a long Prolegomenon to bring the information on the inscriptions up to date.

central to Jewish life than were the synagogues of ancient Palestine, located where Jews comprised a much higher percentage of the population, where indeed the town itself might be largely Jewish.

V

The earliest of the six buildings, at Delos, was not much more than an assembly hall or prayer hall; there is no evidence of architectural embellishment or of a formal liturgy. The evidence from Stobi is not yet complete, but at the remaining four sites one might assume that scriptures dominate the religious life of the community; at least, some provision for the physical objects, the scrolls, is architecturally very important. At Priene the niche is the main feature in an otherwise plain room. At Ostia the visitor is bracketed between the *bema* on the west wall and the monumental Torah shrine on the east. At Sardis the focus of worship was a massive lectern, shown in the plan between the first pair of piers just east of the apse. But the scrolls were kept in the *aediculae* flanking the central door at the east end of the hall; thus it is likely that processions moved back and forth between shrines and lectern during the service. The spectacular Torah shrine and the paintings at Dura also underline the importance of the scripture there.

Along with the scriptures went teaching; that is likely at the other sites and certain for two, Dura and Sardis. The study of the Dura paintings has revealed the complexity of the traditions behind them. At Sardis an inscription commemorating Samoe, a local "priest and teacher of wisdom" was placed precisely in the center of the main hall; its location indicates his importance to the community.

The details of this teaching in each case are less clear, but some contours are visible. Sardis and Dura are particularly well attested; here the Jews boldly took over some of the ideological vocabulary of the local society and turned it to their own purposes. At sardis the most striking examples are iconographic: the appropriation of Lydian lions and Roman eagles. These "pagan" images have such a preeminent location in the west end of the building that one must suppose that they also had a place in the religious thought and popular piety of those who used the building. The idea of "divine Providence" or *pronoio*, unattested in Jewish inscriptions elsewhere in the Diaspora, is so common in the Sardis inscriptions that it must have had a local, thus gentile source, probably in the philosophical language of Sardis' well known schools.[12] This sug-

---

12 The emphasis in the Dura paintings is on the great events in the life of the nation, the "Chosen People." If the Sardis Jews favor such an idea as *pronoia* in their inscriptions, it perhaps indicates a swing to a more individualistic, less corporate understanding of Jewish identity, a wholly predictable development when viewed against the background of the gentile piety of this period.

gests that Samoe was something like a latter-day Philo, and would have been more at home in Alexandria or Rome than in the rabbinic communities farther east.

The Dura paintings are strange to those who know only synagogues; they are spectacular but somehow appropriate when seen against the rest of the Dura evidence. And their message is *Jewish*; they are not merely decorative, nor are they crypto-pagan. The representation of the Ark and the Temple of Dagon is the clearest example: in this "biblical" scene the gods of *third century Dura* are included, tumbled before the Ark of the Covenant.

Four distinct religious traditions competed in Dura: Greco-semitic, Jewish, Mithraic and Christian; none dominated. Their religious buildings are nearly side-by-side in the small city. Jews here were well aware of the competition; proximity did not breed "syncretism" but rather a clear understanding of where they stood, of the distance between the true religion and the gentile cults. Dura Jews decided to tell the biblical stories with the visual vocabulary of their city and their time; the alternative was to risk becoming incomprehensible, misunderstood by the new generations of Jews whose only world was pluralistic Dura.[13] The Sardis evidence points in the same direction.

VI

Such buildings as these require a staff, and the community itself must be organized to maintain them and to maintain itself. They stood at a time when the self-contained religious organization was an important and familiar element in Greco-Roman society; it was not only the Jews of the Diaspora who formed themselves into well-articulated groups, witness the score of different offices and the hundreds of members in the Bacchic community of Tusculum, just south of Rome in the second century C.E.[14] Elders and *archisynagogoi*, archons and scribes are well attested to in the Jewish inscriptions of the Diaspora generally, and may be assumed for these sites; the evidence from Dura and Sardis is ample, less so from Stobi and Ostia. Delos and Priene have produced no epigraphic evidence, but the famous throne on the west wall of the Delos building proves some kind of organization there; this is the earliest of the six buildings, but these offices are attested elsewhere in this period and it seems reasonable to assume something similar for Delos.

---

13 Hopkins (note 6 *supra*), 254f., 260 points to the pressure in this direction elsewhere in Dura caused by intermarriage; could that have happened in the synagogue community as well?

14 M.P. Nilsson, *Geschichte der griechischen Religion* (Handbuch der Altertumswissenschaft V.2.2, Munich, 1961.2), 359f., cf. his *The Dionysian Mysteries of the Hellenistic and Roman Age* (Acta Inst. Atheniensis Sueciae, 8o, Lund, 1957) 46f. 5lf.

Three other points should be noted in this regard. First, there are "priests" at Sardis and Dura,[15] this is a status worth possessing even long after the destruction of the Jerusalem Temple. Second, the Stobi community is dominated to some degree by one person, "the father of the synagogue at Stobi," Klaudios Tiberios Polycharmos, who donated the space for the earlier synagogue and lived with his family in its upper rooms; his heirs may well have had a similar status and stature in the later building. Third, at Sardis there are several synagogue offices mentioned, but the important titles were those which derived from local or provincial government: city counselor, procurator, count. In the synagogue inscriptions, read chiefly by fellow Jews, it is one's sociopolitical status in the city which is stressed.

VII

"Relations with gentiles (or: with Christians)" in the Greco-Roman world was a topic of somewhat less importance to Jews in the Diaspora than it has been to many who have studied them since.Among these six sites there is considerable variation in what the data say. At Ostia a Greek donor inscription for the Torah shrine begins with the Latin religious-political formula *pro salute Aug(usti)*, a surprising phrase best known in the context of ruler-cult; somewhat similar good wishes for the ruler's well-being are known from earlier synagogues in Egypt.[16] For Delos and Priene there are no data. At Dura cultural and religious pluralism was so marked that no one tradition seems to have dominated; in such a situation relations may have been difficult generally, or tolerance may have been the rule.[17] In any case there is no indication that Jews were singled out for opposition; and the gutting of the synagogue (which put an end to its life but preserved it in part at the same time) was a military necessity not an anti-Jewish act—buildings of other religions suffered the same fate.

Stobi and Sardis appear to be at opposite poles, thus they call into question any sweeping statement about "the situation of the Jews under Rome" or about "the gentile (or Christian) view of Diaspora Judaism." The later Stobi synagogue was deliberately supplanted in the fifth century by a Christian basilica built immediately on top of it. The power of the Christians in this city

---

15 At Sardis, Samoe the Priest; at Dura, Samuel the Priest, cf. C.H. Kraeling *The Synagogue* (The Excavations at Dura-Europos, Final Report VIII.l; New Haven, 1956), 263, Aramaic inscription la.

16 Ostia: Kraabel, "Diaspora Synagogue" (note 1 *supra*), 499 note 76. For Egypt, the inscriptions are as follows (the first number is that of Frey, the second that of Lifshitz, see note 10 *supra*): 1432 = 86, 1440-1444 = 92-96.

17 Hopkins (note 7 *supra*), 95f., favors tolerance for at least part of this period, the result of the influence of the Emperor Alexander Severus.

increased steadily; apparently traditional paganism was not strong enough to withstand them, nor was the Jewish community substantial and stable enough to resist. This need not mean that the Jews of Stobi were always under pressure from gentiles; they had built two synagogues, after all, one in the third century and another in the fourth, and their patron Polycharmos, "the father of the synagogue in Stobi," must have been a person of some substance in the city.

The most powerful community known from the Diaspora Judaism under Rome was located at Sardis. In the second century it infuriated the local bishop, Melito; the hostility was that of the leader of a small Christian group, all but impotent over against the synagogue. There is no evidence that the Sardis Jews knew of Melito's wrath; indeed later evidence indicates that Jews and gentiles here were generally on better terms than Christian leaders like Melito might wish. They lived and worked side-by-side; Sardis lacks a "Jewish quarter" or ghetto. The synagogue was a "display piece"; gentiles could not miss it, looming over a main road intersection. They could see into it; the colorful forecourt was right in front of anyone following the colonnade toward the main entrance of the magnificent city gymnasium-baths, and if the synagogue's main doors were open, passers-by would be able to see through the main hall to the apse 90 meters away. It seems likely that the entire building was open to gentiles on occasion:[18] the apparent harmony between Sardis Jews and gentiles, and the prominence of the building suggests it. This might be the reason that *public* offices (rather than synagogue offices) are so frequently mentioned in the synagogue inscriptions; they may have been intended to underscore to gentile visitors the place of Sardis Jews in the public life of gentile city and province.

The Sardis situation may be an anomaly in late antiquity, the result of a coalition of unusually powerful Jews and pagans against a divided Christianity. But the Jewish community here was a very old one. Generations of Sardis Jews were native Anatolians, not refugees, immigrants or slaves from the troubled lands farther east; by the time synagogue and city were sacked by the Persians in the seventh century the Jews had lived there for nearly a millennium, perhaps more, and from the beginning they had enjoyed a standing with various governing authorities. As many inscriptions emphasize, they are *Sardianoi*; they belong there, and apparently they were treated as such.

This was all but unknown before 1962 when the Sardis synagogue was discovered. Evidence for previously unknown or all-but-unknown Diaspora Jewish communities still appears, e.g. in 1976 at Aphrodisias and in 1977 in

---

18 This may have been the case at Dura, if (as Geiger believed) the visitors, who at one point inspected the synagogue paintings, were not Jews, see Kraeling (note 14 *supra*) 296-300, and Hopkins (note 7 *supra*) 142, 166.

Athens;[19] still more may be expected, and Sardis may turn out to be less the exception than it once appeared to be.

The Dura synagogue at one point at least welcomed distinguished Iranian visitors from across the Euphrates.[20] The Sardis Jews may have welcomed gentiles from the city (and beyond?) into their building. Such openness may have been assumed by many of the people in these two locations and at least two others, Delos and Ostia, since all four are relatively open communities, accustomed to new faces—traders, travellers, soldiers, government officials— and to changes within their population. If this is the case also for local Jews —as seems possible—it would be another, major example of the influence of gentile society upon Diaspora synagogue life.

Despite the power and importance of Jerusalem and the Temple in biblical and post-biblical theology, the Jews of the Diaspora did not come to the aid of Jerusalem and the Temple when they were in grave danger in the first century, during the first revolt.[21] The outcome of the second revolt appears to have convinced most Jews that the Temple would not soon—if ever—be rebuilt. Yet the symbolic power of the Temple did not die out in the Diaspora, witness its prominent place in the Dura paintings and the priests attested to there and at Sardis, and elsewhere in the inscriptions. These facts suggest that by the first century Diaspora Jews under Rome had learned to separate the symbols of Temple and Jerusalem from the physical building and the geographical location—thus they do not aid in the revolts—and that this spiritualization is a concomitant of their sense of being at home in the Diaspora.[22]

VIII

Thanks to the fourth-century Christian historian Eusebius, later ages have had an image of ancient Christianity which is overly monolithic and a view of post-biblical Judaism which is overly lachrymose;[23] perhaps we should have

---

19 Aphrodisias: M. Mellink, "Archaeology in Asia Minor," *American Journal of Archaeology*, 81 (1977) 306; the epigraphic evidence is to be published by J.Reynolds and O.Masson. Athens: Kraabel, "Diaspora Synagogue" (note 1 *supra*), 505-507.

20 See note 17 *supra*. Whether or not they were Jews is still disputed.

21 E.M. Smallwood, *The Jews under Roman Rule* (Studies on Judaism in Late Antiquity, 20; Leiden, 1975) 356f. Similarly, Babylonian Jews did little or nothing to support the First and Second Revolts, see J. Neusner, *A History of the Jews in Babylonia*, I (Studia Post-Biblica 9.1: Leiden, 1969.2) 67-70, 79.

22 Christians on occasion were able to do something similar, witness the Montanist conviction in the second century that the "New Jerusalem" would be established in Phrygia (Epiphanius, *Haer*. 48.1), a great deal closer to Sardis or Priene than to ancient Palestine.

23 B. Bachrach, *Early Medieval Jewish Policy in Western Europe* (Minneapolis, 1977), 144; the adjective and the idea go back to Salo Baron. On the "historicizing" of theology by such histo-
(continued...)

known better, since he sets out his concerns and his biases on the very first page of the *Ecclesiastical History*. The picture of Diaspora Judaism under Rome is further complicated by the fact that for more than a thousand years the overwhelming bulk of the written evidence, the rabbinic texts, led to the impression that the rabbis *were* Judaism after the destruction of the second temple; the rabbis' disinterest in the Diaspora Judaism west of them allowed the distortions of Eusebius and other Christian writers to be accepted as fact, as all of the facts. Written texts and puzzling scraps of epigraphic evidence appeared to give all of the story.

The archaeological evidence which has become available in the last half-century provides a counter-balance. For the Diaspora, at least, it argues for diversity, symbolized in the various shapes and sizes of buildings on the plans. (A similar diversity has become evident in the Christianity of the same period, though here the new conclusions are the result chiefly of new literary evidence and the reexamination of well-known texts; the recent advances in the under-standing of ancient Judaism on the basis of the non-literary data argue that more attention be paid to the archaeological evidence for various Christian communities as well, in their ancient context.) Unlike Christianity, the Judaism of late antiquity lacked the control of a regional hierarchy; to judge only from these buildings, the closest thing to a central authority was the scripture itself. The Diaspora Jewish communities were more remote from each other in space and time; there were fewer of them, and as much as half a millennium separates the first Jewish settlers at Sardis from the first generation at Priene. The many more Diaspora Christian communities which existed at the time of Constantine's conversion had all been founded in a period half that long.

The archaeological data reviewed here suggest that *the most important factors* shaping a Diaspora synagogue *building* are *local*; location, size, deco-ration, architectural features and even symbolism depend in large part on the forces at work and the patterns available in a particular gentile city or town. I suspect that the Diaspora synagogue *communities* were subject to similar formative influences. The date the first Jews arrived, their status at that time (traders? merchants? slaves? prisoners-of-war? refugees?), their economic level, their relationship, positive or negative, to the authorities—and in the later period, the strength or weakness of traditional paganism,[24] the solidarity

---

23(...continued)
rians as Eusebius, see R.M. Grant, "Eusebius, Josephus and the Fate of the Jews," paper pre-sented at the annual meeting of the Society of Biblical Literature, Nov. 16, 1979, especially p. 79; see also his *Eusebius as Church Historian* (Oxford: Clarendon Press, 1980).

24 On Sardis in this regard, see my "Paganism and Judaism: The Sardis Evidence," in *Pa-ganisme, Judaïsme, Christianisme ... Mélanges offerts à Marcel Simon*, eds. A. Benoit, M. Philo-nenko and C. Vogel (Paris, 1979) 13-33.

of disunity of Christianity *in this particular location*: such things as these go a long way towards explaining the differences among these six buildings, and among their owners.

At the same time, this diversity does not mean they were Jews any less. They acted as though their form of Judaism was authentic; the burden of proof is now on those who would argue that it was otherwise.

A comprehensive picture of Judaism under Rome will take another generation, and will require a mastery of many methods and all the evidence, hitherto housed comfortably in several faculties of the academy: classics, archaeology, ancient history, art history, religious studies and Jewish studies. One sure result of the discoveries at these six sites and others like them is that "Diaspora Judaism" (as we thought we understood it) will never be the same again.

Impact of the Discovery of the Sardis Synagogue[1]

A.T. Kraabel

The Old Consensus and the Sardian Evidence

The importance of the discovery of the Sardis synagogue is simply that it reveals a Jewish community of far greater wealth, power, and self-confidence than the usual views of ancient Judaism would give us any right to expect. The older consensus is found in academic and (even more) in popular publications, by scholars, gentile or Jewish; if it is correct, then Sardis is a glaring exception—but we suspect that the consensus itself will soon undergo revision, with Sardis as catalyst.

This consensus, the usual view of the Jews under Rome, (1) tends to concentrate on ancient Palestine, (2) bases itself on the abundant literary evidence, and (3) often assumes that after Jesus, Judaism is compromised and drops into the background, unimportant, impotent—an ancient Christian bias still marvelously alive today.

If one assumes the first point of the consensus, then Jews outside ancient Palestine, that is, in the "Diaspora," are a ghetto people, without power, never "at home," outnumbered 10 or 20 to 1 by gentiles hostile to them. In this view, the only Jew at home in the Diaspora is the one who has compromised himself and assimilated to gentile society. But Jews were at home in Sardis; their ancestors had lived in the city for centuries *before* this synagogue was built. The first Jews to settle in the Sardis area probably did not come from Israel or Judah at all, but from exile communities in Mesopotamia and Babylonia; that is, they moved from one part of the Diaspora to another. The Sardis synagogue shows unmistakably that these Jews did not abandon their ancestral heritage, but affirmed it and gloried in it; at the same time they flourished among gentile neighbors who greatly outnumbered them.

The foundation of the old (consensus) view is the abundant literary evidence for the Jews of the Roman Empire, from the rabbinic literature to the writings of early Christianity to the brief and scattered references by pagan authors. This evidence is not so much incorrect as it is biased and incomplete —as might be expected in antiquity or in our own day when members of one racial or religious group write about another. And in the case of the rabbis, the evidence is for communities geographically distant and socially dissimilar, with few parallels to Sardis; yet most characterizations of the Jews who are contemporary with Roman Sardis turn out to be based on these nearly irrelevant data.

---

1 Editor's note: This article first appeared in *Sardis from Prehistoric to Roman Times: Results of the Archaeological Exploration of Sardis 1958-1975,* edited by G.M.A. Hanfmann (Cambridge MA: Harvard University Press, 1983) 178-190, 284-285. We have left the references to the figures (=figs.) in this essay and encourage the reader to refer to those figures in Hanfmann's *Sardis,* "Illustrations," 292-456.

The third element of the consensus might be called a "Christian" bias, though for most students of this period it is a "given," an academic presupposition rather than a sectarian view. It occurs in the unexamined assumption that Judaism all but passed from the scene as Christianity moved out into the Roman Empire; or, alternatively, that the Jews of the late Roman Empire are not that much different from those in the New Testament, or even the Old Testament, so that what was true for an earlier era is valid too for this later one. A related assumption is that Jews from this period were preoccupied with their relation to non-Jews, to gentiles, and especially to Christians: trying to make converts, fearful of being converted themselves, cravenly adopting gentile practice and belief to a degree which amounts almost to apostasy.

The abundant Sardis evidence challenges this consensus at nearly every point, as will be made clear in the chapter which follows. Sardis may be only an exception to the norm; we predict, though, that it is more than that, and that this site will make a major contribution to establishing a new "norm," or rather, a new group of norms, a display of perhaps a dozen major forms which Judaism assumed under Roman rule in the first centuries of the common era. The result will be a more broadly documented, better understood image of Roman Judaism than students of the ancient world have ever seen before.[2]

History of the Jewish Community at Sardis

The first Jews known to have visited Sardis were refugees from the Babylonian destruction of Jerusalem in 587 B.C.E.; they are mentioned in passing in Obadiah 20, where Sardis is called by its Semitic name, Sepharad. It is possible, then, that the Sardis Jewish community began as early as the sixth century B.C.E.

A large group of Jews settled in the area in the late third century B.C.E. In an effort to pacify Lydia and Phrygia to the east, the Seleucid king Antiochus III brought in 2,000 loyal Jewish families from his holdings in Babylonia and Mesopotamia, provided them with houses, and gave them a decade's relief from taxation.[3] Since Sardis was the headquarters of the

---

2 Other parts of the old consensus are being dismantled from the side of Jewish studies, chiefly by Jacob Neusner of South Florida University and his students. Neusner's work begins with the history of the large Jewish community in Babylonia, beyond Roman control; see his *History*. Increasingly and inevitably, however, it has a direct impact on our understanding the Judaism of the Roman Diaspora; see for example the articles on Jewish symbolism and the Dura synagogue collected in Part 3 of his *Early Rabbinic Judaism*. In what follows, general statements are not usually footnoted; rather reference is made here to the following studies: Avi-Yonah, *Jews*; P.R.L. Brown, *World; Compendia*; Leon; Smallwood, *Jews*.

3 Josephus, *AJ* 12.147-153.

Seleucid governor responsible for the immigrants, it is likely that some of them came to settle in the city.[4]

By the first century B.C.E. Jews were well established in Sardis; the information provided by the Jewish historian Josephus makes the community come alive before our eyes. These Jews are an influential group: some of their rights are confirmed by an official of Rome itself, others by the city council of Sardis.[5] They also control their own meeting place, provided by the city; here religious ceremonies are carried out, and decisions are made on communiry matters, religious and nonreligious.[6] This meeting place could have been an entire building, an assembly hall, the forerunner of the mammoth synagogue described above;[7] or it may have been nothing more than a designated space in some public building. In any case, these Jews enjoyed a considerable autonomy in the gentile city.

Finally, these Jews, so far from ancient Palestine in time as well as space, manifested some remarkably traditional religious practices; they faithfully transmitted the annual half-shekel tax for the support of the Temple in Jerusalem, a privilege guaranteed them by the Roman government.[8] They insisted on a supply of proper food for themselves; in all probability the food supply concerned them because they were observing the laws of *Kashrut*—the food was to be kosher.[9]

For the next century there is no direct information about the Sardis Jews; it may be assumed, however, that they lost their meeting place when the city "collapsed" (Tacitus) in the terrible earthquake of 17 C.E.[10] It is equally likely that some other place was assigned to them soon after for the same religious and communal purposes. Thus the present synagogue must have had at least two predecessors, one before the earthquake and one sometime thereafter.

In the late first century and into the second,the life of Sardis Jews appears to have continued as before; at least their status in the city remains undiminished. If Rabinowitz correctly interprets one of the few Hebrew inscriptions, they formally honored the emperor Lucius Verus during his visit to the city in about 166 C.E.; the city as a whole erected a statue of the young Verus in the gymnasium, and (Rabinowitz suggests) the Jews set up a commemorative

---

4 L. Robert, *Nouvelles inscriptions de Sardes*, Fascicule 1 (Paris 1964) 9-21.

5 Kraabel, "Paganism," 14-18.

6 Josephus, *AJ* 16.235 = J.G. Pedley *Ancient Literary Sources on Sardis* (Cambridge, MA 1972) no. 275; *AJ* 14.259-261.

7 See A.R. Seager "The Synagogue and the Jewish Community" in G.M.A. Hanfmann *Sardis* (Cambridge, MA 1983) 168-177.

8 Josephus, *AJ* 16.171 = Pedley *Sardis* (1972) no. 212.

9 Josephus, *AJ* 14.201.

10 Tacitus, *Ann.* 2.47 = Pedley *Sardis* (1972) no. 220.

inscription in Hebrew as well, probably in the community's meeting place or Synagogue.[11]

At the same time the bishop of Sardis, Melito, is castigating "Israel" in his famous sermon *On Pascha*; the pointed and personal language of this bitter attack suggests that he has in mind Jews whom he knows personally, his neighbors at Sardis, as much as the Jews of the gospels. This does not mean a Jewish-Christian conflict in late second century Sardis; there is no evidence from the Jewish side for that, and in addition Jewish wealth and influence at Sardis in this period are such as to suggest Christian envy of the Jews from afar rather than an actual confrontation with them. The power of the Jewish community is perhaps even stronger than it had been earlier; before long they will control the largest synagogue ever found in the Roman world.

Not all Jews of this period are so fortunate: in ancient Palestine the century following the destruction of the temple (70 C.E.) is difficult indeed, and after the Bar Kochba revolt (132-135) Jews are forbidden even to live in Jerusalem; nationalistic political activism is discredited, and more and more the attention of Judaism here turns to its own inner development, under the leadership of some of its greatest rabbis. The "consensus" discussed at the beginning of this chapter would suggest that the Diaspora Jews too felt the pressure of Rome and lived a precarious existence as a result. Sardis is one exception to the consensus—and in the large Roman Diaspora there were probably others.

From this point on the history of the Sardis Jews is the history of their synagogue. This building, originally a public structure, came under their control and was turned into a synagogue in the third century, if not before. It was extensively remodeled late in the fourth century, and continued in use with minor repairs and alterations until the destruction of most of the city in 616.[12]

This period, "late antiquity," is of course when Christianity moved into a position of great influence in the Roman world, putting many Jews very much on the defensive. At Sardis, however, the Jews' continuing prosperity suggests that they retained their old power despite Christian advances. The synagogue itself is our best evidence: it would have made a superb church, and synagogues and temples elsewhere were being taken over by Christians for that purpose; but not at Sardis! Until the city fell, the building remained a synagogue.

The relative prosperity of Sardis Jews in the late Roman Empire is probably the result of the interplay of power among Jews, Christians, and the

---

11 Rabinowitz in *The Synagogue and Its Setting* (forthcoming), no. 1 (*Inscriptions* 62.79); *BASOR* 187, 25.

12 C. Foss, "Late Antique Sardis" in *Byzantine and Turkish Sardis* (Cambridge, MA 1976).

remaining citizens of Sardis, here called "pagans" for lack of a better term. The strength of Sardis Jews and pagans together appears to have counterbalanced the Christians, resulting in a greater stability and security for the Jews here than was usually the case in this period.

The story comes to an end with the fall of Sardis in 616 C.E. The destruction by troops of Chosroes II was so severe that Sardis simply ceased to be a city for a considerable period. And after a life of perhaps a thousand years the Jewish community disappeared as well.

Sardis Jews and the Judaism of the Roman World

One of the best known incidents in the life of Anatolian Jews occurred in the first century B.C.E.: it is the attempt by the Roman governor Lucius Valerius Flaccus to divert to his own use the gold they were sending to Jerusalem to support the Temple. When prosecuted, Flaccus engaged Rome's most famous lawyer, Marcus Tullius Cicero, whose successful speech in Flaccus' defense, the *Pro Flacco*, may still be read.[13] Jewish funds deposited in four cities are mentioned, two in the interior, in Phrygia, and two in Mysia on the northwest coast. The speech reveals several things relevant to our story. These Jews took their traditional obligation seriously; far from ancient Palestine, they had not cut their ties to Jerusalem. Collectively they had substantial disposable income; over 200 pounds of gold were brought together. Inevitably their life in the Diaspora involved them with Roman authorities, officials who were in a kind of "diaspora" of their own; Flaccus held the office for the usual term of one year before returning home. (As it happens he was replaced in Asia by Cicero's younger brother.) Thus even at this early date Jews were a part of the normal life of some, perhaps many, Anatolian cities. Roman provincial officials may have expected to have dealings with them, and venial ones may well have tried to exploit them; their vulnerability to Flaccus in this case, however, is not necessarily a sign of weakness, since he misappropriated funds from gentile communities as well, and even from Roman citizens.

Anatolian Synagogues

Several dozen Jewish communities have been identified in the Roman province of Asia; the important ones will be described briefly below, to fill in a picture of the Anatolian Judaism of which Sardis is a part.

Perhaps the most widely known synagogues from this area are the ones mentioned in the New Testament in Acts and Revelation. In several places in Acts (13:13; 14:1; 16:13; 18:19, 26; 19:8) Christian missionaries are described as beginning their work in Anatolian synagogues; this is due to the author's

---

13 Cicero, *Flac.* 66-68.

conviction that, in the very beginning of Christianity, missionary work in the Diaspora started with Jews for theological reasons. In Revelation 2:9 and 3:9 there are attacks on "synagogues of Satan" in Smyrna and Philadelphia, but these may be rival Christian groups. Thus the New Testament "evidence" must be used with great caution, perhaps with a substantial discounting of the Jewish-Christian hostility which they appear to reflect.

The following evidence is arranged roughly in chronological order, and may thus be put beside the account of the history of Sardis Judaism given in the previous section.

Miletus

By about the second century B.C.E. the coastal city of Miletus was so well known to Jews that a reference to it was inserted (at Ezekiel 27:18) into the Septuagint, the famous translation of the Hebrew Bible into Greek. The Miletus Jews of the Roman period were patrons of the magnificent theater there; an inscription reserves fine fifth-row seats for them.[14]

Acmonia

Of the dozen synagogues attested by inscriptions for this area, the earliest was at Acmonia in inland Phrygia; it is securely dated to the first century C.E. The Jewish community here must have been an attractive one, of social status equal perhaps to Sardis, since the Acmonia synagogue was a gift to the Jews from a gentile woman, Julia Severa, a magistrate of the city and at one time a priestess in one of the local pagan cults.[15] Beyond this we know very little about her, and nothing further about her philanthropic activities. Inscriptions indicate that the Jewish community was a large one, with a life extending over several centuries. Hebrew was known there; the only Hebrew inscription found in Asia Minor outside Sardis comes from here, perhaps from the synagogue given by Julia Severa. It is a "biblical" blessing: "(May there be peace upon) Israel, and upon Jerusalem and (upon this place to the time of) the end." It is also bilingual; the text is given in Greek as well.[16] Probably knowledge of Hebrew was limited to a few traditional blessings and other formulae; the Sardis fragments and the absence of Hebrew inscriptions elsewhere mean that in general the Jews of this area were at home only in Greek.

---

14 *CII*, 748.

15 *MAMA* VI = *Momumenta Asiae Minoris Antiqua* VI, *Monuments and Documents from Phrygia and Caria*, ed. W.H. Buckler and W.M. Calder (Manchester 1939) no. 264 = *CII*, 766.

16 *MAMA* VI, no. 334.

Aphroaisias

Aphrodisias in Caria is probably typical of more cities in this area than one would at first suspect: only a few years ago there was no indication at all of a Jewish presence there; now two lengthy inscriptions[17] of about the second century give names and occupations of a great many men of the Jewish community, and a graffito in the Odeum indicates the seats of certain Jews, as at Miletus.[18] These new data suggest that the Jews of this well-known Roman city may have been as influential as those of Sardis, and that other ancient cities in this area may also have had Jewish minorities, perhaps substantial ones, evidence for which has yet to be unearthed.

Hierapolis

For Hierapolis in Phrygia, just north and east of Aphrodisias, the evidence is more abundant—a good number of epitaphs from the second or third century. The Jewish community itself is designated a *Katoikia*, suggesting that it had a clear identity as a social unit within the city. Many citizens of Hierapolis were members of trade organizations, and the Jews were no exception; the city's Association of Purple-dyers and the council of the Association of Tapestry-makers were made responsible for memorial ceremonies for deceased Jewish members on Passover and Pentecost![19] These organizations contained gentiles as well as Jews; the conclusion must be that the Jews of this city maintained their Jewish identity and *at the same time* participated fully in the life of their city.

Apameia

Apameia, also in Phrygia, is east of Hierapolis; the two cities are connected by one of the main Roman roads. Apameia had a Jewish community of some size by the early first century B.C.E. It was one of the places where Flaccus confiscated funds intended for the Temple tax. The fascinating evidence here, though, is several centuries later—a series of coins minted in the first half of the third century, showing Noah and the Ark (*kibotos* in the Septuagint) from the biblical flood story. On each coin the scene is actually double: first Noah and his wife in the Ark (*kibotos*), which is shaped like a chest (also *kibotos*) with open lid; then Noah and wife standing outside the Ark with their right arms raised in thanksgiving. The name Noah appears on

17 Mellink, "Archaeology" (1977) 306, and J. Reynolds and R.F. Tannenbaum, *Jews and God-fearers at Aphrodisias* (Cambridge, England, 1987).

18 Cameron, *Circus Factions*, 315.

19 *CII*, 775, 777.

the Ark on the coins, making identification certain.[20] The background is fascinating and complex: there is literary evidence for the existence of pagan flood-legends in this area, and for their conflation with the biblical story. It is clear also that Apameia had a second name: it was sometimes called Apameia Kibotos, *kibotos* here meaning "chest," "container," "packing box," a reference to the city's importance as a commercial center. The various meanings of *kibotos* allow the link between the city's second name and Noah's Ark, and also led to the representation of the Ark as a chest on the coins. Some of the mint-masters who struck the coins may have been Jewish, although it is unlikely that all of them were who did so over a period of half a century. Because the imagery on the coins does not change over time, it has been suggested that there was a single pattern for them--a local painting, one on public view. Exactly contemporary with the Sardis synagogue, the coin is impressive evidence not just of close contacts between Jews and gentiles, but of something more: some sort of "official" acknowledgment of a traditional mythological bond of some antiquity between them.

Laodiceia

Nearby Laodiceia is also one of the cities where Jewish gold bound for Jerusalem was seized by Flaccus. Much later, in the middle of the fourth century, it was the site of a council of Anatolian bishops; the council's formal decisions or "canons," still preserved, are among the most anti-Jewish known from the ancient Church. Canon 16, for example, stipulates that only New Testament texts are to be read on the sabbath (Saturday); possibly some Christians were following the synagogue practice and reading only the Old Testament at Saturday services, perhaps together with local Jews. Canon 29 orders Christians not to "Judaize" by resting on the sabbath; they are to rest instead on Sunday. Canon 36 forbids the making of Jewish ritual phylacteries. Canon 37 forbids keeping festivals with Jews or heretics, and receiving from them such gifts as are associated with these festivals. Canon 38 is more specific on the same point: Christians are not to receive unleavened bread from Jews. The conclusion of James Parkes regarding the canons seems plausible: "Taken together (they) certainly leave a strong impression that even in the fourth century there were not only Judaic practices in the Church in Asia, but that there was actual religious fellowship with the Jewish inhabitants," despite the opposition of church leaders.[21]

---

20 A.A. Kindler, "A Coin Type from Apameia in Phrygia (Asia Minor) Depicting the Narrative of Noah," Museum Haaretz, *Bulletin* 13 (1971) 24-32; Kraabel "Paganism," 23; Goodenough, *Symbols* 2:119, 3:700.

21 Parkes, *Conflict*, 175.

Priene

A dozen synagogues are known from the Jewish inscriptions of this area, but the only two buildings definitely identified are at Sardis and at the hillside, seacoast city of Priene, located between Ephesus and Miletus. Priene is a small place and its synagogue is small as well; it would fit easily into the forecourt of the Sardis synagogue. The Jews of Priene were less powerful, or perhaps less bold: their building was on a side street, not easily identified, surrounded by small rooms which may have also been under the control of the Jews. The synagogue itself was a plain room, 14 m. wide and 10 m. deep, with a niche in the east wall to contain the Torah-scrolls.[22]

Relations of Anatolian Communities with Palestine

There is some general evidence of communication among these Jewish communities (and others in the area omitted in this brief survey); since the cities were relatively close together and the road system was a good one, such contacts are to be expected.

Links with Jerusalem or (later) with the rabbinic authorities in ancient Palestine are more problematic. Before the destruction of the Jerusalem Temple in the first century, the two obvious connections between ancient Palestine and the Diaspora were the Temple tax and the pilgrimage to Jerusalem, the latter incumbent on Jewish men three times a year. We have already seen that the Jews of Asia Minor did contribute to the Temple by paying the tax. The obligation of pilgrimage three times a year could not be maintained in this period when the majority of Jews lived outside of ancient Palestine; pilgrims came as they were able, and as their piety demanded, and there is clear evidence that some who came were from Asia. Sardis was located on the main land route for pilgrims coming from the west,[23] and members of the Sardis Jewish community must have been among the pilgrims on occasion; the only Sardian who claims to have traveled to the Holy Land, however, is the second century bishop Melito.

The revolts in Palestine in the first and second centuries must have sent Jewish refugees and slaves into Asia Minor. There is no indication that Anatolian Jews took an anti-Roman position in these conflicts, or took part in the actual battles. Perhaps they viewed the revolt as nationalistic and political struggles which did not concern them; perhaps they did not want to endanger their own favorable position with the government. The Romans apparently made a distinction between the Jews in revolt and those Jews in

---

22 Kraabel, "Diaspora Synagogue," 489-491.

23 See Map V in *Compendia Rerum Iudaicarum ad Novum Testamentum* I.1, 2 editions, ed. S. Safrai and M. Stern (Assen 1974, 1976), 196.

other parts of the Empire who remained peaceful; at least, those in the latter group were not punished or restricted because they had a common religion and heritage with the former.[24]

After the Bar Kochba revolt the situation of the Palestinian Jews is greatly different from the way it had been a century earlier. The Temple with its cult no longer exists, and hope for its restoration is all but abandoned. There is no need for a priesthood, no goals for pilgrimage, no purpose for a Temple tax. The synagogue is now the central religious building, the rabbi is the community leader, and in Palestine the patriarch is recognized by Jews and Roman authorities as the head of the Jewish nation. The Temple tax from Diaspora Jews had been diverted to a special Roman treasury during the first revolt, but before long funds are coming in again from the Diaspora, this time in support of the patriarch; these voluntary contributions are collected by the patriarchs emissaries, called *apostoloi*.

Could such *apostoloi* have come to western Asia Minor, or Sardis? This area was surely on the edge of the rabbinic world; little attention is paid to it in rabbinic literature. Even the meaning of the term Asia in the literary evidence is unclear; sometimes it designates what we have been calling Asia (Minor), sometimes a single city, sometimes a non-Anatolian location. For example, rabbinic texts tell of rabbis sent into the Diaspora as *apostoloi* of the patriarch, to collect funds and to keep the official ritual calendar synchronized with that of the partriarch. The famous second-century rabbi Meir once went to "Asia" for the second purpose, and when he found the community without a copy of the book of Esther (for the Purim festival) he wrote one out from memory. Meir is also reported to have died in Asia. Did these two events take place in the same area of the same city? If an Anatolian community lacked Esther, was it because the community was so far out of touch with the majority of Jews as to even lack a complete text of the scriptures? Or was it because the people of Asia refused to accept the festival of Purim because of its political and anti-gentile emphases, that is, not because they were marginal Jews but because their kind of Judaism was self-consciously independent of the nationalism of the Palestinian homeland?[25]

In the last analysis, it is unlikely that the patriarch or the rabbis maintained any significant, systematic supervision over the Jews of Asia. The evidence available at present suggests that the *apostoloi*, the only body which might have carried out this function in the west, lacked the manpower and influence for so substantial a task.

---

24 Smallwood, *Jews*, 356-357.

25 Babylonian Talmud, *Megillah* 18b; N. Cohen, "Rabbi Meir, A Descendant of Anatolian Proselytes," *JJS* 23 (1972) 51-59. Generally on the *apostoloi*, see *Compendia*, 205-210; Smallwood, *Jews*, 475.

The single piece of evidence on this issue from the Sardis excavations is the important mosaic inscription of Samoe, "priest and *sophodidaskalos*."[26] The second title means literally "teacher of wisdom" or "wise teacher," but in the Judaism of this period it is most likely the equivalent of "rabbi." The inscription is probably later than 429, by which date the patriarchy had been suppressed in Palestine. Thus the inscription may not be used as evidence for strong ties between Sardis Judaism and the patriarchate.

Two well-known features of Sardis Judaism may provide the most helpful clue about the relations between this city and Palestine: the first is the use of Greek in the inscriptions, nearly to the exclusion of Hebrew; the second is the great age of the Jewish community here. These points, when taken with the other evidence reviewed in this chapter, lead almost inevitably to a picture of this community as strong and independent, with its own traditions, and "at home" in the Roman world; the Jews of Sardis had enduring respect for the homeland of their religion, but were not under its control. During centuries of life as a minority in the Diaspora, they must have worked out a form of Judaism more in keeping with that context than rabbinic Judaism could have been. If we knew more about Samoe, he likely would recall the earlier theologian and philosopher Philo of Alexandria, rather than any leader of the "rabbinic world" farther to the east.

The Jews in Gentile Sardis

Only three large cities of the Roman world contain Jewish minorities for which there is broad documentation. In the Empire's capital many Romans were put off by any foreigner: a Greek, a Briton, a Gaul, or a Jew. But in addition, Jews here were without political status and financial power; they lacked polish, often they were all but illiterate. Jews had lived in Alexandria in large numbers since its founding by Alexander the Great; the Septuagint and the writings of Philo are evidence for their intellectual activity in philosophy and theology. But the unstable Alexandrian citizenry was given to riot, and Jews frequently got caught up in clashes between local gentiles and the Roman authorities.

Before our excavations, the evidence for Sardis came chiefly from Josephus; the texts have been discussed above, and they could well give the impression that the Sardis Jews were a distinct group with strange practices and particular rights which must be protected by the authorities. One might assume that the status of the Jews in Sardis was not much different from the status of the Jews in Alexandria or Rome. But part of Josephus' purpose is to stress the long-held rights of Jewish communities, and the protection of

---

26 *BASOR* 187, 38, fig. 48. On Samoe, see G.M.A. Hanfmann, *Sardis* "Illustrations" fig. 267.

those rights by the authorities. The result is to underemphasize the Jews as accepted members of a city's society. For Sardis at least, the picture changes considerably when archaeological evidence is added. Perhaps the situation of Sardis Jews improved after the period described by Josephus; all of the evidence to be discussed below comes from after the earthquake of 17 C.E.

Let us look again at Figs. 207, 240, 251-253;[27] they show clearly the place of the Synagogue in Roman Sardis. As Seager notes, the upper walls and roof of the building must have been clearly visible above the shops and road colonnades (Fig. 239). The interior of the entire building could be seen by gentiles walking by when the doors were open. The Forecourt (Fig. 251) may have contained a municipally licensed fountain and may have been accessible to all.

The evidence from epigraphy buttresses the evidence from architecture. There are over eighty inscriptions from the Synagogue, and they differ strikingly at one point from the hundreds of other Jewish inscriptions known from the Roman world. Elsewhere, for example at Rome, the texts may emphasize one's status within the *Jewish* community; the Sardis inscriptions stress rather the status of Jews outside the Jewish community, in the city and its government, and even beyond. Many donors proudly identify themselves as *Sardianoi*, "citizens of Sardis," and no less than nine may use the privileged title *bouleutes*, "member of the city council;" perhaps because of their wealth, the latter must have possessed considerable social status. In addition, three donors held positions in the provincial administration: one was a comes ("Count"; Fig. 278), another a procurator (Fig. 272), another an assistant in the state archives.[28]

The inscriptions refer to more than thirty donors (Figs. 254, 268, 275, 278); only two names are Hebrew (Fig. 267), and one of these is followed by an additional name which is Hellenized Roman: 'Samuel, known also as Julian"; this practice is found in other Jewish inscriptions and also in the New Testament, for example, "Saul . . . known also as Paul" (Acts 13:9). This preference for non-Jewish names is not surprising. Only 13% of the Jewish inscriptions of Rome display only Semitic names, while 46% have Greek names only, and 32% Latin names only; the rest have a mixture of Greek and either Latin or Semitic.

The few Semitic names from Sardis are fascinating in themselves: for example, the person of greatest religious importance in the synagogue bears a Semitic name, Samoe, the priest and *sophodidaskalos* whose dedication was discovered squarely in the center of the Main Hall (Fig. 267). It is not

---

27 Editor's note: The "Figures" which Kraabel is referring to here and *infra* in this article are found in Hanfmann, *Sardis*, "Illustrations."

28 On the inscriptions, see "The Building," in Hanfmann, *Sardis*, 171 nn. 24-25.

surprising that a "rabbi" would manifest something traditional when other Jews were using names more common in the larger and largely gentile community. Four additional names are known from graffiti in the shops, three of Hebrew origin: Jacob, John, and Sabbatios. Perhaps the graffiti reflect more familiar names, the inscriptions more formal ones.

One synagogue inscription mentions "the tribe of the Leontioi." It is unclear whether this refers to a group within the synagogue community, or to the Jews as a whole within the larger Sardis community.[29] The choice of the term *Leontioi* was an inspired one, whatever the extent of the group to which it refers. *Leontes* is the Greek for "lions," a powerful symbol to those who speak Greek but think in biblical terms. In the Bible the tribe of Judah (Gen. 49:9), the tribe of Dan (Deut. 33:22), and finally all of Israel (Num. 23:24; 24:9) are all pictured as "lions." The great hero Judah the Maccabee could be described as a lion (1 Macc. 3:4-6), and in the Eagle Vision of fourth Ezra the lion is the Messiah himself (4 Ezra 12:31f.). The lion is a popular Jewish symbol in art as well as literature; the excavated synagogues of ancient Palestine have produced a score of examples. But in Greek literature the lion is associated with Sardis since the days of Herodotus. Lions are the subject of approximately one-third of all the sculpture published from Lydian and Persian Sardis, prompting Hanfmann to remark that "the Lydians suffered from a regular *leontomania*."[30]

The recent excavations show very clearly what the Jews did with this powerful Sardis symbol. A massive Lydian lion (Fig. 240)—or possibly a pair of lions--was installed just outside the Synagogue Forecourt, and two pairs of lions from the Persian period (Fig. 256) bracket the great Eagle Table in the front of the Synagogue.[31] But the Jews were not simply "reusing" the lion statues; they were actually associating themselves in some way with this traditional Sardis image, combining it with the biblical one, using it as the story of Noah was used at Apameia in Phrygia. The culmination of this process appears in a Hebrew graffito to be published by Rabinowitz; the writer is a *ben Leho*, "son of Ieo."[32] Apparently the lion became such a popular image among Sardis Jews that one of their number was given the name Leo, the *Latin* for "lion"; but in the graffito it is written in *Hebrew* characters!

The occupations of Jews in this part of the ancient world are not much different from those of gentiles; there is no clear indication that particular

---

29 L. Robert, *Nouvelles* (Paris 1964) 45-46, pl. 5, considers it "certain" that the Leontioi were not a municipal tribe.

30 G.M.A. Hanfmann and N. Ramage, *Sculpture from Sardis: The Finds through 1975* (Cambridge, MA, 1978) 15, 20-23.

31 Ibid. nos. 31, 25.

32 Rabinowitz in *The Synagogue and Its Setting* (forthcoming), "Hebrew Inscriptions."

crafts were associated with Jews. Goldsmiths must have been in demand; three of the synagogue donors were Jews of that occupation. Others were merchants; some sold glass, some paints and dyes. One may have been a sculptor. As already mentioned, others held government positions.[33]

Since this is a sketch of the life of Jews in a gentile city, one final matter must be considered: what about anti-Semitism, gentile hatred of Jews? Our impression is that there was no anti-Semitism at Sardis while this synagogue was in use. (The special case of Melito, Christian bishop of Sardis, will be discussed below.) Modern descriptions of ancient anti-Semitism tend to generalize too quickly; on the basis of specific texts and incidents from particular locations, they extrapolate toward "*the* gentile attitude toward the Jews." But gentile attitudes toward Judaism were anything but monolithic! At about the time one gentile (a Roman general soon to be emperor) was destroying the Temple in Jerusalem, another gentile (an ex-magistrate named Julia Severa) was donating a synagogue to the Jews of Acmonia, in Phrygia not far from Sardis. In accounts of ancient anti-Semitism the Jew is a stranger and a threat; his religion forces him into an odd diet, peculiar work schedules, and strange cultic practices. He is forced to keep to himself, to live by himself, to avoid contact with gentiles. And yet he is eager to proselytize; it is an indication of his own insecurity that he must try to convert gentiles, or at least turn them into "sympathizers." His targets are the gullible of the gentile world: women, children, and the uneducated. Such a reconstruction of the past will not fit the Sardis presented in this volume; and because the Jewish community of Sardis is so well documented, the new evidence has the effect of calling into question long-held views of the relationships between Jews and gentiles in the entire ancient world.

Sardis Jews and Paganism

Until the discoveries at Sardis, the evidence for Judaism in western Asia Minor had been scattered and fragmentary. It was examined usually by those more interested in Christianity: Asia Minor is the first part of the Diaspora which Christianity penetrated, and it spread rapidly. In the Diaspora the Christian attitude toward Jews soon became generally negative. The idea grew up that Diaspora Jews had not remained true to biblical faith; particularly in Asia Minor, it was claimed, Jews adopted the vocabulary, the imagery, and even the theology of pagan piety. They came under the spell of the Anatolian god Sabazius; perhaps they thought that *Sabaz*ius was the *Sabba*th. They sometimes used the eagle as a religious symbol; this too was seen as a descent into pagan ways, since the eagle was used as a religious and political emblem

---

33 *BASOR* 187, 32.

by Roman gentiles. Their cultic use of wine suggested that the Jews were secretly followers of Dionysus; according to Euripides, this god comes from Mt. Tmolus, immediately south of Sardis. In the Septuagint, God is frequently called "the highest one," *hypsistos*; in Anatolian inscriptions one deity or another may be called *hypsistos*, offering Jews here still another opportunity for syncretism, mixing their religion with pagan piety. Some Jews did these things because they were not very smart—they did not know any better; but most were deliberate, pathetically attempting to make themselves more "gentile." Thus the old view.

But if syncretism among Jews was as widespread as we have been told, there should be clear evidence for it in the Sardis data. From Lydia and from Sardis itself there is abundant evidence for Sabazius and Dionysus: was any of it found in the Synagogue? The Sardis Jewish community can now be extensively documented; is there any indication that mixtures of traditional Judaism and pagan piety were being concocted there? The answer to both questions is no.[34]

Frequent and generally friendly contact with gentiles must have been an accepted part of the daily life of Sardis Jews; clearly they worked, shopped, and lived side by side, and—like Philo—some Sardis Jews must have studied with gentiles. The Synagogue inscriptions provide strong evidence that they may have had a technical, philosophical vocabulary in common. Eleven inscriptions, dating from the third to the fifth centuries, use the term *pronoia*, "Providence"; the donors are stating that their gifts to the Synagogue are paid for out of resources bestowed by Providence. In an expression which seems strangely modern, the Sardis Jews used Providence to mean God. *Pronoia* is exceedingly rare in inscriptions for other synagoges, and never means "divine providence" (that is, God). Since the Sardis Jews use the term in a quasi-liturgical fashion in their inscriptions, it is probable that this use of *pronoia* became common in the synagogue community sometime before these inscriptions were composed. How did this idea reach Sardis, and why is it found only here, out of all the Jewish communities known in the Roman Diaspora?

The most likely possibility is gentile philosophy. In the thought of this period the concept of a systematic divine control over human events—a combination of plan and power building the cosmos—was an attractive alternative to the anthropomorphism of earlier Greek and Roman mythology. A number of treatises entitled *On Providence* were produced by pagan philosophers in this period, the most comprehensive by Plotinus in the third century.

---

34 Generally, see Kraabel, *"Hypsistos"* (1969); "Paganism" (1978); C. Foss *Byzantine and Turkish Sardis* (1976) "Late Antique Sardis."

If Jews and pagans studied together and lived side by side, it is possible that they joined forces against the Christians in Sardis' final religious conflict. Such a coalition would help to explain how the Synagogue building remained Jewish and was not expropriated, even during the reigns of such aggressively pro-Christian emperors as Constantius II (337-361), Theodosius I (378-395), Theodosius II (408-439), and Justinian (527-565).

The hypothesis which best explains the data is as follows: the religious situation of Sardis in the last two centuries of the city's existence was characterized by a coalition of Jews and pagans opposing a frequently divided Christian community that gradually grew to include a majority of the population. Because of this coalition the Synagogue did not pass into Christian hands. But this Jewish-pagan alliance did not lead to the "paganizing" of Sardis Judaism; the Synagogue itself remains our best evidence of that.

Sardis Jews and Christianity

Moving out from ancient Palestine, Christianity made a significant penetration into Asia Minor in the first century.[35] The New Testament contains letters written to Christian groups in Ephesus and Colossae, both on the Roman highway which runs south of Sardis, and the Christian missionary Paul directed one of his most important letters to Christians in Galatia, east of Sardis, in the interior. Revelation, written at the end of the first century, begins with brief letters to Christian communities at Sardis (Rev. 3:1-6) and six other nearby cities; people in Sardis had been Christian for some time by then, since the text pointedly contrasts their present low spiritual state with the good reputation which they had earned in the past. Other early Christian texts, still extant though not in the New Testament, come from authors personally familiar with Christianity in the Sardis area: the letters of Ignatius were written a decade or two after Revelation; the letter of Polycarp, Bishop of Smyrna, and the *Martydom of Polycarp* are from about the middle of the second century.[36] These texts and later evidence indicate that Christianity took several competing forms in Western Asia Minor; it was inchoate and still very young when it reached this area, and its often independent missionaries addressed different audiences in a variety of ways. There were conflicts not only with Jews, but also with "Judaizers," Christians who manifested more of Jewish belief and practice than Church authorities would prefer. Judaizers need not be converted Jews: apparently Jewish or Jewish-Christian practices were brought to the attention of some Anatolian gentiles when they became Christian, and they adopted them to the dismay of the Christian leadership.

---

35 Generally, see S. Johnson, "Asia Minor and Early Christianity," in *Christianity, Judaism and Other Greco-Roman Cults: Studies for Morton Smith at Sixty*, ed. J. Neusner (Leiden 1975).

36 Ignatius, etc., in *Apostolic Fathers*.

By the end of the first century there were many more Christians outside of ancient Palestine than within the Christian and Jewish homeland, and by the end of the second century the new religion was overwhelmingly gentile; "Judaizers" were increasingly unwelcome.

The best known Christian of ancient Sardis is the enigmatic Melito,[37] bishop there in the latter part of the second century; in Christian tradition he is one of the "great luminaries" of the early church in this area, along with the disciples Philip and John and the martyr Polycarp. The background of Melito's work has become much clearer thanks to the Sardis excavations, but the resulting picture is of a tangled set of relationships between him and second century Judaism, including the Sardis Jews in all probability. Consider the following: (1) the Old Testament was so important to Melito that he made a journey to the Holy Land to secure an accurate list of its precise contents; he is thus the first Christian pilgrim to Palestine of whom we are informed; (2) he was a quartodeciman, like many other Anatolian Christians of his time: the Easter lie celebrated was dated according to the Jewish Passover each year, and might thus fall on a day of the week other than Sunday. This practice has its roots in the Gospel of John but was repeatedly condemned as "Judaizing," particularly by western churches; (3) Melito's one extant sermon, the *On Pascha*, is an intricate, ornamented, often florid interpretation and application of the Passover story in Exodus 12, so central to Jewish piety.

None of this means that Melito was on good terms with Jews. Quite the reverse: in his *Apology* he calls them "barbarians," outside the boundaries of Greco-Roman culture. The *On Pascha* is a bitter attack on the Jews as responsible for the death of Christ; for this Melito has been called "the first poet of deicide" or "God- killing," the monstrous charge that all Jews and Jews alone are responsible for the death ofJesus. The attacks on the Jews in the *On Pascha* are bitter and prolonged; the section denouncing "Israel" occupies nearly a third of the whole text. There is nothing in quartodeciman Christianity which requires taking such a position; indeed, a quartodeciman sermon closely related to Melito in date and theology contains but a few references to Judaism—they are negative but quite brief. It is true that ancient Christianity produced substantial anti-Jewish literature, attacking Jews on theological grounds; but that tradition was just beginning at the time of Melito and he did not benefit from it.

The new Sardis evidence will permit Melito to be understood fully for the first time, by allowing us to see clearly the context out of which he wrote. Apparently he was battling on two fronts simultaneously. Among Christians he had to defend quartodeciman practice; what better way to meet the charge of "Judaizing" than by preaching sermons attacking "Israel"? But at Sardis the

---

37 Kraabel, "Melito," 77-85; *Melito of Sardis*.

enemy must have been the Jews; the newly revealed Jewish community apparently had far more power locally than did Melito's Christians. There is no firm evidence that Sardis Jews were even aware of Melito, or that a direct hostility on their part provoked his attacks. But the present synagogue or its immediate predecessor, and the people who controlled it, made a profound and profoundly negative impression on him; of that there can be little doubt.

Two Christian martyrs are known from third century Sardis, but their conflict was apparently with the pagan state rather than with the Jews; there is no evidence whatever of Jewish contribution to Christian persecution at Sardis, although something of the kind had taken place in Smyrna, not far to the west.

With the reign of Constantine (306-337), relations among pagans, Jews, and Christians at Sardis become more complex. The substantial Church EA (Figs. 288-291) was built in a necropolis near the Pactolus River in about the middle of the fourth century; it is two-thirds the size of the Synagogue, an indication of Christian strength. But Christians were still divided into factions; there were reports of riots and violence among Sardis Christians into the fifth century. The laws of the now-Christian state bore down with increasing severity on pagans and Jews, but enforcement varied considerably from period to period and location to location. In Sardis, the combination of a still-living paganism and a divided Christianity may well have made it impolitic for local officials to apply sanctions on the Jews.

There are hints as well that relations between Sardis Jews and the Christian laity were not always hostile. The shops which were built against the outside of the Synagogue south wall are described in Chapter VIII[38]; excavation has shown that shops owned by Christians existed side by side with shops owned by Jews (Figs. 239-243). The shops front on the main east-west street of the city, where Christian and Jewish shoppers and merchants encountered one another every day. There is no sign of a "Jewish quarter" or ghetto; from all indications Sardis Jews, Christians, and pagans lived side by side.

As a quartodeciman leader resident in Sardis, Melito the bishop was close to Jews in some points of theology and practice, and close to them also in his daily life; for his own reasons he attacked them strongly, making extreme statements which later become detached from their historical situation and made a substantial contribution to Christian anti-Jewish vocabulary. For Sardis Jews, he must have been an unpleasant person to have around. But the Jews also had Christians for neighbors, laity unlike Melito, and they may have had a more positive attitude toward them. We suspect that the larger history of

---

38 Editor's note: Kraabel is referring to G.M.A. Hanfmann and Fikret K. Yegül and John S. Crawford, "The Roman and Late Antique," in Hanfmann, *Sardis* 109-138.

Jewish-Christian relations at Sardis is something like this: something between antagonism and openness is to be assumed between the two groups. If the *On Pascha* is to be used as evidence, then the situation between Jews and Christians reflected in canons of the nearby council of Laodicea is also part of the picture--or so the new evidence would suggest.

Jewish Religious Life in Sardis

It is possible to enter the ancient Synagogue of Sardis; there has been extensive reconstruction (Figs. 251, 256-258, 280; cf. 253), so that visitors may examine the entire building, from front steps to apse. Anyone with more than a casual interest in this structure will surely want to know the answer to two central questions: How was this building used? And what does it tell us about Sardis Judaism? The simplest way to answer is to take an imaginary tour;[39] more questions will suggest themselves in the process.

Like the gymnasium itself, the Synagogue was designed to be entered at the east from the East Road colonnade (Figs. 239, 240, 243). What we see now is the fourth and last stage of the building (Fig. 271), from the fourth century; but in the latter part of stage three the building was already a synagogue, and even stage two could have been made to serve as such by blocking the northern passage in the apse, the only direct link in stage two between this building and the pagan gymnasium. In general, then, the building entered from the colonnade may be said to reflect the religious life of Sardis Jews' from the third century until the destruction of the city in 616. But it did not serve the religious life alone. The ancient synagogue was a building of many uses. Particularly in the Diaspora, it may well have been the only large space in a gentile city where the Jewish community could assemble. In the first instance, it is the place where Jews gathered to pray and to hear the Scripture read; these tasks were the responsibility of the congregation and the community in general. The ancient synagogue had no professional priesthood, no formal liturgy of the kind associated with Christianity, no trace of any sacrificial rite as had been practiced in the Temple in Jerusalem. This synagogue was also a school, and it may have been used on occasion as a dining hall; since a main highway from the Aegean to the east was just outside, Jewish travelers must often have spent the night in the synagogue itself, or perhaps in a loft over one of the Jewish shops built against the outside of the south wall (Figs. 207, 239- 242) next to the highway. It was pointed out above that one of the predecessors of this building was used by Sardis Jews for their own discussions and for the resolution of communiry differences, practices which must have continued in this building. Several

---

39 A review of the plates and plans in Seager's description of the building, (See Hanfmann, *Sardis* 168-177), will serve to stimulate the imagination.

features of the Sardis synagogue recall the famous Diplostoon, the "double-
-colonnaded synagogue at Alexandria destroyed by Trajan.[40] The Talmud
indicates that people were seated in the Diplostoon by trades—all the goldsmiths together, all the weavers together, all the carpetmakers together—so
that a new person in the community thus associated himelf with others in his
profession in order to gain employment; the Sardis Synagogue too may have
functioned as a kind of hiring-hall.

The first thing which strikes the visitor is the size and grandeur of the
building, still inescapable today. The few other Diaspora synagogues which
have been excavated are on the scale of a private dwelling;[41] the scale of this
building is that of the great gymnasium and Marble Court of which it is a part
(Fig. 207). In view of its central location, its size, and its embellishments, it is
hard to avoid the conclusion that the building was intended to be a showplace
of Judaism for Sardis gentiles. The richness of the Dura synagogue in Syria
was hidden from strangers, walled off behind a complex of community meeting rooms; in contrast, this building appears to be "on display." The space
which the Jews had received was substantial, and they could have used it more
"efficiently," had they wished, or had they been following practices known from
other Diaspora synagogues. The crosswall dividing the Forecourt from the
Main Hall (Figs. 253, 266,' 271) is a new feature in the fourth stage; it could
have been erected much farther to the west, closer to the apse, and the space
thus freed could have been devoted to a number of new, small rooms for
various synagogue purposes. The present Forecourt too is more attractive than
efficient: there were sunlight and shade, splashing water, brightly decorated
floors and walls (Fig. 251), all in full view of anyone on his way from the Main
Avenue to the gymnasium. To passersby, it all must have said quite good
things about Sardis Judaism; we believe that was by design.

The Main Hall (Figs. 252, 253) is accessible only from the Forecourt,
which may be entered through the main doors on the east or by a smaller
passage from the south, convenient to the Jewish shops. It was customary to
wash one's hands on entering the synagogue; a trough-like basin of marble for
that purpose stood between the south entrance to the Forecourt and the south
door leading from the Forecourt to the Main Hall. Water from the fountain
might also have been used. Just before entering the Main Hall, the visitor
would notice four comemorative inscriptions set into the mosaic floor on the
west side of the Forecourt (Fig. 257), the first of many to be encountered in
the building.

Just inside the Main Hall are the two marble shrines or aediculae, one on
each side of the central entrance (Figs. 258, 266). The south shrine was evi-

---

40 Goodenough, 2:85.

41 Kraabel, "Diaspora Synagogue," 489-491.

dently the more important (Fig. 274); the construction is of better quality, and the few fragments of Hebrew inscription (Fig. 269) from the building were found here. The shrines are in reuse; the capitals of each were notched so that a screen or curtain could be hung between them. In this way a wholly gentile architectural element became a synagogue furnishing, with all the essential features of the Torah Shrines known from other synagogues and from Jewish art.

When the Scripture was to be read aloud from the Eagle Table at the west end of the building (Fig. 256), the proper scroll must have been brought, perhaps in a formal procession, from the shrine over 40 meters away (Fig. 258); afterward it would be returned in the same fashion. This is perhaps as close to a formal liturgical activity as the Sardis community might come. The Sardis Jews erected two shrines for reasons of symmetry; there is no reason why both of them could not have been used as receptacles for scrolls. The crosswall and shrines are new to the fourth stage of the building; they indicate architecturally the increasing importance of the scripture in Diaspora Judaism, and permit the scrolls to be stored on the wall closest to Jerusalem, a feature seen also in Diaspora synagogues at Ostia outside Rome, and at Priene and Dura. The Sardis Jews had a significant name for such a structure; in one of the inscriptions it is called "that which protects the Law" (*nomophylakion*). The term is rare, and the choice of it revealing. The usual Hebrew, Aramaic, and Greek names for the Torah Shrine reflect biblical imagery. This word does not; rather it underscores the purpose of such a structure at Sardis, and witnesses to the importance of the Law in this community.

Another inscription from the Synagogue makes the same point; it is not a dedication, but a kind of motto in formal, liturgical language: "Having found, having broken, read! observe!" The plaque bearing this inscription (Fig. 276) is designed to be free-standing, on a pedestal or perhaps on the Eagle Table itself (Fig. 257). "Breaking" may refer to "breaking open" a text, that is, discerning its meaning; or perhaps to breaking the seal of a scroll in order to open it. Both inscriptions are carefully done, intended to be impressive; each text is framed in a *tabula ansata*. The *nomophylakion* inscription was carved in raised relief; the depressed background was originally painted red (Fig. 275).

West of the aediculae in the center of the Main Hall is the Synagogue's most important inscription, the dedication by "Samoe, priest and *sophodidaskalos*"; the inscription is framed by four stone slabs set in a square, perhaps supports for a decorative baldacchino to mark the location (Fig. 267; cf. 252, Bay 4).

Samoe was a priest, although the Sardis Jews had no ritual of sacrifice; such things ended with the destruction of the Temple centuries before this inscription was created. A priest is not essential to the function' of the synagogue, but Samoe was a descendant of the biblical high priest Aaron and bore the title proudly. *Sophodidaskalos* means "wise teacher" or "teacher of wisdom"; given the prominent location of the inscription, it is likely that he was the teacher for the synagogue, the closest thing that Sardis had to a rabbi. The inscription is in Greek, and Samoe must have taught in Greek, to judge from the overwhelming preference for Greek over Hebrew in the Jewish inscriptions of Sardis and of Asia Minor as a whole. (There is a higher percentage of Hebrew in the decorations of the typical American synagogue of today!) The precise center of the Main Hall is marked with this inscription and its baldacchino(?) (Fig. 252, Bima?) probably because this is just where Samoe taught, with his students around him, when the building was not given over to formal services. In synagogues in Asia Minor in this period, the Bible was read and then interpreted in Greek; probably Samoe's teachings were homiletical and in some sense "haggadic," intended to instruct or to edify—but more than that we cannot say.

The west end of the Synagogue is the architectural focus of the building, and must be seen as a unit (Fig. 253); it is the culmination of this tour of the structure and this story of the Jews of Sardis. For the services, important members of the community and honored guests were seated on the benches of the apse; the wall behind them was decorated with colorful designs in cut marble and long commemorative inscriptions (Fig. 256). These personages looked out across a semicircular mosaic (Fig. 260), over the apse railing and the Eagle Table and out to the rest of the community. The table was flanked by pairs of marble lions (Fig. 256). The "Socrates" menorah (Fig. 268) may have stood on a small, carefully carved monument in the shape of a Corinthian round temple that was placed against one of the north piers (Fig. 256).[42] Eagles, lions, and menorah were all rich in symbolism for the assembled community. The scroll of the Scriptures was unrolled on the Eagle Table; a member of the community stood on a small pedestal at the tabled his back to the apse, and read aloud the text designated for the day.

For centuries these are the things which characterized the ancient synagogue of Sardis and the community for which it was the center. In the Roman Empire there were many kinds of Jews, in different locations, on different social levels. About some of them we know a great deal: the rabbinic communities, Qumran, Palestine generally, Alexandria. Now with a directness which

---

42 G.M.A. Hanfmann and N. Ramage, *Sculpture from Sardis: The Finds through 1975* (1978) nos. 25, lions: 217, Eagle Table (supports); 226, Socrates menorah. "Corinthian" monument base (SYN 62.20), restored 1970-1971, is described by A. Seager, *The Synagogue and Its Setting* (forthcoming), "Main Hall," pier N 1. It consists of a hexagonal structure with attached Corinthian half-columns capped by an architrave with Ionic dentils, height 1.30 m., diameter 0.70 m. According to G.M.A. Hanfmann, it dates ca. 200 C.E. A cast is on display in the Sardis Synagogue. Original parts are at Sardis camp and in the Manisa Museum.

written evidence alone cannot convey, the Sardis building and its contents illuminate a Judaism almost unknown before. And because these Jews lived as they did in a city so important to the Greco-Roman world, they have a claim on our attention unmatched by remote Qumran with its Dead Sea Scrolls, or by the border village of Dura, despite its spectacular art. This must be the single most important building left to us by the Jews of the ancient world.

Religion, Power and Politics:
Jewish Defeats by the Romans in Iconography and Josephus[1]

Douglas R. Edwards

Diaspora Judaism in parts of the Roman empire operated for the better part of a century (63 B.C.E.-81 C.E.)[2] within an environment in which Roman victories over Judaea helped further the prestige and power of Roman leaders. In certain cases, even the iconography showed a degree of continuity as evident in the images commemorating the Flavian victory over the Jews in 70-71 C.E. and the defeat one hundred years earlier of the Hasmonaean Antigonus by C. Sosius, quaestor and later consul. Iconography displaying Jewish defeats boosted the power and prestige of Roman leaders up through the year 81 C.E. and provided evocative images that shaped and were shaped by the general and regional climate of the Roman world.[3]

The paper examines the role Jewish military defeats played in the acquisition and promotion of power and prestige among Roman leaders with special attention to the iconographic and rhetorical displays on coins, architecture and statuary of Sosius, the city of Aphrodisias in Asia Minor, and the Flavians. Such public and private displays provide important clues about the network of power in which the emperor and his subjects operated.[4] Analysis of iconographic and rhetorical presentations of victory over Judaea also provides a framework in which to evaluate how one of the newest members of the Diaspora, Josephus, dealt with an environment that moved Judaea's military defeats from their previous peripheral positions to become an integral part of public displays of Roman and more particularly Flavian power. Indeed, the subjects most often displayed in iconography generally parallel Josephus' own

---

1 The paper was made possible by generous grants from the University of Puget Sound and the National Endowment for the Humanities. It was completed during my tenure as Visiting Scholar at the Oxford Centre for Postgraduate Hebrew Studies (1990-1991), drawing on the excellent resources of the Ashmolaean Museum. My thanks to Martin Goodman, Fergus Millar, and Simon Price for valuable comments and advice on earlier versions of this paper and to Michael Crawford, C. J. Howgego, and Andrew Burnett who provided direction on aspects of the numismatics material. I, of course, must take responsibility for the final product.

2 By convention B.C.E. (="before the common era") is equivalent to B.C. and C.E. (="common era") to A.D.

3 Cf. P. Zanker, *The Power of Images in the Age of Augustus* trans. A. Shapiro (Ann Arbor: University of Michigan Press, 1988) and the review by A. Wallace-Hadrill, "Rome's Cultural Revolution," *JRS* 79 (1989):157-164 who recognizes the varied response that can attend such images.

4 See S. Price, *Rituals and Power: the Roman Imperial Cult in Asia Minor* (Cambridge U.P., 1984): 234-248; F. Millar, "State and Society: The Impact of Monarchy," ed. F. Millar, E. Segal, *Caesar Augustus: Seven Aspects* (Oxford: Clarendon Press, 1984):37-60.

summary of the significant events.[5] The study explores the "words, gestures, rituals and monuments" that express the "language of power" by Roman leaders and their affiliates and the Diaspora Jew, Josephus. Such visual and verbal language defines as well as reflects power.[6]

Roman Power and Jewish Defeats

The defeat of Judaea became a symbol for Roman leaders as early as 63 B.C.E. when Pompey placed Palestine under the tutelage of Roman rule. Pompey's defeat of the Jews was one of many victories celebrated in his triumph in Rome and furthered his power and prestige in both Rome and the defeated countries. Pliny mentions that Pompey placed fourteen bronze statues depicting nations around his theater in Rome, although their identity is not mentioned (NH 36.42).[7] A coin issued from Rome in 54 B.C.E. may be associated with Pompey's victories in the East (which included Judaea) or possibly with his agent Gabinius (57-55 B.C.E.) who defeated the Hasmonaean Alexander (plate 1).[8] The coin shows a supplicant Bacchius Judaeus (who is otherwise unknown), next to a camel extending the olive branch of peace.[9] The curule aedile Aulus Plautius who issued the coin associates Pompey's arrival in the East with the submission of military figures such as the unknown Bacchius Judaeus. Even so, as H. Hart notes, the event is probably 'incidental' from the Roman perspective.[10]

More explicit evidence comes from Cicero who used Pompey's defeat of the Jews to argue for his client Lucius Valerius Flaccus who while governing Asia between 62-61 B.C.E appropriated Jewish funds intended for the temple in Jerusalem. "Their armed resistance against Pompey was an affront to Roman rule and to the immortal gods as evidenced by its [Judaea's] conquest, payment of taxes, and slave status" (*Pro Flacco* 28.69). Even allowing for

---

5 "... how their descendants [Hasmonaeans], in their quarrel for the throne dragged the Romans and Pompey upon the scene; how Herod, son of Antipater, with the aid of Sosius, overthrew the Hasmonaean dynasty; of the revolt of the people, after Herod's death, when Augustus was Roman Emperor and Quintilius Varus provincial governor; of the outbreak of war in the twelfth year of Nero's principate ..." (*BJ* 1.19 (Loeb)).

6 A. Wallace-Hadrill, "Roman Arches and Greek Honours: The Language of Power at Rome," *Proceedings of the Cambridge Philological Society* 216 (New Series 36) (1990): 147.

7 Cf. Diodorus Siculus, *Bibliotheca Historia* 40.4; see R. Smith, "Simulacra Gentium: The Ethne from the Sebasteion at Aphrodisias," *JRS* 78 (1988): 72-74.

8 M. Crawford, *Roman Republican Coinage* (Cambridge University Press, 1974), volume I: 454-455; volume II: plate 52.7; H.A. Gruebner, *Coins of the Roman Republic in the British Museum* (hereafter *BMC Republic*) (London, 1910) I: 490, fn. 2; *BJ* 1.167ff.

9 H.St.J. Hart, "Judaea and Rome: The Official Commentary," *The Journal of Theological Studies*, (New Series III) (1952): 178-179; plate 2, #2.

10 H. Hart, "Judaea and Rome," *JTS* (1952): 179.

Cicero's rhetorical flourish in defending his client[11] the message is clear. The Jewish defeat legitimates and demonstrates Roman power.[12] Nevertheless, commentary on Jews much less their defeats for this period by extant contemporary Greek and Latin writers is small.[13] This may be an historical accident but more likely from the Roman perspective, the country's defeat was simply one among many and merited no more comment than any other defeated country on the periphery of the empire.

The next revolt proved more crucial certainly for Marc Antony and the quaestor or magistrate C. Sosius.[14] The Parthians had lent their support to several claimants of thrones in the East, including Antigonus, a Hasmonaean who sought and gained the throne of Israel (40-37 B.C.E.).[15] Sosius, then governor of Syria, backed Herod against Antigonus and after a lengthy and bloody battle succeeded in capturing Jerusalem in 37 B.C.E.[16] The battle was significant in that it helped consolidate Antony's position in the East at a time when he was vying for power with Octavian. It also provided an opportunity to display indirectly the power and prestige of Antony whose man Sosius celebrated a triumph in Rome, one of several by the Antonian faction in this period.[17] Again a Jewish defeat became the occasion for the display of the power and prestige of Roman leaders, in this case Sosius and indirectly Marc Antony (Dio Cassius 49.23.1-3).[18]

Iconography played an important role in the presentation of power by the Roman officials in the triumvirate. C. Sosius minted a bronze coin on the island Zacynthus commemorating his selection as imperator (plate 2).[19] The

---

11 Cf. M. Stern, *Greek and Latin Authors on Jews and Judaism*,I (Jerusalem, 1974):193-195.

12 Cf. Plutarch, *Vita Pompei* 45.1-2, 5.

13 M. Stern has the few relevant references in his *Greek and Latin Authors on Jews and Judaism*, I; cf. T. Rajak, "Was there a Roman charter for the Jews," *JRS* 74 (1984): 107-123.

14 For a summary of the literary sources on Sosius see Pauly-Wissowa, *Real-Encyclopaedia*, series 2, III (1929): 1176-1180.

15 E. Shürer, G. Vermes, F. Millar, *The History of the Jewish People in the Age of Jesus Christ (175 B.C.-A.D. 135)* I, (Edinburgh: T&T Clark, 1973): 281-286; for Sosius' consulship see A. Degrassi, "Fasti Consulares et Triumphales," Inscriptiones Italica 13.1 (1947): 510-511.

16 Ibid:252, 284; for a coin issue dedicated to M. Antony by C. Sosius as quaestor see *BMC Republic*, II: 504; III: plate 114, #5.

17 R. Syme, *The Roman Revolution* (Oxford: Claredon Press, 1952):241.

18 Cf. F. Shipley, "C. Sosius, his Coins, his Triumph, and His Temple of Apollo," in *Papers on Classical Subjects in Memory of J. M. Wulfing* (Washington University Studies, 1930): 73ff.

19 Gruebner, *BMC Republic* II: 508-509, fn.2; III: plate 114, #9; F. Shipley, "Building Operations in Rome," *Memoirs of the American Academy in Rome* 9 (1931):25-28; P. Gardner, "Zacynthus," *Numismatic Chronicle,*third series 5 (1885): 81-107, plate 5, #8; M. Bahrfeldt, "Provinziale Kupferprägung aus dem Ende der Römischen Republik: Sosius, Proculeius, Crassus," *Journal Intérnational D'Archeologie Numismatique* 11 (1908): 216-222; plate 13, #3,4.

obverse shows Antony's head, with whom Sosius sought to associate (and derive) his power and prestige.[20] The reverse of the coin depicts a military trophy with two captives at its base. To the right of the trophy sits a female figure symbolizing Judaea with her head resting on her hand; to the left sits a male captive, apparently nude, perhaps symbolizing Antigonus. The image though probably not the coin itself served as the prototype for one of the Flavian Judaea Capta coin series.[21] The words C. Sosius *IMP(erator)* on the reverse and Antony's portrait on the obverse establish Sosius' association with Antony and with the Jewish defeat.[22] The coin is found on the island of Zacynthus but does not appear to have had wide circulation beyond it.[23] Nevertheless, the island, just west of the southern portion of Greece, was an important and strategic trading center (especially with Sicily) and a military base so that the range of Sosius' display of power, if not the coin itself, no doubt went beyond the confines of the island.[24] The coin certainly bolstered Sosius' local prestige and probably played a minor role in the increasing competition of visual and architectural displays of power between Antony and Octavian and their respective advocates.[25]

Sosius' celebration of his triumph in Rome no doubt displayed more explicitly the integration of his power with the Jewish defeat. The degree and date of Sosius' exhibition of power in Rome, however, remains a matter of debate. Initially some argued that Sosius refounded a temple to Apollo, located at a strategic section in the Campus Martius, as part of the celebration of his triumph in Rome.[26] If the temple is dated prior to 31 B.C.E., as Shipley argues,

20 Cf. F. Millar, "Triumvirate and Principate," *JRS* 63 (1973): 62.

21 A close parallel to the Sosius' issue (*BMC Republic* III, plate 114; #9) can be found in an issue by Titus (plate 3). Both issues have a hooded woman on the left, a trophy in the middle, and a bound male seated on the right. See also T. Reinach, *Jewish Coins*, translated by Mary Hill (London: Lawrence and Bullen, 1903): 30; plate 3, #5; F. Madden, *Coins of the Jews* (London, 1903): 99, fn.3; D. Barag argues that the Sosius coin was too localized to serve as a prototype for the Judaea Capta series in "The Palestinian 'Judaea Capta' coins of Vespasian and Titus," *Numismatic Chronicle,* seventh series 18 (1978): 14-23. Hart suggests that both series imitate an earlier coin of Caesar (54-47 B.C.E.) that celebrates his victory over the Gauls; "Judaea and Rome," *JTS* (1952): 180.

22 H. Gruebner, *BMC Republic* III: plate 114, #9; cf. *CIL* 9.4855.

23 D. Barag, *Numismatic Chronicle* 18 (1978): 18-19, fn. 21.

24 M. Grant, *From Imperium to Auctoritas: A Historical Study of AES Coinage in the Roman Empire 49 B.C.-A.D.14* (Cambridge University Press, 1946): 393; Gruebner, *BMC Republic* II: 504, fn. 1.

25 M. Grant, *From Imperium to Auctoritas*: 40-41.

26 P. Zanker, *The Power of Images in the Age of Augustus*, translated by A. Shapiro (The University of Michigan Press, 1988): 66-67; E. Nash, *Pictorial Dictionary of Ancient Rome*, volume (continued...)

Sosius associates Apollo with the Jewish defeat, not surprising since the deity also appears on another coin celebrating Sosius' appointment as Consul designate (around 37 B.C.E.) (plate 4).[27] Sosius' interest in archaizing, that is reclaiming older religious traditions, which is clearly evident in one of his coin issues would be a factor as well if he refounded the Apollo temple.[28] Thus, it is argued, Sosius as a friend of Antony countered Octavian's own archaizing efforts, most notably his dedication of an Apollo temple on the Palatine in 36 B.C.E.[29] Apollo, in fact, was the protecting deity of Octavian so Sosius' intention to rehabilitate the ancient temple of Apollo would have significant if not ominous overtones.[30] Further, the political and religious overtones were obvious if, as Shipley argues, the temple served as the senate meeting house, holding an impressive array of statuary that included a wooden statue of Apollo dedicated by Sosius.[31] From this perspective, therefore, a marble frieze found in the interior of the temple showing part of a triumphal procession with two bound captives on either side of a trophy displays Jews in Sosius' triumph (plate 5).[32] Thus, Shipley concludes that the temple and its iconography reflect "'jockeying for position' between the friends of Octavian and the agents of Antony."[33]

26(...continued)
I: 28-29; F. Shipley, *MAAR* 9 (1931): 25-28. For more recent discussion of the finds associated with the temple see E. La Rocca, "Der Apollo-Sosianus," and A Viscogliosi, "Die Architektur-Decoration der cella des Apollo-Sosianus-Tempels," in *Kaiser Augustus und die Verlorene Republik* (Berlin, 1988): 121-136; 136-148; E. La Rocca, *Amazzonomachia: Le Sculture frontonali del tempio di Apollo Sosiano* (Rome: DeLuca, 1985).

27 Zacynthus had a long association with the cult of Apollo: P. Gardner, "Zacynthus," *Numismatic Chronicle* third series 5 (1885): 83-92; Gruebner, *BMC Republic* II: 524.

28 Gruebner, *BMC Republic* I: 524. Greek prototypes found in P. Gardner, *Catalogue of Greek Coins. Peloponnesus* (London, 1887): 94-97 and plate xix, #17,23.

29 F. Shipley, "Building Operations in Rome," *MAAR* 9 (1931): 27, f.n. 3; for the temple on the Palatine as well as description of the Apollo temple on the Campus Martius see E. Simon, *Augustus: Kunst und Leben in Rom um die Zeitenwende* (Munich, 1986): 104-109. See also P. Zanker, "Klassizismus und Archaismus. Zur Formensprache der neuen Kultur," *Kaiser Augustus und die Verlorene Republik* (1988): 622-635; for a recent discussion of Augustus' promotion of himself as the son of Apollo see F. Kleiner, "The Arch in Honor of C. Octavius and the Fathers of Augustus," *Historia* 37.3 (1988): 347-357.

30 R. Syme, *The Roman Revolution*: 241.

31 Cf. Pliny, *NH* 13.53; 36.28; Shipley, *MAAR* 9 (1931): 28.

32 F. Shipley, *MAAR* 9: 25-28; I. S. Ryberg, "Rites of the State Religion in Roman Art," *MAAR* 22 (1955): 144-146, plate 51; E. Nash, *Pictorial Dictionary of Ancient Rome*, I (London, 1961): 28.

33 F. Shipley, *MAAR* 9: 27, fn 3.

Recent studies now question a pre-31 B.C.E. date for the temple of Apollo.[34] Additional excavations suggest that the style of the temple better reflects the period between 30-20 B.C.E.; thus, its iconography may refer to one of Augustus' triple triumphs in 29 B.C.E. (perhaps over Dalmatia, at Actium, or over Egypt).[35] Further, the dress and appearance of the captives on the frieze may indicate one of the northern barbarian tribes defeated by Augustus[36] although this is not conclusive. The evidence for the temple's provenance and its iconography, therefore, remains ambiguous at best with the evidence leaning against association with Sosius' triumph. Despite the uncertainty surrounding the temple of Apollo Sosianus, the coinage of Sosius and his celebration of a triumph over the Jews [EX IUDAEA] in Rome[37] exploits the defeat of the Jews and demonstrates his power and prestige at a critical time for the nascent Roman empire, the struggle between Octavian and Antony.[38]

Sosius' victory had yet another part to play in the portrayal of Roman power albeit a minor one as the Fasti Triumphales Capitolini inscription indicates (plate 6).[39] The inscription consisted of a long list of triumphs beginning with the ancestral founder Romulus (plate 7) that was prominently displayed on an Augustan arch built in 29 B.C.E. (plate 8) or an arch built in 19 B.C.E. celebrating the return of lost Roman standards from the Parthians.[40] In either case, the list, which included Sosius' EX IUDAEA displayed prominently and publicly a succession of Roman triumphs moving from Romulus himself to Augustus, who appeared as "the latest—and greatest—of a long line

---

34 E.g. E. La Rocca, *Amazzonomachia. Le sculture frontoniali del tempio di Apollo Sosiano* (Rome, 1985) and the relevant articles in *Kaiser Augustus and die Verlorene Republik* (1988).

35 E.g. P. Gros, *Aurea Temple: Recherches sur L'Architecture Religieuse de Rom a L'Epoque D'Augusta* (Rome, 1976): 188, 211.

36 E.g. P. Zanker, *The Power of Images in the Age of Augustus*: 70; E. La Rocca argues that the frieze celebrates not Sosius' triumph but Octavian's over the northern tribes in "Der Apollo-Sosianus-Tempel": 125; cf. P. Zanker, op. cit.: 70 who suggests Illyria (not mentioned in his English edition).

37 *CIL* I.2 (1893): 50, 70.

38 The coinage clearly demonstrates this power struggle between Antony and Octavian as M.H. Crawford shows in *Roman Republican Coinage*, II (Cambridge: Cambridge University Press, 1974): 742-744.

39 "*C. SOSIUS. C.f. T.N. PROCOS . EX IUDAEA. AN.DCCXIX III. NONAS . SEPTEMBR*" in *Inscriptions Italiae* 13.1 (1947): 86- 87, line 34; cf. pp. 342-343.

40 For a recent discussion of the problems involved with identifying these arches and the relation of the fasti or lists see F. Kleiner, "The Study of Roman triumphal and honorary arches 50 years after Kahler," *Journal of Roman Archaeology* 2 (1989): 195-206; see also E. Kunzl, *Der römische Triumph: Siegesfeiern im antiken Rom* (Munich: C. H. Beck, 1988): 52-60.

of distinguished men who had brought honor and glory to the Republic"[41] (plate 9). It would not be the last time that a Jewish defeat was incorporated by Roman officials or their affiliates as part of a visual and verbal rhetoric of power.[42]

Josephus portrays an Augustus well known for his benefactions and tolerance toward the Jews (cf. Apion 2.37, 61-62; Ant. 19.283), a portrait no doubt rosier than Augustus' actual response.[43] Judaea played a part in at least two defeats associated with the reign of Augustus, the first his victory over Antony, which included the defeat or at least the return to the fold of the Jews,[44] and the second the quelling of a revolt in Judaea by Varus after the death of Herod in 4 B.C.E (cf. Jos., Ant. 17.273-285).[45] The revolt of 4 B.C.E. was substantial and, according to Josephus, occupied three legions from Syria, the entire force (Ant. 17.286). The Sebasteion or imperial cult complex at Aphrodisias in Asia Minor shows how one group in the Greek East took advantage of a Jewish defeat by Rome (plate 10). The Sebasteion was apparently begun during the reign of Tiberius and additions occurred into the reign of Nero.[46] Several dedications to 'Aphrodite, Theoi Sebastoi, and the Demos' by the two Aphrodisian families who sponsored the complex establish the framework in which to understand the complex.[47]

Of particular interest are the ethne bases and reliefs, which include a base for ETHNOUS IOUDAION (plate 11). The ethne series include areas that Augustus had either defeated, defeated and added to his empire, or brought back to the empire.[48] As persons entered through a magnificent propylon on the west, they would see a long courtyard bounded on the north and south sides by two storied porticoes that led to an imperial temple serving the cult

---

41 F. Kleiner, The Arch of Nero: A Study of the Roman Honary Arch Before and Under Nero (Rome: Giorgi Bretschneides, 1985): 27.

42 Cf. S. Price, Rituals and Power: 248.

43 See T. Rajak, "Was there a Roman Charter for the Jews?" JRS 74 (1984): 115.

44 J. Reynolds, "Further information on Imperial cult at Aphrodisias," Studii Clasice 24 (1986): 116 argues for this defeat as the reason for Judaea's inclusion in an ethne series found at Aphrodisias.

45 R. Smith suggests a third possibility, the establishment of the province of Judaea under direct control of Roman officials in 6 C.E. JRS 78 (1988): 58.

46 R. Smith, "Myth and allegory in the Sebasteion," in C. Rouche and K. Erim (eds.) Aphrodisias Papers: Recent work on Architecture and Sculpture (Ann Arbor, MI, 1990): 89.

47 See R. Smith, JRS 78 (1988): 51.

48 R. Smith, JRS 78 (1988): 59; cf. J. Reynolds, "Further Information on Imperial Cult at Aphrodisias" Studii Clasice 24 (1986): 115-116 who argues that they all represent Augustan victories.

of Aphrodite and the imperial family.[49] At the monumental gateway, the visitor first encountered a series of sculptures that included a number of Julio-Claudians as well as Aeneas and Aphrodite Prometor (=Venus Gentrix), images that clearly connected the Aphrodisian Aphrodite with the Imperial family.[50] Large relief panels between the columns of the upper two stories of the north and south porticoes presented a visual display of Roman victories and power drawing often on Greek mythology and images.[51]

The South portico had emperors and gods in the upper story and scenes from Greek mythology directly below, while the north portico had allegories and emperors in the upper story with the ethne reliefs in the second story.[52] The south portico emphasizes the victory of the emperors, their divinity and their association with the gods while the upper row of the north portico displays an "empire without end, imperial conquest by land and sea, night and day."[53] There seems little question that the ethne figures on the reliefs directly below, which included one for the Judaeans,[54] display overtones of conquest and capture.[55]

The Sebasteion presents the subjection of Judaea along with as many as forty-four other countries in the series[56] amidst potent displays of imperial and divine power that illustrate the extent of Roman power across the *oikoumene*.[57] Local elites among the Aphrodisians sought and effectively managed to associate the power of their city goddess, Aphrodite, with Augustus and the Julio-Claudian line.[58] The defeat of Judaea along with other ethne provided

---

49 R. Smith has a fine reconstruction of this complex in *JRS* 77 (1987): 93-95 (esp. figure 3, p. 94) (plate 10).

50 R. Smith, *JRS* 77 (1987): 95; J. Reynolds, *Aprhodisias and Rome* (1982): 182-183.

51 R. Smith, *JRS* 77 (1987): 98.

52 R. Smith, *JRS* 78 (1988): 51 and 53, figure 3, which reconstructs the placement of one *ethnos*.

53 R. Smith, *JRS* 78 (1987): 96.

54 R. Smith *JRS* 78 (1988): 52, 55, 57; plate 8.5; R. Smith, "The Imperial Reliefs from the Sebasteion at Aphrodisias," JRS 77 (1987): 90; J. Reynolds, "Further Information on Imperial Cult at Aphrodisias," *Studii Clasice* 24 (1986): 111.

55 R. Smith, *JRS* 78 (1988): 58; *JRS* 77 (1987):95-96; J. Reynolds,"New evidence for the imperial cult in Julio- Claudian Aphrodisias," ZPE 43 (1981): 326-327.

56 R. Smith, *JRS* 77 (1987): 96.

57 R. Smith suggests that the inspiration and even the pattern for the various ethne may have come from Augustus' *Porticus ad Nationes*, which displayed a series of people in the empire; "Myth and Allegory in the Sebasteion," *Aphrodisias Papers* (1990): 92; see also *JRS* 77 (1987): 96.

58 As evidenced repeatedly in the material found associated with the walls of the theater at Aphrodisias; see J. Reynolds, *Aphrodisias and Rome JRS Monographs* 1 (1982): 78- 80; 91, 109,

(continued...)

an opportunity for one small town in Asia Minor to promote Roman power and victories[59] and in the process symbiotically bolster the prestige of their community.[60] The clearest association of Jewish defeat with Roman power and prestige, of course, comes from the Flavians.[61] Private and public iconographic displays occurred in a variety of forms, most notably the *Judaea Capta* coins,[62] the arches of Titus,[63] the arch to Isis (*ARCUS AD ISIS*),[64] and the Olympia[65] and Sabratha imperial sculptures.[66] Unlike earlier periods, however, when the Jewish defeats represented one among many groups defeated by the Romans,[67] the Flavian propaganda program through the reign of Titus drew almost exclusively on the Jewish defeat.

58(...continued)
113, 182-183; op. cit., "Further information on Imperial Cult at Aphrodisias," 113-114; D. Edwards, "Chariton's Chaereas and Callirhoe: Religions and Politics Do Mix," in K. Richards (ed.) *Society of Biblical Literature 1985 Seminar Papers* (Atlanta, Ga.:Scholars Press, 1985): 175-181.

59 Paralleling the Romans own activity; see E. Gruen, "Augustus and the Ideology of War and Peace," in R. Winkes (ed) *The Age of Augustus 1982 Archeologia Transatlantica* 5 (Louvain and Providence, RI, 1986): 51-72.

60 S. Price, *Rituals and Power*: 206; cf. R. Smith, *JRS* 78 (1988): 77; J. Reynolds, "Further information on Imperial Cult at Aphrodisas," *Studii Clasice* (1986): 116.

61 H. Hart, "Judaea and Rome," *JTS* (1952): 172-198.

62 For excellent depictions of the coins see *BMC Rome* II: plates 1, 2, 10-13, 18-20, 23-26, 30, 32, 33, 36, 37, 39, 40, 42, 48, 57; F. Madden, *History of Jewish Coinage and of Money in the Old and New Testament* (London, 1864): 183-197 and Hart, *JTS* (1952): 172-198 (with plates).

63 M. Pfanner, *Der Titusbogen Beiträge zur Erschliessung hellenistischer und Kaiserzeitlicher skulptor und Architector*, Band 2 (Mainz: 1983); E. Nash Pictorial Dictionary of Ancient Rome volume I : 133-135.

64 See F. Castagnoli, "Gli Edifici Rappresentati in un Rilievo del Sepolcro degli Haterii," *Bullettino della Commissione Archeologica Communale di Roma* 69 (1941): 59-69, esp. plate 2.

65 S. Stone, "The Imperial Sculptural Group in the Metroon at Olympia," *Mitteilungen des Deutschen Archaeologischen Instituts Athenische Abteilung* 100 (1985): 378-391; K. Stemmer, *Untersuchungen zur Typologie, Chronologie und Ikonographie der Panzerstatuen* (Berlin, 1978): 33, plate 17, #4.

66 K. Stemmer contains the best photos; op. cit.: 62, plates 38.1-2; for a discussion of the finds see G. Caputo, "Sculture dallo scavo a sud del Foro di Sabratha, 1940- 1942)," *Quaderni di Archeologia della Libia* 1 (1950): 7-28 (esp. 16-17; plate IV a & b; cf. H. Niemeyer, *Studien zur Statuarischen Darstellung der Röemischen Kaiser* 7 (Berlin, 1968): 93-94; no. 40; pl. 14, 1; H. Hart, "Judaea and Rome," *JTS* (1952): plates II, IV.

67 Smith places the number of possibilities that could be selected for inclusion in the Sebasteion in the low hundreds, *JRS* 78 (1988): 74; cf. H. Hart, "Judaea and Rome," who notes that dealings with Judaea were not "front line news." *JTS* (1952): 180). In short, the Jewish experience was not unique. Other groups' defeats served to bolster the power and prestige of particular emperors (e.g. Claudius over Britannia and Nero over Armenia).

Common was the minting of the *Judaea Capta* coin series, which was produced in large amounts in commemorative gold, silver and bronze denominations in major imperial mints and local mints across the Roman empire (including Rome, Spain, Bithynia, Syria, Caesarea, and Gaul).[68] The coin represents the message of the Flavians in forceful tones.[69] While other types of iconography had a geographically limited space, these coins were spread throughout the empire and minted at various times for over twelve years (70-81 C.E.) reaching nearly every level of society.[70] The coins indicate that the disastrous defeat of the Jews in Judaea and their subsequent captivity occurred because of the might of the Flavians, most particularly Vespasian and Titus.[71] The coins have a variety of presentations.[72] On the obverse is generally a large portrait head of the Emperor, mostly Vespasian and, to a lesser extent, Titus. On the reverse one commonly finds the depiction of a woman (Judaea) sitting or standing next to a palm tree, now the symbol in the Roman empire for the Jewish nation. Often included are Vespasian or Titus in military garb standing over the sitting female figure (plate 12); sometimes a male Jewish soldier with hands bound behind his back accompanies the defeated Judaea (plate 13). Several coin types have a victory signing a shield against a palm tree either with or without a bound captive (plate 14). One unusual type has the emperor holding a small Nike in his palm with a kneeling man and a woman appealing to him (plate 15).[73] The iconography on the various coin issues reflects a similar message. The head of the emperor on the obverse symbolizes where the central authority of the state rests, the emperor Vespasian (and later Titus).[74] The reverse displaying the Jewish defeat emphasiz-

---

68 Y. Meshorer, *Ancient Jewish Coinage*, volume II (Jerusalem: Amphora Books, 1982): 191; H. Hart, "Judaea and Rome" *JTS* (1952): 184; Y. Meshorer, "Notes on 'Judaea Capta' Coins," *Israel Numismatic Bulletin* 3-4 (1962): 98; H. Brin, "Note on Rare Judaea Capta Sestertius," *Israel Numismatic Journal* 8 (1984-85): 12-13.

69 Vitellius, however, first used the Jewish defeat on his coins. See C. Sutherland, *Roman History and Coinage 44 B.C.-A.D. 69* (Oxford: Clarendon Press, 1987): 121-123; Ibid., *The Roman Imperial Coinage*, volume I (London: Spink, 1984): 277, plate 32, #169; H. Hart, "Judaea and Rome" *JTS* (1952): plate 2, #1.

70 H. Hart, "Judaea and Rome" *JTS* (1952): 174-186.

71 Cf. M. Goodman, *The Ruling Class of Judaea: The Origins of the Jewish Revolt Against Rome A.D. 66-70* (Cambridge University Press, 1987): 235.

72 Y. Meshorer lists the major types in *Ancient Jewish Coinage*, volume II (1982): 192.

73 Conveniently summarized and displayed by H. Hart, "Judaea and Rome," *JTS* (1952): 184-191; plates II-IV.

74 A. Wallace-Hadrill argues persuasively that the obverse and reverse of coins must be seen in tandem and together represent a significant message to the viewers, *JRS* 76 (1986): 66-87; contra M. Crawford, "Roman imperial coin types and the formation of public opinion," in C.

(continued...)

es the power of the Flavian line during the rule of Vespasian and later Titus. These coins, often issued not by the emperor but rather by those who wished to associate with his imperial authority, reaffirm for the viewer that power resides with the Flavians and those associated with him. In short, the issuing authority draws on "value-laden symbols that can command assent in the society within which they are to circulate."[75] The Jewish defeat served as a 'value-laden symbol' that clearly filtered into the empire at large.[76]

Additional evidence comes from two cuirassed figures, plausibly identified with Vespasian and Titus, which formed part of an imperial sculptural group found in the Metroon at Olympia in Greece (plate 16).[77] One of the statues, presumably Vespasian, has at its feet a hooded female captive whom S. Stone persuasively argues is Jewish;[78] the display of the statue visibly associates the Jewish defeat with Flavian power. Even clearer is the famous sculpture of a cuirassed Vespasian found in Sabratha, Libya, the home of Flavia Domitilla, wife of Vespasian (plate 17).[79] The sculpture, found in the exedra of a basilica in the forum, shows on Vespasian's cuirass a victory signing a shield attached to a palm tree with a bound male Jewish captive to the right.[80] Such examples leave little doubt that the association of the Jewish defeat with Flavian power was "internalized and absorbed"[81] throughout a significant portion of the Roman empire, especially among local elite classes who sponsored such displays.

74(...continued)
Brooke, I. Stewart, J. Pollard, T. Volk, *Studies in Numismatic Method Presented to Philip Grierson* (Cambridge University Press, 1983) who does not see coin iconography as a "massive effort to mould public opinion" (p. 59), especially the reverse which he feels is extraneous.

75 A. Wallace-Hadrill, "Image and Authority in the Coinage of Augustus," *JRS* 76 (1986): 69-70.

76 The Caesarean mint certainly reflects this. Regional differences, however, were bound to influence the message. As Meshorer argues, the Caesarean mint wrote the legend in Greek (*IOUDIAS EALOKUIAS* = 'captured Judaea') and deleted some of the symbols offensive to Jewish sensibilities (e.g. the half naked captives). The stress, he argues, falls on Roman victory rather than the Jewish defeat (*Ancient Jewish Coins*, volume II (1982): 75-76, 78, 194. The distinction seems finer than that made in antiquity (especially when the rhetorical language stresses 'captured Judaea' rather than victorius Rome). Nevertheless, the coins stress the power and prestige of the Flavians, especially Titus who figures prominently on a large number of the coin issues.

77 S. Stone, "The Imperial Sculptural Group in the Metroon at Olympia," *MDAIA* 100 (1985): 389-390; fn. 68-75.

78 S. Stone: 389; see plate 84.2.

79 G. Caputo, *Quaderni di Archeologia della Libia* 1 (1950): 7-28.

80 K. Stemmer: 62; Niemeyer: 93; C. Vermeule III, "Hellenistic and Roman Cuirassed Statues," *Berytus* 13 (1959): 44.

81 Cf. A. Wallace-Hadrill, "Rome's Cultural Revolution," *JRS* 79 (1989): 159.

The images of imperial power and Jewish defeat become even more explicit as one goes to the core of the empire, Rome. The Flavians used the Judaea Capta imagery on the arch of Isis (*ARCUS AD ISIS*), probably built to
celebrate their triumph (plate 18).[82] Here the connection between religion
and the triumph becomes explicit. The tomb of the Haterii, builders of many
of the Flavian projects, which depicts the Isis arch has at the top of the arch
a palm tree with a bound captive, a clear reference to the victory over Judaea.[83] Josephus' describes the Flavians spending the night in the temple of
Isis and starting their triumph from there, indicating that the Flavians associated their victory in some manner with the Isis cult (*BJ* 7.132-157). Indeed, the
Isis cult played an important role through most of the Flavian rule, especially
during the time of Domitian, a point that created problems for Martial (2.14.
7-8; 11.47.3-4) and Juvenal, *Sat.* 6.488-89; 9.22-23).[84]

The arch of Titus that celebrated his triumph (no longer standing) was
located next to the Circus Maximus. It occupied a prominent position as can
be seen from a coin of Trajan (plate 19).[85] An inscription apparently associated with the arch proclaims Titus's victory over the Jews and his destruction
of Jerusalem.[86] Such visual and verbal associations of imperial power and
prestige with the Jewish defeat would be difficult to miss.

The second arch of Titus currently standing on the Via Sacra reflects in
many respects the culmination of the public iconographic posture of the Flavians toward the Jewish defeat (plate 20). Built by Domitian sometime after the
death of Titus in 81 C.E. it commemorates the virtue, honor, and victory of
Titus his brother.[87] The arch effectively symbolizes the end of one regime
(Vespasian/Titus) and the beginning of another, Domitian's, who had little

---

82 F.S. Kleiner, "The Study of Roman Triumphal and honorary arches 50 years after Kaeh-
ler," *Journal of Roman Archaeology* 2 (1989): 197; E. Nash, *Pictorial Dictionary of Ancient Rome*,
volume I:18-19.

83 F. Castagnoli, *Bullettino della Commissione Archeologica Communale di Roma* 69 (1941):
59-69.

84 S. Heyob, *The Cult of Isis among Women in the Graeco-Roman World* (Leiden: E.J. Brill,
1975): 23-28; 112-118; W. Van Unnik, "Flavius Josephus and the Mysteries," ed. M. Vermaseren,
Studies in Hellenistic Religions (Leiden: E. J. Brill, 1979): 254-258. A Vespasian coin depicts the
facade of the Isis temple on the Campius Martius prior to its destruction by fire in 80 C.E. See
A. Roullet, *The Egyptianizing Monuments of Imperial Rome* (Leiden: E.J. Brill, 1972): 30; plate
15.

85 H. Hart, "Judaea and Rome," *JTS* (1952): plate IV, #7.

86 *CIL* 6.944; H. Newton, "Epigraphical Evidence for the Reigns of Vespasian and Titus,"
Cornell Studies in Classical Philology 16 (1901): 9-14.

87 M. Pfanner, *Der Titusbogen*: 103; B. Jones, *The Emperor Titus*: 156; N. Hannestad, *Roman
Art and Imperial Policy* (Aarhus University Press, 1986): 126.

direct involvement in the Jewish defeat or the *Judaea Capta* Series.[88] Domitian, in fact, minted a Germania Capta coin series that replaced the *Judaea Capta* coins, while still using some of the same iconographic symbols (plate 21).[89] Further, the *Judaea Capta* coins appear to be discontinued around 81 C.E.[90] Perhaps as some argue Josephus and Jews in general found increased hostility by Roman rulers during Domitian's reign.[91] To be sure Domitian established stringent if not oppressive collection practices for the *Fiscus Judaicus*, practices that were changed under Nerva.[92] Such activities by Domitian, however, probably had little additional impact on those who professed their Jewish heritage and religion.[93]

In summary, Jewish defeats at the hands of the Romans provided ample grist for Greek and Roman iconographic and rhetorical displays from Pompey through the Flavians. Displays promoting Pompey's, C.Sosius/Antony's, and Augustan' victories placed the Jewish defeat amidst many others. The defeat of the Jewish nation intertwined with the presentation of Roman power, particular Roman leaders, and those who wished to associate with their power as each consolidated their local, regional or international power base in a turbulent and formative period of the Roman empire. Even a Greek city such as Aphrodisias of Caria entered with its iconographic contribution.

In the Flavian period, however, the defeat of Judaea took on much greater significance as it became one of the primary symbols for Flavian power and prestige under Vespasian and Titus, unlike the earlier presentations, which were often local or diluted by their association with other defeats at the hands of the Romans.[94] To be sure Philo and Josephus indicate that tension existed between Greeks and Jews and even between Jews and the Romans in the per-

---

88 Y. Meshorer, *Ancient Jewish Coins*, volume II (1982): 197.

89 For coin evidence see R. A. G. Carson, *Coins of the Roman Empire* (London: Routledge, 1990): 31-33. The *Germania Capta* series has a seated woman on the left and a male bound captive on the right of a trophy. Domitian appears to be redefining the iconography for his own reign. *BMC Rome* II: plates 70, #8; 72, #8; 75, #4; 76, #6.

90 Y. Meshorer, *Ancient Jewish Coinage*, volume II (1982): 190. An exception appears to be a one-time issue commemorating the twentieth anniversary of Titus' victory by Agrippa II in 89/90 C.E. (Y. Meshorer, *Ancient Jewish Coinage*, volume II (1982): 89).

91 Margaret H. Williams, "Domitian, The Jews and the 'Judaizers'—A Simple Matter of Cupitas and Maiestas?" *Historia* 39.2 (1990): 196-211; S. Cohen, *Josephus in Galilee and Rome: HisVita and Development as a Historian* (Leiden: E.J. Brill, 1979): 236.

92 M. Goodman, "Nerva, The Fiscus Judaicus and Jewish Identity," *JRS* 79 (1989): 41-44.

93 See F. Millar, *Emperor in the Roman World* (London: Duckworth, 1977).

94 N. Hannestad, *Roman Art and Imperial Policy* (Aarhus University Press, 1986): 21. Hannestad calls the victory the "cornerstone of Flavian propaganda;" cf. Valerius Flaccus, *Argonautica* I.1- 20 and Silius Italicus, *Punica* 3.597-606 who glorify the Flavians by citing their victory over the Jews. See M. Stern, *Greek and Latin Authors*, I:502-506 for discussion.

iod between Augustus and the Flavians (e.g. Tiberius' expulsion of Jews and the Claudius edict).[95] But never had Jews as a nation and an ethnos had to deal with symbolism that singled out their defeat with consistent iconographic and rhetorical displays across the breadth of the Roman empire for the better part of twelve years.[96]

Josephus and the Jewish Defeats

When Josephus, now a Jew of the Diaspora, writes about the Jewish War toward the end of Titus' reign[97] he operates within a public environment that places his country in the uncomfortable position of a conquered people whose defeat coincided with a new house and family taking over the reins of power in the Empire. The Flavians needed a prime venue to display Flavian power and prestige and the defeat of Judaea provided it.

Josephus remained a member of the elite class and retained a connection to the land of Palestine by accepting property there from the Flavians (Vita 1-6; 422-423, 426, 429). Josephus does not respond directly to iconographic portrayals of the type discussed earlier (with the exception, of course, of his description of the Flavian triumph). There can be little doubt that he was aware of such images and the atmosphere they reflected (and fostered). This section can only take a brief look at how Josephus depicts the Jewish defeats displayed in the iconography discussed earlier. Nevertheless, it should become clear that Josephus as a member of the Jewish elite of the Diaspora redefined the nature of the power network in which the defeats were to be understood.[98]

In the period preceding Pompey, Josephus argues, the Judaean kings alone remained the sole friends and allies of Rome, a clear reference to Greeks, some whose ancestors, of course, had revolted in this period (*Apion* 2.134). When Rome does intervene in Judaean affairs, Pompey comes, Josephus argues, because of squabbles between the Hasmonaeans Hyrcanus and Aristobulus (*Ant.* 14.77). Moreover, Sosius' victory is viewed as a replay of the Pompey victory even to the point of the city of Jerusalem being captured on

---

95 E. M. Smallwood, *The Jews under Roman Rule* (Leiden: E.J. Brill, 1976); ibid., "Philo and Josephus as Historians of the Same Events," in *Josephus, Judaism, and Christianity* ed. L. Feldman and G. Hata (Leiden: E.J. Brill, 1987): 114-129.

96 With the death of Titus, however, the iconography of defeat against the Judaeans ceases. Hadrian portrays his victory over the Jews in the Bar Kochba rebellion in a much different vein iconographically. See the discussion in H. Hart, "Judaea and Rome," *JTS* (1952): 193-194.

97 S. Cohen, *Josephus in Galilee and Rome*: 90; see the summary with bibliography in P. Bilde, *Flavius Josephus between Jerusalem and Rome* (Sheffield: JSOT Press, 1988).

98 I intend to examine Josephus more thoroughly in a book that explores the role of religion and power among local elites and their affiliates in the Greek East.

the same day (*Ant.* 14.487). And the revolt against Augustus and Varus, which occurred after the death of Herod, was led by *lestai* or brigands (*Ant.* 14.285). In short, the victories of Pompey, Sosius and Augustus came as a result of the nation's sins against God and internecine warfare between various factions in Judaea and do not reflect a general tendency on the part of Jews to rebel against Rome (*BJ* 5.398-401; 407-409). Josephus' "rhetoric of power" focuses on the abrogation of responsibility by the leadership in losing power rather than on the Roman intervention in gaining it. As I argue elsewhere, for Josephus the ultimate power broker in the conflict is the Jewish God.[99] The apostasy of the Jews who lead the revolt cause the necessary intervention of the Romans, the abandonment of the nation by God, and the disastrous defeat. Even Titus acknowledges that the Jewish God aided the Roman victory (*BJ* 6.39-41; 411).[100]

When Josephus writes Antiquities the Roman iconographic program, at least, has changed if not the hostility still evident in Greek and Latin authors.[101] Josephus' portrait of the Isis cult in Antiquities contrasts sharply with the positive association it has in the Flavian iconography.[102] Josephus paints a distinctly unflattering portrait of the Isis cult during the reign of Tiberius. Josephus indicates the basically perverse nature of some of its important practitioners, the temple priests as they connive to aid in the seduction of Paulina, a Roman matron (18.65-80).[103] The account stresses the corruption (and destruction) of a significant cult with whom the Flavians associate their victory and power. In effect, Josephus' verbal portrait displays a cult that disrupts the social and cultural fabric of Tiberian society. A Flavian public would be hard pressed to miss the relevance of this episode for their own

99 D. Edwards, "Surviving the Web of Roman Power: Religion and Politics in the Acts of the Apostles, Josephus, and Chariton's Chaereas and Callirhoe," in Loveday Alexander (ed), *The Image of Rome in Literature of the Late Antiquity* (tentative title) (JSOT Press, forthcoming).

100 Cf. *BJ* 2.390; 5.377-378; 390; 5.412. See M. Stern, "Josephus and the Roman Empire," in L. Feldman, G. Hata (eds.) *Josephus, Judaism, and Christianity* (Detroit: Wayne State University Press, 1987): 76-77; N.R.M. de Lange, "Jewish Attitudes to the Roman Empire," in P.D. Garnsey and C.R. Whittaker (eds.) *Imperialism in the Ancient World* (London: Cambridge University Press, 1978): 263-264.

101 See M. Stern, *Greek and Latin Authors* for the relevant passages.

102 Josephus describes the Flavian triumph beginning at the Isis temple on the Campus Martius. The reader, however, learns as much about the wealth of the Jewish nation as they do the prestige of the Roman leadership (*BJ* 7.132-157). In one sense Josephus elevates the power and prestige of the Jewish nation (an important issue for Josephus) and, by their defeat of the nation, the power of their conquerors, the Flavians.

103 H. Moehring, "The Persecution of the Jews and the Adherents of the Isis Cult at Rome, A.D. 19," *Novum Testamentum* 3 (1959):293-304; D. Edwards, "The Social, Religious, and Political Aspects of Costume in Josephus," in J. Sebesta (ed), *Roman Costume as a Historical Source* (tentative title) (University of Wisconsin Press, forthcoming).

period.[104] The portrait of Isis highlights the Jewish cult, a movement noted, according to Josephus, for its antiquity and sagacity, strong moral and ethical codes, and the superiority of its god.[105] The latter point is also made quite explicit in *BJ* in which the victory of the Romans occurs because of the rule of the Jewish God.[106] Both his *Bellum Judaicum* and *Antiquities* are meant to show clearly who runs the cosmic show.[107]

Josephus and no doubt other Jews of the Diaspora, especially those from or associated with the elite classes, interpreted their current condition within the larger framework of the Jewish God's plan. The Greek historians' vision of power, roundly condemned by Josephus (e.g. *BJ* 1.7-8; *Ant.* 1.5) has been supplanted, giving those who identify with Josephus' portrait a greater degree of power (even if psychological). It is within this cosmic framework that Josephus' conception of power and prestige must be understood. Josephus summarizes his position succinctly in his final work:

"I would therefore boldly maintain that we have introduced to the rest of the world a very large number of very beautiful ideas. What greater beauty than inviable piety? What higher justice than obedience to the laws? What more beneficial than to be in harmony with one another, to be prey neither to dissension in adversity, nor to arrogance and faction in prosperity; in war to despise death, in peace to devote oneself to crafts or agriculture; and to be convinced that everything in the whole universe is under the eye and direction of God?" (*Ap.* 2.134).

No clearer example of the 'language of power' that defines power as well as reflects it[108] could be given.

---

104 This becomes especially clear when compared to the account of Jewish skullduggery that immediately follows. In Rome, four Jews deceive Fulvia, another woman of high rank who had become a proselyte (*Antiquities* 18.81-84). When she discovers what happened, she has her husband report the incident to Tiberius, the emperor, just as Paulina had done with her husband. Tiberius held the entire Jewish community responsible and ordered them from Rome. In both cases corporate punishment was exacted. Yet, only in the case of the Jews, Josephus makes clear, do numerous Jews keep the Jewish law even on pain of punishment and recognize that the Roman law is proper and, on the whole, good. Further, only four persons not the entire Jewish population were responsible; (cf. Van Unnik, "Flavius Josephus and the Mysteries," in M. Vermaseran (ed.) *Studies in Hellenistic Religion* (E.J. Brill, 1979): 256-257).

105 Cf. R. McL. Wilson, "Jewish Literary Propaganda," in *Paganisme, Judaïsme, Christianisme Mélanges offerts à Marcel Simon* (Paris: E. de Boccard, 1978): 70.

106 D. Edwards, "Surviving the Web of Roman Power," in *The Image of Rome in Late Antiquity* (forthcoming); F. Bruce, "The Romans Through Jewish Eyes," in *Paganisme, Judaisme, Christianisme*: 11-12.

107 Cf. S. Cohen, *Josephus in Galilee and Rome*: 232-242.

108 A. Wallace-Hadrill, "Roman Arches and Greek Honours" *PCPS* 216 (1990): 147.

The importance of visual and verbal displays of power was not lost on either the Romans or Josephus. Each placed the ultimate rubric of power under traditions and powers (most notably particular divine ones) that demarcated their place in the Roman world. Jewish defeats played an important role in the conqueror's and conquered's assorted interplays between religion, power, and politics, a process that helped shape the fabric of the early Roman empire.

PLATES

1. Bacchius Judaeus coin. Ashmolaean Museum. (Cf. H. Hart, *JTS* (1952): plate 1, #2.
2. C. Sosius, imperator coin minted at Zacynthus. *BMC Republic* 3, plate 114.9 and H. Hart, *JTS* (1952): plate 1, #6. My coin is an enlarged version (2x) of the *BMC* specimen.
3. A Titus *Judaea Capta* issue. *BMC Rome* 2, plate 45. 4, 5.
4. Sosius coin celebrating his appointment as Consul designate with Apollo head on obverse. *BMC Republic*, p. 524. My photo from the British museum is previously unpublished.
5. Marble frieze from Apollo temple depicting two bound captives as part of a triumph. Inez Scott Ryberg, "Rites of the State Religion in Roman Art," *Memoirs of the American Academy in Rome* 22 (1955): plate 51, a and b. Obtain original photos from *Sopraintendenza all antichita*, Rome. *Museo dei Conservatori*.
6. Reconstruction of a pillar that contains an inscription from *Fasti Triumphales Capitonlini* showing Sosius' section. Take from *Inscriptiones Italiae* 13.1 (1947): plate 51 (Sosius is on group XL, the third line from the bottom).
7. First part of *Fasti Triumphales* inscription showing Romulus entry. Excellent example in E. Nash, *Pictorial Dictionary of Ancient Rome*, volume I. plate 103 (p. 101).
8. Reconstruction of the Augustan arch with placement of the triumph and consular inscriptions. Found in *Inscriptiones Italiae* 13.1 (1947): plate 9; see also E. Nash, *Pictorial Dictionary of Ancient Rome*, volume I: plate 102 (p. 100).
9. Reconstruction of arch of Augustus with placement of inscribed pillars. See *Inscriptiones Italiae* 13.1 (1947):
10. Proposed construction of Sebasteion. See *JRS* 77 (1987): 94, figure 3.
11. The base for *ETHNOUS IOUDAION*. See *JRS* 78 (1988): plate 8, #5.
12. *Judaea Capta* with woman sitting under palm tree. Found in *Royal Imperial Coins* from the Hunter Cabinet. Vespasian, plate 32, #36; cf. H. Hart, *JTS* (1952): plate 1, #17, 19; plate 3, #10-13.

13. Male Jewish soldier accompanying female Judaea. Found in *Royal Imperial Coins* from the Hunter Cabinet. Vespasian, plate 34, #90; cf. H. Hart *JTS* (1952): plate 3, #3, 4, 5, 6, 7.

14. Victory signing a shield against palm tree. Found in the *Royal Imperial Coins* from the Hunter Cabinet. Vespasian. plate 34, #98; cf. H. Hart, *JTS* (1952): plate 2, #2-3.

15. Emperor holding small *Nike* before kneeling man and a woman appealing to him. In *British Museum of Coins* in Rome, p. 147; cf. H. Hart, *JTS* (1952): plate 4, #? .

16. Cuirassed statue of Vespasian with hooded female captive at his feet from Olympia. S. Stone, "The Imperial Sculptural Group in the Metroon at Olympia," *Mitteilungen des Deutschen Archaologischen Instituts Athenische Abteilung* 100 (1985): plate 84, #2. For a negative contact the *Deutsches Archaologischen Instituten* at Athens (Olympia #2128).

17. Cuirassed statue of Vespasian from Sabratha, Libya. Klaus Stemmer, *Untersuchungen zur Typologie, Chronologie und Ikonographie der Panzerstatuen* (Berlin, 1978): plate 38, #1, 2.

18. *ARCUS AD ISIS* (arch of Isis) on tomb of the Haterii. F. Castagnoli, *Bullettino della Commissione Archeologica del Governatorato di Roma e Bullettino del Museo Dell'impero Romano* 69 (1941): plate II. For a negative contact the *Deutsches Archaologischen Instituts* in Rome.

19. Coin of Trajan showing the position of the arch of Titus (on the left side of the circus as you face the coin). *Royal Imperial Coinage* p. 54, #326; plate 12.326.

20. Two shots of the Titus arch. The first shows the east facade. The second shows the procession with the material from the temple. Michael Pfanner, *Der Titusbogen* (Mainz: Philipp von Zabern, 1983): plate 13; plate 54.

21. Two Domitianic coins. The first shows *Germania Capta*. The second a victory writing on a shield. *Royal Imperial Coinage, Domitian,* 53.120; 54.137

On The Meaning of The Term "Jew"
In Greco-Roman Inscriptions[1]

Ross S. Kraemer

The Greek terms 'Ιουδαῖος/'Ιουδαία and their Latin equivalents *Iudaeus/ Iudaea* have rarely posed serious translation problems for scholars.[2] Whether in masculine or feminine form, singular or plural, regardless of declension, these terms have usually been taken as straightforward indicators of Jews, at least when applied to individual persons.[3] Only recently A.T. Kraabel has suggested that these terms, uniformly translated "Jew" or "Jews," might have other significance, in particular as indicators of geographic origin, that is, "Judaean(s)."[4]

A careful look at the occurrence of these terms in Greek and Latin Jewish inscriptions suggests that rather than sustain only one uniform translation, *Ioudaia/Ioudaios* may have had a range of connotations. In this article I suggest that, in addition to Kraabel's interpretation of the term as a geographic indicator, it may also indicate pagan adherence to Judaism. In still other cases, the masculine and feminine singular may represent a proper name, but even in those cases, the use of the name may still evidence pagan attraction to Judaism.

The subject of pagan attraction to Judaism is a complicated one, as John Gager and others have demonstrated.[5] Ancient Christian writers found pagan

---

1 Editor's note: This article first appeared in *Harvard Theological Review* 82.1 (1989) 35-53.

2 For the sake of convenience, I will refer primarily to the Greek terms; in general, the reader may assume that general comments hold true for both Greek and Latin forms, unless I indicate otherwise. On the meaning of these terms, see Solomon Zeitlin, "The Names Hebrew, Jew and Israel: A Historical Study," *JQR* n.s. 43 (1952-53) 365-79. See also Peter J. Tomson, "The Names Israel and Jews in Ancient Judaism and in the New Testament," *Tijdschrift voor filosophie en theologie* 47 (1986)120-40.

3 Of course, *Ioudaia* has uniformly been translated "Judaea" when it occurs in a manifestly geographic context. For some examples of the assumptions behind the translation of these terms, see Jean-Baptiste Frey, "Inscriptions inédites des catacombs juives de Rome," *Rivista Archaeologia Cristiana* 7 (1930) 235-60. Frey distinguishes between "une indication de *race* et de *nationalité*" and "une indication de *religion*." See also H.Z. (J.W.) Hirschberg, A History of the Jews of North Africa, vol. 1: *From Antiquity to the Sixteenth Century* (Leiden: Brill, 1974), who assumes that in the North African inscriptions, the terms are simply ethnic appellations: "The authors of the inscriptions mostly did not try to conceal the religious and national identity of the buried. In comparatively many cases we find the ethnic appellation 'Jew' or 'Jewess'" (69).

4 A. Thomas Kraabel, "The Roman Diaspora: Six Questionable Assumptions," *JJS* 33 (1982) 445-64.

5 John G. Gager, *The Origins of Anti-Semitism: Attitudes Toward Judaism in Pagan and Christian Antiquity* (New York: Oxford University Press, 1983). The literature on the degrees of pagan attraction to Judaism in the Greco-Roman world, and the possible distinctions between God-fearers, pagan sympathizers, and "formal" converts is considerable. Kraabel has argued strongly

(continued...)

interest in Judaism virtually inexplicable after the advent of Christianity, since Christianity was supposed to supersede Judaism once and for all. Modern scholars have also developed a myopic view of the subject, one manifestation of which has been a tendency to talk about degrees of adherence to Judaism as a way of minimizing pagan (and even Christian) attraction to Jewish practices and beliefs. The whole debate about whether or not there were formal degrees of adherence to Judaism, as evidenced by the designation of some individuals as God-fearers, probably should be viewed in this light. When we distinguish between various degrees of adherence to Judaism in antiquity, what we often intend are distinctions of practice. But whether such distinctions have useful implications for the self-conceptions of the people who performed these practices, we simply do not know. When Philo chides those Jews who attend synagogue only on Yom Kippur, he may think they are not "good" Jews, but they may think otherwise. In our time, the parallel is significant.

The diversity among modern Jews is not about degrees of adherence to Judaism; it is about fundamentally different understandings about what it means to be Jewish. And I suspect this was true also in antiquity. Since I will look at inscriptions in which the evidence for adherence to Jewish practices (and beliefs, althoug¹ ·⁀ ;e are generally harder to document in inscriptions) may seem at odds with much scholarly appraisal of "good" or "orthodox" Jewish practices and beliefs in antiquity, and will suggest that these inscriptions may reflect the interest of non-Jews in Judaism, it is important to keep in mind that I have no commitment to a particular brand of normative Judaism in the Greco Roman period, and that I perceive Judaism in this time to have been extremely varied and diverse.⁶

That the obvious interpretation of the terms *Ioudaia/os* may not be sufficient quickly becomes apparent after even a cursory review of the patterns of usage in ancient inscriptions. Out of approximately 1700 extant Jewish inscrip-

---

5(...continued)
(above, n. 3) that the various phrases translated as God-fearers, *sebomenos/ē phoboumenos/ē theosebēs, metuens,* etc., cannot be construed as technical terms. See also A. Thomas Kraabel, "The Disappearance of the God-fearers," *Numen* 28 (1981) 113-26; idem, "Greeks, Jews, and Lutherans in the Middle Half of Acts," in George W.E. Nickelsburg and George MacRae, eds., *Christians Among Jews and Gentiles: Essays in Honor of Krister Stendahl on his Sixty-Fifth Birthday* (=HTR 79 [1986]) 147-57. Others have construed the evidence quite differently; see, e.g., John G. Gager, "Jews, Gentiles, and Synagogues in the Book of Acts," ibid., 91 -99, and Tom Finn, "The Godfearers Reconsidered," *CBQ* 47 (1985) 75-84. Additional bibliography can be found in all four articles. A newly published inscription from ancient Aphrodisias has been read by a number of scholars as the definitive evidence against Kraabel's interpretation, but there will doubtless be additional discussion. See Joyce M. Reynolds and Robert Tannenbaum, *Jews and God-fearers at Aphrodisias: Greek Inscriptions with Commentary* (Cambridge, England: Cambridge Philological Society, 1987).

6 I am indebted to Tom Kraabel for hammering away at me on this point!

tions, these terms occur in only thirty-four epitaphs and ten miscellaneous inscriptions.[7] They are absent altogether from the Greek donative synagogue inscriptions compiled by the noted Jewish epigrapher Baruch Lifshitz.[8] Obvi-

---

7 Given the haphazard state of Jewish inscriptions, there may be a few more in obscure publications which I have missed. I would appreciate hearing from anyone with additional references to individuals in inscriptions. My approximation of the number of Jewish inscriptions at 1700 is based on the numbering in *CIJ* (which gave 1539 inscriptions, but did not include certain geographic areas), taking into account those regions not included in Frey, together with new inscriptions. I have not attempted to count all the relevant inscriptions.

The majority of known Jewish inscriptions are collected in Jean-Baptiste Frey, ed., *Corpus of Jewish Inscriptions: Jewish Inscriptions from the Third Century B.C. to the Seventh Century A.D.*, vol. 1: *Europe* (New York: Ktav, 1975),with prolegomenon by Baruch Lifshitz, originally published as *Corpus Inscriptionum Judicarum* (Rome: Pontifical Institute of Christian Archaeology, 1936) in 2 vols. Vol. 1 covers Europe: vol. 2 (which has not been updated) covers Asia Minor, Syria, Judea, and Egypt. More recently, donative inscriptions were compiled by Baruch Lifshitz, *Donateurs et fondateurs dans les synagogues juives* (Paris: Gabalda, 1967).

The Roman inscriptions were revised and translated into English in an appendix to Harry J. Leon, *The Jews of Ancient Rome* (Philadelphia: Jewish Publication Society, 1966). A small number of additional Jewish inscriptions were published by Umberto M. Fasola, "Le due catacombe Ebraiche di Villa Torlonia," *Rivista di Archaeologia Cristiana* 52 (1972) 7-63.

The Jewish inscriptions from various towns in North Africa (Cirta, Cyrene, Tocra, etc.) were never compiled by Frey, who died before he could assemble the planned third volume of *CIJ*. Some of these are published in John Gray, "The Jewish Inscriptions in Greek and Hebrew at Tocra, Cyrene and Barce," in Allen Rowe, ed., *Cyrenaican Expedition of the University of Manchester, 1952* (Manchester: Manchester University Press, 1956), or in A. Fetron, "Inscriptions juives de Carthage," *Cahiers de Byrsa* 1 (1951) 175-206, and most recently in Gert Luderitz, *Corpus judischer Zeugnisse aus der Cyrenaika* (Weisbaden: Reichert, 1983). Others from North Africa are only in *CIL* or even less accessible. See also Alfred Louis Delattre, *Gamart ou 1a necropole juive de Carthage* (Lyons, 1895); P. Monceau, "Les colonies juives dans l'Afrique romaine," *REJ* 44 (1902) 1-28; Hirschberg, *Jews in North Africa*, and Shimon Appelbaum, *Jews and Greeks in Ancient Cyrene* (*SJLA* 28; Leiden: Brill, 1979). See esp. Yann Le Bohec, "Inscriptions juives et judaisantes," and " . . . remarques onomastiques," *Antiquités africaines* 17 (1981) 165-207, 209-29.

The inscriptions from Egypt were edited and translated by David M. Lewis in Victor A. Tcherikover and Alexander Fuks, ed., *Corpus Papyrorum Judaicorum*, vol. 3 (Cambridge: Harvard University Press, 1964). Notices of new Greek Jewish inscriptions occur frequently in *Bulletin épigraphique*, while *L'année épigraphique* reports Latin Jewish inscriptions. In the last few years a new publication, G.H.R. Horsley, ed., *New Documents Illustrating Early Christianity* (=*New-Docs*; North Ryde: MacQuarie University, 1981 currently 4 vols., has included notices of newly published Jewish inscriptions. Small numbers of Jewish inscriptions from the Greco-Roman period may occasionally be found in such works as Alexander Scheiber, *Jewish Inscriptions in Hungary* (Leiden: Brill, 1983).

For inscriptions from Asia Minor, one needs to search extensively through Louis Robert, *Hellenica*, as well as in *Monumenta Asiae Minoris Antiqua*. Still helpful is William H. Ramsay, *The Cities and Bishoprics of Phrygia* (Oxford: Clarendon, 1895-97; reprinted New York: Arno, 1975).

Finally, extremely helpful, though not exhaustive in bibliography, is Larry Kant, "Jewish Inscriptions in Greek and Latin," *ANRW* II.20.2 (Berlin: De Gruyter, 1987) 671-713.

8 Lifshitz, *Donateurs et fondateurs*.

ously, Jews did not normally indicate their Jewishness by the use of such words, at least not when burying their dead, or making dedications in the local synagogues. On the contrary, it would seem that Jewishness was either manifestly apparent, as in persons buried in demonstrably Jewish catacombs, or in synagogues, or through the use of incontrovertibly Jewish symbols or else not considered appropriate, necessary, or desirable to mention. Jean-Baptiste Frey thought that the term "Jew" was used on burial inscriptions to distinguish a Jewish tomb from surrounding pagan ones.[9]

Ioudaios/Ioudaia as an Indicator of Pagan Attraction to Judaism

Europe

Twelve inscriptions from Europe designate a person with a form of these terms. One, from the Via Nomentana catacomb in Rome, explicitly identifies Crescens Sincerius Iud(a)eus as *prosélytos* (*CIJ* 68). A marble fragment on a sarcophagos from the Via Appia catacomb contains the terms *[io]udea proqsé[lytos]* (*CIJ* 202).

A third inscription contains the term *eioudea* and *proselytos*, but it is not at all clear whether both terms refer to the same individual within the inscription (*CIJ* 21). A very problematic inscription, it comes from a marble plaque found at the Villa Torlonia, as a memorial to a three-year-old girl.

Εἰρήνη (θ)ρε<ζ>πτὴ προσήλυτος πατρός καὶ μητρὸς Εἰουδέα Ἰσ/δ/ραηλ-
ίτης ἔζησεν (ἐ(τ)γ'μ(ῆνας) ζ'ἡμ(έ)ρ(αν)α'

The precise translation of the inscription depends upon the resolution of several issues, in particular the objects of the terms *prosélytos, eioudea,* and *Is[d]raélités*. Harry Leon took *prosélytos* and *Is[d]raélités* to modify *Eirene*, while he thought *eioudea* described the parents, with the following translation:

1) Irene, foster child, proselyte, her father and mother Jewish, an Israelite, lived three years, seven months, one day.[10]

Frey, on the other hand, thought that all three terms referred to the child, and translated:

2) Irene, pupille, prosélyte, par son père et sa mère, Juive Israelite, a vécu 3 ans, 7 mois, 1 jour.

Neither translation exhausts the possibilities. My colleagues in the Philadelphia Seminar on Christian Origins and elsewhere have offered such translations as:

3) Irene, foster child, her father a proselyte, her mother Jewish, an Israelite (that is, the mother) ...

---

9 Frey, "Inscriptions inédites," 251.
10 Leon, *Jews of Ancient Rome*, 267.

4) Irene, foster child, proselyte, by her father and her mother, a Jewish Israelite (again, the mother) ...

5) Irene, foster child, Israelite, her father a proselyte and her mother a Jew

In fact, the only combination no one has suggested, understandably, is one in which Israelite modifies her father. All the others have some claim to feasibility, yet none is without difficulty. Case agreement might favor application of all four terms (*threpté, prosélytos, eioudea,* and *is[d]raelités*) to the deceased child, assuming all these are meant to be nominatives, but their location in the inscription, while not crucial, creates some doubt. Then, too, there are enough spelling errors in the inscription to make the determination of cases questionable.

It may be helpful to sort out the possibilities by considering that the deceased child is called *threpté* while the dedicators identify themselves as her parents. *Threpté/os* carried a range of meanings in antiquity, from a slave raised in the owner's household, to a child given by its parents to be raised by others, to a child abandoned and raised by parents who discovered the foundling.[11] A. Cameron indicates that *threptoi* could be given by their parents to be raised by others, and John Boswell has informed me that parents might sometimes reclaim abandoned children at the time of their death. Thus it might be that Irene's real parents dedicated this inscription. This raises a number of significant problems. First, why would her biological parents have indicated on her gravestone that she was a foster child? Second, assuming that it is Irene who is the proselyte, what can this mean? If both her real parents were Jews, then she could not be a proselyte; if neither of her real parents was a Jew, why did they indicate her conversion, and bury her in a Jewish catacomb? Were they, too, proselytes? Given Irene's age, this cannot be a case of meaningful voluntary conversion; therefore, adults must have imposed the conversion on her. If her real parents were also proselytes, presumably they

---

11 Cameron, "Threptos and Related Terms in the Inscriptions of Asia Minor," in W.M. Calder and Josef Keil, eds., *Anatolian Studies Presented to William Hephurn Buckler* (Manchester: Manchester University Press, 1939) 27-62. See also T.G. Nani, "THREPTOI," *Epigraphica 5-6* (1943-44) 45-84; John Boswell, "Expositio and Oblatio: The Abandonment of Children and the Ancient and Medieval Family," *AHR* 89 (1984) 10-33; and Beryl Rawson, "Children in the Roman Familia," in idem, ed., *The Family in Ancient Rome: New Perspectives* (Ithaca: Cornell University Press, 1986) 170-200. *CIJ* 3 records a male *threptos,* but the exact relationship between this Justus and Menandros, who dedicates the inscription, is unclear.

According to *m. Ketub.* 1.2-4, a female child who converted to Judaism past the age of three years and one day was not considered a virgin for the purposes of reckoning her dowry, and so on, but I see no way in which that clarifies the presence of a three-year-old proselyte, even if we could be sure that Jews in Rome at this time would have subscribed to rabbinic views on such matters.

converted after her birth, thus accounting for the need to convert the child as well. This would seem to be the scenario presumed by Leon's translation (no. 1).

Frey's interpretation is perhaps even more problematic, for it postulates either a three-year-old Jewish child of non-Jewish parents, which is puzzling, or Jewish parents with a three-year-old proselyte child, which might be accounted for if the parents were also newcomers to Judaism, presumably after the child's birth.

Some of the difficulties are eased if we prefer translation no. 4, reading Irene as the proselyte, her mother as Ioudaia Israélités and the father as not Jewish, which would be sufficient to account for the designation of Irene as a proselyte. Shaye Cohen has shown that the matrilineal principle of Jewish identity, whereby a child is considered Jewish if the mother is Jewish, is a relatively late rabbinic development, prior to which a child was considered Jewish if the father was Jewish.[12] If the father of Irene was not Jewish, but her mother was, we might very well have epigraphic evidence here for the operation of the patrilineal principle. The uncertain date of the inscription, and its Roman provenience would support rather than undermine that interpretation.

Translation no. 3 is also plausible, but leaves ambiguous the status of the child herself, and may divorce the terms *Ioudaia* and *prosélytos*, making the inscription somewhat less obviously pertinent to my concerns. It would, however, constitute epigraphic testimony to intermarriage, where a non-Jewish man marries a Jewish woman and adopts her religion. Translation no. 5 envisions a similar scenario, yet designates the child as Israelite, which is itself problematic. To the best of my knowledge, this term is a *hapax legomenon* in the Jewish corpus, although it does occur in a Samaritan inscription.[13] If it applies to the child, it is hard to tell what distinction it is intended to imply. Koenig reports that converts were called Israelites in rabbinic literature,[14] so that perhaps it attests a Jewish mother, a proselyte father, and a proselyte child. Alternatively, if both *Ioudea* and *Israélités* apply to the mother, we might

---

12 Shaye J. D. Cohen, "The Origins of the Matrilineal Principle in Rabbinic Law," *AJSRev* 10 (1985) 19-53; idem, "The Matrilineal Principle in Historical Perspective," *Judaism* 43 (1985) 5-13.

13 Philippe Bruneau, "Les Israelites de Délos et la juiverie délienne," *Bulletin de correspondance hellénistique* 106 (1982) 465-504; A.T. Kraabel, "New Evidence of the Samaritan Diaspora Has Been Found on Delos," *BA* (March 1984) 44-46.

14 Stanley B. Hoenig, "Conversion During the Talmudic Period," in David Max Eichhom, ed., *Conversion to Judaism: A History and Analysis* (New York: Ktav, 1965) 33-66; the reference is to *t.Ned.* 2.4.

argue that both mother and father were newcomers to Judaism, and that these terms are the signatories of such transition.

So far, we have presumed that the parents of Irene are her biological parents. If this is not the case, if the dedicators are her adoptive parents, more scenarios are possible, for we could then understand how Jewish parents could have a proselyte child. Since, however, there is no way to resolve these questions definitively given the present evidence, we must go on to consider the other relevant inscriptions.

Two inscriptions display features which have led scholars to postulate that the women in question may not have been born Jewish, or remained Jewish. The first of these is an inscription (*CIJ* 678) with substantial significance for the criteria by which one identifies Jewish inscriptions:

> D(is) M(anibus)
> Septim(i)a Mariae
> Iudeae Quae Vixit
> Annis XVIII Actia
> Sabinilla Mater

Although it clearly begins with the invocation *dis manibus* ("to the gods of the lower world"), the inscription refers to the deceased Septim(i)a Maria as *Iudea*, so that Frey, despite his assumption that Jews did not use *dis manibus* on their funeral inscriptions, was forced to include it in the main portion of his *Corpus*. Frey, unfortunately, did not take seriously the methodological implications of this inscription, considering it instead one of the few genuinely Jewish inscriptions to use the pagan invocation to the gods of the dead. Although I would generally agree with E.R. Goodenough (against Frey) that Jews could and did use this invocation on occasion,[15] it also seems plausible that Septimia Maria and her mother were not born Jews; for them the common invocation *dis manibus* would not have seemed in any way incongruent. It is particularly interesting that Actia Sabinilla did not refer to herself as *Iudea*, leaving us to wonder what the term might mean in reference to her daughter.

The combination of the pagan invocation with the term *Iudea* leads Alexander Scheiber to consider the possibility that Actia Sabinilla was not Jewish, whereas her daughter was, in which case conversion by the daughter seems the most likely, though not the only, explanation.[16] Yet the fact that Actia Sabinilla acknowledged her daughter's affiliation with Judaism by publicly

---

15 E.R. Goodenough, *Jewish Symbols in the Greco-Roman Period* (13 vols.; Princeton: Princeton University Press, 1953) 2. 137-40.

16 Scheiber, *Jewish Symbols in Hungary,* 45.

calling her *Iudea* on her burial inscription would seem to indicate some sympathy or acquiescence on the mother's part.

Also of interest here is Septimia's age, which suggests that she converted to Judaism at a relatively young age. The fact that her mother commissioned her burial inscription rather than her father may suggest additional significant factors for the study of pagan adherents to Judaism. If her father was simply not living, the dedication may mean less. But the dedication by the mother may imply that the daughter was illegitimate or that the daughter's attraction to Judaism had created a conflict within the family. The likelihood of either being a slave is undermined by their double names.

Septimia's second name, Maria, is attested as pagan, Jewish, and Christian.[17] Since there is evidence elsewhere that Jewish converts took on an additional name, Maria could be understood in that context.[18] If Actia Sabinilla herself had become interested in Judaism, the name Maria might be understood as an indicator of the mother's affiliation, as I will discuss below in greater detail.

The second inscription (*CIJ* 77*) poses similar difficulties for Frey's assumptions about what Jews did and did not do.

Iunonibus. Annia L(ucii) l(iberta) Iuda pro suis v(otum) s(olvit)

The dedication to Iunones (which Frey translates as Junean goddesses, although "goddesses" may be too precise) by a woman named Annia Iuda was considered sufficiently un-Jewish by Frey to be placed in his category of paganizing Jews: "Outside of the word *Iuda*, everything in this inscription smacks of paganism" (*CIJ* 1. 576). But it seems odd that Annia would have identified herself as *Iuda* if she had truly renounced her affiliation with Judaism, as Frey speculates.[19] On the other hand, if Annia was not born Jewish, but later subscribed to Jewish practices, as indicated by her epithet *Iuda*, her simultaneous attachment to Judaism and her dedication to the Iunones seem considerably less incongruous.

It might also be the case that Annia Iuda was born a Jew and still considered herself a member of the Jewish community, in which case we would have to conclude that Jewish women were not above making offerings to pagan spirits. It would be especially interesting if the Iunones, related to Juno, could be connected with situations of special concern to women, such as childbirth. But given the connections of *Iuda* with proselytism and adherence to

---

17 See "A Problem Like Maria," *NewDocs* 1979 [1987] no. 115 for a detailed discussion of the name Maria in inscriptions.

18 E.g., the proselyte Beturia Paulla takes on the name of Sarah (*CIJ* 523). See G.H.R. Horsley, "Name Change as an Indication of Religious Conversion in Antiquity," *Numen* 34(1987)1-17.

19 *CIJ* 1.576.

Judaism in other instances, it seems equally plausible that Annia was not born Jewish, but eventually identified with Judaism.

What can be deduced from the fact that in the European inscriptions women are designated *Ioudaia/Iuda* twice as many times as men are designated *Ioudaios/Iudeus*? Overall, women represent about only forty percent of those whose gender is identifiable in Jewish burial inscriptions.[20] Since there is considerable evidence that women were prominent, if not predominant, among non-Jewish adherents to Judaism in the Greco-Roman period,[21] does this strengthen the possibility that *Ioudaia/os* may designate a non-Jew who has adopted some degree of Jewish observance?

Asia Minor

The picture changes somewhat in the inscriptions from Asia Minor where *Ioudaia/os* occurs thirteen times, referring in all but three cases to males.[22] Interestingly, five of the inscriptions come from one town, Corycos in Cilicia. One other comes from the nearby town of Olba, also in Cilicia. These six inscriptions account for eleven of the fourteen men so designated in the Anatolian inscriptions. Nothing in these epigraphs indicates that any of the men were pagan adherents to Judaism. Perhaps inscriptions from Asia Minor utilize the term more along the lines that Kraabel envisions, namely, as a geographic indicator.

Two other inscriptions from Asia Minor, however, lend additional credence to the hypothesis that *Ioudaia* signified pagan adherence to Judaism. The first is a third-century C.E. epitaph from the necropolis of Termessos in Pisidia:[23]

> Marcus Aurelius Ermaios, son of Keues, (himself) son of Keues, (set up) a funerary urn for his daughter, Aurelia Artemeis *Ioudea*, only. No one has the right to bury anyone else (in it). Anyone who attempts to will pay 1,000 denaria to the most sacred

---

20 See Ross S. Kraemer, "Non-literary Evidence for Jewish Women in Rome and Egypt," in Marilyn B. Skinner, ed., *Rescuing Creusa: New Methodological Approaches to Women in Antiquity* (=*Helios* 12 [1986]) 85-101. For some discussion of the methodological problems in using epigraphy for demography, see Keith Hopkins, "On the Probable Age Structure of the Roman Population," *Population Studies* 20 (1966) 245-64.

21 I have discussed this at length in a paper delivered at the annual meeting of the Society of Biblical Literature, Dallas, 1983, "The Conversion of Women to Judaism in the Greco-Roman Period," which is condensed from a larger unfinished manuscript.

22 *CIJ* 741, 750, 753, 764, 778, 786, 789, 790, 791, 793, 794, 795, and *TAM* 3 (1941) 448 (discussed in Robert, *Hellenica* 11-12 [1960] 386); *BE* (1971) 645. *CIJ* 741 refers to Rufina *Ioudaia* (on which, see above); *CIJ* 750 refers to Getiores, who is actually called *Ebraia*, not *Ioudaia*.

23 *TAM* 3 (1941)448, also in Robert, *Hellenica* 11-12 (1960) 386.

treasury, and will be liable for [the crime off breaking into graves.

This epitaph suggests that Aurelia Artemeis was a Jew, but that her family, or at least her father, was not. Either she was a convert or her father was originally married to a Jew, her mother—this is essentially the interpretation offered by R. Heberdey, the editor.[24] The absence of the mother from the inscription may suggest that she predeceased her daughter, a not uncommon occurrence. But if this is so, the fact that Ermaios set up a special tomb for his daughter is puzzling. If a separate tomb was needed for his daughter because of her Jewishness, and if the mother was also Jewish, why did he not bury his daughter in the tomb with her Jewish mother? Does the new tomb suggest that Aurelia Artemeis had chosen her Jewishness of her own accord? Alternatively, perhaps the mother and father were divorced. If Aurelia Artemeis was a Jew because her mother was Jewish, we would have evidence for intermarriage, for the matrilineal principle of Jewish descent, and for a child of a pagan father who nevertheless follows the religion of the mother.

Finally, with regard to this inscription, I am not sure how to interpret an accompanying inscription, where M. Aurelius Molis Ermaios, also son of Keues, set up an inscription for himself, his wife Aurelia Artemeis, and their daughter Korkaina.[25] Since the wife's name is the same as that of the daughter in the first inscription, it might seem that she was in fact the mother of Aurelia Artemeis, which might also suggest that the two men were in fact one and the same. Heberdey believed that the two men were brothers, in which case there are either two women named Aurelia Artemeis, or perhaps Aurelia Artemeis, the mother of Korkaina, was first married to one brother, and then to the other. If the two inscriptions are by the same man, the fact that he buried Aurelia Artemeis, his daughter, in a separate grave from the rest of the family would mitigate against the notion that Aurelia Artemeis *mater* was Jewish by birth, or even that her mother's proclivity to Judaism was expressed by naming her daughter *Ioudea*. If the Aurelia Artemeis in the second inscription is the mother of the Aurelia in the first, the evidence would suggest that the daughter was an adherent to Judaism for whom *Ioudea* functioned as the signatory of her Judaism which distinguished her from the remainder of her family.

It seems unlikely that Ermaios set up a separate grave for his daughter simply because she was the first to die. If Ermaios had not wished to establish two separate tombs, at most his daughter's death would have been the impetus

---

24 Quote in French translation in Robert, *Hellenica* 11-12 (1960) 386.

25 Ibid.,386n.2.

for him to demarcate the whole family tomb, as is frequently the case with other inscriptions from Asia Minor, Jewish or otherwise.

We should also consider an inscription (*CIJ* 74I) from Smyma which is a key inscription for the study of women leaders in ancient synagogues.

> Rufina *Ioudaia*, president of the synagogue, constructed the tomb for her freedpersons and for the slaves raised in her household; no one else has the right to bury anyone [in it]. Anyone who ventures to do so shall give 1500 denaria to the sacred treasury and 1000 denaria to the Jewish community. A copy of this inscription has been placed in the [public] archives.

Unfortunately, little in this inscription allows us to determine the significance of the epithet *Ioudaia* in this case. That Rufina identified herself as Jewish is evident from her title as president of the synagogue, and from the fact that tomb violators are liable not only to the imperial treasury,[26] but to the Jewish community as well. Precisely because those factors adequately identify Rufina's Jewishness, we must consider what else the term may signify. As in the case of most other inscriptions from Asia Minor, it may signify geographic origin, in which case we would read: "Rufina, the Judean..." Conceivably it is a name, although this seems less likely.[27] Could it signify that Rufina did not begin life as a member of the Jewish community? Although I do not think we can establish this with any cerrainty, what may we deduce from the fact that Rufina constructs a tomb for her freedpersons and for those abandoned infants raised in her household?[28] There is evidence from elsewhere that Jews in the Greco-Roman period felt some obligation to proselytize among their households, and that slaves and freedpersons were particularly likely to adopt the religious affiliation of their Jewish masters and mistresses.[29] Is this more likely to have been the case with householders who were themselves newcomers to Judaism?

Is there any significance in the fact that the penalty for violating the tomb is a fine both to the imperial treasury and the Jewish treasury? Split penalties

---

26 Bernadette J. Brooten, *Women Leaders in the Ancient Synagogue: Inscriptional Evidence and Background Issues* (BJS 36; Chico: Scholars Press, 1982) 10.

27 *CIL* 8. 7710, for another Rufina who may be called Judea, from Theveste in North Africa.

28 See Brooten, *Women Leaders*, 10 for this interpretation of *thremmata*.

29 Hirschberg, *Jews in North Africa*, 181. See also Frey, "Inscriptions inedites," 239, who claims that "half" the actual proselyte inscriptions are to slaves or *threptoi*. He thinks that Rufina was the instrument of conversion here. In the Ps.-Clem. *Homilies* 13.7.3-8.1 two men are hought by a convert to Judaism named Justa, who adopted them and educated them in worship and study.

occur in a few other Jewish inscriptions.[30] In the majority of cases, though, the penalty is to be paid to the Jewish community or treasury alone. Does this suggest anything about Rufina's ties to the non-Jewish community, and would this be more unusual for someone born a Jew than for someone entering the Jewish community voluntarily?

In the absence of any other evidence linking the term *Ioudaia* with pagan adherence to Judaism, we could hardly conclude from this inscription alone that such a connection existed. But given the evidence discussed earlier in this article, it is not inconceivable that Rufina was a convert. Her synagogue title would not mitigate against this, since we know of at least one demonstrable convert who held titles in two Roman synagogues.[31] Her Roman name might also support this, although certainly we know of Jews in Asia Minor with Roman names.

Egypt

Only two inscriptions from Egypt designate individuals as *Ioudaia/Ioudaios*. Both are votive inscriptions found in the Temple of Pan at Resediyeh.[32] The first records the gratitude of Theuodotos Dorionos *Ioudaios* for being saved from disaster at sea. The second, by Ptolemaios Dionysios *Ioudaios*, does not record the occasion of the inscription, but these are part of ninety texts found around the Paneion at El-Kanais, most of which are addressed to Pan of the Successful Journey. They are thought to be mid-second to late-first century B.C.E.

Not surprisingly, the presence of votive inscriptions by men who called themselves Jews gave Frey considerable pause: "One is surprised to find Jewish votive inscriptions in a pagan temple" (*CIJ* 2. 445). His explanation is that these may be "due to ... the belief, assuredly not very orthodox, that one could thank Yahweh even in a temple of Pan." Since the inscriptions themselves do not name Pan, but speak only of an unspecified *theos*, such an argument cannot be contradicted by actual wording. Alternatively, he suggested that the two evidence a belief that the god Pan was in fact a universal deity (Pan = *to pan*, "the all").

Perhaps this inscription simply evidences the everyday religious behavior of two Jewish men, and demonstrates that Jews could and did honor other gods under some circumstances. But this leaves unanswered the question of their self-designation as *Ioudaios* and what it means in this context.

---

30 *TAM* 3 (1941) 448; *CIJ* 775 and *CIJ* 779, although in the case of the latter, it is not absolutely clear that this is a Jewish inscription.

31 Beturia Paulla, *CIJ* 523.

32 *CPJ* 1537, 1538. Recent discussion in *NewDocs* 1979 (1987) no. 26 (= pp. 113-17). Republished in André Bernand, *Le paneion de'El-Kanaîs: Les inscriptions grecques* (Leiden: Brill,1972).

North Africa

The designation *Iudaeus/Iudaea* also occurs in eight inscriptions from North Africa.[33] Johannes Oehler, who noted the inscriptions in his collection published in 1909, classed most of them as the epitaphs of judaizing pagans, but his judgment may have been prejudiced by one to Iulia Victoria [Iu]dea, which begins with the invocation *dis manibus* (*CIL* 8. 7530).[34] In fact, two of the North African inscriptions may suggest a more tempered interpretation.

> Caelia Thalassa Iudaea vixit ann(es) XX m(enses) IIII. M. Avillius Ianuarius coniugi karissimae (*CIL* 8. 8423)

> Caelia Thalassa Iudaea lived twenty years, four months. M. Avillius Ianuarius to his dearest wife.

> Avilia Aster Iudea M. Avilius Ianuarus Pater Sinagogae Fil(iae) Dulcissimae (*CIL* 8.8499)

> Avilia Aster Iudea. M. Avilius Ianuarus, father of the synagogue, to his sweetest daughter.

If the two men in these inscriptions, both from Sitifis in Mauritania, are the same, we have here an interesting situation of a man who is demonstrably Jewish (by virtue of his title "father of the synagogue"),[35] whose burial inscriptions to his wife and daughter call both of them *Iudea*, but who does not style himself *Iudeus*. In the inscription to his daughter, one might argue that the synagogue title makes any reference to himself as *Iudeus* superfluous, but that is clearly not the case in the epitaph for his wife.

What scenarios might explain these inscriptions? If the designation *Iudea* indicates adherence to Judaism, we might hypothesize that Avilius, himself born a Jew, married a non-Jewish woman who converted to Judaism, presumably after their marriage, since the daughter is also called *Iudea*, and would only bear the signature of a convert herself if she were born before her mother became a Jew, if we assume a matrilineal principle of descent. If a patrilineal reckoning were still in effect here, this would be moot.[36] Conceivably, even Avilius is a convert (and we do know of one convert at Rome who

---

33 CIL 8. 7150, 7155, 7530, 7710, 8423, 8499, 17584, 20759.

34 Johannes Oehler, "Epigraphische Beiträge zur Geschichte des Judentums," *Monatsschrift für Geschichte und Wissensehaft des Judentums* 53 (1909) 292-302; 443-52; 525-38. Note that the reading [Iu]deae is reconstructed, although it fits better than that offered by the *CIL* editor: [sacerdoti]deae.

35 On the title *pater synagogae* see Brooten, *Women Leaders*, 64-71.

36 See Cohen, "Origins of the Matrilineal Principle," and idem, "Matrilineal Principle in Historical Perspective" (n. 11).

became "mother" of two synagogues),[37] but we should note again that he does not style himself *Iudeus*.

It is even possible that all three persons, Avilius, Avilia Aster, and Caelia Thalassa are Jews by birth, but this still leaves us with the difficulty of understanding why the women were called *Iudea* but not Avilius. In neither inscription could we explain Avilius's failure to call himself *Iudeus* by virtue of the fact that he is the dedicator, for in another Latin inscription from North Africa, it is the dedicator who is called *Iudeus*, not the deceased.[38]

Ioudaia/os as a Proper Name

There is yet another interpretation of *Ioudaia/os* and its Latin equivalents which may clarify the majority of these inscriptions, namely, that the term may be used as a proper name. This is clearly the case in at least two inscriptions in the Jewish corpus. In one (*CIJ* 710, 163 B.C.E.), a slave *hói onoma Ioudaios* (by the name Ioudaios) who is to *genos Ioudaion* (Jewish by race), is manumitted through a fictitious sale to Pythian Apollo. In the other (*CIJ* 711, 119 B.C.E.), a man named Ioudaios manumits a slave named Amyntas through the same device.

Intriguingly, the vast majority of inscriptions in which the term occurs in the singular, whether masculine or feminine, would make at least as much sense if *Ioudaia/os* is a proper name.[39] In three cases, it seems less likely to be a name, since the term is separated from the person's name by other phrases in the inscription.[40] In the problematic epitaph to the foster child

---

37 *CIJ* 523, Beturia Paulla, called mother of the synagogues of Campus and Volumnius. See Brooten, *Women Leaders*, 57-59.

38 *CIL* 8. 7150. It is unlikely but not impossible that the syntax of the second inscription does not follow that of the first, but instead supports the translation: "Avilia Aster Iudea (and) M. Avilius Ianuarus, father of the synagogue, to (his/their) sweetest daughter." Here we would eliminate the difficulties caused by a wife and daughter called Iudea, and hypothesize instead that Avilius was twice married to women who converted to Judaism. If so, this inscription would constitute one of the rare pieces of evidence for a mixed marriage in which a non-Jewish woman converted and married a Jewish man (although not demonstrably in that order). Marriage between a Jewish woman and a non-Jewish man may possibly be reflected in *CIJ* 63*, 69*, 71*; as well as in Scheiber, *Jewish Inscriptions in Hungary*, nos. 4 and 5. She might have married him and then converted, adopting the name Judea. Thomas Drew-Bear (*Nouvelles inscriptions de Phrygie* [Zutphen: Terra, 1978] #20, reprinting Ramsay, *Cities and Bishoprics*, 2. 218) thinks that the marriage of Justa, wife of Dionysius, was mixed. The parents of Irene in *CIJ* 21, discussed above, might also have been a mixed marriage.

39 E.g., *CIJ* 296, 678, 680, 715i, and all North African inscriptions (see n. 32 above).

40 E.g., *CIJ* 693, 665. See also *CIJ* 250: "Marcia bona Iudea . . ."

Irene,[41] if the term is a proper name it is most likely that of the mother; but this seems odd since the father is referred to only by the generic patér.

If *Ioudaia/os* does represent a proper name in these dozen inscriptions, does this contradict the other interpretation I have suggested here? Might one, for example, perhaps simply understand the name as a variant of Judah, a commonly attested Jewish name, or, in the case of slaves, as a descriptive (perhaps pejorative) term? In the European inscriptions, and several others, the connections with other indicators of proselytism and the presence of terms more frequently associated with pagan inscriptions still remain to be explained.

One fruitful direction may be that suggested in another context by Victor Tcherikover, where he explains the prevalence of "Sambathion" names among demonstrably non-Jewish Egyptians.[42] Tcherikover suggests that some Egyptians became enamored of a Sabbath cult in which the female deity Sambathion figured predominantly, and then named their children in honor of Sambathion. These names then evidence not the religious affiliations of those who carry the name so much as those who named them.

A number of the inscriptions under consideration might be construed in this light. The dedication of Actia Sabinilla to her daughter, which combines the pagan *dis manibus* with an apparently indisputably Jewish name, might be less contradictory if Actia Sabinilla were a pagan attached to Judaism who had named her daughter Septimia Maria Iudea. It is not so much that I share Frey's disbelief that a Jew might inscribe her daughter's tombstone with a pagan invocation, as that it seems equally plausible that a woman who sympathized with Judaism might not perceive any conflict. What is significant in this interpretation is that it continues to suggest that the name *Iudea* signifies pagan adherence to Judaism, but on the part of the mother, rather than the daughter![43]

One might equally understand the dedication to Iulia Victoria Iudea as the epitaph of someone whose parent(s) found Judaism appealing, but whose survivors saw no discrepancy between the invocation of the gods of the underworld and whatever ties to Judaism Julia Victoria may have had.

Several of the remaining inscriptions do, however, complicate this interpretation. The inscription from Sitifis in Mauritania by M. Avilius Januarius

---

41 *CIJ* 21.

42 *CPJ* 3. 45ff.11

43 Professor Amy Richlin of the Classics Department at Lehigh University reminds me that we cannot tell from the inscription whether the woman is freeborn or merely freed, and consquently who named Septimia Maria, since someone else, such as the father or the owner, might have named the child if the mother was a slave when the daughter was born, or if the daughter was a slave at birth.

is demonstrably Jewish by virtue of its reference to him as "father of the synagogue." Regardless of how we translate the two inscriptions, the women concerned must have had more link with Judaism than simply the affiliation of their parents, namely, their relationship to Avilius himself.

The dedication to Crescens Sinicerius Iudeus offers a different sort of test case:

> Crescens Sinicerius Iudeus, proselyte, lived thirty-five years and fell asleep. Mother did for her sweetest son what he would have done for me. December 25.[44]

Crescens is clearly called a proselyte by his mother, whose name we do not know. At least in this case, the individual called Iudeus is said to have identified himself with Judaism. Of course, Iudeus could have been added to the young Crescens' name after his mother became interested in Judaism, and his formal proselytism might have come at a later age. Alternatively, though, Iudeus might have been a name he adopted himself upon converting. Finally, in this inscription, *Iudeus* may modify *proselytus* to read "Crescens Sinicerius, a Jewish proselyte," which is how the epitaph is normally interpreted (*CIJ* I. 4I).

We might also consider the fragmentary inscription mentioned earlier, which, as reconstructed, reads Ioudea proselytos[45] Whether it refers to a proselyte named Ioudea, or to an unnamed woman who is a Jewish proselyte, it does demonstrate the plausible connections between the two. If it referred to a person named Ioudea, it, together with the inscription of Crescens Sinicerius, might be construed as evidence that persons named for their parents' attraction to Judaism ultimately adopted that interest as well, perhaps in a more formal way. This, though, is problematic for many reasons, not the least of which is the question about degrees of adherence to Judaism, or whether there were simply different understandings of what it meant to be Jewish, as there are today.[46]

Against interpreting *Iudea/us* as a proper name may be that if such names were then triple names, they would be inconsistent in form with typical Latin and, to a lesser extent, Greek nomenclature. We could, of course, claim that Jewish nomenclature need not follow such customs, but since we would

---

44 *CIJ* 68. One might argue that Crescens is a Christian proselyte born to a mother who initially sympathized with Judaism and thus named her son Iudeus. The terminology of the inscription would not contradict such a reading, nor does the photograph in Frey indicate any Jewish symhols. Diehl classed the inscription as Jewish in *Inscriptiones Latinae Christianae Veteres* (Berlin, 1927) 2. 497.

45 *CIJ* 202. See Mary Smallwood, "The Alleged Jewish Tendencies of Poppaea Sabina," *JTS* n.s. 10 (1959) 329-35. See also Frey, *Inscriptions inédites*, 251-56.

46 Juvenal *Satire* 14. 96-106, in (*inter alia*) Menahem Stern, *Greek and Latin Authors on Jews and Judaism* (Jerusalem: Israel Academy of Sciences and Humanities, 1976-) 2.301 (pp. 102-3).

be dealing with people not born Jewish, it becomes difficult to argue that they would not be influenced by the typical patterns of nomenclature just because they had become interested in Judaism. However, there are a few inscriptions in which this would be less of an issue, since the person involved still has only two names, such as Annia Iuda. In her case, Iuda might have been her slave name: whether it designates her ethnic identity, as in the case of the slave in *CIJ* 710, or whether it reflects the affinity of her owners we simply cannot tell.

Ioudaia/os in Greek and Latin Authors and in the Papyri from Egypt

Although I intend here primarily to consider the patterns of usage for *Ioudaia/os* in Greek and Latin inscriptions, it is useful to consider the ways in which Greek and Latin authors used the term, and to note the patterns of usage in papyri. Greek and Latin authors (Jewish or otherwise) clearly use the term, in the plural, to refer to Jews as commonly construed, whether in Syria-Palestine or in the Diaspora. Josephus in particular uses constructions such as *Ioudaioi men to genos*, "Jewish by race [or: birth]."[47]

But significantly, the term, when applied to specific, named individuals, occurs rarely.[48] In most of these cases, *Ioudaios* is understood to be the eponymous ancestor of the Jews.[49] The sixth-century Greek writer Damascius refers to one Zeno of Alexandria, ἀνὴρ Ἰουδαῖος μὲν γεγονώς (a Jewish man by birth), who apostatized.[50] He also refers to Zeno's teacher, a physician, who he calls Δόμνον τὸν Ἰουδαῖον.

An extremely interesting reference comes from Dio Cassius, whose *Historia Romana* dates from the late second/early third centuries C.E. In addition to referring to Josephus as ἀνὴρ Ἰουδαῖον, he also reports that "this title [Jews] is also borne by other persons who, although they are of other ethnicity, live by their laws," in other words, pagan adherents to Judaism.[51] This may mean simply that those not born Jewish who follow Jewish customs were then called Jews in some general sense, or it may further support my contention that the term is especially applied to such individuals.

The waters may be further muddied by references to Revelation, Ignatius of Antioch, and elsewhere, which may be contrued as evidence that some non-Jews adopted practices and beliefs which they understood as Jewish, and call-

47 E.g., Bell. 2.120.

48 See, e.g., the index to Stern, *Greek and Latin Authors*, vol. 3.

49 E.g., Plutarch *De Iside et Osiride*, 259.

50 Damascius *Vita Isidori* (in Stern, *Greek and Latin Authors*, 2.678-79).

51 Dio Cassius Historia Romana 66.1.4 (in Stern, *Greek and Latin Authors*, 2.371), and 37.17.1 (ibid., 349-51).

ed themselves Jews, to the consternation of their Christian antagonists.[52] In a recent article, Lloyd Gaston concludes that "some uncuircumcised Christians in Asia referred to their own teaching and practice as 'Judaism,'"[53] which if true, might have signigicant implications for our reading of inscriptions from this area. However, Gaston's analysis is itself built on problematic assumptions and needs further study before it could be used profitably in this discussion.[54]

In the papyri, the term *Ioudaios* occurs with some frequency, often as an ethnic or geographic indicator. It is much more common in the Ptolemaic period,[55] after which it rarely occurs until the papyri from the Byzantine period.[56] It is my sense that the different functions of papyrus documents (many of these are commercial, tax, and military documents) as opposed to burial and donative inscriptions may account for the different patterns of usage, and also the different conotation. In particular, the papyri do not all emanate from the Jews themselves, while most of the inscriptions represent self-designation.

Conclusion

This brief study, when added to the work already done by Kraabel, suggests that the terms *Ioudaia, Ioudaios, Iudaeus,* and *Iudaea,* especially when applied to individiuals, must be interpreted with care. While inscriptions demonstrate that one could be called Jewish by ethnicity, or Jewish by religion or belief, some lend themselves to Kraabel's suggestion that geographic origin

---

52 See Lloyd Gaston, "Judaism of the Uncircumcised in Ignatius and Related Writers," in Stephen P. Wilson, ed., *Anti-Judaism in Early Christianity,* vol. 2: *Separation and Polemic* (Waterloo, Ontario: Wilfred Laurier University Press, 1986) 33-44.

53 Ibid., 44.

54 Gaston's underlying hypothesis is significant: Gentile Christians who *falsely* call themselves Jews are the cause of unfair Christian slander of Jews. "Not all Judaisms are Jewish, and it is unfair for Jews to be tarred with the brush of Gentile Christian judaizers" ("Judaism of the Uncircumcised," 44). The issues here are quite complex. When the author of Revelation says that these people say they are Jews, but they are not (Rev 2:9; 3:9) what exactly is at stake? What makes the people *not* Jews? All the conceivable problems of definition may be raised in attempting to understand this passage. When Ignatius claims that it is better to hear Christinaity from the circumcised that Judaism from the uncircumcised (*Phil.* 6.1), does this mean that Gentiles are teaching Judaism, or could it coneivably be evidence of the presence of born Jews who do not practice circumcision? The answers to these questions are regrettably beyond the scope of this paper, if not incapable of resolution given the available evidence.

55 E.g., *CPJ* 8, 9, 18, 19, 20, 22, 23, 30.

56 E.g., *CPJ* 500, 505, 508, 509, 511, 512. Se also *CPJ* 451 (and 151), which is of particular interest in some respects because it refers to a man name Hellenos, son of Tryphon, who apparently referred to himself as an Alexandrian, only to have the scribe cross that out and replace it with the phrase "a Jew from Alexandria." The editors conjecture that when the scribe had the full facts before him, he disagreed with Hellenos's original phrasing, and replaced it with a more legally accurate terminology.

is intended. Most of the other inscriptions lend themselves to the explanation that non-Jews who affliated with Judaism either took on the term, perhaps as a self-designation, or gave the term as a proper name to their children. And it may well be that the term was necessary especially in situations where the Jewishness of the individual might not be apparent, not only in cases of burial near pagan graves (as Frey suggested) but in cases where the individual did not begin life as a Jew.[57]

57 I am indebted to the National Endowment for the Humanities for a grant during 1982-83, which enabled me to do the basic research and some of the writing for this ariticle. A portion of this paper was read in the fall of 1986 before the Philadelphia Seminar on Christian Origins, members of which provided much helpful critique. Robert Kraft read an earlier draft and offered several helpful observations, which a detailed written critique by Tom Kraabel was especially important in producing the final version.

New Evidence of the Samaritan Diaspora has been Found on Delos[1]

A.T. Kraabel

Delos is one of the Cyclades islands just south and east of the Greek mainland. Its place in Greco-Roman history is an honored and an one. In Homer's *Odyssey* [book VI, line 162], Odysseus recalls a visit he made to the altar of Apollo at Delos, and Virgil's hero Aeneas praises "this most pleasant island" [*Aeneid*, book III, line 73]. Delos is also significant in Jewish history in that the oldest synagogue yet discovered in the Mediterranean Diaspora was found there. Philippe Bruneau, who conducted the final excavations of the building, has dated its earliest phase to the first century B.C.E.[2] Now we have the first evidence for the existence on Delos of a community of people related to the Jews—the Samaritans, well known from a number of New Testament references. Bruneau has recently published two steles with inscriptions of considerable importance because of the new understanding they provide of the early history of the Samaritans and their spread throughout the ancient Mediterranean world.[3]

The first inscription is wholly preserved, and Bruneau dates it to between 150 B.C.E. and 50 B.C.E. It reads:

Οἱ ἐν Δήλῳ Ἰσραελεῖται οἱ
ἀπαρχόμενοι εἰς ἱερὸν Ἀργαριζεὶν
στεφανοῦσιν χρυσῷ
στεφάνῳ Σαραπίωνα Ἰάσινισ
Κνώσιον εὐεργεσίας
ἕνεκεν τῆς εἰς ἑαυτούς

> The Israelites on Delos who make offerings to hallowed *Argaizein* crown with a gold crown Sarapion, son of Jason, of Knossos, for his benefactions toward them.

Bruneau is correct in interpreting *Argarizein* as equivalent to *Har Garizim*, Hebrew for Mount Gerizim, the holy mountain of the Samaritans. He refers to John 4:20. Jesus is speaking with a woman of Samaria, who says "My Samaritan ancestors worshiped God on this mountain, but you Jews say that Jerusalem is the place where we should worship God" (Today's English Version). The mountain is Gerizim.

---

1 Editor's note: This essay first appeared in *BA* 47 (March 1984) 44-46.

2 P. Bruneau, *Recherches sur les cultas de Délos à l'époque hellénistique et a l'époque impériale*, Bibliothèque des Écoles françaises d'Anthènes et de Rome 217, (Paris:Editions E. de Boccard, 1970). A.T. Kraabel, "The Diaspora Synagogue," *Aufsteig und Niedergang der römischen Welt: Geschichte und Kultur Roms im Spiegel der neueren Forschung*, II.19.1 (1979) 477-510.

3 P. Bruneau, "Les Israélites de Délos et la juiverie délienne." *Bulletin de Correspondance Hellénistique 106* (1982) 465-504.

The other inscription, which Bruneau believes to have been a century earlier than the first (around the period of 250-175 B.C.E.), is not complete, but it is certain that the group responsible for it thought of themselves in the same way. They described themselves as:

/Οἱ ἐν Δήλῳ/
Ἰσραηλῖται οἱ ἀπαρχόμενοι εἰς ἱερὸν
Ἀργαριζεὶν . . .

> (the) Israelites (on Delos) who make offerings to hallowed,
> consecrated *Argarizein* . . .

The words in parentheses are restored on the assumption that this inscription was structured in a manner similar to the first. In this inscription, Gerizim is bother "hallowed" (*hieron*) and "consecrated" (*hagion*), while only one adjective is used to described Mount Gerizim in the first inscription. This is a minor variation, and essentially the same wording is used to designate the group that erected the steles. Both inscriptions were found only one hundred meters from the synagogue.

As a classicist I was struck by how properly Greek both steles are. The same design is found time and again across the Mediterranean world: a rectangular shaft of white marble with find wreath carved in high relief, the inscription below it. The honor was a double one: the gold wreath ceremonially bestowed on the benefactors,[4] and the inscription that records the honor in a public and permanent fashion. Jews also used this traditional form. In about the third century C.E., Tation, daughter (or wife) of Straton, son of Empedon, donated an entire synagogue to the Jewish community of Phocaea on the Ionian coast of Asia Minor. She was honored both with a gold crown and with the right to a seat of honor in front of the congregation.[5]

Bruneau holds that these Samaritans and the Jews of the nearby synagogue lived in a kind of "ghetto" [he uses the French term juiverie], but that should not be taken in the medieval or eastern European sense. It is unlikely that they were restricted to this area by the Delian Gentiles or that only Jews and Samaritans were permitted to live on this part of the island. What we know about Jewish life in the Greco-Roman world suggests that the term *ghetto* would be an anachronism here.

---

4 For this custom see F.W. Danker, *Benefactor: Epographic Study of a Greco-Roman and New Testament Semantic Field,* (St.Louis:Clayton Publishing House, 1982) 467-71.

5 *Corpus Inscriptionum Iudaicarum: Recueil des inscriptions juives qui vont du IIIe siècle avant Jesus-Christ au VIIe siècle de notre ère,* ed., Jean-Baptiste Frey. (Vatican: Pontificio Instituto di Archeologia Cristiana, 1936-1952) 738, which is also inscription number 13 in B. Lifshitz, *Donateurs et fondateurs dans les synagogues juives* (Paris: J. Gabalda, 1967); Tation's status is ably discussed in B.J. Brooten, *Women Leaders in the Ancient Synagogue: Inscriptional Evidence and Background Issues* (Chico,CA: Scholars Press, 1982) 143-44.

Why did the Samaritans call themselves "Israelites"? Aren't Israelites Jews? Not necessarily! The term *Israeletai* can also mean "those from [the Northern Kingdom] Israel."[6] Since the Samaritans came originally from the Hebrew Bible's northern kingdom, Israel, rather than from Judah in the south, they have as much right as the Jews to that title, perhaps more. I suspect too that on Delos they are using the term for a second reason as well—that is, to lay claim to it, lest the Jews of Delos gain full possession of it. The fact that both inscriptions refer to "Israelites" *associated with Mount Gerizim* may indicate that this has already occurred. Without the reference to Gerizim most Delians might have thought that these "Israelites" *were* Jews.

Is the Delos synagogue Samaritan? Bruneau says no, and he has the numbers on his side. There is only one known Samaritan synagogue in the Mediterranean Diaspora, that at Thessalonica from a much later period,[7] but all the other excavated synagogue buildings, the fragmentary synagogue remains [mosaic floors, architectural members], and the many synagogue inscriptions outside Palestine appear to be Jewish.[8] The Samaritan Diaspora was not extensive. Further, we know from Josephus that there was a Jewish community on the island at the time this synagogue was established (see the end of this note). There are, however, no *unmistakably Jewish* features to the building or its inscriptions. Indeed, there has never been full agreement that the building was a synagogue.[9] I am persuaded by the evidence that it is,[10] and if so, it is not impossible for it to be a Samaritan synagogue rather than a Jewish one.

What were the Samaritans and Jews doing on Delos? The evidence indicates that they were inhabitants, not just a transient population. The island is small, less than two square miles, but significant in cult (it is the legendary birthplace of Artemis and Apollo), in political and military history, in international relations and international trade. Its foreign colony in this period

---

6 There is an exact parallel in *CII* 742, which is an inscription from Smyrna in Ionia of the second century C.E. Here a long text mentions *hoi pote Ioudaioi.* This is usually translated "the former Jews," leading to the conclusion that these were a group of apostates. They are, rather, "people formerly of Judea," that is, immigrants, not native of Smyrna. Here, as on Delos, the term is geographical, not religious, A.T. Kraabel, "The Roman Diaspora: Six Questionable Assumptions," *JJS* 33 (1982) 445-64.

7 B. Lifshitz and I. Schiby, "Une synagogue samaritaine à Thessalonique, *Revue Biblique* 65 (1968) 368-78; the inscriptional evidence is dated to the fourth century C.E.

8 E.R. Goodenough, *Jewish Symbols in the Greco-Roman Period.* 13 vols. (New York: Partheon Books, 1953-1968); H. Shanks, *Judaism in Stone: The Archaeology of Ancient Synagogues,* (New York: Harper & Row, 1979); M.J.S. Chiat, *Handbook of Synagogue Architecture,* BJS 29 (Chico, CA: Scholars Press, 1982); B. Lifshitz, *Donateurs et fondateurs dans les synagogues juives,* (Paris: J. Gabalda, 1967); A.T. Kraabel, *The Diaspora Synagogues,* 1979.

9 See the summary in H. Shanks, *Judaism in Stone,* 43-45.

10 A.T. Kraabel, *The Diaspora Synagogue,* 491-94.

included many Romans, and others from various locations in the Aegean and the Mediterranean. I suspect that it was trade and, to a lesser extent, international politics that brought Samaritans and Jews here to settle.

Our previous knowledge of the Samaritan Diaspora in this period was limited to Josephus, who noted the presence of a Samaritan community in Egypt.[11] The Delos inscriptions now suggest a Samaritan presence over a much wider geographic area and at an earlier time than previously thought. This raises a number of questions about the extent of the Samaritan Diaspora and the relationship between Jewish and Samaritan diasporic communities.

I would like to close with two comments about the relationship of Samaritans (and Jews) with "Gentiles." First, Sarapion, son of Jason, of Knossos, need not have been a fellow Samaritan. He could have been a pagan benefactor, someone who aided the Samaritan community for his own reasons, political, economic, or personal. In this same period Jews in Egypt were honoring benevolent pagan rulers with inscriptions in their synagogues and prayers on their behalf, and during the reign of Nero, Julia Severa, a Gentile of high status in Acmonia, Phrygia, underwrote the cost of a synagogue there.[12] Neither in Phrygia nor in Egypt were these patrons converts to Judaism.

Second, it is important to note that life outside Palestine, in the Greek world, did not corrupt these Samaritans and Jews, or lead them from the traditional piety. The Samaritans of Delos still sent their offerings to Mount Gerizim, and the Jews (if that building is theirs) established a synagogue. And two decrees preserved by Josephus specifically protect the rights of Delos Jews to observe their ancestral customs, sacred rites, and common meals,[13] and exempt them on *religious grounds* from military service.[14]

---

11 For example, *Jewish Antiquities*, book XI, paragraph 345; book XII paragraph 7 and following; book XIII, paragraph 74 and 78.

12 The inscription from Egypt are Lifshitz, *Donateurs* (1967) number 86 (*CII* 1432), number 92 (*CII* 1440), number 93 (*CII* 1441), number 94 (*CII* 1442), number 95 (*CII* 1443), number 96 (*CII* 1444), and number 99. The donations of Julia Severa is recorded in Lifshitz, *Donateurs* (1967) number 33 (*CII* 766). See also Brooten, *Women Leaders*, (1982) 144 and the text and translation on 158.

13 *Jewish Antiquities*, book XIV, paragraph 213 through 216.

14 *Jewish Antiquities*, book XIV, paragraphs 231 and 232.

"The King has Become a Jew." The Perspective on the Gentile World in Bel and the Snake

John J. Collins

Bel and the Snake is an apocryphal story appended to the Book of Daniel in the Greek and other versions. It tells how Daniel contrives to destroy the temple of Bel and have its priests put to death, and then kills a live serpent worshipped by the Babylonians. These actions provoke the wrath of the Babylonians, who coerce the king to hand over Daniel, whom they then throw into the lions' den in Daniel 6. Daniel survives, nourished by the prophet Habakkuk, who is transported from Judea for the purpose. When the king finds him alive after seven days, he releases Daniel, extols his God and throws his enemies to the lions.

The relationship of this story to the Hebrew-Aramaic Book of Daniel is disputed.[1] The most obvious point of contact concerns the episode of Daniel in the lions' den in Daniel 6. This motif was probably older than either story in which it now occurs. Both stories portray the Gentile king in exceptionally positive light. They also have some minor motifs in common, such as the use of the king's ring as a seal and the execution not only of Daniel's enemies but of their entire families. These latter motifs, however, are not very distinctive. On the whole, the differences between the two stories are much more impressive than the similarities. It is unlikely that either story depends directly on the other. In any case, *Bel and the Snake* does not appear to be derived from Daniel 6.[2] There are two Greek versions of the apocryphal book, the Old Greek and Theodotion. It is generally agreed that the OG is the older of these.[3] One of the peculiarities of that version is that Daniel is identified as a priest, who was a companion of the (nameless) king of Babylon.[4] The story does not presuppose the identity of Daniel as established in Daniel 1-6, and

---

1 James A. Montgomery, *Daniel* (ICC; Edinburgh: Clark, 1929) 270, suggested that *Bel* was an earlier, popular form of the story. L.F. Hartman and A.A. DiLella, *The Book of Daniel* (AB 23; Garden City: Doubleday, 1977) 21, regard it as obvious that the apocryphal story was influenced by Daniel 6. Carey A. Moore, *Daniel, Esther and Jeremiah. The Additions* (AB 44; Garden City: Doubleday, 1977) 147-9 holds that the two stories have only a kernel of tradition in common.

2 See Lawrence M. Wills, *The Jew in the Court of the Foreign King* (HDR 26; Minneapolis: Fortress, 1990) 129-38. Wills attaches more significance than I do to the motifs of the king's seal and the slaughter of the priests' families, and holds that Daniel 6 borrowed motifs from *Bel and the Snake*.

3 J. Schüpphaus, "Der Verhältnis von LXX-und Theodotion-Text in den apokryphen Zusätzen zum Danielbuch," *ZAW* 83(1971) 49-63.

4 Theodotion's version of the opening verses can be understood as a reworking of the OG, designed to incorporate it into the Book of Daniel, since Cyrus is named in Dan 6:28 and 10:1. The redactor must have realized that Darius the Mede was problematic, and substituted the name of an actual Median king, Astyages.

the failure to name the king of Babylon suggests that the story circulated independently.

The Court Tale Tradition

Bel and the Snake bears some generic similarity to the Aramaic tales in Daniel 2-6, in so far as it describes the adventures of Daniel at the Gentile court. It retains some typical features of the Court-Tale genre:[5] the king is gullible and Daniel's opponents are villainous and murderous. However, *Bel and the Snake* also differs from the Aramaic stories in several significant respects:

First, the courtly elements of the story are reduced. Daniel's enemies are not rival sages, but priests and the Babylonian populace. Since Daniel is also identified as a priest in the OG, the conflict here is between priests of rival religions rather than between courtiers. This suggests a different *Sitz-im-Leben* for this story from that of the tales in Daniel 1-6. The court setting is retained because of the traditional associations of Daniel, and because of the persistent interest in the king, but some aspects of the court context have lost their significance.

Second, the story of *Bel and the Snake* places less reliance on legendary features, or on interventionist theology, than the Aramaic tales. Of course the episode of Daniel in the lions' den, and of the miraculous transportation of Habakkuk to feed him there, is highly legendary, but such features are notably absent in Daniel's encounters with Bel and the snake. The exposé of Bel has the character of a detective story. Daniel traps the priests by sprinkling ashes on the floor of the temple. Again, he disposes of the snake by feeding it a strange concoction which causes it to burst. No divine intervention is necessary in these cases. The commonsense, rational approach of these stories is typical of Jewish polemic against idols, which often takes the form of *reductio ad absurdum*.[6]

Third, the polemic against idols is much more central in this story than in any of the tales in Daniel 1-6. More importantly, the context of the polemic is different. In Daniel 1-6, as in Esther, the Jewish exiles pursue their careers without malice towards the Gentiles or their religious practices. If Daniel lectures Nebuchadnezzar and Belshazzar on true worship, it is only because he has been called in to address their problems. Belshazzar, moreover, is guilty of abusing the Jewish temple vessels. Daniel is not crusading against idolatry. The confrontations in Daniel 3 and 6 concern the rights of the Jews to be faithful to their own religion. In *Bel and the Snake*, in contrast, Daniel takes

---

5 The best account of the genre is that of Wills, *The Jew in the Court of the Foreign King*.

6 Wills, *The Jew in the Court of the Foreign King*, 132, who cites the story attributed by Josephus to Hecataeus of Abdera about the Jewish archer Mosollamus, who shot a bird which pagan soldiers were watching to see if their campaign would be auspicious (*Ag Ap* 1.22 §201-4).

the offensive, and sets out to destroy the pagan idols, without provocation. There is no parallel for such aggressive action by a Jew in the other court tales. Even the idol parodies, such as Isa 44:9-20 or the *Letter of Jeremiah*, do not narrate or call for the destruction of the idols.

Finally, despite the polemic against the idols, the Gentile king is portrayed in very positive light. It is, of course, typical of these stories that the Gentile king comes to acknowledge the God of Israel in some way. *Bel and the Snake*, however, introduces a new idea in the genre of Jewish Court Tales when it has the Babylonians say, after the death of the snake, that "the king has become a Jew." It is not apparent that this accusation is justified in the context of the story and it is not endorsed by the author, but it is striking that such a possibility is even considered.

Each of these points suggests that the apocryphal story reflects a rather different *Sitz-im-Leben* from the Aramaic Daniel stories, and invites some reflections on the setting of this intriguing work in Second Temple Judaism.

For much of the Second Temple period the Jewish people lived in harmony with Gentile overlords, both in the Diaspora and in the land of Israel. The Court Tale, which describes the adventures of Jews in the service of foreign kings, is one of the typical literary products of the period. The biblical prototype of the genre is found in the Joseph story; the main examples are found in the books of Esther and Daniel. The genre was not peculiar to Judaism. Stories of a foreigner at court seem to have flourished especially under the Persian empire and several can be found in Herodotus. Many of these stories show what Larry Wills has called the "ruled ethnic perspective," and were a means for subject peoples to express their aspirations and dignity in fictional form.[7]

The Jewish stories of this type are characterized by two features: loyalty to the King, on the one hand, and a strong sense of Jewish identity on the other. Esther and Mordecai show their exemplary loyalty to the King by exposing a plot to assassinate him (Esth. 2:19-23). Daniel flatters Nebuchadnezzar as the head of gold (Dan 2:38) and wishes that the king's dream be for those who hate him and its interpretation for his enemies (4:19). Conflict is usually ascribed to the envy or malice of other courtiers, rather than to the king himself. In the Book of Esther, the danger is stirred up by Haman. Both Daniel and his three companions are victims of plots by rival courtiers (chaps. 3, 6). In each case the Jews arouse envy or resentment not only by their success at court, but by the fact that they are different. In the words of Haman: "There is a certain people scattered and separated among the peoples in all the provinces of your kingdom; their laws are different from those of every other people and they do not keep the king's laws, so that it is not appropriate

---

7 Wills, *The Jew in the Court of the Foreign King*, 55-74.

for the king to tolerate them" (3:8). In fact, Jews only had problems with Gentile laws in matters of religion and worship. The accusations against the Jews in Daniel 3 are more specific:"There are certain Jews whom you have appointed over the affairs of the province of Babylon. . . These pay no heed to you, O King. They do not serve your gods and they do not worship the golden statue that you have set up" (3:12).

Idolatry and Conversion

Rejection of idolatry was, of course, one of the trademarks of Judaism in the post-exilic period.[8] The famous idol parodies of Second Isaiah are in the context of the overthrow of Babylon and the restoration of Judah, and are understandably colored with nationalistic fervor. Rejection of idols, however, did not necessarily imply the rejection of Gentile sovereignty. In the fragmentary *Prayer of Nabonidus*, found at Qumran, the king recounts how he was smitten with an evil disease for seven years by the decree of God. For those seven years he was praying to gods of silver, gold and other materials, until a Jewish diviner taught him to honor the true God. While the conclusion of the document is missing, it is evidently implied that the king comes to the knowledge of this God.[9] It is well known that the historical Nabonidus (556-539 B.C.E.) sojourned for several years in Teman in the Arabian desert. This mysterious exile was construed in Jewish tradition as divine punishment. What is remarkable, however, is that it also becomes the occasion for a story of the king's conversion, for which, of course, there was no historical basis whatever.

The Jewish adaptation of the Nabonidus tradition was taken further in the Book of Daniel. Here Nebonidus is replaced by the more familiar figure of Nebuchadnezzar. The king is driven away from human society for "seven times" to teach him a lesson: "that the Most High has sovereignty over the kingdom of mortals and gives it to whom he will" (4:32). In the end, Nebuchadnezzar "blessed the Most High and praised and honored the one who lives forever" (4:34). In the following chapter Belshazzar is berated for failing to learn from the example of Nebuchadnezzar and reverting to the worship of gods of silver and gold (5:23). Belshazzar meets a sudden fate, but he is exceptional among the Gentile kings in Daniel 1-6. The king who succeeds to the kingdom, the fictional "Darius the Mede," is sympathetic to Daniel, even

8 H.D. Preuss, *Verspottung fremder Religionen im Alten Testament* (BWANT 12; Stuttgart: Kohlhammer, 1971). On the critique of idolatry in the Hellenistic period see M. Gilbert, *Le critique des dieux dans le Livre de la Sagesse (Sg.13-15)* (Rome: Pontifical Biblical Institute, 1973); J.J. Collins, *Between Athens and Jerusalem. Jewish Identity in the Hellenistic Diaspora* (New York: Crossroad, 1983) 137-74.

9 The most complete study is still that of R. Meyer, *Das Gebet des Nabonid* (Berlin: Akademie Verlag, 1962).

when he is coerced by his courtiers to throw him to the lions. When Daniel survives the ordeal Darius is quick to recognize the God of Daniel as the living God. One of the lessons of Daniel 1-6 is that even Gentile kings must worship the God of heaven, who is the God of Israel, if their sovereignty is to endure. Conversely, these stories do not envisage any imminent overthrow of Gentile dominion. Their hopes and fantasies center on the sympathies, if not the outright conversion, of the Gentile monarchs.

These stories do not define in detail the kind, or degree, of conversion expected of the kings. At the end of Daniel 2, Nebuchadnezzar tells Daniel "Truly your God is God of gods and Lord of kings and a revealer of mysteries . . ." (vs. 47). Nonetheless, in the next chapter he proceeds to set up a golden statue, and demand that his officials worship before it. While there are often problems of continuity between the individual stories in a book like Daniel, it is clear that the king's acknowledgement of the God of gods in Chap. 2 does not necessarily entail the renunciation of idols. Nebuchadnezzar seems to make a fresh discovery of the true God in Chap. 3, and again in Chap. 4. The last of these, which is an adaptation of the Nabonidus tradition, is especially interesting. In the *Prayer of Nabonidus*, the king confesses that he used to pray to idols, and this would seem to imply that he had now renounced the practice, but it does not necessarily mean that he had become a monotheist. In Daniel 5, when Daniel berates Belshazzar for failing to learn from the example of Nebuchadnezzar, he points to the worship of idols, but not of the true God. This could be construed to mean that Nebuchadnezzar had renounced the worship of idols, but it may only mean that he acknowledged the superiority of the God of heaven. Interestingly enough, in the story of Nebuchadnezzar's madness in Daniel 4, the king is not told to renounce idolatry. Daniel simply counsels him to "atone for your sins with righteousness, and your iniquities with mercy to the oppressed" (vs. 27). Eventually, of course, the king acknowledges the sovereignty of the Most High, but he does not explicitly reject all other gods. Cyrus of Persia had acknowledged "the Lord, God of Heaven" as the one who had given him dominion (Ezra 1:2) without prejudice to his continuing polytheism. Josephus claims that even the mighty Alexander the Great acknowledged the God of Jerusalem.[10] Such acknowledgement is little more than a gesture of respect and does not imply conversion in any exclusive sense.[11]

---

10 *Ant* 11.8.5 §333. S.J.D. Cohen, "Alexander the Great and Jaddus the High Priest according to Josephus," *AJSRev* 7-8 (1982-3) 41-68. There are numerous examples of such praise of the God of Israel by Gentiles, dating back to Hiram of Tire in the time of Solomon (2 Chron 2:11).

11 On the spectrum of different ways in which a Gentile might be attached to Judaism see S.J.D. Cohen, "Crossing the Boundary and Becoming a Jew," *HTR* 82(1989) 13-33.

The accusation of the Babylonians against the king in *Bel and the Snake* raises the possibility of a more serious conversion: "The king has become a Jew." In pre-exilic Israel, one only became a member of the people by intermarriage.[12] There were laws regulating the alien and the sojourner, but they were recognized as distinct categories. In the post-exilic period it became more common for people to attach themselves to the Jewish people for religious reasons (e.g. Isa 56:3,6), and *ger*, alien, took on the meaning of proselyte.[13] Not until the second century B.C.E., however, do we hear of people becoming Jews. On three occasions the Maccabees compelled the Gentile inhabitants of recently conquered areas to adopt the Jewish way of life, including circumcision.[14] Among them were the Idumeans, from whom the house of Herod came. While some people regarded the later Idumeans as "half-Jews," they accepted and persevered in their Jewish identity. In the Book of Judith, which is probably of Hasmonean date,[15] when Achior the Ammonite "saw all that the god of Israel had done, he believed firmly in god, and was circumcised, and joined the house of Israel, remaining so to this day" (14:10). Here again the way to become a Jew was to be circumcised. The Epic of Theodotus, which says that the inhabitants of Shechem were required to adopt the Jewish way of life by being circumcised (*peritemnomenous ioudaisai*) should also be taken as a reflection of the policies of the Hasmoneans.[16] The expression "to become a Jew," however, is found, to my knowledge, in only one pre-Christian text besides *Bel and the Snake*. That occurrence, surprisingly, refers to Antiochus Epiphanes, who according to 2 Macc 9:17, resolved on his deathbed "to become a Jew and visit every inhabited place to proclaim the power of God."

There are some noteworthy parallels between these two occurrences of the motif of becoming a Jew. Both involve Gentile kings, and both arguably reflect a Gentile perspective on what it means to become a Jew. Neither mentions circumcision, or any practice of Jewish law. Antiochus promises only to proclaim the power of God. The king in *Bel and the Snake* is said to have

---

12 J. Milgrom, "Religious Conversion and the Revolt Model for the Formation of Israel," *JBL* 101(1982) 169-76.

13 D. Kellermann, "gûr," *TDOT* 2.439-49; K.G. Kuhn, "*proselytos*," *TDNT* 6(1968) 728-30.

14 Josephus, *Ant* 13.9.1 §257; 11.3 §319; 15.4 §397; S.J.D. Cohen, "Conversion to Judaism in Historical Perspective: From Biblical Israel to Postbiblical Judaism," *Conservative Judaism* 36 (1983) 36.

15 G.W.E. Nickelsburg, *Jewish Literature Between the Bible and the Mishnah* (Philadelphia: Fortress, 1981) 109.

16 J.J. Collins, "The Epic of Theodotus and the Hellenism of the Hasmoneans," *HTR* 73 (1980) 93-104. The expression may be a paraphrase by Alexander Polyhistor rather than the phrase of Theodotus.

become a Jew because he has apparently rejected idolatry. Neither would necessarily have been accepted by a Jewish community,[17] and they would certainly not have been accepted as Jewish by the Hasmoneans. Both stories, however show the emerging definition of Judaism in the Hellenistic world. Later, in the Roman period, such authors as Tacitus (*His* 5.5.2) and Juvenal (*Sat* 14.96-106) would regard circumcision as an essential mark of conversion to Judaism.[18] In the Hellenistic period, however, Jewishness was less strictly defined, at least in some circles.

It is interesting to compare these cases of "becoming a Jew" with the story of a king who actually did convert to Judaism, Izates of Adiabene, in the first century C.E. The king's mother, Helena, who had already converted to Judaism, discouraged him from being circumcised, for fear that his subjects "would not tolerate the rule of a Jew over them." He was also assured by a Jew, Ananias, that he could worship God even without circumcision, but another Jew, named Eleazar, gave a stricter interpretation of the law and the king was circumcised.[19] This story, however, implies that Izates was not really a Jew, and would not be considered a Jew by his subjects, until he underwent circumcision. The difference between Izates and Cyrus in *Bel and the Snake* reflects different historical settings—the story of Izates is considerably later. While *Bel and the Snake* is a fiction, and not an historical report, it presupposes that the king's subjects would consider him to have become a Jew if he rejected idolatry, even if he had not been circumcised.

There is, however, also a notable difference between the king in *Bel and the Snake* and Antiochus Epiphanes in 2 Maccabees 9. Antiochus makes his promise under duress, having been brought to his knees by the disease with which he is smitten by God.[20] Cyrus is persuaded of the futility of idols by Daniel's demonstration. For Antiochus, "becoming a Jew" is an act of repentance, and a dramatic reversal of his earlier attitude. Cyrus had been a sympathetic figure from the start. Moreover, Antiochus' death-bed resolution can

---

17 This point is validly emphasized by Cohen, "Crossing the Boundary," 27. It does not necessarily mean that circumcision was considered necessary for salvation. See J.J. Collins, "A Symbol of Otherness: Circumcision and Salvation in the First Century," in J. Neusner and E.S. Frerichs, eds., *To See Ourselves as Others See Us: Christians, Jews, "Others" in Late Antiquity* (Atlanta: Scholars Press, 1985) 163-85.

18 M. Stern, *Greek and Latin Authors on Jews and Judaism* (Jerusalem: The Israel Academy of Sciences and Humanities, 1980) 2.26, 103. See also W. Gutbrod, "Israel," *TDNT* 3(1965) 370.

19 *Ant* 20.2.4 §38-48. See L.H. Schiffman, "The Conversion of the Royal House of Adiabene in Josephus and Rabbinic Sources," in L.H. Feldman and G. Hata eds., *Josephus, Judaism and Christianity* (Detroit: Wayne State, 1987) 293-312.

20 Doron Mendels, "A Note on the Tradition of Antiochus IV's Death," *IEJ* 31 (1981) 53-6 has argued plausibly that 2 Maccabees account of Antiochus' death is modelled on the Nabonidus tradition, which also underlies Daniel 4.

hardly inspire much confidence in the context of 2 Maccabees and it is not in fact carried out. Cyrus is judged by others to have become a Jew, and while his conversion was not complete by Hasmonean standards, the narrative credits him with a significant move in permitting the destruction of the idols.

The Destruction of the Idols

Bel and the Snake is exceptional among Jewish court tales by Daniel's aggressive attitude towards the pagan idols. Even stories like the Prayer of Nabonidus and Daniel 4-5, which are clearly critical of idolatry, do not describe or demand the destruction of the idols. The destruction of idols was commanded by the Book of Deuteronomy, but the command concerned "the nations whom you are about to dispossess" and so the land of Israel. The zealous action of Elijah, and the reform of Josiah, were also directed against idolatry in the land of Israel. For an attack on idols outside of Israel we must wait for the *Book of Jubilees*, an apocalypse composed in Israel in the second century B.C.E.[21] In Jubilees 12:2 Abraham upbraids his father: "What help or advantage do we have from these idols before which you worship and bow down?" His father advises him to "be silent, my son, lest they kill you." Abraham, however, "arose in the night and burned the house of idols. And he burned everything in the house. And there was no man who knew" (12:12-13).[22]

The spirit of the *Book of Jubilees* is very different from that of the Court Tales of Esther or Daniel. It exhibits hostility not only to idolatry, but to the Gentiles. Abraham exhorts Jacob to "Separate yourself from the gentiles and do not eat with them, and do not perform deeds like theirs" (22:16). Intermarriage with foreigners is condemned at length (30:7-17). Levi and his sons are blessed "because he was zealous to do righteousness and judgment and vengeance against all who rose up against Israel" (30:18). This militant nationalism reflects the setting in which Jubilees was written, either the time of the Maccabean revolt or the subsequent campaigns of the Hasmoneans.

In *Bel and the Snake*, however, we find no such hostility to the Gentiles. Daniel is the loyal servant, and honored friend of the king. His efforts are directed towards enlightening the king, and delivering him from the deceptions of the Babylonian priests. There is no objection to Gentile sovereignty as such.

---

21 For different positions on the date of Jubilees see J. VanderKam, *Textual and Historical Studies in the Book of Jubilees* (Missoula: Scholars Press, 1977) 207-88, who favors the early Maccabean era and D. Mendels, *The Land of Israel as a Political Concept in Hasmonean Literature* (Tübingen: Mohr, 1987) 57-88. See also the cautionary observations of R. Doran, "The Non-Dating of Jubilees," *JSJ* 20(1989) 1-11.

22 The legend of Abraham's destruction of the idols subsequently became widespread. See e.g. *Apoc Abraham* 1-8. Compare the analogous action by Job in T. Job 2-5.

Bel and the Snake, then combines some features which are otherwise associated with diverse settings in Judaism. On the one hand the acceptance of Gentile sovereignty is typical of Diaspora literature in the post-exilic period; on the other hand the aggressive attitude towards idols is otherwise associated with nationalistic or exclusivistic strands in the Hellenistic period. In fact, there is no consensus as to the provenance of this document.

The Provenance of Bel and the Snake

It is generally agreed that the Old Greek translation of Daniel was completed no later than 100 B.C.E.[23] If we may assume that *Bel and the Snake* was incorporated into the Book of Daniel by the OG translator,[24] then the date can be no later than the second century B.C.E. Moreover, the simple paratactic style and occasional Hebraisms (e.g. *kai egeneto*) suggest that the story was composed in a Semitic language, probably Hebrew rather than Aramaic in view of the apparent use of the waw consecutive.[25] Since the translation was included in the Old Greek of Daniel, the original date of composition can hardly be later than 150 B.C.E. The fact that the OG version makes Daniel a priest, in contradiction to Daniel 1, also suggests a date before MT Daniel had become authoritative, therefore before the mid-second century. On the other hand, the idea that a Gentile could "become a Jew" is not attested before the second century. There are then, reasonably strong indicators of date, which point to the first half of the second century B.C.E.

The place of origin is more elusive. The ostensible setting is Babylon, but the story shows no familiarity with Babylonian life and religion. The story of the statue of Bel is a crude parody, and there was no prominent cult of a live serpent in Babylon. Yehoshua Grintz has argued that the story was composed in Babylon "when Bel was no longer worshipped," so between the destruction of the temple of Bel by the Persian king Xerxes and its restoration by Alex-

---

23 Sharon Pace Jeansonne, *The Old Greek Translation of Daniel 7-12* (CBQMS 19; Washington: CBA, 1988) 19, argues that "the translation of the Semitic text of Daniel into Greek is possible and plausible at a point shortly after its written composition."

24 Moore, *The Additions,* 128.

25 See Moore, *The Additions,* 119-120. Moore suggests that the original composition was in Aramaic but that Theodotion was based on a Hebrew translation. This solution seems unduly complicated. Recently Klaus Koch, *Deuterokanonishe Zusätze zum Danielbuch* (AOAT 38/1-2; Klevelaer: Butzon & Bercker/Neukirchen-Vluyn: Neukirchener Verlag, 1987) has argued for the essential authenticity of the Aramaic text found in the Chronicles of Jerahmeel, and published by Moses Gaster, "The Unknown Aramaic Original of Theodotion's Additions to the Book of Daniel," *Proceedings of the Society for Biblical Archeology* 16 (1894) 280-90, 312-17; 17 (1895) 75-94 (reprinted in *Studies and Texts* [New York:Ktav, 1971] 1.39-68). I will offer a critique of Koch's arguments in my forthcoming commentary on Daniel in the Hermeneia series.

ander the Great.[26] This theory does not account for the episode of the Snake, which suggests that the author had only the most superficial familiarity with Babylonian religion. Wolfgang Roth, in contrast, gave primary consideration to the polemic against idolatry, and assigned the book to Egyptian Judaism in the first century B.C.E.[27] This date is too late, however. Moreover, if the original language was Hebrew or Aramaic, then an origin in the Egyptian Diaspora, in the Hellenistic period, is very unlikely, since there is no clear example of Egyptian-Jewish literature from this period in a Semitic language. If the original language was Hebrew rather than Aramaic, the land of Israel is by far the most likely place of composition.[28] Composition in Aramaic is also quite compatible with composition in the Jewish homeland in this period.

Witton Davies argued that the story reflects bitter persecution, and so associated it with the time of Antiochus Epiphanes.[29] In fact, however, it is Daniel, not the Babylonians who initiates hostilities in this story, and the Gentile king is sympathetic to the Jew throughout. Such a portrayal of a Gentile king is more plausibly dated before the time of Antiochus Epiphanes rather than later. We may suggest then that the original document was composed in Judea in the first quarter of the second century B.C.E., in circles different from those that collected the tales of Daniel 1-6. Since this is the only source in which Daniel is identified as a priest, we might suppose that the author, too, belonged to priestly circles.

If this reconstruction is right, then the story of *Bel and the Snake* can illuminate another facet of a poorly documented period of Jewish history. The only document that is firmly dated to the first quarter of the second century is the Wisdom of Ben Sira. That book, too, has a deferential attitude towards rulers,[30] and is glowing in its praise of Simon the Just, "in whose time the house of God was renovated" by the beneficence of the Seleucid king, Antiochus III.[31] Sirach also knows the uselessness of offerings to idols that can neither eat nor smell.[32] The wisdom teacher, however, lacks Daniel's zeal for the destruction of idols and pays little attention to specifically Gentile kings.[33]

---

26 Yehoshua M. Grintz, "Bel and the Dragon," *EncJud* 4(1971) 412.

27 W.M.W. Roth, "For Life, He Appeals to Death (Wis 13:18). A Study of Old Testament Idol Parodies," *CBQ* 37(1975) 21-47.

28 So also T. Witton Davies, "Bel and the Dragon," APOT 1.656.

29 Davies, ibid.

30 E.g. Sir 10:5: "Sovereignty over everyone is in the hand of God, who imparts his majesty to the ruler."

31 Sir 50:1, compare *Ant* 12.3.3 §129-44.

32 Sir 30:19.

33 The glaring exception is found in the prayer in Sir 36:12: "Smash the heads of the hostile
(continued...)

Bel and the Snake represents a more purist, less tolerant, strain, emerging in Judaism in this period.

What is of interest in this document, however, is that religious intolerance did not necessarily entail political rebellion. It expresses the hope for the triumph of monotheism even within the domain of Gentile sovereignty. The hope was that destruction of idols might be accomplished if the king, even in a loose sense, were to become a Jew.

33(...continued)
rulers . . ." The authenticity of this prayer is disputed. See T. Middendorp, *Die Stellung Jesu ben Siras zwischen Judentum und Hellenismus* (Leiden: Brill, 1973) 113, 125.

Afterword
by A.T. Kraabel

I. Introduction

I understand our subject to be the Greek-speaking Jews of the Greco-Roman world who lived outside the Holy Land. I took my first look at this topic as a college student, with a senior thesis on Philo Judaeus. I took it up again a decade later when Krister Stendahl and Helmut Koester pointed me to Sardis, and the passion and excitement of Erwin Goodenough and George Hanfmann for the excavation made it irresistible. Sardis then brought me to Diaspora Judaism and showed how it might be understood. My interests had long divided up about equally among Classics, Jewish Studies, early Christianity and archaeology. All four of those fields came together in this site, the only Diaspora Jewish community I claim to know very well.

The beginnings of the synagogue we excavated are somewhere in the third century C.E. By that time there had been Jews in Sardis for at least 500 years. Indeed, Hanfmann, who discovered the building, argues in an unpublished paper that Judaism at Sardis began with Jewish prisoners freed from captivity by Cyrus of Persia in about 538 B.C.E. It is probable that the community was in continuous existence thereafter.[1] The excavation took three seasons, three summers. The interpretation of the building has been going on for nearly thirty years and shows little indication of being completed anytime soon. I propose to use that problem as the entree to this concluding essay.

One approach to puzzling out the life of this community is to look at the external evidence available for the period when the last building began to be used as a synagogue. (It had previously been a public basilica.) I begin with the pagan and Jewish sources, but it is characteristic of them that they tell us almost nothing about the Jews who lived in this part of the Roman Empire. To take one pagan example from western Asia Minor, the famous letter of Pliny the Younger to the emperor Trajan about the Christians of Bithynia (*Ep.* 10. 96). In it Pliny makes no reference to Jews of any sort. As a provincial administrator in the eastern part of the Empire he would have been aware of the first Jewish War and the continuing restlessness of Jews in the eastern Mediterranean. Yet he makes no connection between that dangerous nation and the small group of religious trouble-makers about whom he wrote the emperor at some length. Nor did Trajan, in his much briefer reply (*Ep.* 10. 97).

Christian sources are a bit more helpful. A fair number of Christian texts were written between, say, 50 and 250 C.E. relating to western Asia Minor. Some have little or nothing to say about Judaism: the letters of Ignatius from around the year 113, or the earliest known Christian inscription, the tomb-

---

1 "Jews and Lydians at Babylon and Sardis," a manuscript I am preparing for publication.

stone of bishop Abercius from Hieropolis in Phrygia, from around the year 200.

One Christian document where Diaspora Jews appear frequently, of course, is the Acts of the Apostles. When I did some research into early Anatolian Christianity before I went off to dig at Sardis, the handbooks assured me, based on Acts, that not only had there been Jews in western Asia Minor, there had also been a good number of God-fearers. The handbooks took Acts literally, and so did I, and so that set a theme as I began: perhaps artifacts of the God-fearers would appear in our excavation. Starting in this way distorted the picture for a while, until I began to realize that the traditional, text-based picture of the God-fearer—and of Diaspora Judaism itself—could not stand up to the *realia* of that site.

Of the Christian authors outside the New Testament who do make reference to Jews, the one closest to this synagogue in time and geography is Melito, bishop of Sardis in the second half of the second century. The fierce attacks on Judaism, on "Israel," in his Paschal Homily are provoked chiefly by the power of the Jews of his city, especially when contrasted with his tiny band of believers.[2] (His vituperation may also be a backfire set to defend himself from the charge by fellow Christians that, as a Quartodeciman who followed the Jewish calendar annually in setting the date of Easter, he was "Judaizing.")

I doubt that the Jews of Sardis knew much about Melito. They would not have accepted his sermon, indeed they probably would not have understood what the fuss was all about. But Melito was a man of great influence, in his own time and even more in the later Church. In about the year 190 Bishop Polycrates of Ephesus referred to him as one of the "great luminaries of the Church" now lying in his grave in western Asia Minor. One of the others on Polycrates' short list of heroes was "John, the one lying close to the breast of the Lord" (Eusebius, *HE* 3.21.3). Further, it is the Fourth Gospel which provides the timetable of the Passion Story followed by Melito's (eventually heretical) Quartodecimanism, a chronology incompatible with that in the Synoptics. Thus as I began at Sardis, not only the God-fearers of Acts, but also the Beloved Disciple from the Fourth Gospel, had tantalizing associations with this site; since, as the Polycrates text makes clear, by this time in the Christian

---

2 Feldman agrees, "Proselytes and 'Sympathizers' in the Light of the New Inscriptions from Aphrodisias," *REJ* 148 (1989) 271, hereafter "Feldman *REJ*." Further on Melito, II.7 above, and R.S. MacLennan, *Early Christian Texts on Jews and Judaism*. BJS 194. Atlanta: Scholars Press, 1990, chap. three.

tradition, the Beloved Disciple[3] had the name John. Melito was buried in Sardis, "John" in nearby Ephesus.

II. The Place of *Acts*

The Fourth Gospel may be put to one side for the present purpose, but Acts clearly has a particular and direct importance to any study of this topic. For that reason I need to present my own view of that work, beginning with some comments on several relevant publications which have appeared since the submission of a recent article to the *Festschrift* in honor of Helmut Koester.[4] First, Colin Hemer's 1989 posthumous work, *The Book of Acts in the Setting of Hellenistic History*.[5] Heavily documented and containing much of value, it is essential reading for anyone interested in Acts. But it might better be called "Arguing for the Historicity of the Acts of the Apostles." Hemer is able to sustain his very conservative views only by taking up those topics where his case is most easily made, and largely avoiding the points where he would run into the greatest difficulty.[6]

Next, Heiki Räisänen's *Beyond New Testament Theology*.[7] Particularly important here is the emphasis of the *history of the influence* of a biblical text, its *Wirkungsgeschichte*. Räisänen notes that if the amount of attention devoted today to a particular New Testament document were commensurate with the degree of its importance *in later history*, bibliographies in New Testament studies would have a different look. He points out correctly that if we gave proportionate attention to those "writings that were really formative of subsequent developments"[8] in the history of the Church, we would spend a good deal more time on the Pastorals than we do, and on Acts. Räisänen includes Acts because, for most people, first the beginnings of the Church and then the career of Paul happened just as they were described in the Book of Acts. Those two Lukan stories have been immensely influential in our understanding of what the Church is, how Christians relate to Jews, just what it

---

3 See A.T. Kraabel, "The God-fearers Meet the Beloved Disciple," in *The Future of Early Christianity: Essays in Honor of Helmut Koester*, edited by B.A. Pearson with G.W.E. Nickelsburg and N.R. Petersen, (Minneapolis: Fortress Press, 1991) 276-284, (= "Beloved Diciple" below).

4 See n. 3 above.

5 Edited by Conrad H. Gempf. *WUNT* 49. Tuebingen: Mohr/Siebeck, 1989.

6 See my review of Hemer, forthcoming in *CBQ*. Generally on Acts, Hans Conzelmann, *Acts of the Apostles*. Trans. J. Limburg, A.T. Kraabel & D.H. Juel. Hermeneia series. Philadelphia: Fortress Press, 1987. For a very different view both of Acts and of Hemer, see W.W. Gasque, "The Historical Value of Acts," *Tyndale Bulletin* 40 (1989) 136-157.

7 London: SCM Press / Philadelphia: Trinity Press International, 1990.

8 Räisänen, 104.

means to be a Christian—and what the Greek-speaking Jews who lived outside the Holy Land were really like.[9]

L. Michael White's *Building God's House in the Roman World*[10] provides a striking example for a *Wirkungsgeschichte* of Acts. The book is about the earliest Christian communities and the buildings they used as centers. When he tries to clarify the social and architectural setting of the first generations of Christians, White is driven back time and again to what the author of Acts tells us. For the early period there is no more important source.

Finally, J.G.D. Dunn's *Jesus, Paul and the Law*[11]. About this volume I would make only two points. The first has to do with the "new perspective on Paul" to which Dunn devotes a great deal of attention. It is striking how much this "new perspective" has to do with the new understanding of Judaism, the result of the work of a new generation of scholars in Jewish Studies, particularly in North America. (And what Dunn says for Paul in this regard, Räisänen has said for the theology of the entire New Testament.[12]) Many things within New Testament studies no longer look the same just because we have a different, clearer picture of the Jews of the Roman Empire, most of whom lived in the Diaspora.[13]

My second comment on the Dunn book in particular has to do with some of the points where we differ. Those differences have something to do with the fact that we begin in different places and do our work for different purposes. New Testament exegetes start with Palestine and with Jesus, I work out of the Mediterranean Diaspora and Judaism. Where you stand often depends on where you sit. Dunn and I—and Räisänen, for example, or Louis Feldman[14] or Jacob Neusner—each sit in different places. Things look different as a result. For that reason I need to be as clear as possible in laying out my own view.[15]

---

9 For a case history of later interpretation with special reference to this topic, see Paul S. Stuehrenberg, *Cornelius and the Jews: A Study in the Interpretation of Acts before the Reformation* (diss., University of Minnesota, 1989).

10 The ASOR Library of Biblical and Near Eastern Archaeology. Baltimore: Johns Hopkins, 1990, cf. my review in *RSR* 17 (1991) 258.

11 London: SPCK, 1990.

12 Räisänen, pages 110-112, 120, 122f. etc.

13 To take Matthew as an example, see J.A.Overman, *Matthew's Gospel and Formative Judaism*. Minneapolis: Fortress Press, 1990.

14 See his *REJ* article, and especially *Jew and Gentile in the Ancient World*. Princeton: Princeton University Press, forthcoming (hereafter "Feldman ms."), which he kindly made available to me in ms. form.

15 I have not seen Paul R. Trebilco, *Jewish Communities in Asia Minor*. SNTSMS, 69. Cambridge UK: Cambridge University Press, 1991, but see the review by N. de Lange in *Bulletin of Judaeo-Greek Studies* 8 (1991) 26-31.

What kind of a document is Acts? What was its purpose? When Hemer takes up this topic, he moves too quickly to split Acts off from the Third Gospel: "Luke and Acts are themselves different in type," he says; they are not of the same genre.[16] Perhaps, but didn't Luke put them very much together? Aren't they in fact carefully linked, one work in two volumes? If publishing technology had permitted, would it not have been written as one long story?

I suggest that in the present two volumes Luke had a single purpose: to present the Jesus-story and the Church-story, the two-part foundational and normative account of the first two generations of the new religion. For Luke, and for Luke alone of the evangelists, the latter is essential to complete the former. Acts, understood in this way, will not lack "historical" content. But those "historical" specifics will always be conformed to Luke's kerygmatic purpose, just as they are in his gospel. And we remember that the Third Gospel has more explicit links to contemporary history than the other three canonical gospels combined.

As in the Fourth Gospel, so in the Book of Acts, the narrative has been embellished, drama has been added, to make a point important to the author. Characters appear in each document to carry out its author's agenda, characters who are not on stage anywhere else. The Beloved Disciple and the God-fearers are not known by the rest of the New Testament; that does not bother the author of the Fourth Gospel or of Acts, nor should it bother us.[17]

---

16 Hemer, 33.

17 The Beloved Disciple and the God-fearers may be unique only in the magnitude of the roles they play. In fact all four gospel writers offer us actors peculiar to one text only, shadowy figures not in evidence elsewhere. In traditional exegesis it was sometimes asserted that each of the evangelists secretly "signed" his work by writing himself into his account in a unique text, producing episodes which were not paralleled in the other Gospels. If we take up that idea, the "author's signature" in the Fourth Gospel would be the figure of the Beloved Disciple. In Matthew it is the "scribe who has become a disciple to the Kingdom of Heaven and, like a householder, brings forth out of his treasure things new and old" (13:52). In Mark it is a follower of Jesus who was present at Judas' betrayal, the Young Man in the linen cloak, who was almost seized himself, but left the cloak behind in his captors' hands and fled naked (14:51f.). Luke, in writing a two-volume work, has left us two signatures. These are the "We-passages," of course, and the God-fearers. (Hengel is one of those who suggest that the author of Luke-Acts was a God-fearer himself, see M. Hengel, *Acts and the History of Earliest Christianity*. London: SCM Press, 1979, page 107.) This provides a vivid image of each of the four evangelists: Matthew the Scribe, Mark the Young Man, John the Beloved Disciple, and Luke the God-fearer carrying his travel diary. It appears that all four authors employed the same techniques and perhaps shared the same understanding of what they were creating. It is just that the third and fourth evangelists did a great deal more with character and plot development here than did the second and first. Classicists will recall a not dissimilar issue, that of identifying the "historical Socrates" behind the accounts of Plato, Aristotle and Xenophon; on this most recently, Gregory Vlastos, *Socrates, Ironist and Moral Philosopher*. Cornell Studies in Classical Philology, 50. The Townsend Lectures. Ithaca NY: Cornell University Press, 1991, see my review forthcoming in *RSR*.

This also makes clear why Acts ends where and as it does. Paul, as Luke presents him, is at the same time fully the observant Jew and fully the Roman citizen. He is a crucial symbolic figure. When this symbol reaches Rome, Luke's goal has been attained. The new Christian movement, represented by Paul, has progressed from Jerusalem to the very center of the known world. (Acts could end nowhere else than in Rome.) In Rome the new religion now flourishes "unhindered," ἀκωλύτως —Luke's goal, and thus the last word of Acts' final verse.[18]

III. Problems in the Research into Diaspora Judaism

The centuries-old propensity to use Acts, a Christian text whose theology opposes Judaism, as a source for *Jewish* history and practices may serve to introduce the premier issue in the study of Diaspora Jews. When we are confronted with an artifact, text or symbol, how can we tell whether it was produced by Jews? What are the criteria? What is it that makes something Jewish? This is a much more serious problem in the Diaspora than it is for rabbinics (which, all too often, sets the criteria) or, for that matter, for Church history. "Is this Christian?" is a matter of theological debate; but in the Diaspora "Is this Jewish?" is usually a question of identification, simple but often maddeningly difficult.

Consider the example of Ezekiel the tragedian. I cannot use traditional rabbinic criteria to fault his *Exagoge* on its orthodoxy, since I see him as working out of very different concerns and at an earlier time.[19] He wanted to tell the central story of Judaism, Passover/Exodus, in a way accessible and attractive to the educated of his community, the Jews as much as the gentiles. He is no less fully a Jew in this task than the LXX translators were in theirs.

The wealthy Julia Severa in Phrygia (*CII* 766) raises a related issue, alleged conversions to Judaism.[20] The sources commonly used to provide information about the criteria for and the rituals of conversion in antiquity are almost always rabbinic, even though their relevance for Diaspora Judaism is

---

18 Most recently on the general topic, J.T.Sanders, "Who is a Jew and Who Is a Gentile in the Book of Acts?" *NTS* 37 (1991) 434-455, hereafter "Sanders *NTS*." He concludes: to describe "the complexion of Judaism and Christianity in the Roman province of Asia around the year 100 C.E....much more accurately is the outstanding task in the study of Acts."

19 Feldman, ms. page 108; Howard Jacobson, *The Exagoge of Ezekiel.* Cambridge UK: Cambridge University Press, 1983; P.W. van der Horst, "Some Notes on the *Exagoge* of Ezekiel," *Mnemosyne* 37 (1984) 354-375; E. Schürer, *The History of the Jewish People in the Age of Jesus Christ.* Rev. ed. by G.Vermes, F. Millar & M. Goodman III.1 London: T. & T. Clark, 1986, pages 563-566, hereafter "Schürer."

20 See pages 11 and 12 above, orig. page 456. Feldman ms., page 579.

dubious at best.[21] To call Julia Severa a convert or even a "sympathizer" is misguided. In her particular case the correct *classical* label is "benefactor," a common hellenistic idea[22] which goes the farthest toward explaining her support for the Acmonia synagogue, and makes her donation instantly understandable in the context of the social history of the first century.

A further example comes from a current project, near completion: the occurrence of the Greek term *pronoia* (foresight, oversight, Providence) to mean "God" in a number of dedicatory inscriptions in the Sardis synagogue. The usage is all but unparalleled in other Jewish inscriptions,[23] and uncommon in the LXX and other Greek literature produced by Jews. My hypothesis is that the conception was presented to some Jews at Sardis in the course of their education in that city, and that it comes directly from popular philosophy, not from Jewish sources at all. They used it in the inscriptions because it said something they wanted to say in a conceptual language which made sense to them and to those Jews and non-Jews who were expected to see the inscriptions.[24]

Examples are as small as a single, broken artifact, or as vast and complex as an entire ancient community. When I look at Sardis, for example, I cannot accept that that community endured *for a millennium* as a *Jewish* community if in the crucial second half of its life it was changing its composition, indeed its essence, by "winning...many converts and 'sympathizers'," as Feldman has suggested.[25] And those who try to turn the Sardis story on its head, by suggesting that *only* because it contained "many converts and 'sympathizers'" did it endure in a gentile world at all, doubly dishonor these Jews, first by questioning their commitment to their traditions and, second, by not allowing that

---

21 Most recently on these issues, S. McKnight, *A Light among the Gentiles: Jewish Missionary Activity in the Second Temple Period.* Minneapolis: Fortress Press, 1991. In addition, Shaye Cohen has a major project on conversion and intermarriage in antiquity which has already resulted in a series of articles, of which the best-known is "Crossing the Boundary and Becoming a Jew," *HTR* 82 (1989) 13-33; and Martin Goodman is at work on a monograph tentatively titled *The Concept of Mission in Late Antiquity.*

22 F.W. Danker, *Benefactor.* St Louis: Clayton Publishing House, 1982, cf. my review in *CurrTM* 10 (1983) 107-110.

23 For a new instance from Philippopolis (now Plovdiv, Bulgaria), E. Kesjakova, "The Ancient Synagogue of Philoppopolis," *Arkeologia* 1 (1989) 20-33, published in Sofia in Bulgarian. I owe this reference to Gidon Foerster.

24 Kraabel, "*Pronoia* at Sardis," to appear in the proceedings of "The Jewish Diaspora in the Hellenistic and Roman Periods," a colloquium held in January of 1991 at Tel Aviv University.

25 Feldman ms., page 803.

they could have participated authentically in the larger gentile culture around them while continuing to retain that commitment.[26]

One final problem: the study of Diaspora Judaism is unavoidably interdisciplinary. That is why it is so easily misunderstood by anyone approaching it from any single specialization. Whoever takes it up from a particular discipline will need to learn a new way of doing research; and since it requires skill in many areas, anyone interested in the topic will need allies. No one will work it very fruitfully alone.

This was one of the advantages of approaching Diaspora Judaism first archaeologically, as I did. Some scholars are uncomfortable not being "experts" in the subject of their research, but archaeologists have to be team players. Hundreds of researchers in a score of disciplines have worked at Sardis, for example, over the last three decades; each of us was an amateur in the approaches we knew least. It was and remains essential to work together. (Happily, such cooperation is becoming easier all the time. Satellite networks and electronic mail—and the possibility of a more friendly world—make colleagues in Leningrad or Berlin or Tel Aviv or Oxford more accessible now than ever before.)

But teamwork can go only so far. At some point, after going over the evidence and weighing the views of specialist colleagues, you have to make your own judgments in the areas for which you are responsible. That is how I finally arrived at an interpretation of the synagogue community at Sardis. Beginning with their building, indeed working *within* that building, I could not accept that the people who controlled it and expressed themselves in its architecture and inscriptions fit the conventional image of Diaspora Judaism.[27] For the same reason, I could not see clusters of God-fearers in that building either.[28] Curious gentiles? Surely. Business associates, neighbors or friends of one Jew or another who were not Jews themselves? Why not? But the semi-converts of the handbooks? Unlikely!

IV. The Future of Diaspora Judaism

The immediate future of this topic centers in the most important Jewish inscriptions discovered in this century, those from Aphrodisias. We are far

---

26 A recent epigraphic example of the larger issue, I. Levinskaya, "A Jewish or Gentile Prayer House? The Meaning of ΠΡΟΣΕΥΧΗ,"*Tyndale Bulletin* 41 (1990) 154-159, cf. Kraabel, "Υψιστος" and the Synagogue at Sardis," *GRBS* 10 (1969) 81-93.

27 Further on this issue, I.1 above.

28 Feldman suggests that its "huge size...was necessary to accommodate" the large numbers of God-fearers it attracted, *REJ* 279.

from a consensus yet as to what they really have to say about the Jews of that city.[29] But my concerns here are more programmatic.

Who will study Diaspora Judaism in the future? A diversity of fields will continue to be represented, as in this volume; and a diversity of journals, as in our bibliographies. But most new research will come from the students of earliest Christianity. For one thing, they far outnumber the folks in Classics, Jewish Studies, and Greco-Roman archaeology and history. More important, the Judaism contemporary with the new religion but outside the Holy Land is going to turn out to be more central to that field than it is to the other disciplines.

The multi-disciplinary, team approach which will be required has several important methodological implications, especially for those coming from the study of the earliest Church:

1) Paying full attention to the archaeological *realia* of Judaism will seem unusual to many, given that Judaism, particularly in Late Antiquity, has for centuries been a text-based discipline. But understanding Diaspora Judaism requires a social history of the richest and most complex kind. The ancient Jews I find most fascinating, because they are all but unknown to us, are not the writers—the Ezekiels, the Philos and the Josephuses, or the rabbis—but merchants and donors and other kinds of "average" people. At Sardis I think of those who rebuilt that basilica into a proper synagogue, owned or frequented its shops and, in a later period, sat at the feet of Samoe, the priest and *sophodidaskalos*. Since texts are not my speciality, when I work with them I take my lead from colleagues for whom that is their major concentration. Especially is this true for the rabbinic literature where, of the many things I have learned from Jacob Neusner and Geza Vermes, the most important is to be wary of using such texts too quickly and too directly as historical sources.

2) It is only through patient participation in a many-sided dialogue that a clear picture of these particular Jews will begin to emerge. We should not be surprised when what we write on this topic is misunderstood. The audience is diverse, much more so than in the scholarship within a single discipline. There is no common store of technical terms. Explanations have to be more elaborate, definitions more frequent, as a result. Clarity will first be reached on a site-by-site, city-by-city basis; only after that —possibly long after—will the topic as a whole fit together.

3) On occasion, in this interdisciplinary undertaking, one insight or another will appear to be a threat to a particular discipline's integrity, since when

---

29 See above, section II, and add Feldman, *REJ*, and I. Levinskaya, "The Inscription from Aphrodisias and the Problem of God-fearers," *Tyndale Bulletin* 41 (1990) 312-318, neither of which convinces me.

it is read back into that discipline, the new conclusion will alter traditional presuppositions—by deepening them, say, or by correcting instances of parochial narrowness. This is likely to happen most frequently in the study of the earliest Church, where the study of Judaism in general and Diaspora Jews in particular has been heavily influenced by theological issues.[30]

4) The data are such as to make anyone cautious of generalizations, of extrapolating from any single ancient author or any one site (even one as rich and well documented as Sardis) to speak of "*the* Diaspora" or "*the* Greek-speaking Jews," somewhat as gentile writers in antiquity were wont to do. The one generalization I would make is that each of the excavated Diaspora synagogues is so different from the others as to make any *other* generalization about Diaspora Judaism hazardous indeed.[31] To give just one example: although Feldman has asserted that "there was no such thing as ghetto Jews" in the Greco-Roman Diaspora,[32] the synagogues at Dura, Priene and Ostia were carefully concealed from outside view. Sardis, on the other hand, doesn't fit that pattern at all; the synagogue there is right on Main Street, one of the best locations in town. It could not be the center of a Jewish quarter or "ghetto," though any one of the other three might have been.

One of the results of the study of the history of the early Church in the last half-century has been to uncover theological and ethnic diversity where a pristine doctrinal uniformity had been assumed before. This new religion took many forms despite the controls to be found in strong bishops and a well organized communications network. Judaism in the Mediterranean Diaspora had a weaker network, no bishops, apparently far fewer organized communities—and many more years to assume new forms. I expect that too to become more clearly attested in the future.[33]

....

The intent of this Afterword was not to present a comprehensive treatment of Diaspora Judaism or the scholarship upon it. (Feldman's forthcoming

---

30 See particularly n. 3 above. Further on this, with special reference to New Testament studies, Sanders, *NTS*.

31 Further on this, Kraabel, "The Diaspora Synagogue," *ANRW* II.19.1 (1979) 477-510, and III. 2 above. Underestimating this diversity is one of the shortcomings of H. Bottermann, "Die Synagoge von Sardes," *ZNW* 81 (1990) 103-121.

32 Feldman *REJ*, page 288.

33 This despite the insistence of Feldman (*REJ*) and Reynolds and Tannenbaum (in the *editio princeps* of the inscriptions) that the Aphrodisias texts attest rabbinic control over this Diaspora community (and others as well?).

monograph is chiefly on that subject, and the bibliography alone is nearly fifty ms. pages.) It is rather an invitation to scholars and students of antiquity to consider this underpopulated area of research. The subject has its own importance, of course, but for many its greatest value will turn out to be the way it enlivens and opens up the traditional disciplines which impinge on it. In my own case it has provided a perspective on Classics, earliest Christianity, archaeology and Jewish Studies which significantly increased my understanding of all four fields. Carefully—and cooperatively—done, it can serve to deconstruct disciplines, link them up and assemble them again in ways which make them clearer and more comprehensive and complete.[34] And satisfying, as any true vocation ought to be.

July 26, 1991

---

34 Two final examples: first, Jacob Neusner's recent probe into Jewish symbolism, *Symbolism and Theology in Early Judaism* (Minneapolis: Fortress Press, 1991), in which he compares the vocabulary of symbolic discourse in iconic form (as found in the art of the ancient synagogues of the Holy Land) and that of the same mode of discourse carried on in verbal form in certain rabbinic texts, notably *Song of Songs Rabbah*. The next step, of course, is to bring his method and results to bear on the Diaspora. Second, along with the new methods, there are also "new" sources, that is, known texts not fully examined for what they might tell us about Diaspora Judaism, for example, the pagan, Jewish and Christian evidence (often contemporary with the Sardis synagogue and the Aphrodisias inscriptions) to be found in the *Sibylline Oracle*, see Schürer III.1 (1986) 618-654; J.J. Collins, *The Sibylline Oracles of Egyptian Judaism. SBLDS*, 13. Missoula MT: Scholars Press, 1974; and D.S. Potter, *Prophecy and History in the Crisis of the Roman Empire: A Historical Commentary on the Thirteenth Sibylline Oracle*. Oxford Classical Monographs. Oxford: Clarendon Press, 1991, cf. my review forthcoming in *RSR*.

A Bibliography of Works by A. Thomas Kraabel

Books

The Future of Early Christianity: Essays in Honor of Helmut Koester. Edited with B.A. Pearson, G.W.E. Nickelsburg and N.R. Petersen. Minneapolis: Fortress Press, 1991.

Goodenough on the Beginnings of Christianity, A.T. Kraabel, Brown Judaic Studies, 212. Atlanta: Scholars Press, 1990.

Ancient Synagogue Excavations at Khirbet Shema', Upper Galilee, Israel 1970-72, (Annual of the American Schools of Oriental Research, 42). E.M. Meyers, J.F. Strange and A.T. Kraabel. Durham: Duke University Press, 1976.

Articles

"Judaism at Sardis," in A.R. Seager et al., *The Synagogue and Its Setting.* Archaeological Exploration of Sardis. Cambridge: Harvard University Press (forthcoming).

"Christianity at Sardis," in Hans Buchwald et al., *The Churches of Sardis.* Archaeological Exploration of Sardis. Cambridge: Harvard University Press (forthcoming).

"*Pronoia* at Sardis," to appear in the proceedings of "The Jewish Diaspora in the Hellenistic and Roman Periods," a colloquium held in January of 1991 at Tel Aviv University.

"The God-fearers meet the Beloved Disciple." Pages 276-284 in *The Future of Early Christianity: Essays in Honor of Helmut Koester,* edited by B.A. Pearson, A.T. Kraabel, G.W.E. Nickelsburg and N.R. Petersen. Minneapolis: Fortress Press, 1991.

"The Myth of Greece and the Liberal Arts." Inaugural Lecture, Orlando W. Qualley Chair of Classical Languages. Decorah, Iowa, 1989.

"Model, Scale, and Difference," *AGORA, A Journal of Interdisciplinary Discourse* (Spring 1989) 17-20.

"The Synagogue at Sardis: Jews and Christians." Pages 62-72 in *Sardis: Twenty-Seven Years of Discovery.* Papers Presented . . . at the Oriental Institute March 21, 1987. Edited by Eleanor Guralnick. Chicago, 1987.

"Unity and Diversity Among Diaspora Synagogues." Pages 49-60 in *The Synagogue in Late Antiquity,* edited by Lee I. Levine. A Centennial Publication of the Jewish Theological Seminary of America. Philadelphia: The American Schools of Oriental Research, 1987.

"Archaeology, Iconography, and Nonliterary Written Remains." Pages 175-210 in *Early Judaism and its Modern Interpreters,* R.A. Kraft and G.W.E. Nickelsburg (edd.), vol. II of *The Bible and its Modern Interpreters,* Douglas A. Knight (ed.). A Society of Biblical Literature Centennial Publication.

Scholars Press, Atlanta/Fortress Press, Philadelphia, 1986. [with E.M. Meyers]

"The God-Fearers—A Literary and Theological Invention?" *Biblical Archaeology Review* 12 (1986) 46-53, 64 with R.S. MacLennan—with responses by Robert F. Tannenbaum (54-57) and Louis H. Feldman (59-63, 64-69).

"Greeks, Jews, and Lutherans in the Middle Half of Acts." Pages 147-157 in *Christians Among Jews and Gentiles: Essays in Honor of Krister Stendahl on His Sixty-Fifth Birthday.* Edited by G.W.E. Nickelsburg with G.W. MacRae, S.J. Philadelphia: Fortress, 1986 [=*Harvard Theological Review* 79.1-3].

"*Synagoga caeca.* Systematic Distortion in Gentile Interpretations of Evidence for Judaism in the Early Christian Period." "*To See Ourselves As Others See Us*": *Christians, Jews, "Others" in Late Antiquity.* Edited by Jacob Neusner and Ernest Frerichs. Chico, CA: Scholars Press, 1985, pages 219-246.

"A Bibliography of the Writings of Erwin Ramsdell Goodenough." In *Religions in Antiquity: Essays in Memory of Erwin Ramsdell Goodenough.* (Supplements to *Numen*, 14), edited by Jacob Neusner, 621-632. Leiden: Brill, 1968. Reprinted in R.S. Eccles, *Erwin Ramsdell Goodenough: A Personal Pilgrimage.* Chico CA: Scholars Press, 1985, 177-185.

"New Evidence of the Samaritan Diaspora has been found on Delos," *Biblical Archaeologist* 47 (1984) 44-46.

"Impact of the Discovery of the Sardis Synagogue," in G.M.A. Hanfmann, *Sardis from Prehistoric to Roman Times.* Cambridge, MA: Harvard University Press, 1983, pages 178-190.

"The Roots of Christmas," *Dialog* 21 (1982) 274-80.

"The Excavated Synagogues of Late Antiquity from Asia Minor to Italy," *XVI Internationaler Byzantinisten-kongress, Akten II/2 = Jahrbuch der Osterreichischen Byzantinistik* 32.2 (1982) 227-36.

"The Roman Diaspora: Six Questionable Assumptions," *Essays in Honour of Yigael Yadin,* edd. G. Vermes & J. Neusner (=*Journal of Jewish Studies* 3.1-2, 1982) 445-464.

"The Disappearance of the 'God-fearers'." *Numen* 28 (1981) 113-126.

"Social Systems of Six Diaspora Synagogues," in J. Gutmann, ed. *Ancient Synagogues: The State of Research,* pages 79-91 + fig. 19. Chico, CA: Scholars Press, 1981.

"The Diaspora Synagogue: Archaeological and Epigraphic Evidence since Sukenik." In *Aufstieg und Niedergang der römischen Welt* II.19, edited by H. Temporini and W. Hasse. Pages 477-510, one plan, one plate. Berlin: de Gruyter, 1979. Excerpted and reprinted in Hebrew in *The Ancient Synagogue: Selected Studies.* Edited by Zeev Safrai. Jerusalem: Zalman Shazar Center for Jewish History, 1986, pages 193-198.

"Paganism and Judaism: The Sardis Evidence," in *Paganisme, Judaïsme, Chris-tiansme: Influences et affrontements dans le mond antique. Mélanges offerts à Marcel Simon.* A. Benoit, M. Philonenko, C. Vogel (edd.) Paris, 1979. Pages 13-33.

"Jews in Imperial Rome: More Archaeological Evidence from an Oxford Col-lection," *Journal of Jewish Studies* (1979) 41-58.

"The Open University, *The Myth of God Incarnate* and World Religious Plu-ralism," *Dialog* 17 (1978) 189-195.

"The Shalom Christians — *Requiescant in pace*," *Dialog* 15 (1977) 8-10.

"A Bibliography of the Writings of Morton Smith to December 31, 1973." In *Christianity, Judaism and Other Greco-Roman Cults: Studies for Morton Smith at Sixty.* (Studies in Judaism in Late Antiquity, 12), edited by Jacob Neusner, part 4, 190-200. Leiden: Brill, 1975.

"Synagogues, Ancient,"in *New Catholic Encyclopedia. Vol. 16:Supplement 1967-74.* New York: McGraw-Hill, 1974. Pages 436-439, one plate.

"Khirbet Shema' et Meiron." *Revue biblique* 80 (1973) 585-587 + Pl. 34f.

"Archaeology and Rabbinic Tradition at Khirbet Shema': 1970 and 1971 Cam-paigns." *Biblical Archaeologist* 25 (1972) 1-31. (With E.M. Meyers and J.F. Strange).

"Khirbet Shema' and Meiron," *Israel Exploration Journal* 22 (1972) 174-176 + Pl. 37f. (With E.M. Meyers and J.F. Strange).

"Melito the Bishop and the Synagogue at Sardis: Text and Context," in *Studies Presented to George M.A. Hanfmann*, (Fogg Art Museum, Harvard Uni-versity, Monographs in Art and Archaeology, 2). Edited by D.G. Mitten, J.G. Pedley and J.A. Scott. Cambridge: Fogg Art Museum, 1971. Pages 72-85.

"Khirbet Shema' (Meiron)," *Revue biblique* 78 (1971) 418f. + Pl. 16f. (With E.M. Meyers).

"*Hypsistos* and the Synagogue at Sardis," *Greek, Roman and Byzantine Studies* 10 (1969) 81-93.

"Paul and the Hellenization of Christianity," in *Religion in Antiquity: Essays in Memory of Erwin Ramsdell Goodenough.* (Supplements to *Numen*, 14). Jacob Neusner (ed.). Leiden: Brill, 1968. Pages 23-68. (With E.R. Good-enough)

Translation

Hans Conzelmann. *Acts of the Apostles: A Commentary.* Hermeneia Commen-taries. Translated by J. Limburg, A.T. Kraabel, and D.H. Juel. Philadel-phia: Fortress, 1987.

Index of Authors

South Florida Studies in the History of Judaism

240001	Lectures on Judaism in the Academy and in the Humanities	Neusner
240002	Lectures on Judaism in the History of Religion	Neusner
240003	Self-Fulfilling Prophecy: Exile and Return in the History of Judaism	Neusner
240004	The Canonical History of Ideas: The Place of the So-called Tannaite Midrashim, Mekhilta Attributed to R. Ishmael, Sifra, Sifré to Numbers, and Sifré to Deuteronomy	Neusner
240005	Ancient Judaism: Debates and Disputes	Neusner
240006	The Hasmoneans and Their Supporters: From Mattathias to the Death of John Hyrcanus I	Sievers
240007	Approaches to Ancient Judaism: New Series Volume One	Neusner
240008	Judaism in the Matrix of Christianity	Neusner
240009	Tradition as Selectivity: Scripture, Mishnah, Tosefta, and Midrash in the Talmud of Babylonia	Neusner
240010	The Tosefta: Translated from the Hebrew: Sixth Division Tohorot	Neusner
240011	In the Margins of the Midrash: Sifre Ha'azinu Texts, Commentaries and Reflections	Basser
240012	Language as Taxonomy: The Rules for Using Hebrew and Aramaic in the Babylonia Talmud	Neusner
240013	The Rules of Composition of the Talmud of Babylonia: The Cogency of the Bavli's Composite	Neusner
240014	Understanding the Rabbinic Mind: Essays on the Hermeneutic of Max Kadushin	Ochs
240015	Essays in Jewish Historiography	Rapoport-Albert
240016	The Golden Calf and the Origins of the Jewish Controversy	Bori/Ward
240017	Approaches to Ancient Judaism: New Series Volume Two	Neusner
240018	The Bavli That Might Have Been: The Tosefta's Theory of Mishnah Commentary Compared With the Bavli's	Neusner
240019	The Formation of Judaism: In Retrospect and Prospect	Neusner
240020	Judaism in Society: The Evidence of the Yerushalmi,Toward the Natural History of a Religion	Neusner
240021	The Enchantments of Judaism: Rites of Transformation from Birth Through Death	Neusner
240023	The City of God in Judaism and Other Comparative and Methodological Studies	Neusner
240024	The Bavli's One Voice: Types and Forms of Analytical Discourse and their Fixed Order of Appearance	Neusner
240025	The Dura-Europos Synagogue: A Re-evaluation (1932-1992)	Gutmann
240026	Precedent and Judicial Discretion: The Case of Joseph ibn Lev	Morell
240028	Israel: Its Life and Culture Volume I	Pedersen
240029	Israel: Its Life and Culture Volume II	Pedersen
240030	The Bavli's One Statement: The Metapropositional Program of Babylonian Talmud Tractate Zebahim Chapters One and Five	Neusner
240031	The Oral Torah: The Sacred Books of Judaism: An Introduction: Second Printing	Neusner